All but the People

"That's nothing, Franklin; you ought to read what they said about me." Reprinted with permission from the Philadelphia Record. Cartoon by Jerry Doyle.

All but the People

FRANKLIN D. ROOSEVELT
AND HIS CRITICS
1933–39

George Wolfskill & John A. Hudson

THE MACMILLAN COMPANY

COLLIER-MACMILLAN LTD., *London*

ACKNOWLEDMENTS

Permission has been granted to reprint the following excerpts in *All but the People:*

Adelaide W. Neall's "Through the Looking Glass," in the *Saturday Evening Post.* Copyright 1933 The Curtis Publishing Company.

Second stanza of "H. L. Mencken Meets a Poet in the West Side Y.M.C.A." from *The Fox of Peapack and Other Poems* by E. B. White. Copyright 1936 by E. B. White. Used by permission of Harper & Row, Publishers. Originally appeared in *Saturday Review of Literature.*

Library of Congress Catalog Card Number: 69–10191

FIRST PRINTING

The Macmillan Company
Collier-Macmillan Canada Ltd., Toronto, Ontario

Printed in the United States of America

FOR *Alberta* AND *Jenny*

Contents

Preface

"My god, what are we coming to?" House Speaker John McCormack exclaimed in Washington. It was the kind of question civilized men everywhere asked that day—the day President Kennedy was shot—part prayer, part oath, part disbelief. Within the hour the whole country, the whole world, knew that Americans had murdered their fourth President in less than a century.

Others, perhaps, could not know it and feel it as we did. Dallas, Texas. Less than twenty miles away; thirty minutes on the Turnpike. Commerce Street. Dealey Plaza. The Texas School Book Depository Building. The memory of places long familiar heightened the reality of that wicked, insane deed, forced upon us a feeling of immediacy, of personal involvement that seemed unbearable in the first hours of the tragedy. Going about our usual affairs was out of the question. We gathered with small groups seeking solace, spoke aimlessly of what we had been doing when the news came, tried to reassure students, some of whom had passed the very spot on the way to the Arlington campus of The University of Texas.

Reflecting on those four days in November, on our emotions, our feelings of anger and resentment, of frustration and helplessness and futility, of shame and sadness, we were aware of a nagging question, one that no doubt found its way into the theme of this book. Historians spend much of their adult lives studying theories, cycles, economic and social conflicts and forces, war and diplomacy, geopolitics, and all the rest, the stuff that is supposed to explain history neat and tidily. But what of the lunatic's bullet and the fanatic's bomb? Where did history by assassination fit into the picture?

Where, for that matter, did history by character assassination fit? Or history by rumor, by distortion, by falsehood? What effect did these things have on the course of events and the principal players in the events? Granted that an opposition, free to organize and free to criticize without fear of reprisal, was essential to the democratic process in the United States, and granted that politics was a contest for power not a course in ethics, was there no limit? Did anything go, short of physical assault and bodily harm?

In the United States, we have often behaved as if it did, behaved as if anything was fair, as if all forms of opposition, all views, all positions were equally valid. We have often pretended that this did not create a climate in which even intelligent, constructive criticism degenerated into gossip, and that the honor, the integrity, the spirit of public servants (including Presidents), could not be mortally wounded by unrelenting, unreasoning attack just as surely as their flesh would yield to the assassin's bullet.

All this is something quite different and apart from what one President, Harry Truman, had in mind when he remarked, "If you can't stand the heat, stay out of the kitchen." There is criticism that is just and criticism that is unjust; there is more than one kind of heat. For the well-being of the country and the soundness of the democratic process, men should learn the difference and adhere to an etiquette, a protocol of criticism; they should learn to behave like civilized men and confound the cynic who insists that most people prefer less than the truth.

Perhaps it was some kind of tribute to his importance that Franklin Roosevelt was the center of so much controversy, that his New Deal was the object of so much criticism; men are not likely to quarrel over that which does not matter. Roosevelt was accused of just about everything except starting the Civil War. Some of the criticism was by decent and honorable men, by wise men, by men who sincerely disagreed with Roosevelt, by men whose motives were above reproach. Much of it was by strange men, men obsessed by twisted and sinister motives, by men who would have applauded a public execution of the President. Some of the criticism was deserved; much of it was not. Running through the latter like a leitmotiv were two themes. One was an incredibly vicious, intensely personal abuse of the man, his family, and those close to him. The other, and infinitely more serious, was the accusation that Roosevelt was willfully subversive, that he was deliberately betraying the country, seeking to destroy the Republic, striving to remake it into a tyranny either of the Right or of the Left.

Critics and criticism. That is what this book is about. It is in the nature of a case study, a cross-section of the critics and their criticism of a Chief Executive, an attempt to identify the opposition forces a President must likely contend with, the enemies he is likely to encounter. It is not a history of the New Deal or of the Roosevelt years, although there is a lot about Franklin Roosevelt and the New Deal in it. It is a study of the Roosevelt critics, who they were and what they were, what they criticized and why, and what (if anything) they tried to do about it. It is an effort to see Roosevelt and the New Deal through hostile eyes; to let his enemies speak for themselves. It is also an attempt to delineate a certain streak of madness in American political criticism which has received scant attention and to appraise the adverse effects of such criticism on the course of events.

The period covered is 1933 to 1939, one in which domestic affairs—depression, recovery, reform—strained the energies, riveted the attention of the country. It is with domestic affairs that this book is concerned, those matters in which the country seemed to have the maximum opportunity to shape its own destiny. From 1939 and after, the domestic New Deal was over; foreign policy took priority. The book is not concerned with this. Criticism of the Roosevelt foreign policy and his leadership as a wartime President is quite another story.

While the nature of the subject seemed to require a topical format, the sequence of topics is entirely arbitrary. In general, we have moved along the spectrum from the irrational to the rational, from criticism that made little sense to criticism that made a great deal of sense. The first section samples personal criticism of Roosevelt and those close to him. Section two examines the extravagant criticism of the native Fascists and those flirting with fascism. Interesting, dangerous (but perhaps not so important as some others over the long haul), the Fascist crowd occupies a disproportionate space here because of the nearly endless variations of its themes. Sections three and four are an analysis of the Communists and others of varying degree of radicalism, the business community and its allies, the press, and the two major political parties. In the final section, we have attempted a tentative interpretation of the critics, Roosevelt's response to them, and the ultimate effect of the critics on the course of the New Deal. In this last, an "iffy" proposition (as Roosevelt might have said), we believe we have provided some fresh insights into Depression America and the New Deal. And, with customary academic modesty, we assume full responsibility for the results, both good and bad.

In this narrative of New Deal criticism the indecent and the obscene have been purposely omitted.

We owe much to many. Mrs. Shirley Baker, Mrs. Mary Welch Greene, and Mrs. Mary Stoddard Hitt shared the unpleasant chore of typing the first draft of the manuscript. Mrs. Evelyn Thiessen typed the final draft and, amazingly, remained tolerant and cheerful through many changes and revisions. Mr. Jimmy West of The University of Texas at Arlington Library staff endured the thankless task of transcribing many of the notes. We are indebted to the friendly people at The University of Texas at Austin Library and the Roosevelt Memorial Library, Hyde Park, New York, for many kindnesses that made our research easier. Harry Ransom, Chancellor of The University of Texas, and F. W. Roberts, Director of The University of Texas Humanities Research Center, made it possible for us to use the Valentine Collection. A modest research grant from The University of Texas at Arlington eased the financial burden.

Collaboration was a new and satisfying experience. There are obvious advantages in a historian and a librarian working together. We have emerged from the endeavor with a stronger bond of friendship than when we first began. Not all collaborators can say as much.

GEORGE WOLFSKILL
JOHN A. HUDSON

The University of Texas at Arlington
January 15, 1968

An overwhelming proportion of the material power of the country was arrayed against him [Andrew Jackson]. . . . The great media for the dissemination of information and the molding of public opinion fought him. . . . Haughty and sterile intellectualism opposed him. Musty reaction disapproved him. Hollow and outworn traditionalism shook a trembling finger at him. . . . It seemed that sometimes all were against him—all but the people of the United States.

—FRANKLIN D. ROOSEVELT

PART I
Below the Belt

T UESDAY afternoon, April 5, 1938. Debate was in progress on the Reorganization Bill, legislation intended to streamline the Executive branch of government and introduce greater efficiency into its operations.

The bill was having tough sledding. Opposition, based mostly on the mistaken notion that the proposal would hand the Chief Executive dictatorial powers, was strong, determined and well organized. Debate was bitter, straying often from the bill to the personality of the man who would benefit from it, President Roosevelt. Representative John Cochran, the Missouri Democrat from St. Louis, was addressing the chair:

Mr. Chairman, lest we forget, let us remember another occasion when a great Man, a Man whom the world worships today, walked along the Calvary road to Golgotha and was put upon a crucifix. There, while the Roman centurions were driving nails into His hands and feet, letting the blood run, and while the burning sun was parching His sad and smiling face, He looked upon those who tortured Him, who misunderstood His mission, and spoke to them in language that has come down through the ages: "Father, forgive them, for they know not what they do." So I say today that throughout the length and breadth of our land, through misguided, poisonous, destructive, and unfair criticism, there is being put upon the cross of propaganda the greatest emancipator and the greatest humanitarian this country has ever known. While the nails of bitterness, rancor, hatred, and prejudice are being driven into his soul he must be weeping inwardly as he contemplates the tragedy of suffering humanity. Our great President of the United States, Franklin Delano Roosevelt, will go down in history as one of the noblest and finest characters this Nation has ever elected to office, and as he envisions the Republic he loves and the people he trusts, he, too, must be silently praying to the God of Creation: "O Lord, Father, forgive them my traducers, for they know not what they do."

Cochran was laying it on thick, of course, even by the fluid standards of political oratory; comparing Roosevelt to the gentle Man of Galilee may even have been in poor taste. Roosevelt was not divine. Presidents never are. Like all men born of woman, they embody about the same alloy of vices and virtues. But divine or not, they are Presidents, to whom much is given and from whom much is expected. Their achievements are acclaimed by the multitude; and when the applause dies away those achievements are recorded in books and etched in stone.

Their failures, real and imaginary, have a way of enduring, too. A readiness to criticize is always lurking in the land; it is part of that tendency inherent in a democracy to weaken those figures who exercise authority or who represent authority. Were Presidents perfect the people would have to invent faults, fashion feet of clay. It is also part of that tendency, it seems, to subject Presidents to hatred and to lies, to faultfinding without charity, to unfair criticism, intensely personal criticism, building

3

up in some men, building up like a biological urge, as inevitable as hunger or thirst. More durable than books or stones is the pettiness of the human heart, the meanness of the human spirit that perpetuates such rubbish as: Theodore Roosevelt was a drunk; Chester Arthur was an accomplice in the murder of Garfield; Woodrow Wilson had a loathsome social disease; Jackson was an adulterer; Lincoln was a common thief; Cleveland beat his wife; Washington wished to be king.

Perhaps Cochran's figure was not so overdrawn at that, considering what people have, on occasion, done to their leaders. They must be cut down to size; some people, it would appear, must reassure themselves that Presidents are not higher than the angels. So, Presidents of the United States—good men, for the most part, honorable men who pretended to be no more than men—have been insulted, vilified, reviled, and, on occasion, done to death by their fellows without just cause. Sometimes without cause at all.

It was that way with Franklin Roosevelt. Roosevelt was the object of hatred, of lies, of ridicule and irrational criticism. That he was not assassinated still seems a miracle. Nor was the torrent of personal abuse directed at him alone; his wife, his family, and others close to him all received their share. Sometimes it was spontaneous and uncalculated, sometimes purposeful and deliberate. Often it was by famous people, the well-known and the high-born; more often it was by people obscure and anonymous, people of no consequence. Occasionally, only occasionally, did it display any sense of humor. Always it betrayed an ungenerous spirit lacking in decency, good taste and fair play.

But that is the way it is being President.

CHAPTER I

If You Were
a Good Honest Man...

In all history, however, no President has been the subject of so much unfair criticism and such concentrated venom as has President Roosevelt.
—Adolph J. Sabath

Never in our history has an attack been so bitter. . . . No newspaper or journal would dare put into cold print even a hint of the charges about Mr. Roosevelt's mind and outlook. . . . —The Nation

. . . the whispering campaign against Franklin D. Roosevelt increases in virulence. —Common Sense

No slander is too vile, no canard too preposterous, to find voice among those who regard the President as their mortal enemy. —Marquis W. Childs

AUGUST 5, 1935, was a bad day for E. P. Cramer of Plainfield, New Jersey. He was fired from his job. Maybe he deserved to be fired for what he did. In any case, it was Franklin Roosevelt's fault.[1]

Cramer was an advertising man with the Thomas A. Edison Industries of Orange, New Jersey. As a minor stockholder in the Electric Bond and Share Company and a member of the American Federation of Utility Investors, he had more than a passing interest in the Wheeler-Rayburn Public Utilities Holding Company Act. For Cramer, passing interest meant opposition, and opposition meant writing a 2,000-word letter to Clarence E. Groesbeck, chairman of the board of Electric Bond and Share, offering a four-point program for counteracting the utilities legislation and "for destruction of the New Deal. . . ."[2]

Three of those points did not matter; the fourth got him fired. Groesbeck, Cramer suggested, should help launch "a whispering campaign designed to create popular suspicion that the 'new dealers,' and especially the 'New Dealer in Chief,' are either incompetent or insane. . . ." Cramer was willing to leave to Groesbeck the methods for starting "the ball rolling" without endangering the reputation of the company. "Ways to meet this requirement," he wrote, "will readily suggest themselves to you." Groesbeck never saw the letter. But a young assistant, George Walker did, and in reply, volunteered that Cramer's suggestions were "very pertinent."[3]

Possibly it was coincidence that shortly afterward tales about the President's mental condition began to appear, a mere trickle at first, then a torrent. There was no evidence that Walker had acted on Cramer's suggested slander. But with or without Walker's help the stories spread, growing more extravagant with the telling. "All over the country tongues waggled," was the way *Newsweek* put it, ". . . in smoking cars, taprooms, and country general stores rumor sprouted." In banks, too. Elliott V. Bell, in "The Decline of the Money Barons," relates an experience in which the head of one of the largest banks in New York remarked that he thought Roosevelt was insane. "You don't really mean that?" Bell asked. "Yes, I do. I think the man is absolutely unbalanced." Bell might have paid little notice had another banker not made the same remark a few hours later. "You don't really mean that?" he again asked. "Yes, I do," the gentleman replied. "I mean I think he's a pathological case."[4]

Others, who should have known better, passed the word along. Charles Benedict, writing for *The Magazine of Wall Street*, dwelled on Roosevelt's mediocre intellect and "irresponsible tendencies"; and Robert H. Hemphill, who handled financial news for the Hearst papers, called the President "incompetent" and "irresponsible." Even Congress interrupted its serious business to give the rumor a hearing. "Whom the gods would destroy, they first make mad," quoted Hamilton Fish, Jr., Republican representative from Roosevelt's home district. At the other end of the Capitol, Republican Senator Thomas D. Schall of Minnesota, who had courageously overcome his own handicap of blindness, flourished a business newsletter that alluded to Roosevelt's "inane replies" and "mental vagaries" which were "beginning to fulfill our predictions." Schall likened the President to the "weak-minded Louis XIV" (which proved, among other things, that Schall knew very little about Roosevelt and a lot less about Louis XIV). The weekly newsletter in Schall's possession was one privately circulated around Washington reporting choice gossip from Capitol corridors and cloakrooms that Roosevelt was "emotionally unstable."[5]

In the hinterland the stories got earthier. Roosevelt was not emotionally unstable, pathological, or even insane; Roosevelt was crazy. The after-effects of polio had made him so, according to one story. In the unexpurgated version he was hopelessly addicted to narcotics which he had begun using to relieve pain. Less plausible tales had Senator William E. Borah of Idaho coming upon Roosevelt cutting out paper dolls in his White House study, and Owen D. Young, board chairman of General Electric, finding him, on another occasion, babbling to himself and unable to talk coherently.

Or, to add a touch of mystery, the President was not Roosevelt at all. The real Roosevelt had gone completely berserk, had been spirited away, and his aides had quietly installed an impostor. Another story had Roosevelt suffering a mental breakdown while a press conference was in progress. Without warning he had burst into hysterical laughter. For fifteen minutes (while a roomful of newspaper reporters gaped, of course), the mad laughter continued until White House personnel wheeled the President away. The reason Roosevelt was so erratic and unpredictable, according to another yarn, was because he suffered from a strange disease, a malady that made him literally the mental captive of "the last man to see him at night." A more titillating explanation of the President's peculiar behavior, one with both sinister and sexual implications, had Roosevelt suffering a pathological Oedipus complex, or "silver cord" complex in the less sophisticated version. Meanwhile, the Chief Executive was under constant surveillance by psychiatrists (disguised as White House servants in one embellishment) and spending ever longer periods in a straitjacket to keep him from hurting himself.[6]

These and countless other stories circulated, multiplying, dividing, gaining new twists, new fillips, some funny, some vicious, a few obscene, all improbable, "roaring through the country in whispers," according to *Time* magazine, but sometimes by the more formal chain-letter system. For weeks Washington correspondents received urgent queries from their publishers and editors, queries, said the *Time* article, which invariably began: "Is the story true that . . . ?"[7]

The whisper campaign of 1935 reached floodtide by mid-July; then reaction set in. The Pulitzer Prize-winning writer of *The New York Times*, Arthur Krock, in his column of July 9 scotched the whole sordid business. "The only facts," wrote Krock, "are simple and not sensational . . . he is just the same Franklin Roosevelt." Stanley High, a preacher-turned-journalist and, at the time, a young NBC news broadcaster, followed a few days later with this appraisal for his radio audience: "The shrewdest newspapermen I met . . . declared that the country right now has the best and most alert mind in the White House . . . since the day of Roosevelt the First." And the Senate majority leader, Joseph Robinson, picked an appropriate spot, a peach-crop celebration at Forrest City, Arkansas, to brand the stories "lies" and the rumormongers "cowards and malicious falsifiers."[8]

With the whisper campaign out in the open, the Associated Press White House reporter, Francis Stephenson, confronted the President with it at a press conference. A *Newsweek* reporter described the scene: "The President toyed with his long cigarette holder . . . leaned back . . . laughed. Back to the roomful of correspondents he tossed the question. How did they think he looked? 'Okay from here.' "[9]

Early in August, the whisper campaign trail led back to where it may have started, back to Mr. Cramer of New Jersey. The Special Committee to Investigate Lobbying Activities, a Senate committee headed by Hugo Black of Alabama, having come into possession of the Cramer letter, invited him to appear before the committee on August 1. It was all very embarrassing and unpleasant. Black was relentless with his conscience-stricken witness:

THE CHAIRMAN (Black):   Had you seen the President of the United States?
MR. CRAMER: No.
THE CHAIRMAN: How long since you saw him?
MR. CRAMER: I don't know that I ever did.
THE CHAIRMAN: You have never seen him? Had you seen anybody that had seen the President of the United States when you suggested a whispering campaign?
MR. CRAMER: No.

· · · · · ·

THE CHAIRMAN: Do you claim that you had any basis on earth to try to circulate a report to the people of the United States that their President was insane, and if so give it now?
MR. CRAMER: No; none whatever.

· · · · · ·

THE CHAIRMAN: Are you ashamed?
MR. CRAMER: Certainly.
THE CHAIRMAN: Your suggestion was despicable?
MR. CRAMER: Yes.

Four days later, Cramer was fired.[10]

II

The rumors concerning Roosevelt's mental condition that floated around in the summer of 1935 did not die easily; through all the years that Roosevelt was President they kept cropping up with frustrating regularity and sometimes in the least likely places. They were still common, for example, when Marquis Childs wrote "They Hate Roosevelt" for *Harper's* in May, 1936.[11]

Perhaps no other man in the land was so firmly convinced of the President's madness (or did so much to perpetuate the myth) as George Frederick Gundelfinger of Sewickley, Pennsylvania. Gundelfinger, who claimed to have earned a doctorate at Yale in 1909, taught at Yale, the University of Pittsburgh, and later at Carnegie Institute of Technology, had had his troubles, including a sentence of one year and a day at the United States Medical Center for federal prisoners. In a charming little pamphlet entitled *Wooden-Head Son of a Bitch*, he placed the blame for his tribulations on Roosevelt.

Gundelfinger edited *Interquadrangular*, a singularly vicious periodical, and also published pamphlets and articles in an irregular series called Yale's New Fraternity Publications. For undistilled venom, Gundelfinger was hard to top. He first gained national attention in June, 1937, when he took exception to a picnic at Jefferson Island in Chesapeake Bay arranged by Roosevelt for Democratic members of Congress. In a "Message to Democrats," Gundelfinger deplored the idea of good Democrats accepting an invitation "to be gorged with crab meat, mint juleps and the F-rightful D-amnable R-ot of a crippled and imbecile host . . . an un-American president, paralyzed in body and in mind. . . ." Too many congressmen had succumbed to the fake charms of Roosevelt, wrote

"Er—this is Senator McNutney. He's handling our whispering campaign."

Copyright © 1936, 1964, The New Yorker Magazine, Inc.
Drawing by Peter Arno.

Gundelfinger, "with the abandon of brainless harlots"; the President, he insisted, should be impeached and permanently exiled. "Can anyone say seriously that Franklin D. Roosevelt is sane?" was the opening line of an *Interquadrangular* article. "To be candid," he wrote (in an open letter to Senator Robinson during the debate of the President's court plan), "the best example of 'a state of mental and physical decline' in Washington today is President Roosevelt himself. . . ." Robinson forwarded the letter to the President with a note asking if some legal action could not be taken against "this Gundelfinger person."[12]

TRIED EVERYTHING ELSE

Reprinted with permission from the Chicago Daily News.
Cartoon by Vaughn Shoemaker.

In 1938, the whispering began again in earnest. An article in *The Nation* that spring asserted there had never been such a concentrated campaign in our history with the possible exception of that preceding the impeachment of Andrew Johnson. "Have You Heard About Roosevelt . . . ?" was the title of an article in the August issue of *Common Sense*, in which Esther Arthur wrote that "the whispering campaign against Franklin D. Roosevelt increases in virulence. . . . Most of the stories told are far too obscene to be printable." Marquis Childs, in his sequel on the phenomenon, "They Still Hate Roosevelt," wrote that "No slander is too vile, no canard too preposterous. . . ." This was not new, said Childs, "but within the past year it has taken on a more menacing and violent tone."[13]

The old stories that the President's mind was completely gone were still making the rounds; and to the originals about hysterical fits of laughter were now added fits of weeping. There was a new variation on the nonsense about restraints and straitjackets (always reported by a friend of a friend who had just returned from Washington) to the effect that iron bars had been placed on the windows of the White House for fear Roosevelt would throw himself out. One of the more fashionable stories of the season turned on a trip to a psychiatrist. Roosevelt asked if he would live out his term. (It was a natural question because, in addition to being insane, he also had heart trouble, cancer, a stroke, syphilis, or what have you, depending upon who was telling the story.) "You'll survive it," replied the psychiatrist, "but none of the rest of us will."[14]

Even so responsible a writer as Mark Sullivan gave unwitting support to the traducements by referring to the President's "changeableness," a trait, said Sullivan, that is "now so widely understood that no one is going to expect his personality to undergo permanent change and become settled, stable." The colorful General Hugh Johnson, who had broken with Roosevelt shortly after the NRA was shot from under him, trod the outer limits of good taste when he wrote in a *Ladies' Home Journal* article that the President "is unpredictable . . . delights in surprises—clever, cunning, and quick . . . is erratic and impulsive."[15]

But it was one Morris A. Bealle who dared put in bold print what others only hinted at, who confirmed what others only suspected. Bealle was very solicitous; but "if we were squeamish . . . we would be remiss in our plain duty to our readers" regarding "this sorrow of his life." Roosevelt suffered from a condition that "ascends cephalad," he explained. According to Bealle, Roosevelt's "playboy attitude," his "joking approach," his "delusions of grandeur," his "inability to follow any definite course" were not his fault; it was the after-effects of polio, slowly, stealthily creeping upward ("rises toward the head," said Bealle), consuming the brain. The doctors responsible for this recital of medical quackery were unidentified, and for good reason; they did not exist.[16]

III

John B. Chapple was a man apart, one who put fair play ahead of votes in his scale of values. A Republican, Chapple challenged Robert La Follette, Jr., in the Wisconsin race for the Senate in 1934. He lost; but not before he had made it clear that, while he opposed Democrats on matters of policy, he would tolerate no vote-getting efforts on his behalf if it meant personal attacks on Roosevelt. At a rally at Waukesha, John Gay, a candidate for Congress, sneeringly referred to Roosevelt as "a man who can't stand on his own feet without crutches." Chapple shamed Gay for the tactless insult, turned on his heel, and left the rally that was being held in his honor.[17]

Gay had done little out of the ordinary. Roosevelt's paralysis had been legitimate cause for apprehension by many who were concerned, and rightly so, with a very practical question: Would the handicap interfere with the execution of his duties; was his health equal to the strain of the Presidency? The arduous campaign and the first year and a half in office should have dispelled doubts. Instead, his success at minimizing his handicap, the robust health he enjoyed seemed an irresistible challenge to some. There were those who, despite all evidence to the contrary, insisted that Roosevelt was a hopeless invalid. Sometimes the reason was ignorance; too often the reason was malice.

In the skirmishing that preceded the Democratic convention of 1932, Alfred E. Smith, four times governor of New York and rival of Roosevelt's for the nomination, made oblique reference to Roosevelt's health. In language inconsistent with his reputation for fierce forthrightness, Smith reminded the country that a campaign thrust a candidate before the electorate for some months before the election. This, said Smith, "requires a man of great vigor and bodily strength to stand the physical strain of it . . . over so long a period." Smith had not always entertained such doubts about Roosevelt's physical stamina. In 1928, when he was the Democratic presidential candidate and Roosevelt was the nominee for governor of New York, Smith had brushed aside questions about Roosevelt's paralysis. The office, he explained, required only brain work; a governor "does not have to be an acrobat."[18]

In 1935, the whisper campaign that focused on Roosevelt's mental condition also had some equally implausible stories to tell about his physical condition. As Newsweek assayed the situation, if the President contracted a common cold, the gossipmongers sneezed it "into a combination of leprosy, epilepsy, congenital insanity, and moral turpitude." Usually the stories left no doubt that Roosevelt was a helpless cripple. But one, more consistent with Roosevelt's legendary reputation for dissembling deceit, claimed that he was no longer paralyzed at all; the braces, the wheelchairs, the whole business, was a charade, a play on the mawkish sentimentality of the natives to get votes.[19]

Roosevelt's paralysis was the starting point for all manner of gossip about sexual impotence, incontinence, and, of course, creeping insanity— gossip that was spread with much winking, leering, and tongue-clucking; but for most of his enemies, the paralysis in his legs was quite enough. He was a cripple, less than a whole man. One had only to mention it. To point the finger like a malicious schoolboy was a painful reproach. This is what Gay had done. This is what Governor Talmadge of Georgia was doing when he referred warmly to Roosevelt as "that cripple" and complained that the "greatest calamity to this country is that President Roosevelt can't walk around and hunt up people to talk to." Sometimes the reference to his paralysis had Freudian overtones as in the sophisticated prose of Robert Hale's article in *Harper's*, a reply to Marquis Childs' "They Hate Roosevelt!" Some apologists for Roosevelt, wrote Hale, were trying to explain away his shortcomings "as they explain the conduct of the Kaiser by attempting to trace a connection between his unhappy malady and his conduct."[20]

Sometimes the reference was mixed with feigned relief that Roosevelt had thus far been spared from undertaking some presidential function which his condition could not possibly permit. "What a terrible infirmity!" was the opening gambit of a hateful little book, *The House of Roosevelt*. "Fortunately," the writer continued, with mock sympathy, "there is no pain attached to it. . . ." And then the payoff: "We can also be glad that we are living in times of peace . . . it would be absolutely impossible for Mr. Roosevelt to perform the arduous duties of commander-in-chief."[21]

At other times the reference was purposeful, almost sadistic, viciousness. The unhappy George Gundelfinger, in one of his numerous *Interquadrangular* articles, pointed out that America was a humanitarian nation, one that "believes in doing all it can for cripples—but its compassion need not go quite so far as to make them President of the United States." On another occasion, Gundelfinger referred to Roosevelt "limping about the Capital" and to his using a cane "of human living bones." Leonard Fowler, editor of a small-town Illinois paper, *The Fox Valley Mirror*, resorted to a similar approach. Fowler accused the press, the Administration, and the Democratic Party of a "conspiracy to remain mute concerning the infirmities of the President," the excuse being that we should not "take advantage of a sick man." But, wrote Fowler, "a physical cripple is inclined to become an emotional and spiritual cripple"; it was little short of criminal to "indulge them in the handling of a machine [government] where the lives and the liberties and the safety of other thousands are involved." In his libelous satire *The New Squeal*, Edwin T. Whiffen had one of his characters, a none-too-bright office boy, going about reciting a dire couplet: "Let still the land that would be free, Beware a lame and halting sovereignty."[22]

The motives are obscure for what was certainly the most dramatic whisper story about Roosevelt's health. In May, 1937, the McClure Syndicate distributed a "Confidential: Not for Release" report to nearly three hundred newspaper editors across the country. The report related how Roosevelt had been discovered at his desk in a deep coma, had been quietly carried aboard ship and taken to sea under naval convoy to recuperate. At the time all this was supposed to be transpiring, Roosevelt was fishing in the Gulf of Mexico, accompanied by the usual corps of reporters whom he received aboard the U.S.S. *Potomac* for the customary twice-a-week press conferences.[23]

It was not uncommon that Roosevelt's paralysis was linked with religion, the implication being that his affliction was somehow a result of sin. Almost daily, letters arrived in the White House mail from zealots who spoke of such things as "a judgment," "divine wrath," "a visitation," "a just God," and "divine retribution." "If you were a good honest man," one particularly cruel letter began, "Jesus Christ would not have crippled you. . . ." In this instance, Jesus Christ had justly crippled Roosevelt because "the filthy Communist rats" had been keeping "we poor unfortunate Christians out of employment on the W.P.A." Gundelfinger had a slightly different thought on the matter. The "bug of Roman Catholicism" controlled Roosevelt's mind, he told anybody who would listen, just as the polio germ "controls his body." "Perhaps," he wrote ominously, "they are one and the same thing."[24]

The President's paralysis was also indirectly responsible for an attack of another kind. In the years immediately following his bout with polio, Roosevelt had sought help in many directions. In those days he still believed in miracles; he lived in hope of a complete cure. This had led him, in 1924, to Warm Springs, Georgia, to try the soothing baths. Soon after, he initiated a plan for converting Warm Springs into a center for treatment and rehabilitation of polio victims. After he became President, a substantial part of the financing for the enterprise came from the proceeds of balls or celebrations held on his birthday, an annual observance that developed into the March of Dimes.

The Birthday Balls began in 1934; by 1936, the rumormongers were baying at the moon. As might be guessed, the story was that the proceeds went not to the Warm Springs Foundation but into Roosevelt's personal account. Apparently a number of people, disturbed by the rumors, wrote to Governor Talmadge of Georgia for information and reassurance. Talmadge was in no mood to be charitable toward Roosevelt in 1936. In reply, he quite frankly described the foundation as "a racket, being disguised under the name of charity, by the President of the United States" and suggested that they ask William Randolph Hearst to investigate the operation. William Dudley Pelley, leader of the Silver Shirts, one of the more vigorous of the extremist organizations of the 1930's which operated a college in North Carolina and a military camp near Oklahoma City, made a personal project of "exposing" the Warm Springs Foundation. In a leaflet, *Does Roosevelt Get Net Receipts from Birthday Paralysis Balls?*, Pelley wanted to know what conclusion could be drawn from "astounding information coming out of the Deep South, and being widely circulated without convincing contradiction, that all is not on the 'up and up.' . . ."[25]

Pelley had his own unique answer. The President, by racketeering in human suffering, was the "lowest form of human worm—according to Gentile standards." Another of Pelley's leaflets carried a cartoon depicting Roosevelt at his desk, smiling, the desk heaped with money across which is inscribed "Birthday Fund." A forlorn little girl, crippled and on crutches, is peering in the window and saying, ". . . everybody went to the Birthday Balls thinking that they were aiding me!"

As late as 1939, Pelley was still at it with a forty-eight-page booklet entitled *Cripples' Money*, proving to his satisfaction that Roosevelt had pilfered "three to four millions of dollars" of the money raised by the Birthday Balls. "Read it and boil," Stephen Early wrote to Basil O'Connor, head of the Warm Springs Foundation. O'Connor had Roosevelt's consent to proceed with a damage suit if it would serve any useful purpose, Early told him. "Of course, the President cannot act personally," he added.[26]

IV

In his book *Character Assassination*, Jerome Davis related an incident that was sacrilegious perhaps, but hilarious nonetheless. In 1937 he attended the annual banquet of the Military Order of the Loyal Legion in New York, a glittering affair at which Bainbridge Colby, once Secretary of State in the Wilson Administration, was the featured speaker. The dinner began with an invocation by a New York clergyman during which the good man of the cloth prayed for divine blessing upon the President of the United States. But let Davis tell the rest: "At this point a portly gentleman called out, in a voice that could be heard all over the dining room, 'The dirty son-of-a-bitch.' The minister was so dumbfounded by this occurrence that he paused for what seemed a full minute before he regained his composure and finished his prayer."[27]

This was not the first time Roosevelt was called a son-of-a-bitch, nor would it be the last. Over the years he was called this and a good many other things. Some of it was funny; some was lurid, sordid, and obscene. Much of it was tired, uninspired, sad. But not a little showed real spirit, originality, and an inventiveness that was almost admirable.

To the list of Rooseveltian epithets-in-print, the incorrigible George

Gundelfinger added "simpleton" and "this Svengali"; Paul Haber described him as "Lord Fauntleroy in the White House . . . blathering platitudes like a parson on vacation." David Proctor used a different figure, likening Roosevelt to "A modern political Juliet . . . endeavoring to make love to the people from the balcony." The anonymous Mark Granite, in his *A Book of Granitegrams*, a kind of *Poor Richard's Almanac* of anti-Roosevelt material, became lyrical, almost poetic, in describing him. Roosevelt was that "promise-breaker . . . pledge-breaker . . . oath-breaker" that "betrayer of the hopes of youth," that "deceiver of the old." And Lloyd Clark, who turned out reams of anti-Roosevelt literature from his vantage point in Milan, Illinois, on one occasion somehow managed the feat of calling Roosevelt a Communist, Socialist, internationalist, collectivist, and usurper all in the same sentence. In his book *The Roosevelt Road to Ruin*, Robert Morris Pierce used name-calling as a handy literary vehicle, subdividing the book under such headings as "Roosevelt the Demoralizer," "Roosevelt the Tyrant," "Roosevelt the Violator," and so on. As a name-caller, Pierce just about ran Gundelfinger a dead heat. It was the President of the United States that Pierce was describing with such statements as: ". . . animus of an embezzler"; ". . . spirit of a panderer"; ". . . petulant, insolent, rash, ruthless and blundering"; ". . . puts folly before wisdom and wrong before right"; ". . . would cause parasitism, degeneracy and national disruption"; ". . . sorcerer"; "impostor"; ". . . a wholesale dealer in broken promises"; "callow upstart"; "shallow autocrat"; "subjugator of the human spirit." And, as if that were not enough, Pierce had the effrontery to charge that Roosevelt "uses and countenances coarse slang, low epithet, and hot stigma, in place of respectful and cogent words."[28]

Among Roosevelt's name-calling enemies, Howland Spencer had a decided edge on his competitors. Virtually all the others knew Roosevelt secondhand, from a distance, if at all; Spencer knew Roosevelt personally. He should have. The self-styled Squire of Krum Elbow owned the estate across the Hudson River from Roosevelt's Hyde Park home. Spencer could, therefore, speak with authority about "our neighbor" whom he described as "Hyde Park's spoiled, frustrated darling," a "swollen headed nit-wit" with a "Messiah Complex," who had "all the courage of a boy scout—and the brain."[29]

V

All of the name-calling did not come just from little people needing to speak their piece, nor from exhibitionists who had to show off by getting their vituperation in print.

Name-calling, it seemed, was not a virus that infected only the poor, the ignorant, and the low-born. Much of it came from the rich, the educated, the high-born, people who were leaders in every civic enterprise, whose names graced the letterhead of every public charity, who were welcome in any drawing room, candle-lit dining room, or country-club bar. From them the name-calling was perhaps all the more reprehensible because they knew better; they should have been above such pettiness. But they were not. Name-calling was no respecter of persons; it was a disease which caused people like Alice Roosevelt Longworth to refer to her "maverick cousin" as "two-thirds mush and one-third Eleanor." Or Amos Pinchot, in an open letter to Felix Frankfurter, to call Roosevelt "the Great Uncertainty."[30]

The list could be extended indefinitely. At one time or another Roosevelt was called (by members of his own "class") a dictator, Communist, Fascist, revolutionist, destroyer of capitalism, renegade Democrat, coddler of labor, unprincipled charlatan, neglecter of the farmer, "nigger-lover," destroyer of the Democratic Party, President for life, crackpot, weakling, opportunist, politician on the make, man of capricious experimentation, living in a world of make-believe, and suffering from a kind of mental auto-intoxication. It did not matter that a weakling was hardly likely to become a dictator, or that being a Communist and a Fascist simultaneously was a feat of heroic proportions; these were problems only for doubters, not for believers.[31]

Of all the name-callers those with the most transparent motives were Roosevelt's political enemies. Name-calling was part of the political game; any number could play. Some were more adept than others, and occasionally one might actually mean what he said, although sincerity was not a requirement. In the game of vilifying your opponent, skill was what counted; and Roosevelt, himself a master of the art, was kept on his mettle by experts.

From the mouths of Republicans came a steady drum-fire of outrageous sobriquets. Roosevelt was, in their words, the Pied Piper of Hyde Park (Representative Ralph Owen Brewster, Maine); the High Priest of Repudiation . . . the familiar [of] the international money Jews . . . (Representative Louis McFadden, Pennsylvania); Santa Claus (Senator Arthur Vandenberg, Michigan); Franklin "Deficit" Roosevelt (Representative Hamilton Fish, Jr., New York); . . . ridiculous . . . dumb . . . never ran anything but Astor's yacht and a sailboat (Representative Robert F. Rich, Pennsylvania); . . . profligate . . . vacillator . . . springer of surprises (Representative J. William Ditter, Pennsylvania); . . . bitter, vindictive, unreasonable, and abusive . . . who aspires to dictatorial power (Representative Daniel Reed, New York); . . . a Little Napoleon . . . bitter, critical, inconsistent, contradictory [who] can hand out abuse, vituperation, vicious insinuation, and innuendo (Representative Clare Hoffman, Michigan). Alongside Roosevelt, said Senator Chan Gurney of South Dakota, "Barnum becomes a piker."[32]

Representative Dewey Short of Missouri and Senator Schall of Minnesota were the uncontested champion name-callers among Republicans, winning their titles by sheer endurance if for no other reason. It was Short who had once observed that Thomas Jefferson had founded the Democratic Party "and Franklin Delano Roosevelt has dumbfounded it." He could say whatever he pleased about Roosevelt and the Administration, Short liked to say, because "the New Deal outfit will not give me the sweat from their armpit." Short, who could always draw on brains and talent when he wanted to, usually chose to play the plain-talking, cracker-barrel yokel for the benefit of his southwest Missouri constituents. It was in this spirit that he would allow as how Roosevelt was "the smoothest, slickest politician who ever occupied that high office." Yessir, "slick as they make them—something like an eel." That Roosevelt fellow, you "squeeze him here he is over there"; "blows hot and cold in the same breath"; "can say 'yes' and 'no' in the same sentence"; "never letting his right hand know what his left hand doeth"; "the voice of Jacob but the hand of Esau"; "promises that which is not fulfilled."[33]

Schall, however, meant every word of it. Early in 1934, he was already calling Roosevelt a ham actor, full of high-sounding phrases and "great pretense of fierce attack," but really only "a small boy parading as a physician in his father's silk hat." By 1935, the actor had turned to dictator, had "become so great, so godlike, so masterfully minded, so divine, so beyond criticism . . . ," that he may now with immunity entertain "grandiose ideas of dictatorship" and, "with boot and spur," drive "queer un-American legislation" through the Congress. With public funds, Roosevelt behaved like "a drunken sailor," a description that was at least partially correct, because, said Schall, when he faced a problem for which he had no solution he "backs and fills, bluffs and threats, then goes afishing" aboard the *Nourmahal* with that "war profiteer," Vincent Astor.[34]

Before a Chicago Bar Association luncheon in 1935, Schall thought he saw a comparison between the beast of the Apocalypse and Roosevelt, "who set his slimy mark on everything." The President was a Fabian, he said, and the assembled guests (who had drunk a toast to Roosevelt at a banquet the previous evening) "would have to be God-damn drunk to vote for him again." The same high God, he plunged on, who had struck down Woodrow Wilson while he was seeking "the betrayal of America" might also have to strike down "this greater enemy of the liberties of the American people."[35]

VI

Attacking the President was an old story, hallowed by time, made respectable by tradition. Democracy, it seems, would be impossible without it. But few Presidents ever caught hell as Roosevelt did from so many different directions and for such a diverse catalogue of transgressions, large and small, both real and imaginary.

Malcolm Bingay, writing in the Detroit *Free Press*, for example, did not like the way Roosevelt smoked. He disapproved the cigarette holder (which he waved around "as though the thing were a conductor's baton"); he was annoyed by the way he puffed out his cheeks, threw his head back, and self-consciously blew smoke toward the ceiling, all the while flicking ashes ("even when there is no ash"); a performance, seethed Bingay, accompanied by "laughs and smirks and winks."[36]

This minor display of egotism was no doubt in some way related to Roosevelt's background, a background for which critics had a standard glossary of terms including "silver spoon," "wealthy parents," "private tutors," "never suffered privations," "every wish was granted," "wanted for nothing," "never worked," "spoiled child," "pampered youth." A heritage like this was taken as prima facie evidence that Roosevelt was not (nor could he ever be) a man of the people. He was no more capable of understanding the people or of helping the people, according to one pamphlet, "than a ten year old boy from the slums would be to teach etiquette or rhetoric to a class of high school students on the Gold Coast."[37]

This distorted notion of the way people of wealth behaved likewise was a simple way of explaining Roosevelt's predilection for vacationing. It was a doleful picture the critics painted. One could almost see government officials by the thousands drumming their fingers on desktops, and the American people standing dejectedly, hands clasped, eyes turned toward heaven, waiting, patiently yet expectantly, waiting while their President went fishing. Nero fiddled while Rome burned, fumed Congressman Clare Hoffman, but Roosevelt would not even do that. The President just "sits in the White House" and "ponders his next vacation plans." "He knows about and loves to fish and go on extended vacations," said the irascible Michigan representative (accompanied by appropriate remarks about people "living upon an inherited income"). According to Hoffman's absurd calculations, Roosevelt had already spent 42 per cent of his time (as of 1938) on vacations, a mere five months out of each year.[38]

Missouri's Dewey Short also had a few words to say about "the fishingest President that any country ever had" who liked to fish from the decks of "new $10,000,000 cruisers escorted by battleships" or on "a million-dollar yacht of some social high light." Short simply had no idea, he confessed, how much this was costing the taxpayers of the country; but he thought it would make an excellent campaign issue in 1936. Landon, he said, would never fish from a yacht or warship even if he could; ". . . being so plain and simple, he gets a cane pole and a can of worms." This was Short's rustic way of saying that Landon (a millionaire who could have fished any time, any place, and any way he pleased) preferred to "rough it," not with cane pole and a can of worms, but by wading shallow, fresh water with hip boots and fly-rod.[39]

Roosevelt's early years, comfortable years, years free from any bouts with grinding poverty or doubts about the source of his next meal, were grounds for charges of another sort concerning his willingness to work, his ability to work, his never having earned a living, met a payroll, lived within a budget; in short, he had never learned the value of a dollar (or a billion dollars either, according to his critics). Congressman Rich was certain this was the key to the failure of the New Deal. What else could you expect with a man in the White House "who never worked a day in his life . . . never ran a business . . . could not run any kind of business." "You cannot take men," said Rich, "who have inherited things from their forefathers, who do not know the value of a dollar, and have them run a great country like the United States." "I do not mean to be unkind," said New York Representative James W. Wadsworth, Jr., not meaning to be unkind, "but I am wondering if the present occupant of the White House has ever known or ever will know actually himself how a dollar is earned."[40]

Had Roosevelt not had a patrician background it is unlikely that so much would have been said about his being egotistical, arrogant, snobbish. Even if these allegations were true, they were arrived at, in many cases, from false evidence. Some people saw snobbishness in Roosevelt's use of a cape instead of an overcoat, although it should have been self-evident that for a man with paralyzed legs a cape was easier to manage than a coat. Others read the same thing into the way Roosevelt tilted his head and appeared to be looking down his nose at people, a personal habit acquired after long years of maintaining the precarious balance of pince-nez glasses.

At any rate, Congressman Charles Gifford of Massachusetts, in one outburst at "this arrogant President . . . afflicted with a super ego," told the House of Representatives the story of the pupil who, when asked by the teacher to name one thing that did not exist fifty years ago, replied, "Me!" "The pupil," shouted Gifford, "must have been Franklin D. Roosevelt."[41]

But it must be agreed, cried the critics, that the sublime manifestation of the Roosevelt ego was his suggestion in 1939 that Congress build a library at Hyde Park to house the President's private library and state papers. This was done; but not before Representative Harold Knutson of Minnesota registered his protest. The papers should be kept in Washington, he insisted, so future generations could "see how not to run a government." Congressman Short was somehow certain that not even Shakespeare or Milton or Wordsworth would have "the unmitigated gall and brazen effrontery to ask that a monument be erected to them . . . before their death."[42]

For those charitable enough to forgive Roosevelt for the circumstances of birth over which he had no control and for inherited faults, there was more than enough left for the diligent fault-finder. And find fault they did. Early in the Administration the dozen or more clerks who worked in the subterranean sections of the White House Executive offices began a new file of bulging manila envelopes filled with letters, clippings, pamphlets, every known form of written communication imaginable, a file with the strange legend "Below the Belt."

From sampling this file one could learn the worst: that Roosevelt (with a standing order that all Republican speeches on radio be jammed) was taking unfair advantage of his Republican colleagues through modern technology; that Roosevelt had ordered the firing of Glenn Frank, president of the University of Wisconsin; that he was an income tax dodger; that, during the campaign of 1932, he had ordered his motorcycle escort to shoot the locks from the gates of Bennington College, Vermont, where he was to appear for a speech; that, during World War I, he was a slacker and draft-dodger; that he was a thief who had stolen stamps from a rare-stamp dealer during a White House visit; that he was a swindler; and, to round out the list, that he was a kidnapper and murderer.[43]

But with some of it there was just enough truth and ascertainable fact to give it respectability. For more than a year preceding the election of 1936, Roosevelt's enemies had been taking digs at his war record. Letters to the President were usually a good barometer of how effective an anti-Roosevelt story was at any given time. In the spring of 1935, letters began appearing with some regularity that made at least passing reference to Roosevelt's military record, to "his seeing service in the world war," about his "trying to pass himself off as a Legionaire," and asking, "where were you?" One particularly vicious letter (which referred to Roosevelt as "old flat-foot Frankie") said that his war record was spelled "s-l-a-c-k-e-r."[44]

Part of this flurry had been touched off by Roosevelt's attitude toward the veterans' bonus legislation and partly by a much-publicized speech of Huey Long in which the mercurial senator made his point in the form of a hypothetical interview with the President:

"How much money did you get for your services? Of course, sir, we know that you gave your services to the country during the World War as a matter of patriotism only; but how much did you get?"
". . . $10,000 for that year's work."
"How many cannon did you face, sir?"
"None."
"How many nights did you sleep on the ground, sir?"
"None."
"How many nights did you hear the rain on the tents? How many days and nights did you hear the crack of German rifles and endure the smell of poison gas? How many times did you see the flames of the burning fires

of hell and destruction and carnage searing the lives and the souls of men?"
"None."
"And yet you got $10,000, Mr. Roosevelt, for the patriotic services which
you gave to the country in the scourge of that war."[45]

In the hands of the Republican Service League, Roosevelt's wartime
duties as Assistant Secretary of the Navy became virtually the same as
cowardice. In 1936, part of the League's campaign literature included a
leaflet which asked, in bold black type, "What is the Answer? . . . Or,
Isn't There to Be One?" meaning "where [Roosevelt] saw those cities
destroyed, blood running from the wounded, men coughing out their
gassed lungs . . . where, in general, you saw war on land and sea."[46]

Postwar conditions in Germany were partly responsible for the charge
being made that Roosevelt was a swindler; his attempts to regulate banking practices and the stock exchanges did the rest. Our President, Wisconsin Representative John Schafer told the House triumphantly, "is an
ex-international banker of wide experience and a former attorney for
international bankers." The Wisconsin Republican could prove it. "I
hold in my hand" were the familiar words: (1) a photostatic copy of *The
New York Times*, September 14, 1922, page 31, advertising a new issue of
600,000,000 German marks, offered by United European Investors, Limited,
Franklin D. Roosevelt, president; (2) a photostatic copy of *Poor's
Register of Directors*, 1929, page 1480, which lists Franklin Delano Roosevelt as a director of the International Germanic Trust Company; (3) a
photostatic copy of the *Martindale-Hubbell Law Directory*, January, 1933,
volume 1, page 754, showing an advertisement of Franklin Delano Roosevelt, as investment banker; (4) photostatic copies of records of the
Federal International Banking Corporation, which showed that Franklin
Delano Roosevelt wrote the foreword of the prospectus for this company,
a company organized for the purpose of selling foreign securities in the
United States. The purpose of this recital was to prove Roosevelt's involvement in international schemes for "speculating in German marks
during the German inflation. . . ."[47]

Meanwhile, one I. B. Leibson took the time to publish *The Raw Deal;
The Deal Mr. Roosevelt Forgot*, a wretched little book recounting Roosevelt's misadventures in promoting something called Camco (Consolidated
Automatic Vending Machine Company) that ended in bankruptcy
court. Despite the title, the point of the book was to prove that Roosevelt
was simply applying on a national scale the same kind of slipshod practices that had gone on in Camco. In 1933, said Leibson, "there came upon
the land the promotion of Mr. Franklin D. Roosevelt's NEW DEAL, with
the identical methods of the Raw Deal used in a bigger way. . . . Here,
indeed, was a man to drive the wolves out of Wall Street. . . !"[48]

These lesser faults were as nothing compared to the heinous crime
of murder; and Roosevelt was, it seems, a murderer—on two occasions at

the very least. Roosevelt was somehow guilty of the assassination of Huey Long. This was the opinion of the Yorkville, New York, Share-Our-Wealth Society which circulated a mimeographed scandal sheet that arrived at this interesting conclusion using the gossip-columnist technique: "Do you know why Huey Long was murdered?"; "What four men, formerly involved in an attempted assassination of Senator Long, are now on the patronage lists of President Roosevelt and James Farley?"; "What connection was there between President Roosevelt and the murderers of Huey Long?" One did not need the answers to any of the questions; questions and answers were one and the same thing.[49]

Roosevelt also had a hand in the most celebrated crime of the decade, the Lindbergh kidnapping. At least Hal Walton, chairman of something called the Committee of Witnesses, claimed he did. For several years, Walton circulated an article entitled "The New Deal and Lindbergh Baby," an article that Walton advertised in 1939 as being in its twenty-seventh edition and with more than 700,000 copies distributed. It was a complicated story that Walton had to tell about how Lindbergh had earned the enmity of Germans for promoting United States aviation interests in the Far East. The kidnapping was to be his punishment for such mischief, carried out by German agents, and financed from United States sources (Jewish, naturally). The job was bungled; but the bunglers were shielded by Franklin Roosevelt. Bruno Richard Hauptmann, who was tried and executed for the crime, was only the sacrificial lamb. Roosevelt's reasons for protecting the criminals were not altogether clear; but it seemed to have something to do with his participation in an international Jewish bankers' conspiracy. Anyway, Walton had the goods on him; and proposed making March 1, the anniversary of the kidnapping, an annual National Disgrace Day.[50]

VII

Some of the personal criticism of Roosevelt was of less serious nature, taking the form of jokes and stories with at least a trace of humor. "Say, speaking of the W.P.A.," said Mr. Arbuthnot, the cliché expert in Frank Sullivan's delightful satire of an interview with a Roosevelt critic, "did you hear the one about the W.P.A. worker and King Solomon? Why is a W.P.A. worker like King Solomon?" "I heard it," interrupted the interviewer. "Because," insisted Mr. Arbuthnot, "he takes his pick and goes to bed." "Is that the funniest New Deal joke you know, Mr. Arbuthnot?" inquired the interviewer. "Oh, no," he answered; "Here's the funniest. Have you heard there's only Six Dwarfs now . . . ? Dopey's in the White House!"[51]

A number of the funnier stories revolved around Roosevelt's alleged egomania. One concerned a psychiatrist who met an untimely end. Upon his arrival in Heaven he was rushed by St. Peter to attend God Himself. "You see," explained St. Peter, "He has delusions of grandeur; He thinks He's Franklin Roosevelt." Another had Hitler, Mussolini, and Roosevelt attending a conference to decide on a division of the world among them. Hitler announced that he wanted 75 per cent of it. To which Mussolini objected, saying that the good Lord had promised him half of the world. At this point Roosevelt interrupted. "Benito," he said, patronizingly, "you know I never promised you anything of the kind." Another of the more popular stories involving the Heavenly Hosts had Roosevelt arriving in Heaven where he was told by St. Peter that he could do any one thing that his heart desired. Roosevelt announced pleasantly that he would like to rewrite the Heavenly Constitution. In time, Roosevelt brought his new constitution to St. Peter, who looked it over, scratched his wing pit, and muttered, "Seems all right to me; but I wonder how God will like being Vice-President." Although Roosevelt probably held no such exalted opinion of himself, apparently a few did. In January 1939, a poll of fifty thousand students in New York City indicated that Roosevelt was the most beloved man among the school children; God came in a poor second.[52]

To his enemies even his affability became malevolence. Stories of his excessive agreeableness found their way into the halls of Congress where Congressman Gifford told this one to his House colleagues: First Mr. Ickes called at the White House and presented his side. "Mr. Ickes, you are absolutely right," the President told him. Later, Mr. Hopkins came in and presented his side. "Mr. Hopkins," said the President, "you are absolutely right." After Hopkins' departure, someone else who had been quietly listening to the interviews [other versions of the story say it was Mrs. Roosevelt] spoke up and said, "That's silly. They cannot both be absolutely right." To which Roosevelt replied, "You are absolutely right."[53]

Many of his critics confused Roosevelt's agreeableness with vacillation, believing that he had no program, that he was, in fact, an incompetent experimenter who would do anything whether it needed doing or not. This quality in Roosevelt reminded Wisconsin Congressman Stephen Bolles of the story about the veterinarian who was called in to look over a human patient in an emergency when no medical doctor was available. After a superficial examination of the patient the veterinarian drawled: "I don't know what is the matter with him; but I have some medicine here that will throw him into fits, and I'm hell on fits."[54]

Roosevelt's genuine enjoyment of fishing, of sailing, and of being around the water was raw material for a number of jokes. On one occasion, according to a popular Roosevelt fish story, he was fishing alone and ran out of bait. Nothing daunted he heaved the bare hook back in the water, smiled his winning smile and exclaimed, "My Friends!" whereupon a thousand suckers leaped into the boat. On yet another occasion the President was once more fishing alone. "Forgetting that He was not sitting on His throne, He rocked the boat, lost His budget balance, fell overboard and was drowning, when three boy scouts appeared and pulled Him out." With his usual modesty and his famous grin, Roosevelt called the boys "My Friends" and told them that they had done a great thing for their country and for the world, for which they should be rewarded. "Generously He put his practiced hand into the country's pocket and told the boys to name any wish." Two of the boys asked for and received appointments, the one to West Point and the other to Annapolis. "The third boy remained downcast and silent, but upon being pressed, asked for a military funeral." "My boy," said the President, "you are too young to be thinking of such things. Why do you imagine that you are going to need any kind of funeral at this time?" "When I get home and tell my father that I helped pull you out, I'll certainly need one!" the boy sadly replied.[55]

Of all the Roosevelt jokes perhaps the most widely repeated one (although certainly not the most humorous) concerned the Washington committee trying to decide where in the Capitol to erect a statue of Roosevelt. The members decided it would never do to place Roosevelt next to Washington because Washington never told a lie. They could not place him beside Lincoln because Lincoln had freed the slaves and

Can YOU Answer
The $64 Question ?

WHAT MAN SAID TO "THAT" WOMAN?
"You kiss the negroes
I'll kiss the Jews,
We'll stay in the White House,
As long as we choose."

THE PRESIDENT'S WIFE

IS SUING FOR DIVORCE BECAUSE

SHE IS NOT GETTING WHAT HE IS GIVING

THE OTHER PEOPLE

was known as "Honest Abe." They could not place the statue next to the bust of Franklin because, while Franklin's experimental kite was in the clouds, he kept both feet on the ground. The committee was in a quandary. But after careful consideration it was decided to place him next to Columbus, because Columbus did not know where he was going when he started, did not know where he was when he arrived, and did not know where he had been when he returned. Besides, he did it all on borrowed money.[56]

One very common way by which such humor was spread was on business cards. They were everywhere, stuck up over cash registers, along the edges of desk blotters, passed from hand to hand by salesmen calling on customers, and materializing from billfolds wherever men gathered for shop talk and a smoke. "If you don't give me an order, I'll vote for 'That Man' again" and "When in the middle of the stream AND the horse starts *Riding You* it's time to change horses" were among the better ones. The most popular of the funny business cards was one bearing the "new Oath of Allegiance" to the Democratic Party:

I pledge allegiance to the Democratic Party, and to the Roosevelt Family for which it stands, one family indispensable—with divorces and captaincies for all.

Four thousand years ago Moses said to his people: "Pick up your shovels, mount your asses, load your camels, and ride to the Promised Land."

Four thousand years later Mr. Roosevelt said to HIS people: "Throw down your shovels, sit on your asses, light up a Camel: THIS IS the Promised Land."

Probably the most clever of them all, however, was one distributed by the New Jersey Color Card Company which had as its theme the "government handout":

Confidential Report of Conditions of the Nation Under the New Deal

Population of the United States	124,000,000
Eligibles for Old Age Pensions	30,000,000
That leaves to do the work	94,000,000
Persons working for the government	20,000,000
That leaves to do the work	74,000,000
Ineligible to work under the Child Labor Law	60,000,000
That leaves to do the work	14,000,000
Number unemployed in the nation	13,999,998
That leaves to do the work	2

ME AND THE PRESIDENT
HE HAS GONE FISHING
AND I AM GETTING DAMN TIRED[57]

VIII

Why Roosevelt and the New Deal should have inspired so much poetry, parody, and doggerel is a mystery probably not worth pursuing. But they did; some humorous, some mean, not a little scatological, even obscene. If quantity was any sign of depth of feeling, Ulysses Grant Vogan must have hated Roosevelt more than any man in the land. His *A Modern Hudibras; The New Deal in Rime* was a volume of his own poetry, eighty-one pages of it, attacking Roosevelt from every direction. The following is fairly typical:

> A Don Quixote, errant knighting
> Shadows, ghosts, and wind-mills fighting;
> Who sallies forth into the fray,
> Then sallies back the other way,
> And turns so quick from his attack,
> He meets himself a-coming back,
> To boast of monsters he has slain,
> And bigger ones that still remain,
> Till 'twould appear, when all is said,
> The ones he kills do not stay dead.[58]

Some of the anti-Roosevelt poems were quite long, fifteen to twenty stanzas not being uncommon. One of the better efforts, distributed by the Deluxe Stamp Works of Auburn, Nebraska, and entitled simply "Roosevelt," reminded one of Edgar Allan Poe. Its concluding lines were:

> Who ploughed up cotton, corn, and wheat,
> Who killed our pigs, destroyed our meat?
> 'Twas he, the captain of the fleet.
>   'Twas Roosevelt.
>
> Who, with his jesting care-free grin,
> Piles up debts, so our unborn kin
> Must toil in gloom, must die to win?
>   'Twas Roosevelt.
>
> Although in '32 he won,
> Now, judged by all he's said and done,
> PUBLIC ENEMY NO. 1
>   IS FRANKLIN DELANO ROOSEVELT.

In 1938, in the midst of what was called the Roosevelt Depression by his critics, copies of a long, fourteen stanza poem began appearing in the White House mail, deploring the resumption of deficit spending.

> And now that the pump is being primed,
> With what? 'Tis hard to tell;
> But what's the use of priming
> When there's nothing in the well?
> So Frank will have to clatter more
> And swell his chattering bump;
> But with incessant chattering
> How can he prime the pump?[59]

Poems began to appear early in Roosevelt's first term, clever for the most part, light, whimsical and humorous. For example, "His Enigmatic Smile" was the formidable title for this four-line ditty:

> Twinkle, twinkle little Grin
> Up above the world of din.
> Never worried, so serene,
> How I wonder what you mean.

His smile was also featured in this little verse printed as a business card under a caricature of a laughing Roosevelt:

> A Beautiful Voice
> A Wonderful Smile
> With Every Assurance
> Of Nothing Worth While.

The most popular of the early poems was an ambitious effort by an anonymous author entitled "Tired." It seems to have first appeared in print in the August 7, 1935, issue of the *Northwestern Miller*. Later, it was reprinted as a leaflet and as a business card and distributed by numerous companies to their customers. It appeared regularly in anti-Roosevelt pamphlets and books, and eventually was inserted into the *Congressional Record* by Congressman Rich of Pennsylvania.

TIRED

> I'm tired, oh, so tired, of the whole New Deal,
> Of the juggler's smile and the barker's spiel,
> Of the mushy speech and the loud bassoon,
> And tiredest of all of our leader's croon.
>
> I'm tired of the tax on my ham and eggs,
> I'm tired of payoffs to political yeggs,
> I'm tired of Jim Farley's stamps on my mail,
> Tired of my shirt with the tax-shortened tail.
>
> I'm tired of farmers goose-stepping to laws,
> Of millions of itching job-holders paws,
> Of fireside talks on commandeered mikes,
> Of passing more laws to stimulate strikes.

I'm tired of the hourly increasing debt,
I'm tired of promises still to be met,
Of eating and sleeping by government plan,
And calmly forgetting the "Forgotten Man."

I'm tired of every new brain trust thought,
Of the Ship-of-State, now a pleasure yacht,
I'm tired of cheating the courts by stealth,
And terribly tired of sharing my wealth.

I'm tired of seeing Eleanor on page one,
Of each royal in-law and favorite son,
I'm tired of Sistie and Buzzie Dall,
I'm simply—completely—fed up with it all.

I'm tired and bored with the whole New Deal,
With its juggler's smile and its barker's spiel,
Oh, Lord, out of all thy available men,
Please grant us a Cleveland or Coolidge again.[60]

By 1935, with crop control and agricultural relief measures providing payments to farmers for curtailing production of soil-depleting crops and agricultural surpluses, an enterprising wit ran an advertisement in a Joplin, Missouri, newspaper: "Dandy way to make money; buy this thirteen acres for hog raising. Sign up with government not to raise, say 500 hogs. It will pay you $1000. That will pay for the acres and have some left over." Chester A. Davis, AAA Administrator, apparently had a blind spot for humor on this subject, for he exploded: "Preposterous! It's a deliberate misrepresentation and not in any way possible. I shall begin an investigation."[61]

From the strange quirks in New Deal agricultural policy over the years emerged some genuinely funny definitions which, according to *The New York Times*, began with certain United States senators and quickly spread across the country: "SOCIALISM—If you own two cows you give one to your neighbor. COMMUNISM—You give both cows to the government and the government gives you back some of the milk. FASCISM—You keep the cows but give the milk to the government, which sells some of it back to you. NEW DEALISM—You shoot one cow, milk the other and then pour the milk down the sink." Other versions had slightly different definitions of the New Deal. In one, you shoot both cows and milk the government. In another, the government shoots both cows and milks you.[62]

It was inevitable that Roosevelt's New Deal farm policies would also receive their share of ribbing in poetry. Among the first was a poem by Adelaide W. Neall in the *Saturday Evening Post*. The opening stanza set the mood:

"You are wise, Uncle Samuel,"
    the farmer said,
"And there must be a reason, I know,
But why do you lend us money for crops
And then pay us to scrap what we grow?"
"I am told," Uncle Samuel replied with a sigh,
"Big crops are occasion for grief,
And the richer the harvest all over the land
The more there'll be need for relief."

*Copyright 1933, New York Herald Tribune, Inc. Reproduced with
permission. Cartoon by Jay N. Darling*

One of the better ones, a parody of Lord Tennyson's "The Charge of the Light Brigade," was read by a witness before a congressional committee holding public hearings in Sioux City, Iowa, in 1937. Senator Lynn Frazier of North Dakota who had had his differences with Roosevelt over farm policy, preserved it for posterity in the *Congressional Record*.

> Half a league, half a league
> Half a league onward
> Into Sioux City rode
> The crop-control six hundred;
> County agents to right of them,
> Payrollers to left of them,
> Braintrusters back of them,
> Volleyed and thundered.
> Someone had blundered!
> Theirs not to make reply;
> Theirs not to reason why;
> Theirs just to testify.
> So into the valley of death,
> Into the shadow of hell.
> Ready to sell their soul
> For compulsory soil control,
> Valiant six hundred;
> No; not because they felt that way;
> But just to get four bucks a day.[63]

Any number of poems about Roosevelt and the New Deal had a Christmas motif, some of which antedated by several years Al Smith's oft-quoted remark after the New Deal victory in 1936 that one does not shoot Santa Claus. One that had lasting popularity over the years was first presented as part of the annual panning of the Administration at the Gridiron Club dinner in December, 1934.

> 'Twas the night before Christmas
> When all through the land,
> The ballots were ready, the polls fully manned,
> The stockings were hung by the chimney with care
> Because good St. Franklin soon would be there.
> The people were snuggled all warm in their beds
> With visions of alphabet plums in their heads;
> And voters were dreaming of how, the next day,
> They'd march to the polls for old PWA.
> When the jingle of sleigh bells was heard from afar
> And swift through the night roared a big White House car.
> From out of the packages, piled high to see
> Shone the bright, smiling face of the good Saint F. D.
> Each bulging package a dollar sign wore,
> And down every chimney he poured them, galore.

By mantels and chairs he piled dollars so thick,
For he knew, though devalued, they'd still do the trick.
Homes of good little boys, from Curley to Duffy,
And Donahey, McAdoo, Lehman, and Guffey,
He hastened to reach with the glittering stream
Before sleeping taxpayers waked from their dream.
His eyes, how they gleamed; his laughter so gay,
As he thought how good deeds most generally pay!
Every stocking was filled ere the saint turned to go,
And the manna had fallen as thick as the snow;
And they heard him exclaim, as he flew out of sight;
"Merry Christmas to all—and be sure you vote right!"

A Christmas card that was circulated in pay envelopes and with advertising brochures was entitled "Merry Christmas from Santa Claus," or, occasionally, "Advance Notice from Santa Claus":

I am sending this card to tell you
That the New Deal has taken away
The things that I really needed
My workshop—my reindeer—my sleigh
Now I'm making my rounds on a donkey
He's old and crippled and slow
So you'll know if I don't see you Christmas
That I'll be out on my ass in the snow.

There was at least one version of the Christmas carol, "Hark, the Herald Angels Sing," a dreadful parody entitled "Heil":

Heil! the workless workers sing
Glory to the New Deal King.
Loaf on earth while strikes run wild,
Boss and men unreconciled.

Joyful, striking Reds arise,
Smite the U.S. working guys!
Join, My Friends, and then proclaim,
Seldom will we work again.

Soft he tells us charming lies,
Fools us with his beaming smiles.
(Sure to raise class strife on earth,
Bound to cause a dreadful dearth.)

Risen with Postman in His wings,
New (false) hopes to all He brings.
Heil! the workless workers sing,
Glory to the New Deal King.[64]

IX

Much of the anti-Roosevelt poetry was as vicious as other forms of below-the-belt criticism. One ambitious effort that kept turning up with regularity was "Traitors Three," a poem which accused Roosevelt of treason. The author was never identified; but the fictitious imprint read: "Printed in the U.S.S.R., UNITED Subject STATES of Roosevelt." The poem presented Brutus, Benedict Arnold, and Roosevelt in Hell, arguing about who was the greatest traitor of the three. After Brutus bragged that he had betrayed and murdered his friend, Caesar, and Arnold had done him one better by confessing that he had betrayed "a whole bloomin' Army," it was Roosevelt's turn. So impressive was the catalogue of Roosevelt's acts of treasons that:

> Brutus stood there filled with awe,
> Arnold sat with fallen jaw;
> Then Brutus said, "We've had our fling,
> Get up now, Arnold, and salute your KING."

"Rejected," another long poem, was similar to "Traitors Three" in content, tone, and phrasing. It, too, was anonymous. The poem had Roosevelt standing at the gates of Hell applying to Satan for admittance. Satan has posed a question. What sins had Roosevelt committed that were despicable enough to justify his entrance into Hell, Satan wanted to know.

> Then Hyde Park D., with his kosher guile,
> Stepped forth and flashed his toothy smile.

"Hyde Park D." launched into such a recital of sins that Satan finally found it necessary to interrupt him:

> Now Hyde Park talked both loud and long
> While the Devil stood, and his head he hung,
> At last he said: "let's make it clear,
> You'll have to go—YOU CAN'T STAY HERE,
> For once you mingle with the mob,
> I'D HAVE TO HUNT FOR ANOTHER JOB."[65]

There was one or more poems for just about all of Roosevelt's transgressions, specialized poems, poems attacking his farm policy, labor, relief, spending, relations with Congress, and all the rest. One of these, attacking the President for his stand on Prohibition was fairly typical:

OUR BOOZEDOGGLING PRESIDENT

> It's hard to think a man would sink
> So low he'd tell the mob

"Now looka here, I'll give you beer
If you'll give me my job."

He won, 'tis true, as hirelings do,
Yet, winning in that race,
He put a stain upon his name
That time will not efface.

When he espoused the cause of booze
He little thought that day
Of all the human derelicts
He strew along life's way.

The bleary-eyed drunkards everywhere
Now staggering to the grave
The growing host of ruined girls
Now serving as "white slaves."

The countless thousands everywhere
Struck down by cars of steel
Because of drink be-fuddled brains
That get behind the wheel.

The worse than orphaned little ones
Who starve for want of bread
Because the cash which daddy earns
Is spent for drink, instead;

The worse than widowed drunkard's wives
Who feed on tears tonight,
These all can blame our President
Who helped booze win its fight.[66]

Another, a parody of a beautiful hymn, appeared in E. C. Riegel's
Franklinstein, a publication of the Consumers' Guild of America, in
which Roosevelt was portrayed as the mad scientist and the NRA his
monster:

Nira, my God to Thee
Nira to Thee
E'en though I double-cross
Bear with me.[67]

Attacking Roosevelt and the numerous facets of the New Deal through
poetry and parody frequently led into areas of questionable taste, produced
scabrous and sometimes scatological results. One example (in which the
government seemed almost to be inviting such criticism) will suffice.
A program of the CWA (and, later, the WPA) to promote better health
and sanitation was building better outdoor toilet facilities. Whether the
program ever improved health and sanitation is probably unimportant.
At least it gave the country a welcome belly-laugh and opened up all

kinds of possibilities for barnyard humor. The local wit could always raise whoops of laughter with the suggestion that it would take a Privy Council to administer the program; or, better still, a Federal Authority of Rural Transactions (which, like the other alphabetical agencies, would be shortened to F.A.R.T.).[68]

The reason Roosevelt was so interested in privies, the anonymous author explained in *The New Deal Goes to the Privy*, was "perhaps to be found in the fact that most of the carpenters and cement workers on the Federal relief rolls are better fitted for backhouse building than for more enduring or more monumental architectural achievements." At any rate, Roosevelt would long be remembered for a very special reason:

> We who live back in the past, who long for yesterday,
> Can now perk up with dignity and bless "C.W.A."
> For down in North Carolina where nature reigns supreme
> They're licking this depression with a "back to nature" scheme;
> They're building miles of privies on the good old squatter's plan
> With good old fashioned holes and things meant for the real HE man;
> And North Carolina's bound to be the nation's paradise,
> For folks who want real comfort will flock there just like flies.
> And as they sit and meditate, between each groan and grunt,
> They'll thank Roosevelt for bringing
> THE OLD BACK HOUSE TO THE FRONT.

But of all the anti-Roosevelt verses, poems, and doggerel, whether they were meant to be funny, mean, or otherwise, the one that outdistanced all the rest was a parody of the Twenty-third Psalm. It appeared early in his first term, assumed many forms, bore numerous titles, and remained popular for years. Typical was the version entitled the "Twenty-third Spasm":

> Roosevelt is my shepherd; I am in want
> He maketh me to lie down on park benches;
> He leadeth me beside the still factories.
> He disturbeth my soul:
> He leadeth me in the paths of destruction for his Party's sake.
> Yea, though I walk through the valley of recession,
> I anticipate no recovery
> For he is with me;
> His promises and pipe dreams they no longer fool me.
> He preparest a reduction in my salary in the presence of my creditors:
> He anointeth my small income with taxes;
> Surely unemployment and poverty shall follow me all the days of
>   the New Deal,
> And I will dwell in a mortgaged house forever.[69]

What should be done about such a man as Roosevelt? H. L. Mencken had a remarkably simple solution: Make Roosevelt king and then behead him. Decapitating presidents was undignified and without historical precedents; beheading monarchs was time-honored.[70]

Mencken was not serious; but the Washington matron, overheard by Congressman Herbert Bigelow of Ohio expressing the wish that Roosevelt would get a case of double pneumonia, was serious. So were the people who talked loosely of violence, all sorts of dreadful violence, crucifixion, drowning, shooting. "What that fellow Roosevelt needs is a thirty-eight caliber revolver right at the back of his head," was the way one respectable citizen put it. "For the first time in my life I am beginning to feel that in some cases assassination is a patriotic duty."[71]

Of course there were other ways of getting rid of Roosevelt, ways that would weigh easier on the conscience. As late as 1938, Representative Hoffman was threatening impeachment proceedings, a threat that seems to have started back in early 1935, when the first petition reached Congress from an obscure group in New York demanding Roosevelt's removal from office for treason. Glen McNaughton, a Wall Street corporation attorney, had a better idea. He was willing, he said, to lead a campaign to raise $5,000,000 to give to Roosevelt if he would agree to resign. Almost any of these ideas seemed to offer more than the uninspired suggestion of Roosevelt's own Harvard class of 1904 which agreed (by majority vote) that he should be replaced by a Republican.[72]

To be rid of Roosevelt. What a happy thought! Why it was enough to make men shout, ladies weep, and babies smile in their sleep. To be rid of Roosevelt was also to be rid of his wife, his family, the Brain Trust, and all the rest of the New Deal menage.

CHAPTER II

We Don't Like Her, Either

Never before in American History had a respectable woman been subjected to such reckless and relentless attack. . . . —Gerald W. Johnson

Her [Mrs. Roosevelt's] sons and daughter have capitalized upon their father's being our President and have waxed wealthy. They have all the tricks of a carnival or circus outfit. They could not love publicity more if they were a family of acrobats on the flying trapeze. —Robert M. Sperry
Bridgeport Life

All the Roosevelts . . . including all relatives near and remote, male and female, adults and infants, should be disfranchised for three hundred years, rendered incapable of holding office for a like period and, on penalty of the stocks, be denied all access to microphones and loud-speakers. —Carl H. Mote
The New Deal Goose Step

The Roosevelt administration is composed of payrollers and boondogglers; leeches and sycophants; commercial philanthropists and professional social service workers; political climbers and social parasites; eager and ambitious political hoodlums and henchmen. . . . —Ira L. Reeves
Is All Well on the Potomac?

E LEANOR Roosevelt had the redeeming grace of being able to laugh at herself. It was good, being able to laugh; it took the hurt and sting from some things that were not funny.

So she laughed when told about the man who named his clock "Eleanor" because it was "always on the go," and at the story about Admiral Byrd always setting two places for dinner in his South Pole shack "just in case Mrs. Roosevelt should drop in." Her mobile face creased in a wide, toothy grin that would soon be recognized the world over when people related how President Roosevelt had asked that a visitor be taken to see his wife only to be informed by the White House usher, "Mr. President, Mrs. Roosevelt has been out of town three days."[1]

II

Mrs. Roosevelt had not always been so independent. Shy as a child, and embarrassingly homely, she had grown up sheltered and protected, the family wealth providing private tutors and chaperoned travel. Courtship and then marriage to her distant cousin, young Franklin, was an unexpected happiness, a windfall in the life of the unremarkable Eleanor. Those early years of having babies, of living under the critical eye of a strong-willed mother-in-law and her husband's possessive friend, Louis Howe, the painful contrast to a husband as handsome as a greek God, did little to diminish her self-effacing dependency.

But the steel was always there, waiting to be tempered by the fire of near-tragedy, by high fever, the awful truth of lifeless limbs, the hope, the despair of long convalescence. In 1921, when Roosevelt was stricken with polio, she was really needed; for the first time in her life someone was depending on her. Disaster changed her life as it did his, perhaps even more. His extremity was her opportunity to mature as a person, to become eyes and ears and right hand, to walk and even to talk in his place. It was as if the recuperative and regenerative powers of nature, that marvel of nature to compensate for every loss, were being worked through her. By the end of the decade, she was not only a reliable and valuable aide to her husband, but an interesting personality and public figure in her own right.

There had never been a First Lady like her. Many people, instead of getting accustomed to her, simply got annoyed. They had their own image of a President's wife. She was to hang on his arm, grace his table, smile at the right time, stay out of the way, be seen but not heard, like a child on Sunday afternoon when guests come calling.

Mrs. Roosevelt did not fit this description. She was informal. Whether it was rolling Easter eggs on the White House lawn or serving hot-dogs to royalty, she was informal. To many of her critics, informality and lack of dignity were the same thing. She had views on a wide variety of interests, on everything from politics to child care, and did not hesitate to express her views. She engaged in all sorts of projects, from settlement houses to furniture factories. To keep up with her own interests while fulfilling her useful role for the President meant she was often on the move, sometimes turning up in very strange places. She seemed to be everywhere.

"Ubiquitous" was a word used often to describe her. It was a good word; even if one did not know what it meant, it sounded critical and implied more than was really intended. Robert Hale ("definitively, articulately, vociferously, I hate Roosevelt," he had said) could think of no better word in his *Harper's* article, "But I, Too, Hate Roosevelt," to describe the President's wife. Malcolm Bingay, editorial director of the Detroit *Free Press*, also used it, and reinforced it with an appeal to a merciful God that she "light somewhere and keep quiet." Her pace moved Representative Steven McGroarty of California to verse, a masterpiece called "The Lady Eleanor," which began:

The roads that stretch from East to West,
The high roads and all the rest
    The roads that go
    Where all men know
Where men have gone and gone before—
They know the Lady Eleanor.
They hear her footsteps. And the grass
Of fields and meadows sees her pass
On tireless quests, where rivers bend
And oceans wait and wide lands end.
The miles that wind from shore to shore,
They know the Lady Eleanor.
What seeks the Lady Eleanor
In her wide quest from shore to shore?

Another version bearing the same title was a lot less flattering:

THE LADY ELEANOR
(With apologies to Poe's *Raven*)

From the White House of the Nation
Speaking without hesitation,
Comes the voice of unchecked knowledge
From the Lady Eleanor.
In the limelight, basking gaily,
Speaks the Lady nightly, daily,
Like the spring that gushes always
Ever always—ever more!

Speaks the expert of Great Problems;
Home and Children—Love and War—
Race and Liquor—Sex and more;
Speaks the Lady Eleanor.
And this expert ever flitting,
Never sitting, never quitting,
Never tending her own knitting,
Doles her pills of fancied knowledge,
Wisdom from her bursting store.

And there comes a painful sighing
From a people slowly dying
Of a secret lust for gore;
From a hopeless Nation crying
For a surcease and a stilling
Of the sound of Eleanor,
Of the wordy Eleanor,
Of the boresome Eleanor,
Of the quenchless Eleanor.

For despite her global milling,
Of the votes there is not stilling;

With its platitudes galore,
As it gushes on advising,
Criticizing and chastising,
Moralizing, patronizing,
Paralyzing—ever more
Advertising Eleanor![2]

It was not simply that Mrs. Roosevelt traveled a lot, that she was, as they said, ubiquitous. She was always willing to talk when she got there. She liked to talk. To all kinds of people. About any subject. The nicest word used to describe this characteristic was "loquacious." A President's wife both ubiquitous and loquacious was an unbearable combination, especially when she told a nation-wide radio audience that one of the first things a young lady must learn is how much liquor she could drink and then never exceed that amount. Since the repeal of Prohibition had just been accomplished this might have been excellent advice from anyone else; from the First Lady it was intolerable. Can you imagine "the depths of infamy to which this nation has sunk," inquired Lloyd Clark, the shrill voice of Milan, Illinois. It was no wonder, he shouted, that the President's picture "hangs on the wall of every papal booze dive in the nation."[3]

Mrs. Roosevelt's candid observation on females and strong drink also reminded Clark of another of her transgressions. She smoked. Soon after the 1932 election it was "a matter of press reports," Clark explained to his readers, "that Mrs. Roosevelt enjoyed two or more cigarettes with her meals." While unable to discover any papal plot in this bit of information he did equate it with "an informality and breeziness that is somewhat unprecedented at the White House." Nor was Clark the only one to score her addiction. The Women's National Association for the Preservation of the White House, in one of its pamphlets, made quite a thing of it, pointing out that she was the first cigarette-smoking wife of a President. Their advice was that "the mothers of this nation should rise, *en masse*, to do some White House cleaning."[4]

The wide diversity of Mrs. Roosevelt's activities readily invited criticism of another kind. There were those who found it hard to believe that she was simply an able, well-intentioned woman with decent, humanitarian impulses, compassion for the underdog, and an enormous capacity for work, work which was its own reward.

Roosevelt had been in office but a year when Senator Schall began claiming that Mrs. Roosevelt was blackmailing hotels into buying suites of furniture (autographed, no less) from her Hyde Park Val Kill factory at $1,000 each. Charges of Rooseveltian greed were hurled when Mrs. Roosevelt began writing a syndicated column, "My Day" (for which she was allegedly paid $16,000 annually), endorsed a baking powder in one of the women's monthly magazines, delivered a series of radio speeches for a variety of sponsors, and in a radio commercial, extolled the virtues of a patented roofing "at $10.00 per second." "How about a little publicity," one letter-writer asked, "on your ubiquitous wife's income from her writings, lectures, radio contracts, and advertising endorsements?" When an agent suggested that he buy Mrs. Roosevelt's "My Day" column for his paper, Malcolm Bingay exploded. Why, he wanted to know, should he pay his hard-earned money "for a lot of chatter . . . [about] your activities in the White House?" Besides, asked Bingay, "When are you ever in the White House? You seem to be traveling around the world most of the time, telling American mothers how to bring up their children."[5]

The President himself would learn something about what happens when a member of the First Family accepts money. In 1938, Roosevelt agreed to the publication by Random House of his official papers covering the years, 1928–36, edited by his close friend and assistant, Judge Samuel I. Rosenman. The contents would also be made available to the United Features Syndicate, and *Liberty* magazine planned a series of three articles based on them.

While criticism of this literary endeavor became a staple in the whisper campaign of 1938, Congressman Hoffman used the floor of the House of Representatives as a forum to denounce it. Hoffman's attack revolved around the illogically logical question of how much the President's papers would be worth if he were not President. How much would they be worth, he asked, "had not William Randolph Hearst made the deal with Texas and California at the Chicago convention and nominated him for President?" Certainly not $175,000, which he claimed was the amount to be paid by United Features Syndicate and *Liberty*. The deal, said Hoffman, revealed much about the character of the man. "Born to a silk shirt, with the proverbial gold spoon in his mouth, the President can give cards, spades, and big and little casino to the economic royalists and still beat them to the jackpot." When would the country be advised through full-page advertisements of the brand of cigarettes the President smoked, Hoffman inquired disgustedly.[6]

Hoffman's attack triggered one of Roosevelt's few public retorts. "There has been a lot of misrepresentation," said the President in his public statement, ". . . no inquiry and no effort on the part of newspaper commentators or politicians to ascertain the facts. . . ." The truth was that neither he nor Judge Rosenman would receive anything; the proceeds would be devoted "to a useful public purpose under government direction."[7]

It was also true that similar sums received by Mrs. Roosevelt were given to charities or other philanthropic activities in which she was interested. But it might have been better had she kept the money; as it was, her contributions to charities became grounds for accusations that she was a tax-dodger. The charge which originated with a well-known radio news commentator in the spring of 1937, was soon preempted by Congressman Fish who had been insisting for some time that a number of high-ranking New Deal officials, including the President, were holding out on their income taxes.[8]

For about six weeks, Fish waged war for all he was worth, amid charges that the Roosevelts had used tax loopholes, had taken illegal deductions on the Hyde Park property (". . . this is not a farm but a palatial estate"), that his mother had illegally received payment from the government as rent for use of Hyde Park as a summer White House, that Roosevelt had ordered the Treasury to harass and persecute New Deal critics. All this and more he had the evidence to prove, Fish bravely insisted in a letter to Chairman Robert L. Doughton of the Joint Committee for Inquiry into Tax Evasions, evidence which he would gladly provide only if the impending investigation included everyone "from the President and his family on down, and not just the enemies and foes of the New Deal."[9]

Fish's attack was considered serious enough that Roosevelt's secretary, Stephen Early, prepared a day-by-day chronology of Fish's allegations during June and July, 1937, which he sent to the President along with a stack of photostatic copies of newspaper stories and editorials for his information. But the effort to embarrass the Roosevelts aborted when Massachusetts Congressman Allen Treadway, ranking Republican member of the investigating committee, conceded before the show started that he had examined the President's report and considered it "an eminently fair return." Late in July, the committee gave Mrs. Roosevelt a clean bill of health, and the drama was over.[10]

Whether it was endorsing the selection of Secretary Frances Perkins as Charter Day speaker at the University of California, defending the Reedsville project (a disastrous enterprise of the subsistence homestead program), supporting an old friend, Miss Caroline O'Day, in a New York congressional race, or lending encouragement to a student organization (that was almost certainly infiltrated by Communist sympathizers), Mrs. Roosevelt was always the calm eye of the hurricane. On the eve of the 1936 election, Humphrey Shaw, secretary to Congressman Sabath of Illinois, mailed a pamphlet to Charles Michelson, publicity director of the Democratic National Committee which, according to Shaw, was being "scattered all over Chicago." The unsigned, unidentified pamphlet entitled *Some Reasons Why the Present Administration Can and Will Be Defeated* carried a menacing warning on the cover: "Don't read this unless you can stand and understand facts." The facts (twenty in number) consisted mostly of nasty rumors and insults: about "the affected voice," "forced movie actor smile," "disgraceful family life," "assaults on sacred traditions," "irreligion and non-morality of his principal advisors," "drying up the normal source of church funds—thus making the clergy wholly dependent on the State," and other assorted irrelevancies, including one libelous assault on Mrs. Roosevelt for "ridiculing our traditions and stalwart principles . . . [scrapping] the simple homely virtues which built up this country. . . ."[11]

The same year, 1936, there appeared one of the more humorous (and printable) stories about Mrs. Roosevelt. An unidentified speaker, so the story went, was expounding the virtues of Roosevelt when a man in the audience shouted: "I don't like him." The President, the speaker explained patiently, was doing the very best he could when again the man interjected: "I don't like him." Exasperated, the orator added: "He depends on a higher power for guidance." Whereupon the man jumped up and shouted: "I don't like her, either."[12]

The story apparently first appeared in the Greenville, South Carolina, *Observer* which, in a way, was encouraging, almost a left-handed compliment. Many southerners had special reason to dislike Mrs. Roosevelt because of her affinity for minority groups, particularly the Negro. Most southerners, it should be said, were not so extreme as Senator Theodore Bilbo of Mississippi, who, during debate on an anti-lynching bill, suggested that all Negroes be sent to Liberia along with Eleanor Roosevelt, who should be made queen of the Negro nation. But they did resent her frequent association with them, the social and political implications of those associations, and the affront to delicate southern sensibilities on racial relations. "Negro newspapers," said a pamphlet of the Women's National Association for the Preservation of the White House, "are full of Mrs. Roosevelt's pictures and notices of her addresses to their [Negro] meetings coupled with such statements as, 'She waited to hear the address of the Hon. Walter White. . . .'" Walter White, Secretary of the National Association for the Advancement of Colored People, was, according to the pamphlet, "the same little Negro who, like thousands of others, ran the streets of Atlanta a very short time ago. . . ." When Mrs. Roosevelt wrote in one of her "My Day" columns of speaking to the Brotherhood of Sleeping Car Porters at their fifteenth biennial convention in New York, it prompted "A Southern Democrat" to publish a hateful little pamphlet, *Racial Distinction Abolished,* the heading of which began: "President Roosevelt permits Wife to Dine with Negro Porters to Obtain Votes for New Deal." "Southern Democrat," whoever he was, expounded the usual humbug about southern racial integrity, about how "the higher type Negroes" resented "this undue familiarity by the Roosevelts," and how it was all a transparent effort "to get the northern Negro vote."[13]

"Southern Democrat" had a point; Mrs. Roosevelt's activities in this area were symptomatic of the profound effect the New Deal was having on the forgotten men of the South, particularly Negroes, and of the significant changes being wrought in their social, political, and economic status.

Perhaps these changes would not have been so resented had southerners —at least those who had traditionally manipulated the power structure of the South—been in a strong position to control them. But they were not. The programs were federal, which was to lead eventually to the charge that the New Deal was undermining and destroying states' rights. The Negro might be poor, he might be politically quarantined, but he was not all that stupid. The beneficiary of government help and encouragement, the recipient of federal largess, was not likely to forget where to locate the windows of heaven on the map. They were no longer in the offices of the county judge.

Southerners sensed all this and more; which probably explains why, when Talmadge undertook to boom himself for President in 1936, and held an unimpressive "Grass Roots" convention at Macon, Georgia, the delegates found on their seats copies of the *Georgia Woman's World*, a vicious anti-Negro publication. The publication sought to slander Mrs. Roosevelt with what came to be called the "nigger pictures"—pictures that showed her flanked by two young ROTC officers on the occasion of a visit to Washington's Howard University to address the Women's Faculty Club, pictures that continued to crop up in other hate literature including *Racial Distinction Abolished* by the "Southern Democrat."[14]

III

Many people did not like Mrs. Roosevelt (that "Amazon," Leonard Fowler liked to call her); and at least as many did not like the Roosevelt family, either. The Roosevelt children made the headlines with embarrassing frequency, the principal source of their problems being a lack of discipline in love and traffic.

The record of traffic violations included at least ten arrests and one serious accident. The accident, in which, fortunately, no one was hurt, occurred in October, 1935, when John crashed his automobile into the side of a train at a crossing in East Boston. The car was a total loss; and souvenir hunters carried away most of the wreckage. Because the crossing was admittedly poorly lighted, he was exonerated. Roosevelt critics, particularly Massachusetts Republicans, swung into action with indignant letters berating the Roosevelts as well as Frank A. Goodwin, the State Motor Vehicles Registrar, who had held John blameless. "How many times," wrote Constance Lodge Williams, daughter of the late Republican senator, Henry Cabot Lodge, to Goodwin, "does one have to drive through a red light into a train before being disciplined by the registrar of Motor Vehicles? Do the same rules apply to others as to the Roosevelts?" Goodwin, replying with an invitation for Mrs. Williams to mind her own business, left her with the parting thought that there were "a few of you who think they own the party because their relatives at one time or another held important positions therein."[15]

Their frequent encounters with the law provided almost unlimited ammunition for the Roosevelt critics. "Our sons," wrote Malcolm Bingay, "are not spending their Monday mornings squaring themselves . . . in police court because of controversies with traffic cops." Letters to the President made frequent reference to it, one including a box-score of arrests, offenses, convictions, and a projected total of arrests by the end of Roosevelt's first term if they maintained their current pace. The behavior of the Roosevelt boys behind the wheel contributed prominently to the whisper campaign of 1935 when the story began circulating that the family was financially ruined because of lusty blackmail payments to the family of a woman whom young Franklin had run down with his car.[16]

Running red lights and crashing into trains, while they admittedly had nothing to do with solving the farm problem or curing the Depression, were nonetheless inexcusable. So was the distressing marriage and divorce record, with its religious and moral implications, and which was regarded in many quarters as an assault upon the home and an affront to decent and well-organized society. The meaning was well expressed by the Tacoma *News Tribune*, when it said editorially, ". . . two Roosevelt divorces within a year and three months set an example in high places which will not meet with approval in thousands of American homes that still believe in the sanctity of marriage." This is what one correspondent who signed herself "Dixie" meant in her ungrammatical way when she wrote to the President that "your son and daughter by *divorcing* and *remarrying* which is living in adultry [sic]." The apparently cavalier attitude of the Roosevelts toward marriage seemed sufficient justification for a vulgar dig at Mrs. Roosevelt. A neatly printed business card carried this disgusting caption: "The President's wife is suing for divorce because she is not getting what he is giving the other people."[17]

The Roosevelts had hardly gotten their suitcases unpacked at the White House when Elliott separated from Elizabeth Donner, divorced her, and a short time later married Ruth Josephine Googins, a Fort Worth, Texas, girl. Even then, the marriage of Anna Roosevelt Dall was on the rocks. She, her husband, and two children, "Sistie" and "Buzzie," had come to Washington for the inaugural activities, after which Dall departed but his wife and children stayed on at the White House.

This was all the clue necessary for the tongues to begin working overtime. In June, 1934, the rumors made the front page; Anna was on her way to Nevada for a divorce. Elliott's divorce raised many eyebrows but very few alarms; it was a relatively quiet affair. Anna's, according to one contemporary account, was given "the same quiet consideration as Sally Rand's fan-dance, which that summer was wowing patrons of the Chicago Exposition." When, later, she returned to Washington and sought to resume some semblance of a normal life, her every move was treated in the press like "the carefree young queen romping at Trianon among the milkmaids, heedless of the approaching revolution." By 1936, George Gundelfinger was so sick of the Roosevelts that he conceived of a plan he called "speedocity," which meant voting against Roosevelt at the same rate the President was plunging the country into debt ($10,000 per minute, according to his calculations). Such a plan, Gundelfinger guaranteed, would counteract not only Roosevelt's "speedocity" in debt but also his efforts "to usher in 'speedocity' in drinking and driving, 'speedocity' in marriage, 'speedocity' in divorce, 'speedocity' in marrying again . . . 'speedocity' in everything. . . ."[18]

" 'Speedocity' in everything" included using the prestige of their father's office by the Roosevelt children to turn a profit. A New York group, the American Guild, Incorporated, could think of nine reasons why Roosevelt should be impeached, and said so in a pamphlet as early as 1933. Reason number seven was nepotism, the art of putting the Roosevelt family on the public payroll. The Guild was hard put to make the charge very meaningful. It seemed unlikely that anyone would get very excited upon learning that William Phillips, an undersecretary of State, was the husband of President Roosevelt's second cousin, Caroline Astor; or that the minister to Canada, Warren D. Robbins, was another second cousin to the President. Others on the list included a consultant in the writing of the Securities Act, Roland Redmond, who was the husband of Roosevelt's first cousin, Sara Delano; and Frederic Delano, an adviser to the Navy Department, a first cousin. To make the list decently long, the Guild even dipped down into the ranks of third cousins to Mrs. Roosevelt to come up with the name of Henry L. Roosevelt, assistant secretary of the Navy.[19]

Had the Guild waited, it could have bagged bigger game. In 1936, James, the President's eldest son, was granted a commission in the United States Marine Corps Reserve, with the rank of lieutenant-colonel. Senator Rush Holt, Democrat from West Virginia, took violent exception to the appointment, explaining that James (the Crown Prince of the New Deal, Holt called him) had never been in any military service, or even the ROTC, yet he was being given a rank that ordinarily took a man twenty-five years to attain after leaving the U.S. Naval Academy. As if to add insult to injury, President Roosevelt made James an administrative assistant to the President a short time later. His specific assignment was that of coordinating the activities of the independent regulatory agencies, a task that had always been a time-consuming task for every President.[20]

Widespread grumbling greeted the appointment, smoldering resentment that occasionally burst into flame when Republican Congressman Rich of Pennsylvania unburdened himself on the subject of "a boy 30 years of age, to take charge of all the new organizations of government." Rich gave young Roosevelt a severe test: "qualified . . . trained . . . some experience . . . confidence of the American people . . . properly handle this matter . . . administer it efficiently"; and he made zero. But that was to be expected of the President, said Rich; "he has so many incompetent, inexperienced, and radical advisers in his organization. . . . It is most serious, in my judgment."[21]

It was also Congressman Rich who, a short time later, repeated on the floor of the House a slander that had been making the rounds at least since 1935, a slander that involved James Roosevelt using his influence at the White House to peddle insurance. This neat little racket had netted him some $500,000 since his father became President, according to Clare Hoffman in a speech to the Greater Republican Club of Grand Rapids, Michigan. "Let him tell us from whence he derived this sum," Hoffman challenged. In the original version, James had convinced a Boston banker that he needed insurance provided he wanted an RFC loan that was pending at the time in Washington. *Newsweek* related how, on one occasion, when this story was told at a dinner party, the hostess called the banker named and had her guests listen to his denial over the telephone.[22]

Other members of the family were equally guilty of the same sort of thing, so it was said. But more often the foibles, vices, and depravities of the Roosevelts were not asserted. Somehow a knowing question aroused greater curiosity than a simple statement. So, how much was William Randolph Hearst paying Anna "and her for-the-present husband," a Hearst editor? To what extent was Elliott "cashing in" on his radio network in Texas? Were it not for his father, his (Elliott's) "mouthings [on the air] would attract no more attention than a ham sandwich at a family picnic," according to Congressman Paul Shafer of Michigan. How much does Franklin, Jr., get from the du Ponts? How convenient for both sides that young Franklin had married Ethel du Pont. "Is that a bright picture to hold up for the young generation?" a disgusted Texan asked Roosevelt's secretary, Louis Howe. "As an American I am not proud of it, even if set by our first family."[23]

IV

Attacking the New Deal meant more than criticizing the President, his wife, his family. It meant attacking his friends, his advisers, cabinet officers, officials great or small, virtually anyone in government or out who served the President or confessed to knowing him or liking him. The New Deal years were years of open season on the official family, years that were perhaps unparalleled in the ferocity of the attack on public servants of all stations. Had the criticism been confined to ideas advanced, policies pursued, or plans executed, that would have been one thing. This was criticism of another kind, criticism that was intensely, even viciously personal, criticism against which there was no protection, no defense, no chance of refutation by logical answer.

New Dealers were that "crew of bluffers, slicksters and nitwits who mill around his [Roosevelt's] person and infest his bureaus"; "cheapjacks whom he [Roosevelt] takes for sages"; "frantic men . . . determined, ambitious men with such a lust for power as this country seldom sees"; "boy Fridays . . . visionary, impractical and theoretical men and women who are unknown for any outstanding personal achievement"; "little coterie of theoretical, intellectual, professorial nincompoops, who were never elected, and couldn't be elected dog-catchers in any part of our Nation"; "the President's young stormtroopers"; "a collection of freaks and fakers . . . dreamers, clairvoyants, crystal gazers, jugglers, and legerdemain performers . . . the most gigantic aggregation of magicians . . . since the morning stars first sang at creation's dawn"; "Happy-go-lucky play-boys and boon-dogglers"; "spies, snoopers, agents, investigators, and inspectors . . . bureaucratic lilliputians"; "college professors and Harvard dunderheads who [are] long on book learning but guiltless of any ability to apply their booksy brainboxes to the practical problems of life"; "New Deal genii . . . inexperienced, irresponsible zealots . . . shooting craps with destiny"; "this horde of ravenous servants who batten on us, as maggots feed and grow fat on a dead dog . . . these moochers and mendicants . . . these bar-flies and pimps . . . these experimenting flagellants . . . a group of zanies laughing in a frenzied cacaphony, as jackals do"; "paid propagandists, petty peanut party politicians . . . who would sell their patronizing souls for a mess of pottage"; "this New Deal army of political appointees is the American form of the Praetorian Guard of Ancient Rome . . . the officers of an army of ten million voters who receive benefits from the government"; "a group of nitwit carpetbaggers a thousand times more vicious and anti-social than the post-Civil War patriots who plucked what was left of the fallen Confederacy"; "that horde of professors, of theorists, none of whom knows the cause of sweat, the feeling of a blister or a callous; none of whom ever accomplished anything of moment . . . all of whom believe that they are the Lord's anointed, ordained to save the world rather than America."[24]

With hardly a pause for breath, the critics moved from the general to the specific. The cabinet "looks on," wrote Paul Haber, the defender of Brooklyn's virtue against the Roosevelts, "twiddles its thumbs and applauds. Most of them simply don't belong in their seats, just political hacks being rewarded for services rendered." Among the more notorious thumb-twiddling political hacks was Secretary of Agriculture Henry Wallace. Wallace, Colonel Theodore Roosevelt told the state convention of Oklahoma Young Republicans, was "an unbalanced fanatic"; but Congressman Schafer of Wisconsin thought otherwise. Wallace was Secretary in name only; he was "only the Charlie McCarthy of 'braintruster' Mordecai Ezekiel." Wallace was some other things as well, including "the modern Herod, slaughtering and burning millions of innocent piggies," "the honorable Lord destroyer," "the ignoramus of Iowa," "that silly, insulting blabber-mouth." Instead of paying the farmers to raise less, asked Colonel Ira Reeves, why not pay the hungry to eat more? This, he sighed, was too simple for Wallace:

> For Wallace has spoken
> In his words of loud blunder,
> "Don't save for tomorrow,
> Just plow your stuff under."[25]

Postmaster General James A. Farley also took quite a mauling. Farley was that "shyster," "the Nabob of New York," "a typical city-slicker," "the 3-in-1 job magnate," "grubstaker of the ward-heelers," the "Auctioneer of the New Deal." Largely because of his dual role, that of Postmaster General, which meant distributing federal jobs as well as stamps, and national chairman of the Democratic Party, Farley was a favorite whipping-boy. With a man who was Irish Catholic, a New Yorker, an intimate of the prizefight crowd, and who signed his name in bright green ink, you could draw your own conclusion. Senator Schall was drawing one in 1935 when he charged that his outgoing mail was being censored at Farley's orders, a charge which Farley admitted was true because, he insisted, Schall was notoriously flagrant in his abuse of the franking privilege. It was also in 1935, "this third year of our reigning empire of St. Vitus," Huey Long called it, that the Louisiana senator succeeded in having Farley investigated for a series of alleged offenses that included bootlegging stamps to collectors, rigging federal construction contracts, selling supplies to companies with public contracts, protecting a gambling wire service, and commandeering for his personal use facilities of companies seeking loans from the government. "I am being 'whereased' in Washington . . . by Huey Long, but I do not take it seriously," said Farley. When the time came, Farley was cleared on every count.[26]

Time and again Farley was charged with pressuring postal employees to make campaign contributions, buy banquet tickets, attend rallies. That there was substance to these charges is highly probable; for there not to have been would no doubt have made Farley unique in the history of postmasters general. Senator Joseph O'Mahoney of Wyoming was revealing no state secrets when he reminded his colleagues that Walter Brown (postmaster general in the Hoover Administration) had once addressed a national convention of postmasters, telling them it was their duty to participate in political campaigns and to support the President who had appointed them. The Farley character, said his detractors, was no better revealed than in the oft-repeated statement he was alleged to have made about the election of 1936: "Beat $4,000,000,000! Don't be silly."[27]

Secretary of Labor Frances Perkins faced special problems. She was a woman, a female interloper in government, an area traditionally as male as the local barbershop. The circumstances of her marriage were somewhat obscure, and she was allegedly foreign-born (which automatically meant she was Jewish). Representative Schafer thought it was important, and perhaps even sinister, that the Secretary used her maiden name rather than her married name, Mrs. Paul Wilson. In 1913, Miss Perkins had married Wilson, a professional newsman who was secretary to John P. Mitchel, reform candidate for mayor of New York City at the time. Later Wilson suffered a mental breakdown and was confined for years. Schafer thought all this very strange and suggested that it might be illegal for Miss Perkins to sign official documents with her maiden name.[28]

During the whisper campaign of 1935, stories began circulating that she was Jewish or that she was born in Russia. Usually the two were combined. She was a Russian-born Jew, because it is the way of gossip that the whole is significantly greater than the sum of its parts. Although being Jewish or Russian-born were not indictable offenses at the time, these intended slanders became serious enough that during the campaign of 1936 Miss Perkins publicly answered two letters she had received, explaining she was of an old New England family which first came to America in 1630, that she was not Jewish, Russian, or foreign-born, and neither was her husband, Paul Wilson. But a year later, in a speech at Benton Harbor, Michigan, Congressman Hoffman was still referring to Miss Perkins as "the wife of someone, though God alone knows what her true name may be, and no man has yet published the place of her birth." This "tearful woman," "your Old Maid Secretary of Labor," "the first Tootsie Roll of the Cabinet," rates as "the No. 1 donkey on Dr. Roosevelt's merry-go-round" and provides "first-class comedy on the Republic's political stage." "Mr. President," pleaded Stephen Ragsdale, "if you believe Madam Perkins is some sort of Virgin Mary, then why not pray God that she conceive and bear us a man child to become our Secretary of Labor?"[29]

In 1939, Congressman J. Parnell Thomas of New Jersey introduced a resolution calling for the impeachment of Miss Perkins (and some lesser officials of the Labor Department) for her refusal to instigate deportation proceedings against the leader of the West Coast longshore-men's union, the alleged Communist, Harry Bridges. There were, said Thomas, "five hundred thousand reasons" why Bridges was not deported, an oblique reference to his earlier claim that Bridges' union had contributed $500,000 to the Democratic Party.[30]

V

The critics spared no one. Secretary of the Interior, Harold Ickes, "the Chinch-bug of Chicago," was "a fascist dictator," a "totalitarian" who had "repeatedly attempted to promote legislation designed to destroy the liberties of the people." Relief administrator Harry Hopkins was a "wildeyed crackpot," "a vulgar jokester," "a conceited ass," a "profligate spender," who rigged elections by expanding the relief rolls just before the polls opened, who cynically asserted (so it was said) that "we will spend and spend, and tax and tax, and elect and elect." Henry Morgenthau, Secretary of the Treasury, was that "Communist," that "Jew thief." In 1938, Senator Styles Bridges of New Hampshire began a radio speech on the Tennessee Valley Authority with an attack on Charles Michelson, publicity director of the Democratic National Committee, "who reduced the art of political ventriloquism to an exact science," an approach which even the senator admitted was a little unusual. "It was announced that I would talk about T.V.A.," he began, "and I intend to do so. Discussion of the life and works of . . . Charlie Michelson . . . may seem far afield from T.V.A. . . . ." And it was.[31]

Possibly the most extreme and senseless attack upon members of the Administration was that of Bartholomew Dornblazer of Galesburg, Illinois, who referred to himself as a "Typical Prairie Stater," a reminder that James A. Farley had once used the term to describe Alf Landon. During the campaign of 1936, Dornblazer published "PIP: The Raw Deal Jackass," a series of preposterous and incoherent essays. PIP, it turned out, was an abbreviation for a whole series of words beginning with those three letters, a heavyhanded way of ridiculing the New Deal alphabetical agencies (e.g., Personal Initiative Perishes; Parasite's Illogical Policies; Paralyze Individual Performance).

In the essays, dedicated to Roosevelt, "the MASTER INITIALIST," Dornblazer "cussed and discussed the performances of The Four Jackassmen, The President's Piratical Political Parasites." The four "Jackassmen of the Apocalypse" were "Far, Tug, Corn, and Hop." Whenever Dornblazer wished to refer to one of the four—Farley, Tugwell, Wallace (Corn Wallace he called him), or Hopkins—he simply wrote the first letter of the name—ten times. Wallace, then, became "W.W.W.W.W.W.-W.W.W.W." which meant, "Wallace's wasteful, weird, whimsical, wrongful wiles won't worry wakeful wise." Throughout the essays Hopkins was "H.H.H.H.H.H.H.H.H.H." (Hopkins' haphazard, hectic, hodgepodgic, hazy HOCUS-POCUS harasses honest home-loving humanity). The other two were treated similarly. All of which looked very strange in print, but which, for Dornblazer, must have been very soul-satisfying.[32]

But all this was mild compared to the abuse heaped upon that small, kaleidoscopic, largely legendary group, the Brain Trust, a term coined by James Kieran of *The New York Times* during the 1932 campaign to describe people like Raymond Moley, Adolf Berle, Rexford Tugwell, and other academicians and specialists whom Roosevelt consulted with indifferent regularity. Since the Brain Trust was composed largely of men who were (or who had been) college professors, it was absurdly simple to attack them. Everyone knew about college professors, how absent-minded they were, how impractical; soft-handed and soft-headed theorists who had never done an honest day's work in their lives, men naive enough to believe that governments should be run by disinterested intelligence rather than animal cunning, men suspect because they moved in a world of ideas instead of short cuts.[33]

And worse yet, they were radicals. Dreamy incompetent and dangerous radical, that was the Brain Truster and his kind; "the well-known traditional college professor, in his mental daze, whose loving wife must need tie a string about his right index finger . . . visionary, impractical and theoretical men and women who are unknown for any outstanding personal achievement"; the Nation must choose "between the 'brain trust' and common horse sense . . . the lunacy of the 'brain trust' "; a "happy group of experimenters . . . these starryeyed reformers . . . [who] took this country like children with a complicated mechanical toy and proceeded to see what made the wheels go round and the result is much the same . . . the practical hard sense of experienced politicians and businessmen obviously is lacking among them"; "inexperienced and visionary professors . . . day-dreamers . . . magicians . . . wand wavers . . . snake charmers . . . rabbit producers . . . crystal-gazers"; ". . . professor's ideas are theoretical only . . . not burned in the flame of experience, for which there is no substitute . . . with his superior education he may merely dress up in more beautiful diction than the average man what are at bottom wholly fallacious ideas . . . is assumed to know everything, whereas the better educated he is the more he knows about less and less"; ". . . And such men they are! There is not a tried statesman, not a real lawyer, not a well-known economist, businessman, or financier in the whole brainless 'brain trust' . . . just a bunch of ex-assistant professors and tutors . . ."; "A plague of young lawyers . . . all claimed to be friends of somebody or other, and mostly of Felix Frankfurter and Jerome Frank . . . floated airily into offices, took desks, asked for papers, . . . found no end of things to be busy about." When Raymond

Moley, the unofficial leader of the Brain Trust in the early months (and whom one English wit referred to as "Moley, Moley, Moley, Lord God Almighty"), tendered his resignation late in August, 1933, *The New York Times* said, editorially: "Let us not be too sure that the Gotterdammerung of the Brain Trust is at hand. It is too early to speak of the failure of a comic experiment in government by amusing college professors."[34]

Of these amusing college professors, Raymond Moley was, according to Senator Schall, "the witch doctor of the New Deal." And there was no limit to the number of clever things one could do with a name like Felix Frankfurter. It was altogether too obvious why the men in the Administration sponsored by Frankfurter or recommended by him became known as Frankfurter's "Little Hot Dogs." Because of his skill at drafting legislation, the most important of the "Little Hot Dogs" was Benjamin Cohen, who was responsible for no less than seven major bills during the first session of the Seventy-fourth Congress (1935), a feat which led Senator Schall to suggest changing the spelling of Congress to "C-o-h-e-n-g-r-e-s-s."[35]

VI

April 22, 1935. Senator Schall was delivering another of his anti-Roosevelt diatribes which the Senate had come to expect from the blind Minnesota senator. A young constituent from St. Paul, he was saying, a Bible student studying for the ministry, had called on Roosevelt ("our smiling President") urging him to set aside five minutes at some future date as a time for national prayer for the nation's troubles. "The guardians at the portals of his august majesty," according to Schall, told the young preacher that the President "wanted no help from God." "In short," thundered Schall, "if his ambitions are fulfilled, and they seem upon the verge of being fulfilled, he will become God as Lenin has been substituted in the Union of Soviet Socialist Republics for the Divinity."[36]

Tying religion, amorality, and radicalism together in one bundle was a common technique of the Roosevelt critics. The New Deal was Godless, its radicalism was communistic, and the source of both was the Brain Trust; it was the professors who were poisoning the well. E. C. Riegel, in a pamphlet for the Consumers' Guild of America entitled *Brain Trussed*, asserted: "So the professors set about to truss the president's brain . . . none of them is a member of the President's cabinet . . . none was elected to public office . . . the President and his mental kidnappers cared not for a counsel of caution. . . . There was no stemming the professorial putsch and the presidential passion for pyrotechnics."[37]

The Brain Trusters had done more than seduce the President with their sleight-of-hand theories; they had usurped power as well. Hanford MacNider, former American Legion commander and one-time minister to Canada, speaking in Jackson, Michigan, on the eightieth anniversary of the birth of the Republican Party in that city, described the Brain Trust as ". . . brilliant young men of no admitted party allegiance, dizzy with sudden and unrestricted power . . . experimenting with every phase of national life. The industrial and business body of America is securely strapped to the classroom table."[38]

The power of the Brain Trust, said the critics, was achieved by circumventing the legal and constitutional distribution of power. Early in 1933, Frank Kent, the caustic anti-Administration editorialist of the Baltimore *Sun*, lamented: "It is not only that the President has planted a professor squarely behind the more important Secretaries, but the Roosevelt program has—or will—create a group of Federal officials who constitute a new Cabinet with more power and importance than the combined constitutional Cabinet." "They do not outrank the constitutional Cabinet at the dinner table," wrote Kent, "but they do in every other way. In a year's time it is going to be hard to remember who really is in the constitutional Cabinet."[39]

The drive of the Brain Trusters for power was not for reasons that normally motivated men, it was charged; they coveted power to conspire, to betray, to destroy. They were part of a master plan to deliver the United States to her enemies, a Trojan horse draped with doctoral hoods. "It is self-evident," at least to Representative Gifford, "that the plan of the 'brain trust' is that a sick, suffering, and despairing people should be kept in that condition until they shall finally be willing to accept anything. . . ." "Many of us have known for the last two or three years," declared Congressman Hoffman, "that the inner circle of the President's advisers were seeking . . . to prolong the depression, which will produce a better psychological background for the prosecution of their revolutionary designs." "The overturn of our institutions," he insisted, "including the Constitution, is their avowed goal." Republican Senator Vandenberg likewise sensed what was afoot when he told the Senate that "a substantial group, some young in years, all young in practical experience, have gained the ear, not only of the unthinking multitude but of men in high authority, preaching the doctrine that veneration of the Constitution is a form of superstition. . . ." Colonel Reeves, not given to the digressions and indirections of solons, came right to the point. "We have come to the parting of the ways," he wrote. "We have our choice—the Little Red School House of our forefathers or the little 'red Professors' of the Roosevelt administration."[40]

The Communist label was easily the most serious charge leveled at the Brain Trust, and (after some early and fitful confusion with fascism) the most persistent. Congressman Fish and Senator Schall were among the first to spot the Brain Trust for what it was. Roosevelt had been in office less than four months when Fish blew the whistle on their radicalism. "Congress must be deaf, dumb, and blind," the New York congressman told the House, "when it enacts the complicated bills that are coming through the White House from the hands of the 'brain trust' composed mostly of Columbia University theoretical and socialistic professors." Almost simultaneously Schall complained of trying to overcome the Depression "with a cure concocted in the minds of certain professors who have been reading the propaganda of Hitler, Mussolini, and Lenin." By the end of the first year in office, Hanford MacNider was telling the Republican Party birthday celebration at Jackson, Michigan, that "On the Socialist platform their [Brain Trust's] performance for one year is practically one hundred per cent."[41]

The source of this incessant flow of socialistic and communistic legislation was the "little red house down in Georgetown," the residence of Brain Trusters Benjamin Cohen, Thomas "Tommy-the-Cork" Corcoran and James M. Landis. "I referred to a little red house down in Georgetown," said Republican Congressman Frederick A. Britten of Illinois, early in 1934 (as though he were revealing some closely guarded secret). "It is the little red house down in Georgetown where are held the meetings which promote the communistic legislation we all talk about in the cloakrooms. It is in the little red house in Georgetown where every night of the week from ten to eighteen young men of communistic minds meet, so-called young students. They call them Frankfurter's hot-dogs."[42]

Until the United States became engulfed in World War II, until long after the Brain Trust ceased to function as a unit (if it ever did), long after it should have been apparent to everyone that the Brain Trust was at worst unwise or petulantly misguided, the charges of wilful disloyalty continued. In 1935, for example, Hamilton Fish told a nationwide radio audience over CBS that "the recognition of Soviet Russia should be withdrawn, as it was a gigantic hoax perpetrated upon the American people by the President and the 'brain trust.'"[43]

The redoubtable Dewey Short, floundering in such a plethora of words on the floor of the House that spring that syntax failed him completely, shouted: "Are you going to base your future and that of your children upon experience or are you going to follow every unknown, unsolved, unworkable, unconstitutional, dangerous, willful, autocratic, egotistical, tax-eating bureaucrats?" Would the country prefer to follow George Washington and Thomas Jefferson or Raymond Moley and Rexford Guy Tugwell, Short wanted to know. (It was some comfort to historical purists that Short paired Thomas Jefferson with George Washington rather than Alexander Hamilton.) But Short was not finished. "And I should like to know," he inquired, "if we still believe in the genius, courage, and patriotism of Andrew Jackson and Abraham Lincoln or whether we want to overthrow their philosophy to follow the strange and insidious doctrines of Mordecai Ezekiel, Felix Frankfurter, and his 'hot-dog' boys?"[44]

In 1936, Congressman Clare Fenerty, Republican of Pennsylvania, took exception to the processes of the government being "perverted to strange and alarming uses" by men "whose ideas are born in the secretariats of foreign lands"; men "who lay the flattering unction to their souls that they have a monopoly on the brains of America"; men "with the radical theories which they have garnered from the slopes of the Ural Mountains of Russia." And, said Fenerty, if you dare to oppose them you are greeted with such lurid language and name-calling "that one suspects the 'brain trust' of spending its office hours in a searching perusal of the old dime novels and penny dreadfuls."[45]

But perhaps the most picturesque description of the Brain Trust was that of Republican Representative Charles Eaton of New Jersey who, in 1938, described how they "came flying into Washington from the four corners of the country, like crows to a dead horse, strange amorphous creatures, each of them seized and possessed of a complete and entirely different solution for every economic problem in the world." And, said Eaton, completing his interesting simile, "these mysterious New Deal creatures have been roosting near the administration ever since and infecting it with their views, most of them impractical, un-American, and alien."[46]

With Germany poised for the invasion of Poland and the country shuddering at the prospects of global war, Republicans were still shaking their heads and wringing their hands over the Brain Trust. Congressman Schafer was still digressing from discussion of the Reorganization plan to talk in mixed metaphors of Brain Trusters, those "crack-pots" and "nitwits," "these soviet-minded 'brain trust' professors" who have used "the taxpayers' pocketbooks as guinea pigs in the laboratory of New Deal state socialism imported direct from Moscow." The cannons were already belching fire and destruction when Congressman Jacob Thorkelson of Montana took one last backward look at the Brain Trust which had contributed so much to "the greater glory of socialism and destruction of constitutional government." "It is hard to believe," muttered Thorkelson, almost wistfully, "that so many hypocrites can lead a party for six years without being discovered."[47]

VII

The worst of the hypocrites of which Thorkelson spoke was easily Rexford Guy Tugwell, economist, Columbia University professor, and a visitor to the Soviet Union for two years to observe the operation of

Gosplan, the five-year plan. It was Tugwell whom Senator Schall pointedly referred to in conversation as "Comrade Tugwell, Brain Truster No. 1." Of Tugwell, Senator Simeon D. Fess of Ohio quipped that Karl Marx, "would, were he living, necessarily be compelled to apologize for his conservatism to Professor Tugwell." As late as 1936, Congressman Gifford asserted that the four outstanding molders of public opinion at the time were the Reverend Charles Coughlin, leader of the Union for Social Justice, Francis E. Townsend, founder of the Old Age Revolving Pension Plan, Father Divine, the Harlem spiritual leader who claimed ability to walk on the waters or something, and Tugwell; and, like charity, the greatest of these was Tugwell, according to Gifford.[48]

The criticism of Tugwell reached at least a temporary climax in 1934 when President Roosevelt submitted his name to the Senate for appointment as undersecretary of Agriculture. Huey Long was against it because Tugwell "has greater influence with the Chief Executive than any other single man or even group of men" and Tugwell would, if he could, "abolish the Constitution of the United States." Senator Arthur Robinson of Indiana was of like mind. "Abolish the Constitution, and what have we left?" he asked rhetorically. "A dictator—an executive dictator. There is no other way out." Senator Richard Russell of Georgia said he was casting his first negative vote against a confirmation in his five years in the Senate because "we have all but been completely Russianized." "We are at the present time," said Senator Russell, "in the Mensheviki period of the 'revolution' with Dr. Tugwell as the prophet." Senator Schall, needless to say, was not satisfied with Tugwell's answers to his list of twenty-seven questions which he put to him during the four hours of public hearing. Tugwell had taken the oath at the committee hearing "with his tongue in his cheek," he seethed, "knowing as any man must know, and any court in the country having the facts before it would pronounce, that his action is perjury; and perjury in this instance is not only perjury but treason!"[49]

Not everyone, of course, saw commissars under every bed, including the dispassionate New York Times, which wrote editorially of l'affaire Tugwell: "The Republicans will have to try again. Doubtless they will resume their dire whisperings about a conspiracy, shared by the Administration, to overthrow our form of government. But it will be harder than ever to induce people to credit their evidence. Wirt and Tugwell failed them. Who will be the next?"[50]

Perhaps the Times could adopt a calm and rational approach to this and other day-by-day developments of the New Deal years. But there were those who could not, who would not. Some people believed the New Deal was a monstrous plot and Roosevelt a traitor, people who did not hesitate to say so at every opportunity.

PART II

Messiahs, Incorporated

ACCORDING to *Propaganda Analysis* for January 1, 1939, there were in the United States some eight hundred organizations that could be called pro-Fascist. Some had the word "Fascist" in their name. A few used the swastika, or something approaching it, as part of their insignia. Their leaders were frequently preposterous paranoids, insignificant men affecting ridiculous beards and mustaches, pugnacious jaws, comic opera postures, and a rainbow of colored shirts. Most of them had a lot to say about Jews, about ethnic minorities, about Communists, and other favorite scapegoats. All represented a state of mind, a widespread distaste for facing hard, complex facts, and a deep yearning for an easy way out of depression, fear, and defeat. All likewise represented a threat, some more than others, to democratic institutions, despite disclaimers and despite facile talk about wanting to champion democracy and Christianity, protect individualism and free enterprise, and save the country from something or other. Always on their lips was concern for the Bible, for the faith of the Fathers, for the Constitution, and for "the American way of life."

The outbursts of intolerant politics in the 1930's seemed to stem from the frustrations of a severe depression and the sudden appearance of the New Deal, which many believed to be an alien prescription, a revolutionary cure. This might seem to imply that businessmen, industrialists, the well-to-do (those who stood to lose much between depression on the one hand and the New Deal, a dangerous "ism," on the other) would be attracted to Fascist-type solutions as the economic aristocracy had been attracted to Hitler in Germany.

Some were. But they were in the minority. Most of the people representing wealth and business leadership had better sense—call it a deeper social consciousness, perhaps—than their European counterparts. Most of them fought the New Deal and fought it hard. But with only few exceptions they fought with conventional weapons and within the traditional framework of the two-party system. In the United States, Fascist flummery made little headway with the people who mattered, with those who could provide the bankroll and the moral support where it counted. Support for those men aspiring to be America's fuhrer came from the masses, from the little people. The failure to woo businessmen may have been the chief reason why the native Fascist movement, despite all its frantic efforts, produced more fog than lightning.

The Fascist message addressed to the people in the 1930's had to be simple and, alas, irrational. It had to appeal to the lonely, those who felt isolated and uprooted, those who believed life had shortchanged them, cheated them, left them holding the bag. It had to appeal to those who found facing their failures intolerable. For a generation nurtured on the American dream of success, of making good, of opportunity unlimited for him who would work, failure could only imply that there was something wrong with the individual, an implication that shattered the foundations of self-respect. The demagogue's solution had to provide a graceful way out, had to locate the cause for failure some other place. It had to be irrational. There was too much chance logic would lead them back to the unpleasant conclusion that it was their own fault they were nobodies.

Not that it was their own fault. More times than not the victims of the Depression were hard-working, law-abiding, God-fearing, good, honest folks who did not know what hit them. In their distress they were fair game. Impatient with complicated answers to complicated problems, they seemed vulnerable to answers they could comprehend with their bowels and their stomachs rather than their brains.

Those seeking to exploit the people, to play upon their fears and insecurity, their self-pity and self-hate, learned quickly that their best bet was to explain misery by conspiracy. Mixed with their flag-waving and overt patriotism was much talk about anonymous forces (like international banking) and mysterious people wielding great international influence (which was probably why they insisted on remaining mysterious). For some inexplicable reason such people never lived in Omaha or Louisville; it was always Zurich, or Hong Kong, or Belgrade, or some other equally romantic and far-away place. It was never explained why these mysterious people, manipulating enormous but vaguely defined power, wished to oppress the unemployed machinist in Terre Haute or the one-chair barber in Birmingham. They were not pictured as motivated by any rational purpose, but rather by sheer malice, by malevolence; behind their shadowy conspiracies lurked evil for evil's sake.

It was perhaps inevitable that the conspiracy theme for explaining the tribulation abroad in the land would revolve around such things as an international Jewish conspiracy. Anti-Semitism was an important thesis with nearly every native Fascist, because it was the most obvious basis for curtailing civil liberties, just as it had been in Nazi Germany. Anti-communism was another pat hand. Communism could be opposed for its own sake; but it was also easy to link it with Jews, and with the Negro who was the unwitting tool of both. Combining two international conspiracies, Communist and Jewish (as Hitler had done), provided an effective argument for protecting democracy by extreme measures; it was easier to attack them as one than to discredit each separately.

Anti-Semitism and anti-communism were the staples in the native Fascist diet. Accusations against aliens, immigrants, foreigners, munitions-makers, international bankers, college professors, orientals, sometimes against Roman Catholics, and a variety of lesser mischief-makers were thrown in for good measure.

If the native Fascist phenomenon looked like mere atavism, a revival of old-fashioned American nativism, the similarity was purely accidental. While Denis Kearney and his Sandlotters in California were beating Chinese workers to a pulp, or the hooligans of the American Protective

Association were waylaying Irish Catholics, or hooded Klansmen were flogging illiterate Negro sharecroppers, the thought of changing the economic or political system of the United States never crossed their minds. For that matter, neither did changing the social system, except with respect to the status of particular ethnic or religious groups. But during the depression years the native Fascists and their organizations were aiming for a new system. Despite their insistence that they sought only to save and preserve America and its traditional values from the ravages of the New Deal, their goal was revolution, a New Order.

It was one thing to rail against Roosevelt. It was quite another to justify their sentimental attachment to a system that had apparently failed, one that seemed responsible for depression, unemployment, economic insecurity and social disorganization, one that seemed to make the New Deal necessary. Only a moratorium on brains could have kept the American public from realizing sooner or later that they despised the one as much as the other.

In the 1930's, the native Fascists made more headlines than headway. In retrospect it is probably true that no more than a small fraction of the people who may have been ripe for some kind of totalitarian solution to their problems was ever won over. Millions heard but few listened.

A number of plausible explanations for this happy circumstance come to mind. For one thing, the vanity, the overweening ambition, the incredible cheek of the petty would-be Caesars made unity impossible. It is true that they conferred frequently, cooperated informally, quoted each other, made speeches, wrote articles, endorsed pet hates, and hawked literature for each other. But each fancied himself a leader. Each had his own cherished dream and refused to accept second place to anyone. There was not a Goering or a Ciano in the lot.

Probably the psychological barriers that prevented unity likewise explained the inability to build their own organizations. Charismatic leaders, men who could walk on the waters, who steadfastly believed their hour was at hand, had little time or stomach for consolidating their gains or for building stable, effective teams. They lacked the ruthless efficiency of a Hitler; in nearly every instance their organizations were in wild disarray.

The messianic complex meant also that they were incapable of exploiting the traditional avenue to power, the political party. None, with possibly one exception, made any serious effort to capture a major party; nor did third parties figure prominently in their plans, a significant insight into their rejection, their alienation from existing institutions.

If the extremist movement suffered from lack of effective leadership, that weakness was compounded by lack of a coherent ideology. Violent, negative reaction, being against something or somebody, was great for a start. Visions of jerking Roosevelt's wheelchair from under him, of stoning Communists in the streets, or of sterilizing Jews in concentration camps might start beads of perspiration on some foreheads, might cause others to lick their lips. But eventually there had to be a positive program of some kind, one that provided an answer to the most elementary question in politics: "What is in this for me?" They could not, of course, promise glory as Hitler had done; the United States, unravaged by a foreign foe, was already a great power with a glorious tradition. They never seemed able to arrive at a formula that would appeal to both the frightened wealthy and the dirt-poor who learned to hate the world through their pores and under their nails.

The disordered arrogance and neurotic individualism of the native Fascists apparently precluded learning from others how to mobilize their potential followings. It does not appear that any of them studied very seriously, if at all, the work of Lawrence Dennis, the leading intellectual and theoretician of American fascism. Dennis was no Gottfried Feder, and *The Coming American Fascism*, published in 1935, was no *Mein Kampf*. But Dennis' writings were the closest thing to a workable blueprint produced during the decade.

Neither did they appear to pay much attention to Seward Collins whose appeal in the *American Review*, a journal which he began publishing in 1933, was quite frankly aimed at Fascist-oriented intellectuals. Collins, who regarded Mussolini "the most constructive statesman of our age," told his limited audience, with no show of emotion, that the choice was "Communist collectivism or personal liberty under Fascism." *American Review* articles, which were of excellent quality (at least at first), undertook to illumine this singular proposition. But no one was listening. That Dennis and Collins were sons of Harvard and Princeton had nothing to do with it; native Fascists were simply not interested in an intellectual or scientific approach to irrational politics.

Much credit for their relatively ineffectual showing must go to the American people. Not that Americans have some special immunity that will always save them; they may yet sell their souls. But in the 1930's, democracy had a deep reserve, a resolution, a courage, a vitality that was more than a match for the seedy crowd of Fascist sappers. Bad as conditions were, the people never fully surrendered to despair, although it sometimes looked that way. The dream was still intact; and the pluralism of American democracy, the deep roots of equalitarianism, were too strong to yield to totalitarian solutions for vexing problems. Somehow the people knew, perhaps intuitively, that totalitarianism was unlimited, that it demanded everything, that having taken the first step there was no turning back. Only the most dedicated Fascist wished to go that far.

So the country watched—during the depression decade there was a lot of time for watching—fascinated by an ideological fireworks that for sheer entertainment value has probably never been matched in our history; and in the center of it was Franklin Roosevelt.

CHAPTER III

"The Jew Deal..."

Roosevelt inevitably draws upon his Semitic ancestry. It is, therefore, as natural for him to be a radical, as it is for others to be true Americans. . . . HE IS NOT ONE OF US! —Gerald B. Winrod

Pray God, that America shall remain American . . . and escape the servitude so well planned for us by alien factors, the Jew and the New Deal.
—Carl Mote
The New Deal Goose Step

The Roosevelt "New Deal" is not sincere; it is not a recovery movement; it is . . . sabotage . . . with the idea of bringing about . . . the world Jewish state where only Jews will own property and reap profits.—Eugene N. Sanctuary

Not only our individual freedom, but our very lives are at stake. Not only our country, but our civilization is threatened by the formidable sect in control at the White House. —Howland Spencer
Toward Armageddon

WHEN the one-time Pennsylvania Congressman Louis T. McFadden died in October, 1936, the attending physician attributed his death to a stroke. But there were those who knew better than competent medical authority, and said so: Jews had killed McFadden.

The thought of killing McFadden had no doubt crossed the mind of more than one Jew. Some had no doubt lingered on the savouring satisfaction his demise would bring. And not without reason. Since his arrival in Washington in 1915, McFadden had acquired a reputation as an anti-Semite, and little else. Copies of intemperate speeches went out by the thousands over his frank; angry resolutions and counterresolutions were introduced; undignified debates and efforts to get retractions from him (or apologies at the very least) went on in the House to no avail. McFadden eventually became the object of ugly rumors, rumors that were never confirmed, concerning connections with German Nazi agents in the United States.[1]

A climax in the McFadden story came in May, 1934, when he delivered a speech over radio station WOL in Washington D.C. With the uninspired title "Present Day Government" the speech was a delight to every native Fascist in the land. "Present Day Government" was a preposterous tale of "the Jewish plan of a World State," a plan hatched, according to McFadden, by one Israel Moses Sieff, "an Israelite, the director of a chain-store enterprise in England." His was no ordinary chain-store, either; it "handles almost exclusively imports from Soviet Russia. . . ." The agents of Sieff in the United States, the men responsible for engineering the over-throw of the government and of bringing the United States into the Jewish-dominated world system, were, he said, certain members of the Brain Trust. Nor did he shrink from naming names. His list included Felix Frankfurter, Raymond Moley, Rexford Tugwell, Adolf A. Berle, Jr., and "the mysterious Mordecai Ezekiel"—men who were, according to McFadden, "all members of this particular group who are carrying out a world plan."[2]

In the 1930's, McFadden was widely quoted and copies of his radio speech were circulated by demagogues, by anti-Semites and race-baiters, by the fringes of varying degrees of lunacy and, unfortunately, by far too many witless people who knew no better. Even in the 1940's, more than a decade later, copies of McFadden's speech were being reproduced and circulated, fifty for one dollar, by the Crusading Mothers of Pennsylvania. "Present Day Government" had now become "The New Deal Plot to Overthrow Our Constitutional Form of Government." It was perhaps pointless to explain to the Mothers that no dire fate had yet befallen the land or that most of the men whom McFadden had accused ("It is the duty of Congress to seek them out and try them for treason," the Mothers asserted) were no longer in government.[3]

McFadden was adding to anti-Semitism the dignity of the United States Congress, a dignity it did not deserve. But anti-Semitism, perhaps more virulent and more vicious than any time before or since, had lots of friends. The subtle kind of anti-Semitism that was usually associated with country club membership or admission to eastern medical schools, or with a thousand other mean and petty manifestations of racial bias, became in the 1930's an open assault upon Jews (with many of the excesses and the pseudoscientific mumbo-jumbo of the Nazis), and through them upon Roosevelt and the New Deal. The strategic objective of the campaign was to try to convince the unwary that Roosevelt was a Jew, that the New Deal was a Jewish trick contrived to betray the United States into the clutches of international conspirators who were plotting a world state under Jewish domination.

II

Early in September, 1934, the amiable George Deatherage of St. Albans, West Virginia, a successful engineer-turned-crusader and head of the Knights of the White Camellia (an organization which used the swastika for its insignia), wrote to President Roosevelt. There was a time, he said, when he was proud that his son had Delano blood in his veins; but not any more. "I want to assure you," he told the President, "that I am going to take the first opportunity I can to kick it out of him." Deatherage's displeasure and his improbable vow regarding his son were occasioned by his discovery that the Delanos were Jews.[4]

The claim that Roosevelt was a Jew seemed to have started from a genealogical chart, allegedly prepared at the Carnegie Institution in Washington, which first appeared as an Associated Press dispatch in the Tucson *Daily Citizen* on March 7, 1934. This at least was the account given by the Reverend Gerald B. Winrod of Wichita, Kansas. Winrod (the "Jayhawk Nazi" as he was often called), a sometime preacher, an unsuccessful candidate for the Senate in the 1938 Republican primary, and publisher of *The Defender* (a monthly magazine with an unconfirmed circulation of 100,000), was able to draw a number of interesting conclusions from the Roosevelt genealogy. "From the viewpoint of eugenics," wrote Winrod, "it explains his [Roosevelt's] natural bent toward radicalism . . . and proves unmistakably, that the Roosevelt Administration offers a biological, as well as political problem."[5]

What the genealogy seemed to prove was that the Roosevelt family had derived originally from the Rossocampo family, exiled from Spain in 1620. Seeking asylum in the Germanies, in Holland and other countries the family adopted a number of variations on the original family name, variations like Rosenberg, Rosenbaum, Rosenblum, Rosenthal, and Rosenvelt. The President was a direct descendant of Claes Martenssen van Roosevelt (or Rosenvelt, depending on who was telling it) who came to the New World, to New Amsterdam, in 1649. In an attempt to clear up the confusion, the *Jewish Chronicle* of Detroit in March, 1935, asked Roosevelt about his ancestry. The President, in his reply (widely quoted, in *The New York Times* and elsewhere), answered quite candidly that "in the distant past they [Roosevelt's ancestors] may have been Jews. All I know about the origin of the Roosevelt family is that they are apparently descended from Claes Martenssen van Roosevelt."[6]

On the Delano side of the family, Roosevelt was also Jewish because, it was claimed, the Delanos were descendants of an Italian-Spanish Jewish family, the Dilanos (Dilans, Dillanos), who eventually arrived in New Amsterdam via Brazil. Since there was now what many regarded as unimpeachable evidence that Roosevelt was descended from Jews on both sides of the family this made Roosevelt "from the standpoint of Jewish Heredity Law AS GOOD A JEW AS BERNARD M. BARUCH," according to one writer.[7]

Most of Roosevelt's critics on the extreme right played the Jewish angle to the hilt, not the least being Robert Edward Edmondson. Born in Ohio of an old Virginian family, Edmondson was sixty-two years old and modestly successful in the public relations and economic consulting business in New York City when he discovered the Jews. He was comfortable on an annual income of $50,000, he once testified; but he was "all the time running up against a force which he did not understand." The "force," it developed, "was a well-organized international conspiracy . . . the Jews were responsible for it." Once alerted, Edmondson went all out against the "Jewish Conspiracy." Through Edmondson Economic Service, he distributed more anti-Semitic propaganda than any man in America until libel proceedings instigated by Mayor LaGuardia of New York (which were eventually dismissed) prompted him to move his operations to Pennsylvania.[8]

Roosevelt's alleged Jewish heritage was one of Edmondson's favorite topics. As early as March, 1934, only a week after the genealogy appeared, Edmondson had out a broadside entitled "Blame the Rosenvelts." One of Edmondson's contributions to the campaign literature of 1936 was "Moe Roosevelt Wins," in which he asserted that New York Jews had struck a medal with the head of Roosevelt on one side, the six-pointed star on the back and a good-luck greeting in the center which he translated "Good luck and wisdom to Franklin D. Roosevelt, our modern Moses, leading Jewry in the Promised Land." This, wrote Edmondson, was significant evidence that the Roosevelt Administration "is dominated by 'Invisible Jewish Leadership.' "[9]

The leader of the Silver Shirt movement, William Dudley Pelley, a small man with a Van Dyke beard and a mystic who had spent seven minutes in Heaven, talked to God, was the reincarnation of something or other (and who startled Martin Dies of the House Un-American Activities Committee with the information that we "actually choose our parents by our own free will, before entering life as infants"), liked to refer to Roosevelt in his publication, *Liberation*, as the "Kosher President" and to assert that the real President was Bernard Baruch. Gerald L. K. Smith, the devoted lieutenant of Huey Long who usurped the leadership of the Share-Our-Wealth movement after Long's assassination, saw to it that the Christian Nationalist Crusade sent out thousands of copies of the Roosevelt genealogy during the campaign of 1936 from its St. Louis headquarters, with a footnote that read: "Every sensible Christian and loyal American will fight the campaign of Leftists, Communists, Jews and Internationalists to return the Roosevelt dynasty to power." And in his final appeal to his readers on the eve of the 1936 election, Gerald B. Winrod summed up the whole anti-Semitic position in one tortured, anguished cry, "HE IS NOT ONE OF US!"[10]

III

Right-wing extremists worked hard to establish that Roosevelt was a Jew. But had there not been the slightest, remotest possibility that he had a Jewish ancestry they would have invented one. It was important that Roosevelt be a Jew. It was essential to the thesis that Jews controlled the Administration, a prerequisite to an impending betrayal to an international Jewish conspiracy.

Describing the party in power as the "Judocrats" and "Ju-Dealers," Franklin Thompson, who titled his contemptible little book *America's Ju-Deal*, went on to assert that the Roosevelt Administration was "predominantly Jewish." Thompson, a New Yorker who had never been abroad, considered himself a German and made it a point to associate with Nazi sympathizers. "No Administration in the history of the United States," he wrote, "has been under the influence and control of Jews as the present one."[11]

James True, described by Stanley High in the *Saturday Evening Post* as the "number 1 Fascist Braintruster" in the United States and perhaps the most neurotic of all the anti-Semites, was among the first to demonstrate how far Jewish influence extended in the Roosevelt Administration. Roosevelt had been in office only a year, True pointed out, and already "more than 500 men and women have been placed in important positions who are opposed to the Christian religion."[12]

True maintained headquarters in Washington, D.C. Elderly, white-haired, nervous, True feared telephones and worked behind carefully locked doors. From offices in the National Press Building the James True Associates distributed his *Industrial Control Report*, a weekly four- to six-page newsletter with excellent format and carrying no advertising. The newsletter went all over the country, and also down the street where Senator Schall received unanimous consent to enter articles from it in the *Congressional Record*. It was from a True report that Schall picked up the rumor about Roosevelt's mental condition during the whisper campaign of 1935, the report of June 22, 1935, which also included a vicious attack on "that 'Karl Marx' Professor, Frankfurter, and his legal kikes. . . ."[13]

"Kike" was a favorite word with True. In 1935, in a moment of great genius, he conceived the idea for a weapon, a short hardwood truncheon much like the lower end of an axe-handle, with finger grip and leather lanyard. This heavy-duty nightstick (for which True received patent no. 2–026–077 under "Amusement Devices and Games"), he called a "Kike-Killer." Mrs. True, according to the inventor, carried a less hefty one called a "Kike-Killer, Lady's Size."

"For a first-class massacre more than a truncheon is needed," he conceded in an interview. There was going to be a general massacre of Jews in the fall of 1936, True revealed (a national "Jew Shoot" he called it), a piece of arrant nonsense which required the Secret Service to assign guards temporarily to prominent Jewish officials and their families. "We're not going to drive the Jews out of the country," he boasted; "we are going to bury them right here!" According to the reporter True always had a loaded revolver on his desk and kept in practice by shooting at a cake of soap, because "the consistency of soap approximates Jewish flesh."[14]

True was full of tough talk, talk about kikes, killing Jews, and pogroms, all of which found their way into his publications. This kind of talk encouraged similar talk from others, as in the case of a letter in his report of March 21, 1936, a letter from a woman ("a highly educated American of unquestionable integrity") that True quoted at length: "The big shots you know," she began (meaning the prominent Jews in the Administration). "Their understudies are the alien foreigner," she continued, "or the crack-pot American educated in one of our Jewish colleges. Their whole effort is to reduce the white man to a level of degeneracy. . . . These Beasts! . . . The woman I am working under is a Jewess . . . who is also under a Jewess. Both have married Gentiles. But this prostitute . . . the Jewess with an Irish name . . . is the last word in bastardization. I call a spade a spade, and until all Americans take this attitude against the world's common enemy, so long will we be in bondage to this blood-thirsty race."[15]

This, it seemed, was True's personal view, too. Jews had gained control in America, and it was their stranglehold that he was trying to break. This, he told Dr. L. M. Birkhead, national director of the Friends of Democracy, was the purpose of his organization, to defeat the real enemy of the United States, "the Jew Communism which the New Deal is trying to force on America."[16]

William Dudley Pelley thought it would take a mighty host, at least "a million awakened, enlightened Christians" to turn back the Jewish menace. The Jewish threat was the theme of the Silver Shirt membership drive in 1934. "WHAT ARE YOU GOING TO DO ABOUT IT?" was the heading of a Silver Shirt membership advertisement in March, 1934. "Chief Pelley has made it clear . . . that this [Jewish usurpation of power] has been happening. . . . Congressman McFadden must have made it devastatingly clear that it has happened. . . . Again, he [McFadden] throws down the Jewish protocol gauntlet to Congress, to the Jews, *and to you*."[17]

The overwhelming victory of Roosevelt in 1936, and the apparent indifference of the American public to the Jewish danger provoked Pelley to mad talk about a second civil war "to overthrow the Jew-Communist usurpers who have seized the American government. . . ." Victory would be snatched from defeat, Pelley assured his faithful; Gentile would prevail over Jew, but "not before the undisciplined American has run riot in mob spirit and slaughtered Jews wholesale in history's greatest pogrom."[18]

Reviewing for the *Nation* unfair tactics used against Roosevelt in 1936, Paul Ward reported that the list of anti-Semitic literature used in the campaign "could be lengthened interminably." This was literally true;

and Pelley would have earned a place near the top of the list for volume and viciousness. "This present Jewish Administration" became Pelley's favorite way of referring to the New Deal in the weeks preceding the election. In an editorial, "The Final Stroke," on the eve of the election, Pelley took one last wild slash at "this present Jewish Administration . . . in other words, these international Frankfurters . . . who, in the past four years, have turned the Christian United States into a vast civic synagogue."[19]

Edmondson was also busy during the campaign. He distributed a series of charts arranged in the form of a six-pointed Jewish star that listed the ranking Jewish members of the Administration. In the center of one was the legend, "Roosevelt Red Democracy: New Deal Government Of, By and For The Jews." Another was labeled the "FRANKFURTER-BRANDEIS-BARUCH-MORGENTHAU MONOPOLY," which Edmondson described as "America's Invisible Governors." These men, he warned, were only the more prominent among the eighteen thousand Jews "now dictating American policies. . . ." The real power behind Roosevelt, Edmondson insisted in another, was B'nai B'rith.[20]

Of the anti-Semitic literature used during the campaign of 1936 to defame Roosevelt perhaps the *pièce de résistance* was a thirty-five page booklet consisting of editorials by Howland Spencer, the Squire of Krum Elbow, that first appeared separately in Spencer's *Highland Post* (Ulster County, New York), and were then published during the campaign as *Toward Armageddon* by the Militant Christian Association of Charleston, South Carolina.

Like a consummate lover, Spencer gently massaged every erotic muscle. He wrote almost rhapsodically of invisible governments, black inquisitions, Talmudic philosophy, pre-natal necessity, alien-minded groups, old racial dreams, that formidable sect in control at the White House, secret advisers. All of these Jewish vices, said Spencer, were literally combined in one person—"this silent man," "the doctrinaire ear-whisperer, the Iago of this Administration," Felix Frankfurter.[21]

The climax to Spencer's artistry had Roosevelt responsible for what amounted to the ritual murders of New Mexico Senator Bronson Cutting (who died in a plane crash over Missouri in 1934), Louisiana Senator Huey Long (assassinated in the Louisiana state capitol building in 1935), Minnesota Senator Thomas Schall (struck down and killed by an automobile in 1936), and Albert Ritchie, former governor of Maryland (dead of a stroke in Baltimore in 1936). Spencer made it clear that these deaths were part of a Roosevelt-Jewish plot. "Many an historic curse," wrote the Squire of Krum Elbow, "lies in the brains and the blood of a people." What he was saying implied that, in addition to all their other sins, Jews were capable of the black arts as well—voodoo murder, sharp pins in dolls, and all the rest. "The new and terrible curse of sudden death destroys those who disturb the policies of Franklin D. Roosevelt," he said. "Oppose Roosevelt and die! Why is this curse, and from what dark magic does it obtain its potency?"[22]

IV

William Dudley Pelley may have been able to claim that he was first in the race to prove that an international Jewish conspiracy was afoot. By the fall of 1933, Pelley was already appealing for support for his Silver Legion "before it is too late," too late to save the United States from Bernard Baruch, "the Pro-consul for International Jewry in America." Too late to save it from "the Baruchs, Warburgs, Frankfurters, Meyers, Wises, Untermeyers and Franks who have spoken," warned Pelley. "The Judean Horde is on its way!"[23]

By Judean Horde Pelley meant an influx into the United States of three to four hundred thousand Jews from all over Europe who would spearhead the takeover of the government here, an influx to be accomplished by the circumvention of our existing imigration laws. The Jew, Samuel Dickstein, the slight, bespectacled New York congressman, son of immigrants, champion of underdogs and chairman of the House Committee on Immigration, would see to that. Then by "deception, confusion, chaos and collapse," aided and abetted (believe it or not) by the "wholesale inoculation of Gentiles with vaccine syphilitic germs," the Jews would establish a dictatorship as part of the Jewish world government.[24]

Pelley, in a series of pamphlets (e.g., *Hidden Empire*; *There Is A Jewish World Plot, Jews Say So!*; *The Final Stroke*) explained that he had learned the detailed plans of the plot by a small group of Jewish international bankers ("a secret European Money Cartel," Pelley called them) from a "big official" connected with the United States Department of State, whom Pelley did not identify, and who (wouldn't you know it) had subsequently died—or been killed. "As the weeks went by, and [the] New Deal . . . went into operation, I beheld the plan unfold definitely and atrociously, just as my State Department friend had predicted," Pelley wrote. The most obvious clue that the plot was under way, said Pelley, was that "at their bidding" Roosevelt began packing the Administration with Jews, and "firing the Gentiles out of their own government." "There is proof—pressed down and overflowing—" wrote Pelley, "that the New Deal from its inception has been naught but the political penetration of a predominately Christian country and Christian government, by predatory, megalo-maniacal Israelites and their agents."[25]

A world Jewish conspiracy was, almost without exception, an obsessively recurring theme of extremists in the United States. It was, for

ROOSEVELT'S SUPREME COUNCIL

A Non-Partisan Exposure of

AN "ALIEN - STAR" ORIENTAL REVOLUTIONARY - POWER IN CONTROL OF WASHINGTON

The six-point star-picture below, showing **"America's Invisible Governors"** and their allies, gives **only part** of a long list of alien-minded New Dealer "advisors" behind Roosevelt, including unofficial and official "**appointments**," elected "representatives," etc., **all owing allegiance** to the FRANKFURTER-BRANDEIS-BARUCH-MORGENTHAU MONOPOLY. It is estimated that 18,000 of these "key" Internationalists are now **dictating American policies,** directed by Professor Felix Frankfurter, called by General Hugh S. Johnson in the Saturday Evening **Post** of Oct. 26, 1935, "THE MOST INFLUENTIAL SINGLE INDIVIDUAL IN THE U. S."

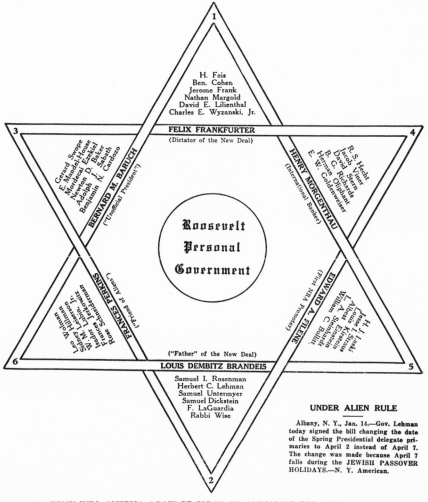

1

H. Feis
Ben. Cohen
Jerome Frank
Nathan Margold
David E. Lilienthal
Charles E. Wyzanski, Jr.

FELIX FRANKFURTER
(Dictator of the New Deal)

3

Gerard Swope
E. Mandel-House
Mordecai Ezekiel
Newton D. Baker
Adolph J. Sabath
Benjamin N. Cardozo

BERNARD M. BARUCH
("Unofficial President")

4

R. S. Hecht
Jacob Viner
David Stern
B. G. Richards
Herman Oliphant
E. W. Goldenweiser

HENRY MORGENTHAU
(International Banker)

Roosevelt Personal Government

FRANCES PERKINS
("Friend" of Aliens)

W. Wolmann
Leo Hillman
Sidney Hillman
W. Jett Lauck
Isador Lubin, Jr.
Frances Schneiderman
Rose Schneiderman

EDWARD A. FILENE
(First NRA Promoter)

Jesse I. Isaac
Adolph J. Sack
William C. Bullitt
A. A. Eberstein
William Green
Alexander Sachs

("Father" of the New Deal)

LOUIS DEMBITZ BRANDEIS

6   **5**

Samuel I. Rosenman
Herbert C. Lehman
Samuel Untermyer
Samuel Dickstein
F. LaGuardia
Rabbi Wise

2

UNDER ALIEN RULE

Albany, N. Y., Jan. 14.—Gov. **Lehman** today signed the bill changing the date of the Spring Presidential delegate primaries to April 2 instead of April 7. The change was made because April 7 falls during the JEWISH PASSOVER HOLIDAYS.—N. Y. American.

WHEN WILL AMERICA AGAIN BE RULED BY AMERICANS FOR AMERICANS?

The above "Seal of Solomon," symbol of Ownership—appearing on all synagogues—is now stamped on (1) *U. S. Post Office dead-letter envelopes;* (2) *U. S. Army Helmets;* (3) *U. S. Navy Dept. seals;* (4) *reverse side of medals of President Franklin D. Roosevelt; and* (5) *on our NEW ONE-DOLLAR BILLS over the American Eagle—the six-point interlaced double-triangle star camouflaged outline being formed of miniature 5-point stars.*

The largest number of the above "SUPREME COUNCIL"—many of whom are foreign-born—owe their positions to Internationalist-controlled **Tammany.** These posts of great importance are filled, NOT by ELECTION, but by ROOSEVELT APPOINTMENTS. Unofficial advisors are **very dangerous** to a free American Government because they cannot be held publicly responsible for their actions.

Descriptions above and on the other side of this sheet are from published records—numbers at the end of star-points referring to groups shown.

(OVER)

NON-PARTISAN DESCRIPTIONS FROM PUBLISHED RECORDS

Group No. 1

FELIX FRANKFURTER of Mass., *foreign-born;* "Unofficial Presidential Advisor"; listed in *"Red Network"* as a member of the Civil Liberties Union, legal advisor of Communists; known as Harvard University's "Karl Marx" (Communist) Professor; called Legal-Master-Mind of New Deal in Simon-Schuster 1934 book, "The New Dealers"; branded as *Bolshevist* by late President THEODORE Roosevelt *for defending Communist* Mooney and "Reds" Sacco and Vanzetti, murderers; placed 100 "key-men" in Roosevelt jobs. *"He has more influence than any other single person in the U. S.,"* says Gen. Johnson in the SaturdayEvening Post of Oct. 26, 1935. Frankfurter has never been *elected* to any public office. He was nominated in 1932 for the Massachusetts Supreme Court, but defeated by 500,000 protests. He is said to be Roosevelt's choice for the next U. S. Supreme Court vacancy.

"Allies"—Herbert Feis of Mo., Asst. Secy. of State. Benj. Cohen of Mass., *wrote Security and Utility Laws.* Jerome Frank of Ill., General Counsel of RFC. Nathan Margold of N. Y., Interior Dept. Legal Advisor. David E. Lilienthal of Wis., Director of TVA. Charles E. Wyzanski, Jr., of Mass., Labor Dept. Legal Advisor.

Group No. 2

LOUIS DEMBITZ BRANDEIS of Mass., "Unofficial Presidential Advisor"; Justice of U. S. Supreme Court; *"Father"* of Communistic New Deal. He is named in *"Red Network"* as supporter of Communistic Commonwealth College of Arkansas. Highly praised by Albert Einstein, expelled from Germany as a *Communist.* The Chicago Tribune of Sept. 22, 1934, printed this statement by Gen. Hugh S. Johnson: "During the whole of this intense experience (building up the *illegal NRA) I have been in constant touch with Justice Brandeis."* The N. Y. Times of Jan. 28, 1934, said: "The underlying philosophy of the New Deal is the philosophy of Justice Brandeis."

"Allies"—H. C. Lehman, Governor of N. Y., *International Banker.* Samuel I. Rosenman, Judge of New York State Supreme Court, whom Roosevelt called *his "Right Arm."* Lawyer Samuel Untermyer of N. Y., "Unofficial Presidential *Public Ownership Advisor,"* listed in *"Red Network"* as endorsing the *anti-patriotic* article, "Professional Patriots," *published in the Communist paper,* "The Daily Worker." Samuel Dickstein, N. Y. Congressman, who radioed on March 18, 1934: *"We Americans must change our laws so they* (GERMAN COMMUNISTIC JEWS) *can come here at once."* N. Y. Mayor F. LaGuardia, "U.official Presidential Advisor," listed in *"Red Network"* as running for Congress on 1924 *Socialist* Ticket. Rabbi Stephen S. Wise, *foreign-born,* of N. Y. City, listed in *"Red Network"* as connected with the Civil Liberties Union, legal advisor to *Communists.*

Group No. 3

BERNARD M. BARUCH of N. Y., called "Unofficial President" by *Rabbi Gross'* Brooklyn Jewish Examiner; *Wall Street speculator and associate of International Bankers;* Wilson-Roosevelt Economic Advisor; admitted to Congress Committee: *"I probably had more power than any other man during the World War."* He called National pride (patriotism) *"A lot of nonsense"* (see Chicago Tribune, Sept. 25). Ford's "Dearborn Independent" of July 25, 1925, said: "The Baruch interest, with others, has planned the Communistic State. It will not be necessary to stage a revolution. Upon commencement of war, the U. S. goes under Communism in one day."

"Allies"—Gerard Swope of N. Y., Roosevelt "Industrial Advisor." Col. E. Mandel-House of Mass., Wilson-Roosevelt International Political Advisor, helped to form The League of Nations. Mordecai Ezekiel of N. Y., Asst. Secy. of Agriculture, one of AAA Law authors. Newton D. Baker of Ohio, "Unofficial Presidential Advisor," listed in *"Red Network"* as *"Communist-recommended author"*—who *urges U. S. to join League of Nations.* Adolph J. Sabath, Illinois Congressman, Roosevelt "Special Investigator." N. Y. U. S. Supreme Court Justice Cardozo, reported in Chicago Tribune of April 26, 1934, as having, with Brandeis, *"led the Supreme Court from conservatism."*

Group No. 4

HENRY MORGENTHAU, SR., of N. Y., *foreign-born;* "Unofficial Presidential Advisor"; *related to International Bankers Seligman and Lehman.* His son is Secretary of the U. S. Treasury and *Dictator of the Two Billion Dollar "Stabilization Fund."* Sigmund Solomon "superintends" for him $5,000,000,000 gold bars in N. Y. Assay Office.

"Allies"—R. S. Hecht of La., *foreign-born,* President of American Bankers' Assn.; "Official Presidential Financial Advisor. Jacob Viner of N. Y., Tax Expert of U. S. Treasury. David Stern of N. Y. and Pa., Member of Federal Reserve Board of Philadelphia and Publisher N. Y. Post; "Unofficial Presidential Advisor." B. G. Richards of N. Y., *foreign-born;* Assistant to National Emergency Council. Herman Oliphant of N. Y., General Counsel to Secretary of Treasury. E. W. Goldenweiser of N. Y., *Russian-born;* Federal Reserve Director.

Group No. 5

EDWARD A. FILENE of Mass., "Unofficial Presidential Advisor; listed in *"Red Network"* as member of American-Russian Chamber of Commerce. His "20th Century Fund" financed NRA's importation from Europe. Filene was in Moscow during the last *Communist International Congress.*

"Allies"—Louis Kirstein of Mass., National Advisory Board member. Jesse I. Straus of N. Y., "Official Presidential Advisor"; promoted Roosevelt Presidential campaign; now Ambassador to France. H. J. Laski, Director of Fabian *Socialist* Society of England; "Unofficial Foreign Advisor." L. A. Steinhardt, Minister to Sweden. Albert Einstein, *expelled from Germany as Communist;* listed in *"Red Network"* as conferring with Roosevelt. W. C. Bullitt, "Official Soviet Advisor"; Ambassador to Russia; listed in *"Red Network."*

Group No. 6

FRANCES PERKINS of N. Y., Secretary of Labor. "The Immigration Crew," a pamphlet of the Amer. Vigilante Intelligence Federation of Chicago, reports: "Frances Perkins says she was born in Boston April 10, 1882. There is no record of her birth in the Boston Register *for* 1882. Her husband's name is given as Paul Wilson. The only record of marriage of Paul Wilson was at Newton, Mass., in 1910, when he married Matilda *Wutski.* Secretary Perkins gave Emma Goldman (*Communist*) permission to enter the U. S. *Secretary Perkins has decreased alien deportation* 60 per cent." She is known as *"The Friend of Aliens."*

"Allies"—Prof. Leo. Wolman of N. Y., Labor Strike Board Chairman; listed in *"Red Network"* as director of Garland Fund (*Communistic*). Sidney Hillman, *foreign-born,* of N. Y.; Labor Advisory Board member; President of "Red" Amalgamated Clothing Workers' Union; listed in *"Red Network"* as Garland Fund director. W. M. Leiserson, *Russian-born;* Labor Board Secretary; listed in *"Red Network"* as member of Socialist Berger Foundation. Isidor Lubin, Jr., of N. Y., Labor Delegate to League of Nations. Frances Jurkowitz of N. Y., Asst. to Secy. of Labor: Rose Schneiderman of N. Y., *Russian-born* Labor Dept. Asst.; listed in *"Red Network"* as member of the Civil Liberties Union, legal advisor to *Communists.*

Roosevelt Congratulates COMMUNISTS on 18th Soviet Anniversary

As reported in the N. Y. Times on Nov. 8, 1935, President Roosevelt cabled Soviet President Kalinin at Moscow on Nov. 7 on "the 18th anniversary of the Socialist (*Communist*) revolution in Russia," saying: *"I am happy to extend sincere felicitations on THIS MEMORABLE ANNIVERSARY,* with my best wishes for Your Excellency's health and happiness." (Thirty Million Christian *Russians* have been killed and starved to death by Soviet.)

New York, Nov. 15, 1935 (Revised Feb. 25, 1936)

Robert Edward Edmondson

(OVER)

example, the theme of Congressman Jacob Thorkelson in his *Is This Nation Ruled by Invisible Government?*, published by Pelley. It appeared in *My Fight for the Right*, in which Gerald L. K. Smith insisted that Roosevelt, "through the cooperation of his pro-Communist pals and the great American Jewish gestapo," had deprived him of access to press or radio.[26]

It was the theme of Colonel Eugene Nelson Sanctuary, an old professional in the ranks of the hate-peddlers, friend of congressmen and senators, a man with numerous German connections, head of the notoriously anti-Semitic American Christian Defenders, and perhaps the only military officer in history to be indicted three times for seditious conspiracy against the United States. Sanctuary probably went farther than most in developing his theme, insisting that both Communism and the New Deal were frauds and hoaxes by which "liberals and other groups . . . will overthrow their governments and put internationalists into power who will establish the world Jewish state." "The Roosevelt 'New Deal,'" Sanctuary could say, straight-faced, "is not sincere; it is not a recovery movement; it is . . . sabotage . . . with the idea of bringing about . . . the world Jewish state where only Jews will own property and reap profits."[27]

Both Edmondson and Howland Spencer leaned hard on the international conspiracy theme. In one of his earlier pieces, "Franklinstein Debt-Bondage," which bore the subheading, "New Deal Secret Goal Unmasked as a Titanic International Monetary Conspiracy," Edmondson warned, "They have captured the Treasury Department." Edmondson arrived at this conclusion by arguing that the "father" of the Federal Reserve System, "the largest central bank in the world," was Paul M. Warburg, a Jew; that the current head of the Federal Reserve Board was Eugene Meyer, Jr., "former partner in the International Banking House of Lazard Freres." This fatuous recital established "beyond controversy the subversive objectives of Roosevelt New Dealers."[28]

As late as 1939 (by which time he could brag that the American Jewish Committee had voted him the most prolific anti-Semitic pamphleteer in the United States), Edmondson was proudly displaying a testimonial signed by leading Jew-baiters "of twenty-four countries" and loudly proclaiming, "The whole nation is now Jew-ruled."[29]

Spencer did not subscribe to the theory that the Jews would take over in the United States by stealth and deceit, although on occasion he peddled the same Israel Moses Sieff conspiracy story that had made Congressman McFadden the darling of the extreme right. The year 1941 was the one set for world domination by the Jews, according to Spencer, and to maintain their time schedule the United States would have to be taken by force, by civil war. "Franklin D. Roosevelt . . . has sold his fellow Americans to the Universal Conspirators," Spencer asserted, sold them "to the blood lust of international anti-Christian assassins."[30]

His prediction that "the zero hour for civil war is to be at dusk on September 15th (1936), when the Zionists begin their new year" was taken seriously by at least one group of Silver Shirts. The Minneapolis *Journal* carried the story of some local Silver Shirts storing up food, enough to last for two weeks. Civil war was to be the grand climax to the inexorable rush of events. "We know Franklin Delano Roosevelt to be what he is," wrote Spencer, ". . . the figure-head of the would-be world destroyers. . . . The light of Shechinah cannot be hidden. The illuminated faces of those seraphim Brandeis and Baruch and reflected faces of the cherubim Frankfurter and Tugwell, *proclaim the ultimate goal of world domination.*"[31]

Of the reams of such fanciful hate literature that appeared in the 1930's from tortured, resentful extremists such as Spencer, Pelley, Edmondson, Winrod, and others, the prize for irrationality and unabashed meanness was *Aryan Americanism* by a Chicagoan, Olov E. Tietzow, who headed the American Guard, The White Man's Party. Tietzow ran the gamut of scurrilous name-calling, omitted none of the anti-Semitic vocabulary and terminology, and dragged in all the customary charges of plot and conspiracy, ritual murder and Jewish deceit. All these things had been said many times and by many people. It was the total effect that was so offensive.

Tietzow raged incoherently about Roosevelt, "that Jew, the New Deal Leader," about "the Jewish New Deal," "that push-cart New Deal," "Jew-controlled finances," "U.S.A. Treasury and Federal Reserve system . . . in the claws of the Jews," "Gentile America," and, of course, about the "international Jewish conspiracy," "the international Jewish cabal," "the sinister Jewish clique." Huey Long, said Tietzow, was the victim of ritual murder. Had he lived "there would now be no person of Jewish blood in the White House. The political beneficiary of that assassination was Roosevelt's Jewish New Deal—draw your own conclusions!"

Tietzow saw only tragedy and sorrow ahead until violence and bloodshed should purge America and set her right. "The continuation of the *Jewish New Deal,*" wrote Tietzow, "has been made possible by gullible masses . . . fascinated . . . hypnotized by an insidious smile . . . deceptive words; the Leader . . . using tricky and cheap political methods . . . to achieve . . . establishment of dictatorial government of, for and by the international Jews and thereby making a second Palestine out of Gentile America." But "a small clique of Jews" could not hope to dominate millions of Gentile Americans forever, Tietzow warned. Some day there would be reaction; the Leader [Roosevelt] would resort to force to maintain Jewish control, and then—"then our country will witness an uprising

of unprecedented proportions and at the end of the civil war that probably would ensue there would hardly be one Jew or New Dealer left
alive in these United States."[32]

Sooner or later, and usually sooner, the anti-Semites who were intent
on proving Roosevelt was a Jew and that his Administration was controlled by Jews would drag out for public display an ancient hoax, the
Protocols of the Learned Elders of Zion, purporting to prove the existence
of an international Jewish conspiracy for world domination.

The *Protocols,* their obscure origins tantalizingly mysterious to the
gullible, had been repeatedly exposed as a fraud. It seemed reasonably
certain that part of the material in them was first published in the 1860's
as part of a satire written by Maurice Joly and directed at Napoleon III.
Another likely source was the work of a German writer, Herman
Goedsche.

Whatever may have been their origin, later accounts which borrowed
from a version published in Russia, in 1905, sought to make it appear
that the plot outlined in the *Protocols* was first hatched at the Zionist
Congress at Basel, Switzerland, in 1897. The 1905 version may have
been concocted by Tsarist police as a political stratagem, deliberately
intended to foment anti-Semitic agitation in a troubled Russia torn by
revolution. But even that is not certain.

In 1934, at a time when the *Protocols* were enjoying enormous popularity with anti-Semites in the United States, two booksellers in Berne,
Switzerland, charged with distributing the *Protocols* for Swiss Nazis,
were losing a libel suit, a suit in which expert witnesses proved once again
that the documents were a disgraceful hoax.[33]

The Swiss decision had no effect on American Jew-baiters; the *Protocols*
continued to carry the authority of holy writ. Colonel Sanctuary published two books on the subject, *The Protocols of the Elders of Zion* and
Are These Things So? Gerald Winrod also relied heavily on the *Protocols.*
During Roosevelt's first term, Winrod printed and distributed about
95,000 pieces of anti-Semitic literature, mostly through the "Defenders
Tract Club," literature that eventually turned up in jails, hospitals, bus
stations, CCC camps, and churches. Included were such titles as, "The
Hidden Hand; The Protocols and the Coming Super Man," "The Jewish
Assault on Christianity," and "The Truth About the Protocols."[34]

While the writings and speeches of others were liberally sprinkled
with mysterious and menacing references to the *Protocols,* perhaps no
one used them as a weapon against Roosevelt more skillfully than
Howland Spencer. Spencer so despised Roosevelt that he sold his 500-acre
estate across the Hudson River from Hyde Park to Father Divine (a New
York Negro evangelist whose salutation "Peace!" became a household
byword in the 1930's), retreated to a self-imposed exile in the Bahamas

(from which he did not return until 1946) with the comment, "We have a 'Messiah' in Washington and now we will have a 'God' at Krum Elbow."[35]

In *Toward Armageddon*, which was used so extensively in the 1936 campaign, Spencer described Roosevelt as "the figure-head of the would-be world destroyers." In this case, the "world destroyers" were the "formidable sect which is behind his policies," "the cabal of Morgenthaus, Lehmans, Frankfurters and Cohens that surround the wheeled chair." The real villain, Spencer made clear, was Felix Frankfurter, the "alien-minded mentor from Vienna," who had brought with him to the United States "an anti-democratic, an anti-individualistic, a definitely European, mental and emotional set-up." Roosevelt, Spencer insisted, was helpless to prevent the execution of this Jewish conspiracy, this plan of "extermination of American business . . . regimented slavery of worker and farmer . . . suppression of all individual leadership . . . complete control by an alien bureaucracy . . . supported by taxes from the native inhabitants," in short, a plan "to wreck these United States so that the mysterious 'they,' who control the money-bund behind the Frankfurter policy, will find us more malleable for 'their' conquest under Roosevelt and 'their' eventual domination—Shiloh."

Spencer knew all this because he had discovered "the key to this designed-destruction . . . in that precis of Talmudic philosophy known as 'The Protocols.'" "That is what gives the Protocols practical political bearing. The plan of destruction here . . . is described in the Protocols."[36]

Attacking Roosevelt and the New Deal obliquely and by inference through anti-Semitism was also used almost as a last resort by one of the most exciting celebrities of the decade, the Reverend Charles E. Coughlin.

The Coughlin story was, in a way, an old and familiar one, a story of rags to riches and back to rags, from obscurity to obscurity in one sensational leap. But it was also new. A priest who was more famous at the microphone than at the Mass, who could woo more men to a convention hall than to a communion rail, and who spent more time in politics than in parish halls, was something new under the sun. That a man who clothed political ambitions in clerical garb had no place to go should have been predictable from the start. But who could have predicted that the way would lead from the mystery of the star of Bethlehem to the conspiracy of the Star of David?

A Canadian and a University of Toronto product, who was better at extemporaneous speaking than at football (but good at both), Coughlin was a humble parish priest when he made his first radio talk over Detroit station WJR in 1926, and was already a star performer on radio when the Great Depression came. His fame spread rapidly when he learned his listeners were more interested in their bellies than their souls, more interested in how to live now than how to die later. People listened, thousands of them, when international bankers, the gold standard, Republicans in general and Hoover in particular began feeling the lash in sermons laced with priestly politics and economics. Coughlin's church, the Shrine of the Little Flower in Royal Oak, Michigan, became a place for the curious to drive by on a Sunday afternoon.

Coughlin was an inspired supporter of Roosevelt and the New Deal. At first. He counseled with Brain Trusters, praised Roosevelt lavishly and extravagantly, could enter the White House without knocking, was on a "Dear Mac" basis with the President's secretary, Marvin McIntyre. Before the election Coughlin was warning the country it was either "Roosevelt or Ruin"; backed him by asserting that "the New Deal is God's deal"; and after six months in office was ready to offer Roosevelt "a niche in the American Hall of Fame equal to the places held by Washington and Lincoln."[37]

During the first year of the Roosevelt Administration, Coughlin was more than generous with advice. He strongly urged the revaluation of gold and remonetization of silver ("the innocents that are marked for slaughter," by "the Herods of high finance [who] already are plotting against the New Deal—plotting among the ruins of their own structure"). He diligently pushed on Administration leaders the implementation of what he would soon be calling his sixteen principles of social justice, which, he claimed, were based on the papal encyclical *Quadragesimo Anno*, a copy of which he sent to Marvin McIntyre urging him to "take time off—if necessary go and sit on the toilet while you read the enclosed book. . . . Then persuade Louis Howe and Stephen Early to do the same thing."[38]

Coughlin's bouquets for the New Deal wilted late in 1934, amid disappointed grumblings, then impatient outbursts, and, finally, uncontrolled invective. He kept the telegraph office busy delivering telegrams of protest against "a proposal of slaughter of approximately six million pigs," which was "as logical as pouring water in a sieve"; of "issuance of more bonds which were aimed at borrowing us out of debt"; against fiscal policies designed "to save the hides of bondholders"; against cowardly economic plans that could only mean "sailing behind the backwash of Wall Street and English propaganda."[39]

The New Deal, he told his radio audience, was making the same economic errors as had Hoover and Coolidge. The Old Deal and the New Deal were only "accidently" different, he charged; "one was the left wing and the other the right wing of the same bird of prey." And in letters to listeners soliciting funds for the radio broadcasts, Coughlin coined the term "Pagan Deal" to describe "laying waste God's bountiful gifts" by destroying wheat and pigs, and plowing under cotton. "Do you want me to preach 'Amen' both to the sins of omission and commission which have been perpetrated in the name of the New Deal?" he inquired; "Do you want me to oppose both reactionary politicians as well as the new type of rubber-stamp sycophants who prefer to follow the dictates of the 'Drain Trust' . . . ?"[40]

The year 1935 found the Coughlin movement short on finances but long on fight. With the radio fund $40,000 in arrears, an urgent plea went out to listeners early in February to contribute what they could, "even if it is a few pennies per month," a plea which evoked from Louis Howe a joyful memorandum to Marvin McIntyre: "Dear Mac, Show this to Franklin." If Howe thought the financial crisis meant the early collapse of the Coughlin movement he was mistaken. In the plea for funds, Coughlin talked optimistically of plans "to drive out of public office those who are supporting and abetting these money-changers." Keep listening, he urged. "How we shall accomplish this," he wrote, mysteriously, "will be told to you some Sunday of a sudden over the air."[41]

Coughlin did not keep that promise; but in the ensuing months, he gave Roosevelt and the Administration a one-man tongue-lashing probably unequalled in American political history. Week after week he raged about stacked decks, old deals and hidden cards; the New Deal, he thundered, "contained the same joker" and "the aces of high finance . . . the kings of big industry were . . . wild!" The first two infamous years of the New Deal would be remembered as years of ". . . compromise . . . social planning . . . endeavoring to mix bad and good . . . surrender . . . matching the puerile, puny brains of idealists against the virile viciousness of business and finance . . . economic failure . . . candy-coated pill of social reform . . . out-Hoovering Hoover . . . keeping American safe for the plutocrats . . . translat[ing] a New Deal into a raw deal."[42]

In March, 1935, Coughlin met his match. General Hugh Johnson ("Old Iron Pants" he was called, everywhere except to his face) was a career soldier who had acquired a tough hide and a vocabulary to match during his years in the cavalry. A hard-driving proven administrator with years of experience with Moline Plow Company, Johnson had been recommended to Roosevelt by the astute Bernard Baruch. To Johnson fell the task of making the NRA work. It did not work; and Johnson drove friend and foe alike to distraction trying to make it work, and got himself fired in the process. In May, 1935, the Supreme Court did the rest. Two months before the Supreme Court sided with the Schechter Brothers and their coopful of chickens, Coughlin and the deposed NRA head locked horns.

In a speech at the Waldorf-Astoria Hotel in New York, sponsored by *Redbook* magazine, Johnson defended Roosevelt ("We could have had a dictator . . . and we would have had one but for the President himself, to whom the whole idea was hateful.") by attacking "the great Louisiana demagogue" Huey Long, and "this political padre" Father Coughlin.

Johnson warmed up to his task by attacking those congressmen who had used Roosevelt to get elected, who "rode in on the horizontal coat-tails of a speeding chief," but had since become "economic kibitzers and political pansies . . . sniping at the President's plans. . . ."

But it was Long and Coughlin, those "two Pied Pipers," "a couple of Catalines," he was really after. Long was "a plausible Punchinello," "an able little devil" with "cast-iron cheek." Coughlin was worse, far worse— "melodious burring . . . [in] a Canadian accent . . . may or may not now be an American citizen . . . calling on the lines and sayings of all the saints and the very precepts of the Master . . . musical blatant bunk from the very rostrum of religion. . . ."

Long and Coughlin, said Johnson, had taken too seriously Marine Corps General Smedley Butler's recent story to the McCormack-Dickstein Committee of an alleged plot to march on Washington, led by some strongman, some "man on the White Horse." "That would be definite to Huey," said Johnson, sarcastically, "because he knows what part of the horse he can be; but we have a right to object most vigorously to the sanctification of such a centaur by having the head wear the collar of Rome and come intoning the stately measures of the Church in pious benediction of such an unholy monstrosity." It was all right with him, said Johnson, if Coughlin "wants to engage in political bundling with Huey Long, or any other demagogue"; but, he insisted, it was "only a fair first move to take off that Roman Catholic cassock."[43]

Expectancy began to mount, the kind of suppressed excitement usually reserved for the latest dance marathon or Amos 'n Andy escapade, when Coughlin announced he had bought time on the NBC network for a reply to Johnson a week later.

Monday, March 11, 1935, 10:15 P.M., Eastern Standard Time, Coughlin, coatless, face flushed, fists clenched, stepped to the microphone and waded in. Johnson, said the outraged priest, fury mounting in his voice, was the "sweet prince of bombast," "a Bourbon," "a comic opera cream puff with an underslung vocabulary," "a red herring, but a dead one," "the first great casualty of the New Deal," "a political corpse whose ghost has returned to haunt us," "the 'Man Friday' of the uncrowned prince of Wall Street [Baruch]," "a cracked gramophone record squawking the message of his master's voice." Coughlin knew what Johnson was up to and who was behind it. It was the opening salvo by the New Dealers in a campaign to silence him, Coughlin shouted.[44]

The name-calling was a standoff; the seminarian gave the commandant of barracks and mule-barn as good as he got. But Johnson had the last word in the free-for-all. Three weeks later, in Chicago, Johnson went for the jugular. "You have not chosen the swastika," he growled, "you have a more sacred device. . . . No swastika for your Nazi—but a cross." Because Coughlin was foreign-born he could never be President, but "you could be a Reichsfuhrer. . . . Are you a Jack-in-the-Pulpit who jumps up one moment in the collar of Rome, ducks and reappears the next moment in a necktie?"[45]

Johnson's attack on Coughlin, whether inspired from the White House or not, did not perceptibly slow down the crusading priest's castigation of the Administration. In April, in a speech launching the campaign to make his Social Justice Movement nation-wide, Coughlin told an overflow crowd of fifteen thousand at Olympia Stadium in Detroit that Roosevelt was "a dictator." But it was his gratuitous insult of Postmaster General James Farley, a fellow Catholic, whom he characterized as "the high commissioner of prostituted patronage" that got most of the attention in the newspapers. He also attacked the Administration for what he claimed were deliberately planted rumors, rumors that he was about to join forces with Huey Long and Milo Reno, leader of the National Farmers Holiday Association.[46]

In May, before a Madison Square Garden crowd of eighteen thousand (with four thousand more assembled in the basement), Coughlin inadvertently took the final plunge: ". . . if this is what we call a New Deal then this plutocratic, capitalistic system must be constitutionally voted out of existence." Coughlin had not expected to say this, probably had not meant to say it. "There was a few moments of silence for this to soak in because it was ad lib," *The New York Times* reporter wrote, "—then a roar broke loose with deafening intensity for a full minute."[47]

Through the summer and into fall, Coughlin kept up the pressure. If there was any who doubted that the priest had a following, one that would do his bidding on cue, they needed only to be in the telegraph office the day after Coughlin asked them to send wires to their senators and congressmen attacking the proposal to join the World Court. The deluge temporarily disrupted telegraph service in Washington.

Or ask President Roosevelt. In a letter to Elihu Root concerning the World Court issue, Roosevelt lamented, "The deluge of letters, telegrams . . . and the radio talks of people like Coughlin turned the trick against us." Coughlin's performance on that occasion led Paul Leach to write, in the Chicago *Daily News*, "Mr. Long with his Share the Wealth Clubbers and the doughty, outspoken Father Coughlin with his National Union for Social Justice are bigger men today politically as a result of the world court vote than they were yesterday morning."[48]

In November, if there was still any doubt in anyone's mind that the priest was through with Roosevelt, Coughlin made the alienation final. My views and those of President Roosevelt are "unalterably opposed," Coughlin told his radio audience. "Today I humbly stand before the American public to admit that I have been in error. . . ."[49]

Now it was 1936, with the chance to rectify that error.

V

The election year began on a note of low comedy and ended in disaster for Coughlin. The alienation between him and Roosevelt did not deter L. B. Ward, Coughlin's right-hand man in the Social Justice movement, from calling on Marvin McIntyre, demanding that the Administration stop interfering in the petition that was circulating in the House to force out of committee the new Frazier-Lemke Farm Mortgage bill, a bill to replace the earlier one declared invalid by the Supreme Court. Ward charged that threats from the White House were causing House members to withdraw their names from the petition. Ward allegedly told McIntyre that he had been able "to keep 'him' [Coughlin] in line last Sunday night but would not answer for him next Sunday."[50]

Ward's blackmail attempt failed, and in his broadcast of February 16, Coughlin condemned the Administration for its tactics in keeping the bill bottled up in the Rules Committee. He also had a few choice words for New York Congressman John J. O'Connor and his private bill, vetoed by Roosevelt, asking for $900,000 for the relief of the International Manufacturers Sales Company, calling O'Connor (chairman of the Rules Committee) "a servant of money-changers." O'Connor took violent exception to Coughlin's remarks, declaring him "a disgrace to my Church." In a telegram, O'Connor invited Coughlin to Washington: "If you will come to Washington I shall guarantee to kick you all the way from the Capitol to the White House, clerical garbs and all."[51]

Coughlin did not accept O'Connor's generous invitation, but not because of physical fear. He had more pressing matters to attend to. Until his break with Roosevelt, Coughlin had played it fairly safe. It had taken little imagination and less courage to attack Hoover, or Prohibition, or the NRA (after the early ballyhoo died down), or even the World Court. These were lost causes anyway. Attacking Roosevelt, an attack which left the country breathless, took reckless confidence—or reckless desperation.

On June 19, Coughlin dropped the other shoe. The National Union of Social Justice, he told his radio audience (estimated at thirty million), was endorsing North Dakota Congressman William "Liberty Bill" Lemke, presidential candidate of the new Union Party, a party which had Coughlin's Social Justice ideas built into its platform. From heckling Roosevelt from the stands, Coughlin had now moved into the field of play. He had, in effect, formed his own party. Less than a month later he announced triumphantly that Francis Townsend and Gerald L. K. Smith were throwing the support of their old-age pension seekers and the remnants of Huey Long's Share-Our-Wealth organization behind

Lemke and his running-mate, Thomas C. O'Brien, a Boston lawyer. This set the stage for a head-on collision with Roosevelt, a contest in which the Detroit priest boasted of being able to deliver nine million votes to Lemke. If he failed to do so, he said, he would retire from the public arena. Actually, what Coughlin seemed to be driving for was a contested election, one in which Lemke would carry enough states to force the choice into the House of Representatives. If Coughlin could ride so strong a race his first time out of the paddock, there was no telling what he might be able to accomplish by 1940.[52]

From July to November, Coughlin provided swashbuckling drama and excitement. But, like the drama and excitement of a ski-run or bobsled race, it was all downhill and quietly subsided at the finish. On July 16, before the ten thousand delegates at the Townsend Convention in Cleveland, Coughlin denounced the President as "that great betrayer and liar —Franklin Double-Crossing Roosevelt." It mattered little that Coughlin followed, a week later, with an open letter to Roosevelt, apologizing for the Cleveland incident; a priest who had not been bashful about telling the princes of his Church where to get off would not hesitate to call the President a liar—or worse—if the moon were right.[53]

And he didn't hesitate; later in the campaign he added to the list. Roosevelt was "anti-Christ" (Cincinnati, September 25) and a "scab President" (Cleveland, October 25). Roosevelt, he said in another speech, was a "dictator"; and his mind wandered to thoughts of gunpowder "when any upstart dictator in the United States succeeds in making a one-party government and when the ballot becomes useless. . . ." In September, on the occasion of the return from Rome of Coughlin's bishop (Bishop M. J. Gallagher of Detroit), Gallagher described Coughlin as "an outstanding churchman . . . it is the voice of God that comes to you from this great orator. Rally around it." The "voice of God" told newsmen "as between Landon and Roosevelt the electorate has only a choice between carbolic acid and rat poison."[54]

This would have been strong talk from anybody; from a priest it was incredible. But the man of the cloth was fast becoming the man of the whole cloth, a man obsessed with his own importance who thought politics meant calling the nation to repentance like an Old Testament prophet. Otherwise, he was a fool to call WPA workers "the greatest army of scab labor in the history of civilization." WPA workers were not sinners who had deserted Yahweh and intermarried with Philistines; they were voters.

Coughlin's sense of divine purpose made it virtually impossible for him to cooperate effectively with others. His coalition began disintegrating almost from the moment it was formed. Coughlin, Townsend, and Smith (a triumvirate which Chester Davis, former AAA administrator and member of the board of governors of the Federal Reserve

System, described as "a mad priest, an impractical dreamer and a political charlatan) were at each other's throats from the beginning.[55]

In July, Coughlin and Smith effectively elbowed Townsend out of the spotlight at his own convention. A month later (as the time approached for Coughlin's convention to assemble in Cleveland), the feuding broke into the open again when Walter D. Davis, Coughlin's major-domo of convention arrangements, announced that Townsend and Smith would "harangue" the convention "only over my dead body." Smith was furious, and the Townsend people threatened reprisals against Lemke if the ban stood. The next day, Coughlin intervened, extending a warm welcome to his allies, but warning there had better be no "oratorical contest" at Cleveland.[56]

There was, however. The eager young Senator Rush Holt of West Virginia, a Democrat who had broken with Roosevelt, was the keynote speaker. Coughlin and Townsend were in peak form; but it was Smith who stole the show. Smith arrived in Cleveland complaining of a Jewish Communist plot to assassinate him. Accompanying him was Eugene Daniel of Boston who had once dropped a stench bomb in the ventilating system of the New York Stock Exchange as an appropriate gesture of his displeasure with Roosevelt.[57]

Communism was Smith's theme before the convention. Roosevelt was a Communist in an Administration shot through with Communists, and the New Deal was a transparent Communist plot. His blue shirt soaked with perspiration, his handsome face contorted with rage, and his two hundred and ten pound frame shuddering with emotion, Smith rammed home his dreadful message—"my real mission is to see that the red flag of bloody Russia is not hoisted in place of the Stars and Stripes—Give that a hand!" And they did.[58]

The convention endorsed Lemke 8,152 to 1. One misguided soul, a John O'Donnell, pled devotion to Coughlin but insisted that Lemke was the tool of William Randolph Hearst and the American Liberty League, an act of treason which caused Charles J. Madden to apologize to the convention for having allowed his delegation to be infiltrated by "one of Jim Farley's stooges."[59]

VI

"Coughlin loused up his chances by shooting off his mouth too much" was the way one disenchanted Coughlinite explained the disaster in November. This was probably as good a way as any to explain how 9,000,000 votes in July became 891,858 in November. Three days after the election, Coughlin announced he was withdrawing from all radio activity "in the best interests of all the people."[60]

Throughout 1937 and early 1938, the country heard little from the Shrine of the Little Flower. By this time, however, the New Deal was running into serious trouble. The court fight, a wave of bloody strikes and sit-downs in the steel and automobile industry and a severe business recession, all took their toll of Roosevelt's popularity.

Coughlin believed the time was auspicious to make a comeback, a comeback with a new twist. Thus far, he had not openly attacked Jews, although anti-Semitism was always just under the surface; "not really and openly," Wallace Stegner wrote in *The Aspirin Age*, "but by implication and innuendo." He had attacked bankers. And he had attacked Communists. But not Jews, although most extremists would have wagered their colored shirts that most bankers and Communists were Jews. And the worst kind were the Jewish international bankers who were engineering the world Communist conspiracy.[61]

Coughlin's plunge into the nether land of Jewish-Communist world plots served only to discredit his cause still further, to drive him into an unfortunate liaison with the Christian Fronters, a palpably anti-Semitic organization (whose leader, John Cassidy, eventually landed in a New York jail for his part in a fantastic plot to seize the government), and into a noisy dispute with Elliott Roosevelt over Coughlin's radio statements. The contention that his remarks were anti-Semitic by "this stripling of the Nation's first family . . . who would never be on the air in the guise of a speaker were he not the son of a President," said Coughlin and his defenders, were merely another attempt by "this New Deal dynasty" to "purge all citizens who dare criticize the New Deal experimentations."[62]

Coughlin could insist all he pleased that he was not anti-Semitic, that his words were misunderstood, that his statements were misinterpreted. But there was one thing that could not be explained away. In July, 1938, Coughlin's publication, *Social Justice*, began printing the *Protocols of the Elders of Zion*.[63]

VII

Those who attacked the New Deal as a Jewish conspiracy were frequently (and almost automatically) anti-Negro as well. The reason was disarmingly simple. Traditionally, Jews in the United States had been friendly to the Negroes, probably because, as persecuted minority groups, they had something in common. But for the anti-Semite the reason was that Jews, dreaming their dreams of conquest, needed allies. They needed somebody who had cause for disenchantment with Gentile America, somebody who did not come lily-white in soap and water, somebody to do their dirty work. By connecting the two groups in this tenuous manner to the discredit of both, and by capitalizing on the built-in animosity toward the Negro in many quarters, particularly in the South, the extremist critic found new ammunition to fire at the New Deal, ammunition that sometimes took the form of doggerel. "Can you answer the $64 question?" the interrogator would ask. The "$64 question," it turned out, was:

> What Man said to "That" Woman,
> "You kiss the niggers,
> "I'll kiss the Jews,
> "We'll stay in the White House
> "As long as we choose?"[64]

It was not difficult to find evidence that the New Deal had done much (and much was being done in its name) for the Negro. For example, in 1936, the Democratic National Convention in Philadelphia was a milestone for Negroes in politics. This was the first national convention to institute a Negro press conference, the first to seat Negroes in the general press box, first to open a convention with the invocation by a Negro, first to seat a Negro woman as a regular delegate; with ten delegates and twenty-two alternates the convention had more Negro representation than any convention in history. And when, on the second night, Congressman Mitchell of Illinois stepped to the microphone in mammoth Convention Hall, it marked the first time in history that a Negro had addressed a national Democratic convention.[65]

When compared to efforts of previous administrations, New Deal attempts to improve the economic well-being of the Negro were impressive. They were not, however, as successful as the efforts to improve the Negro's political status had been. Although some attempt was made at the national level to eliminate racial discrimination in federal employment, local administration of many New Deal agencies meant that Negroes in the South were often the last hired and first fired in government as in private industry.

TVA, for example, adopting the mores of its environs, employed Negroes only for unskilled labor and refused to admit them to its training programs. Under NRA there were differentials between the wages of Negroes and whites even in the same job classifications. Under the crop-reduction policies of AAA, Negro sharecroppers, Negro tenant farmers, and Negro farm workers were the first to lose their land and jobs. Even in the subsistence homestead projects Negroes encountered bigotry. When more than two hundred Negroes applied for admission to the Reedsville (Arthurdale), West Virginia, project, they were told by the manager that the project was open only to "native white stock." But despite problems and failures, the New Deal made great gains in race relations. "In every phase of our national life," a prominent Negro citizen of Indiana,

Dr. W. J. Thompkins, told Senator Sherman Minton in 1938, "Roosevelt's policies have lifted the race higher."[66]

If the New Deal lifted the Negro higher in those years, it may be that in the process its greatest contribution was in hopes raised rather than deeds accomplished. Although the men appointed to newly created Negro advisory positions in the Departments of Interior and Commerce (Dr. Clark Foreman and his assistant Dr. Robert C. Weaver in Interior and E. K. Jones in Commerce) were largely unsuccessful in their efforts to see that Negroes received a fair shake in the AAA and NRA, the fact that these positions had been created gave the Negro the feeling that, at long last, someone cared. By imparting this feeling, the New Deal helped the Negro acquire a new sense of pride and dignity. The great majority of Negroes sensed intuitively that in the Roosevelts they had finally acquired a champion.[67]

They were encouraged that a member of Roosevelt's cabinet, Harold Ickes, had once been president of the Chicago chapter of the National Association for the Advancement of Colored People; they were stirred even more by the "democratic attitude and the uncompromising decency of Mrs. Roosevelt than by the acts of the New Deal Administration," wrote Louis Martin, the Detroit Negro publisher, "because she dared to express some positive beliefs on racial equality." President Roosevelt, despite his failings, meant well, was trying to overcome the odds, his heart was in the right place, was the general feeling among Negroes. "I am at a loss to find a single reason why the Negroes of America should look with disapproval upon the administration of Franklin Delano Roosevelt," said Congressman Mitchell (a former Republican who, like so many of his fellow Negroes, had become a Democrat under the Roosevelt spell); he is "the greatest humanitarian this Nation or any other nation has seen." "He is," said the Illinois representative, "second only to Christ."[68]

Not every Negro agreed with Mitchell that Roosevelt was second only to Christ. Perhaps to Judas Iscariot but not to Christ. There were those who found it hard to break the habit of viewing all Democrats with suspicion and apprehension. And with some justification. As late as 1938, after numerous false starts and much parliamentary footdragging on anti-lynching legislation, the voice of the South, the unrelenting, uncompromising Deep South, was still reverberating in the Negro's ears. The voice was that of one like Senator Theodore "The Man" Bilbo (a Mississippian who, more often than not, saw things Roosevelt's way except on the race issue). ". . . the South," the voice was saying, "may submit sometime to the eradication . . . of the color line . . . may accept, if legally imposed, the principle and practice of miscegenation . . . may subscribe to the social and political equality of the two races . . . in some nebulous age yet to dawn, in the dim vistas of succeeding eons, more distant than the prophetic eye can now envision. . . ." The mocking voice continued:

It is not altogether improbable that she will eventually permit, under the requirements of a Federal statute, the Negro to eat at her lunch counters, her cafeterias, and dining rooms and drink from her fountains; to commingle with the Caucasian; to sit in her church pews by the side of white mothers holding white babes in her arms while listening to a black pulpiteer explain the plan of salvation; to sleep, perchance to dream, in berths of Pullman palace cars adjoining those occupied by the fair daughters of her sunny clime.

And when might these things come to pass? "Mr. President," roared the voice, "this will come to pass only at such an astronomically remote time as when the Prince of Darkness shall have folded his wings on the gravestone of God."[69]

Republicans could not forego such an opportunity to make a point. If the New Deal was such a friend of the Negro, why was it impossible to get a sound anti-lynching bill passed? The reason was not hard to find; it was among the first things a freshman learned in his college government course. Because of the seniority system when the Democratic Party was in power most of the important committees of the Congress were controlled by southerners. This meant that if a Democratic President did not want his legislative program gutted, he must play the Levite who passed on the other side where racial matters were concerned.

That was the message the Republican National Committee had for Negroes in the campaign of 1936. And lest any Negro be misled by New Deal relief programs, the Republicans had an explanation for that. Relief for Negroes was permanent; it was all they would ever get. The New Deal Brain Trusters, with their planned economy schemes, were convinced that several million workers would have to be permanently retired from gainful employment. The Negro worker, said Republicans, "was the one who could be eliminated with the least trouble. . . ." Relief for the Negro, they warned, was the New Deal's version of the Indian reservation.[70]

"THE DEMOCRATIC PARTY OF THE UNITED STATES IS THE IMPLACABLE FOE OF THE NEGRO RACE" was a Republican rallying cry in the 1936 contest. A considerable number of influential Negro leaders concurred. They did not always blame Roosevelt. That things were as they were, that the Negro was a helpless victim of segregation, discrimination, injustice, was not necessarily his fault; the New Deal had not invented these things. But some (perhaps many) did blame him for knuckling under to southern party wheelhorses; they blamed him for timidity, for refusing to risk everything for principle.[71]

A powerful voice of Negro opinion in Pennsylvania, the Pittsburgh

Courier, explained its disappointment. "Thousands of Negroes, who distrust the Democratic party but who have confidence in President Roosevelt," said the *Courier*, "are finding that even the great office of the President has not been able to cope with the malignant influence of the South when the Democratic Party is in power." The *Courier's* able columnist, George S. Schuyler, was less sympathetic. Analyzing Roosevelt's shortcomings on the racial problem, Schuyler wrote that Roosevelt was "a man who could speak systematically about the tortured Jews of Europe, but was too callous or too cowardly to speak likewise about the tortured Negroes of America." In his column "Down the Big Road," W. O. Walker, editor of Cleveland's influential Negro paper, the *Call and Post*, was even more pointed in his criticism: "The South is running the government, it dominates the White House, it controls the Army and Navy, all because President Roosevelt is too weak and probably feeble to do anything to stop them. He has failed to defend his wife or his close friends and party associates from the calumny of southern race hatred." The Philadelphia *Tribune* considered it the last straw when Roosevelt (during the campaign of 1936) asserted that his Administration would become more liberal with the Negro "as it [the New Deal] grows in age." The *Tribune* understood this to mean that while the Administration "was not giving you a square deal now, the NEW DEAL will give you colored people justice after the time becomes ripe." The editorialist's indignation mounted: "Some more Bishops and big shots are telling the colored voters how wonderful the President is. Frankly, he has done a few things, but he has dodged the major issues. . . . And then, to add insult to injury, the President advises colored Americans to wait a little while longer. . . ."[72]

VIII

It would seem worth repeating that by 1936 Roosevelt had succeeded in winning over to the Democratic coalition the great Negro masses; this much seems incontrovertible. But not all Negroes were ardent New Dealers; there was considerable disillusionment and distrust of the Democratic Party—and of Roosevelt—enough to make it obvious to any rational person that Roosevelt was having to compete like everyone else in the open marketplace for Negro support—and not always getting it.

That is why the position of some of the extremists regarding the Negro seemed so absurd. To hear them tell it, the Negroes (after the Jews), were the darlings of the Administration. They delighted in circulating scurrilous pamphlets and cartoons ridiculing those "nigger lovers" in the White House. A popular item was a reprint of a 1936 editorial that was credited to the Rosslyn (Virginia) *Chronicle*. According to the editorialist, Crandal Mackey, prominent local Democrat, it was now "a matter of common knowledge" that Negro men and their wives "attend receptions at the White House . . . mingle with the white guests . . . eat at buffet luncheons with the white men and their wives. . . ." But what was really shocking to the *Chronicle* writer was a recent picture of Mrs. Roosevelt sitting beside a Negro woman at a Negro welfare meeting, "so near together that their bodies touched."[73]

A nasty racial incident occurred in January, 1936, at the Grass Roots Convention in Macon, Georgia. There appeared on the seats of the auditorium copies of the *Georgia Woman's World*. Opposite the first page was the celebrated "nigger picture." Following it was a picture of Negro Congressman Arthur Mitchell of Illinois with the caption: "The Pet and Protégé of James A. Farley." On the first page was an ugly editorial comparing Franklin Roosevelt and Andrew Jackson: "Andrew Jackson didn't have a Negro confidential clerk in the White House . . . didn't try to ram an antilynching bill down the throats of the Southern people . . . didn't put in Republicans, Socialists, Communists and Negroes to tell him how to run these good old United States."[74]

Among the sponsors of the Macon meeting was the indefatigable Gerald L. K. Smith, whose views on Negroes and the New Deal were equally uncharitable. On more than one occasion, Smith had characterized the Negroes as a "child race." According to him, the justification for treating Negroes as inferior was that ageless southern fear, the terror of intermarriage and mongrelization. The white race, said Smith, would fade out into "a sort of Miami tan." "This campaign of mongrelization" Smith blamed on a strange coalition including "modernist churchmen, academic sentimentalists, Communists, and New Dealers, all operating under the leadership of Eleanor Roosevelt. . . . God save us!"[75]

When Senator Hugo Black, chairman of the Senate lobbying investigating committee, gave the Grass Roots Convention a public airing in April, 1936, it was found that the distribution of the anti-Negro material at Macon and its subsequent distribution around the country had been instigated by the Texas lumber and oil man, "fat, freckled, old" John Henry Kirby, through his various patriotic organizations, the Southern Committee to Uphold the Constitution, Texas Taxpayers' League, Texas Election Managers' Association, and the Order of American Patriots, all with headquarters in Houston, Texas. The Macon incident appeared to be part of an organized campaign, a campaign, according to *Time* magazine, that had blanketed the South with "cheap pamphlets . . . blurred photographs of the Roosevelts consorting with Negroes, blatant texts proclaiming them ardent Negrophiles."[76]

Any of the political enemies of Roosevelt, providing they were unscrupulous enough, could exploit the race issue (and some of them did) knowing that this kind of political dynamite might be powerful enough to blow holes in the Democratic Solid South. But the anti-Negro phase of the attack on the New Deal had special meaning to the extremist fringes that haunted the land in the 1930's. In their hallucinations, the Negroes were the allies of the Jews in the grand conspiracy, the strong backs and calloused hands who would do the Jews' bloody deeds. That is what Pelley meant when he insisted that the Jews were behind the Negro CIO organizers, inciting them to overthrow "white supremacy" in the labor movement. That is what James True was talking about in his ridiculous yarns about Jews hiring "big, buck niggers" in the South to rape white women. This is what Edmondson and Spencer meant when the Edmondson Economic Service distributed reprints of Spencer's editorial accusing Roosevelt of inviting "diseased Negro prostitutes to the White House (presumably as an ingratiating gesture to the Negroes— and to infect Gentile public officials). . . . He [Roosevelt] hopes to use the blacks as executioners just as Stalin used his Chinese."[77]

The analogy was particularly appropriate. Like Stalin, Roosevelt was a Jew, a Communist Jew; after all, they had proof, irrefutable proof, did they not?

CHAPTER IV

... And the Red Deal

God Bless America
The Jews own it
The Catholics run it
The Negroes enjoy it
The Protestants founded it
But
The Communists will destroy it.
—Edward James Smythe

Why not pull down the statue of Thomas Jefferson and put Karl Marx in his place? If the New Deal has to have a patron saint, certainly Marx comes closer to filling the bill than the author of the Declaration of Independence.
—George Abbott Winthrop

The Russian newspapers during the last election [1932] published the photograph of Franklin D. Roosevelt over the caption, "The first communistic President of the United States." Evidently the Russian newspapers had knowledge concerning the ultimate intent of the President, which had been carefully withheld from the voters in this country. In fact, the voters of the United States were meticulously misled as to such intentions.
—Senator Thomas D. Schall

O N a Saturday in September, 1934, about one hundred men gathered in a wooded area near Port Chester, New York, a remote spot approachable only by cowpaths or a mile of treacherous wagon-road. It was raining, a soft, gentle rain that made musical sounds among the leaves, a rain that dampened clothing but not enthusiasm.

They were there, the one hundred men, to reactivate the Ku Klux Klan of Westchester County, to breathe life into an organization moribund for more than three years. The meeting was brief. The leader, who refused to reveal his identity, had praise for Hitler, slander for Jews, criticism for the New Deal, and the label of "Communist" for President Roosevelt.

The sparse crowd dispersed, his words still ringing in their ears; they went prepared "to alert the American people."[1]

II

The 1930's produced an alarming number of such people, some of them very strange people, who were in the business of arousing Americans to a new peril, a threat, it had always been thought, that could loom only in Europe or some faraway place. The new danger was a Chief Executive with treason in his soul, a President who had won the hearts of a weary, beleaguered people with his dissembling smile, his charm, and with his promises, for the purpose of delivering them to the enemy. Roosevelt, they would insist, was a Communist and the New Deal a Marxist trick; when the time was ripe the crippled Judas would betray America with a kiss.

The claims from various quarters that Roosevelt and the New Deal were communistic were not of equal value, nor did they always mean the same thing. Who made the charge was important. When a responsible critic, say someone of the caliber of Alfred E. Smith, or John W. Davis (distinguished attorney and Democratic standard-bearer in 1924), or former President Herbert Hoover declared that the New Deal was communistic, he did not mean that Roosevelt carried a party card in his billfold and attended clandestine cell meetings. Or that he had a code name, used blind mail-drops and stole secret documents from the Department of State files. The critic was speaking seriously about certain trends in the New Deal. He was expressing concern over specific legislative proposals. He was alarmed by the influence exerted on Roosevelt by certain New Deal officials whose radical views were common knowledge.

But when the Westchester County klansman and his brothers, the irresponsible critic, the unstable fanatic, the right-wing extremist flirting with fascism, screamed "Communist!" they meant all of these things, and more. In its most mindless form the Communist charge was linked with the Jewish conspiracy and the New Deal became a Jewish-Communist plot, with Roosevelt the central figure.

III

Roosevelt had been in office scarcely a year when the self-anointed began to see Red. In September, 1934, James True launched America First, Incorporated, to give "X-ray Exposure" to the "subversive activities originating within the New Deal." As far back as May, True had been writing about communistic activities in the New Deal, complaining about the New Deal's Communist-controlled press, and warning of a "Red Revolution" that was to follow a paralyzing general strike late in the summer of 1934. Race riots were likewise imminent, said True. Because of the New Deal's "socialistic and communistic agitation" Negroes were "growing restless, belligerent," demanding social equality.[2]

Across country, in Wichita, Gerald Winrod was warning his faithful about the "long, dark, red, sinister shadows" that were falling over Washington, and how Roosevelt's "colossal betrayal, actuated by Satanic genius" was turning the United States "first 'pink,' then 'red.' . . ."[3]

Meanwhile, in Chicago, Elizabeth Dilling, who saw Communists under every bed even during the Hoover Administration, had out *The Red Network: A "Who's Who" and Handbook of Radicalism for Patriots* before the end of the year. Mrs. Dilling had Roosevelt's number early. The question she posed for the reader was simplicity itself: Was Roosevelt "stupid, blind, badly informed and played-upon by radicals, or well informed and deliberately playing the Red game. . . . ?" It took three hundred and fifty-two pages to prove, to her satisfaction, the latter.[4]

The great issue in the off-year election, she said, would be "Marx versus Washington" (George Washington, that is). In the deadly competition between "Socialism versus Americanism," 1934 might be the last opportunity for Americans "to vote 'Karl Marx' out of office." But she doubted that the elections would ever come off; like True, she anticipated before autumn "a united front General Strike culminating in Red seizure of power."[5]

From Westchester County and Washington in the East, to Wichita and Chicago in the Middle West, and into the South, the signal fires began to burn. To Chattanooga, Tennessee, whose people could gaze upward toward Lookout Mountain and dream their dreams of what might have been. They had been unable to save themselves or the South in the great conflict between the states. Perhaps they could redeem themselves, recapture their dignity and self-esteem by saving the country now in its hour of peril.

George W. Christians thought so. Christians believed the alternatives confronting the United States in 1934 were capitalism under economic liberty (he was founder of the Crusaders for Economic Liberty, whose members were called White Shirts) or communism under tyranny. The New Deal, of course, was the latter. Christians had at least toyed with a plan to end that tyranny with dispatch. He had once threatened to cut off the electricity during a visit to Chattanooga by President Roosevelt because, he said, "lots of things can happen in the dark."[6]

In one of his earlier publications, "Freedom of the Press," Christians pressed the urgency of educating the public, of exposing the people to the merits of his economic liberty program (an uncertain and confused brand of National Socialism that emphasized repudiation of the national debt). But the gospel of the White Shirts was being kept from the American people because of a corrupt press, "this damnable perversion of a Public Trust." Christians could not save America from the New Dealers until he could get his message through to the people; and without a free press, this was not possible. There would be no free press, he told his White Shirts, "until certain Publishers and Editors are taken out and HUNG."[7]

He disagreed with True and Dilling in that he believed the attempt by the Communists for an all-out grab for power would not come until after the November elections. Soon thereafter, Christians warned, "things will begin to get rough." There were going to be riots and strikes and marches on Washington. But the White Shirts were not going to take part in any of this; their strategy was to let the Communists and Fascists fight it out in the East. Meanwhile, the White Shirts would take the South and West "which are already practically under our control." Then, in the eastern United States, where the Communists and Fascists had fought to a bloody stalemate, the White Shirts would "close in on them and take control of what is left." They would set up a new capital located in the Middle West and build a new civilization "based upon the Constitution as it is written with Economic Liberty . . . for which Humanity has fought and bled throughout the ages."[8]

In Asheville, North Carolina, William Dudley Pelley, his suspicions aroused by the diplomatic recognition of the Soviet Union ("birds of a feather flock together" was his appraisal), began spreading the word. In what may have been his first publication on the subject, "Communism in Control," Pelley (after paying his customary compliments to the Jews) concluded that the New Deal was "a product of the father and motherhood of Soviet Russia . . . not in harmony with moral standards of Christian intelligence." "There can be no doubt," he wrote, "as to whom [sic] it is that holds the reins in Washington."[9]

It must have been reassuring to Pelley that there were those in Washington who cared what was happening. James True cared. And so did the American Coalition of Patriotic, Civic, and Fraternal Societies, which claimed the right to speak for about one hundred (ninety-four in 1934) patriotic organizations. As late as 1939, the coalition numbered one hundred and twenty-five. Most of these affiliated with the coalition seemed quite honorable and respectable; and it is probably to their discredit that there were so few defections when the extremist position of the coalition leadership became evident.[10]

The coalition's campaign to save the land from New Deal communism began mildly enough with a resolution from its executive committee. President of the coalition, John B. Trevor, heir to a railroad fortune and a seasoned campaigner against the dangers of immigration, an enterprise with strong anti-Semitic overtones, delivered the resolution in person to Senator William Warren Barbour of New Jersey. The resolution, protesting the nomination of Rexford Tugwell for Under Secretary of Agriculture, said that Senate confirmation of Tugwell would amount to "an authorization by . . . and . . . ratification of" Tugwell's efforts aimed at the "destruction of our most cherished institutions."[11]

Before the year was out, Woodrow Wilson's one-time law partner and Secretary of State, Bainbridge Colby, a vice-president of the coalition, told a rally in Portland, Maine, that "submission, not freedom, is to be the future badge of the United States . . . the overturn of our institutions, including the Constitution, is the avowed goal of his [Roosevelt's] immediate advisers." The Portland speech, in September, 1934, was the most vigorous attack yet made upon Roosevelt by one so closely identified with the Democratic Party.[12]

One insight into the character of the coalition came late in December, 1934, when Walter S. Steele, representing the coalition, appeared before the McCormack-Dickstein Committee, the forerunner of the House Un-American Activities Committee. Steele had a pat story to tell, one that kept recurring in the 1930's, a story of general strikes, civil war, and the seizure of power by the Reds. Steele's original contribution to this story seemed to be that in the impending Communist coup Roosevelt would be kidnapped and held while the revolution was executed.[13]

The presence in the ranks of leadership of Steele, publisher of his own independent magazine, National Republic, with its anti-Roosevelt, anti-Jewish editorial line, was a solid clue that all was not what it appeared to be in the American Coalition. Along with Trevor and Steele, one of the original organizers of the coalition was George Sylvester Viereck, whom the McCormack-Dickstein Committee indicated was a propagandist for Nazi Germany and probably in the pay of Germany. Viereck's Nazi sympathies were unashamed. In May, 1934, he had addressed a rally of the German-American Bund at Madison Square Garden in New York where the twenty thousand people were escorted to their seats by a corps of eight hundred ushers wearing storm-trooper uniforms, complete with swastika armbands and jack-boots.[14]

In the long list of organizations belonging to the Coalition were several that made the entire list suspect. One of these was the American Vigilant Intelligence Federation, headed by Harry A. Jung, a man whose unusual background included infiltrating labor unions, professional strike-breaking, and (according to the McCormack-Dickstein Committee) publishing and circulating "great masses of literature tending to incite racial and religious intolerance." Jung was another among those who distributed the fake Protocols and such inflammatory material as "Halt, Gentiles, and Salute the Jews!" and "The Man Behind the Men Behind the President," a slanderous attack upon Felix Frankfurter which he co-authored with Colonel Sanctuary. Jung's magazine kept up a running attack upon Roosevelt, the New Deal, and the Jews. Still another was the organization headed by Colonel Edwin Marshall Hadley, the Paul Reveres, also an anti-Roosevelt, anti-Semitic outfit that had been started originally by Elizabeth Dilling, and had on its advisory board the notorious Jew-baiter, Colonel Sanctuary.[15]

As late as 1938, Steele, representing the coalition, this time before the Dies Committee (his testimony ran to more than 450 pages), was still alerting the American people by citing some six hundred and forty organizations in the United States that were either communistic or "dangerously internationalist," including the Boy Scouts and Camp Fire Girls.[16]

IV

In those days of dramatizing the Red menace, the most celebrated and, at the same time, the most disastrous case was l'affaire Wirt.

William Wirt, superintendent of schools in Gary, Indiana, blundered onto the national scene as if by accident. The setting was a routine hearing on the Stock Market Control bill by the House Interstate Commerce Committee. The last week in March, 1934, the committee called James H. Rand, Jr., of the Remington Rand Corporation, who appeared as head of the Committee for the Nation (an organization agitating for inflation and revision of the gold standard), to hear his criticism of the pending legislation. Rand suddenly enlivened the proceedings, and before the day was out the whole world had heard about a revolutionary plot being hatched by the Brain Trust.

All Rand had done was read passages from a manuscript prepared by Wirt (one of the founders of the Committee for the Nation), which related how, under the most casual circumstances imaginable, Wirt had stumbled upon a plot to overthrow the government of the United States.[17]

It had all started when, some seven months before (September 1, 1933), Wirt had accepted a dinner invitation from Miss Alice Barrows, an employee of the Bureau of Education in the Department of the Interior, and an old friend of Wirt's who had been his private secretary for several years. Among the dinner guests at Miss Barrows' home in nearby Virginia were several interesting small fry of the Administration, people like David Cushman Coyle of the Public Works Administration, Robert Bruere who worked with the NRA, Hildegarde Kneeland from the Department of Agriculture's Bureau of Agricultural Economics, Mary Taylor, editor of the AAA Consumer's Guide, and Laurence Todd, employed by the Tass Agency in Washington.[18]

Amid these unlikely surroundings Wirt was initiated into the fellowship of subversion. According to Wirt, the plan being engineered by the Brain Trusters ("regimenting radicals," Wirt called them) was essentially quite simple. It was by design to prevent recovery, deliberately to perpetuate destitution ("the psychology of empty stomachs" was the way they allegedly described it to Wirt) until, in despair, the American people would accept anything, until they would willingly accept the Brain Trusters' revolution, a revolution that would remake America as a socialist state. "We believe that we have Mr. Roosevelt in the middle of a swift stream and that the current is so strong that he cannot turn back or escape from it," they were supposed to have told him. "We believe that we can keep Mr. Roosevelt there until we are ready to supplant him with a Stalin," Wirt quoted them as saying. "We all think that Mr. Roosevelt is only the Kerensky of this revolution. Eventually he can be easily displaced. . . ."[19]

There was more, much more, of course. Filled with revolutionary fervor, Dr. Wirt's uncommonly candid new acquaintances bent his ear for the better part of an evening with plans of how business would be intimidated, farmers and labor whipped into regimented line, colleges and schools taken over, all the customary trappings of a new order. But the essence of the plot was prolonging the Depression, blaming it on "the traitorous opposition" until a distraught people were willing to accept any solution.

Wirt's story brought forth the usual cleavages. There were those who tried to horn in on the publicity; the scoffers who scoffed; the believers who nodded self-righteously; and the level-headed who merely asked to hear more.

Walter Winchell, syndicated Broadway columnist, sent Postmaster General Farley a telegram naming Paul Douglas, the University of Chicago economist and "a radical," as the guiding genius behind Wirt's hearsay revolution. George Christians of Chattanooga made certain that everyone remembered it was he who had first referred to Roosevelt as "the Kerensky of the Revolution" during an interview with the President-elect at Warm Springs in December, 1932. Silas Strawn, the nationally known Chicago attorney and one-time president of the United States Chamber of Commerce, saw reason to rejoice at the exposure of high-level treachery. Wirt, Strawn told the press, was "the type of man needed to save this country from the intellectual jackasses in Washington."[20]

Republican Congressman Harold McGugin of Kansas was surprised at all the eyebrows which the story raised. Something of the sort had been evident for some time from the way the Department of Agriculture was "communizing and nationalizing" the farmers, McGugin said. Those in control at the Agriculture Department, he reasoned, were "betraying the President and are merely using him in the manner in which Dr. Wirt quotes. . . ." According to McGugin's calculated guess it was Rex Tugwell who was behind the betrayal.[21]

But if McGugin and others were inclined to believe Wirt's story there were others who did not. Mrs. Roosevelt was one who discounted it and at a press conference expressed her view by reading to the reporters a parody of James Whitcomb Riley's "Little Orphant Annie." The parody had the Brain Trust sitting around the fire after dinner at the White House having the "mostest fun" until a goblin (in the form of a huge Russian black bear) materialized and carried off the President.[22]

Others also ridiculed it. Republican Senator Arthur Robinson of Indiana took time in the Senate to read telegrams from various organizations in Gary testifying to the good character and integrity of Wirt and urging an investigation of his charges. When Robinson finished, Senator Bennett Champ Clark of Missouri solemnly asked permission to read a letter from Washington correspondent, Paul Y. Anderson, who agreed that a plot did exist. It took some moments before everyone realized Anderson was putting them on. The plot, he said, was to kidnap Roosevelt and hold him prisoner for a week while Senator Robinson and his neighbor, Senator Fess of Ohio, ran the country "when a revolution would undoubtedly occur."[23]

Dr. Wirt seemed at once dismayed and delighted by all the fuss he had caused, and, in an interview with New York Times correspondent Louther S. Horne the day after Rand's sensational testimony, entered completely into the spirit of the occasion. "If it requires that I be a sacrifice to get the people to thinking about what is going on," the short, stocky, austere schoolman told Horne, "I am willing to be one." But the mood of the martyr passed quickly and Wirt was back to the attack: "There are lists of Congressmen who oppose the Brain Trust program—a blacklist made so that when the time for punishment comes those in power will know whom to punish."[24]

Those who wanted to hear more had their chance. When House Resolution 317 passed with only token opposition, the Select Committee to Investigate Charges Made by Dr. William A. Wirt turned to its task. And what writer of fiction would dared have given to the chairman of a congressional committee a name like Alfred L. Bulwinkle?[25]

Wirt's testimony was considerably less dramatic than his manuscript. In the packed House Caucus room, flanked by the combative ex-Senator James A. Reed of Missouri, Wirt proceeded to absolve Coyle, Bruere, and Miss Barrows of any participation in subversive talk. Nervously fingering his Phi Beta Kappa key, the slow-talking Wirt admitted that much of what he reported was not conversation at all but rather his own deductions from the writings of Rex Tugwell and other New Dealers. One by one, the dinner guests testified that the dinner "was not a success"; Wirt had done most of the talking. Four hours of it. Wirt conceded that perhaps he had done most of the talking, but, he reported ominously, the other guests had "nodded in agreement."[26]

It took less than one day to air Wirt's suspicions. It took less time than that for most people to decide his suspicions were groundless. Arthur Krock, the respected editorialist of The New York Times, called Wirt's performance "the lowest form of public burlesque." The great "plot," said another *Times* editorialist, "is certain to expire in the midst of inextinguishable laughter." When the committee's interrogation of the dinner guests later in the week failed to turn up anything new, the solemn *New York Times* put its tongue in its editorial cheek and wrote:

There is really no question that Dr. Wirt has made out his case. The proof is not in what he said at Washington but in the circumstances under which he said it. We may go further than Dr. Wirt. It is not a question of America being enticed into a revolution. America has already been revolutionized and rendered unrecognizable when a witness at a public hearing is allowed to complete his testimony in one day instead of spending a couple of weeks on the job.

Other damning details are present. The witness appears with only one lawyer instead of a dozen leading members of the American Bar Association. He has to get along without the services of a flock of psychiatrists and a delegation of handwriting experts. He is not permitted to read into the record the minutes of the Council of Four at Versailles. He is not allowed to read from an interesting mystery novel he picked up in the train on the way to Washington. He is deprived of other inalienable rights, privileges, extensions, divagations, excursuses, footnotes, appendixes, elaborations, comments and culs-de-sac which the Constitution guarantees.[27]

That was the way most of the press and magazines handled what the Washington *Post* called the most celebrated dinner since Belshazzer. While reporting the news accurately, *The Editor and Publisher* wrote later, all but a few papers "slanted the story up the spoof alley." In a few cases, notably the Chicago *Tribune*, the Los Angeles *Times,* and the New York *Herald Tribune* (none of which believed the specific charges), the Wirt case was used as an opportunity to criticize radicals and radical trends in the New Deal program.[28]

If the press did not believe the Wirt story, neither did the reading public which seemed willing to settle for the clever verse with which Donald Richberg, the successor of Hugh Johnson as NRA director, dismissed the affair:

> A cuttlefish squirt
> Nobody hurt,
> From beginning to end:
> Dr. Wirt.[29]

V

As the New Deal lengthened into its third year the charges of communism from the violent right-wing became louder, shriller, increasingly extravagant, always more urgent. The familiar native fuhrers, the wearers of shirts, the pamphleteers, those who had, by this time, become an accepted part of the strange political montage of the decade, never let up, never relented. In 1935, they were joined by new voices swelling the chorus, chanting the refrains of New Deal treachery and Red subversion.

Early in February, 1935, Senator Augustine Lonergan of Connecticut made public a letter from The Defenders of the Constitution of the U.S.A. urging his support in the defeat of the pending $4,800,000,000 relief proposal, because, it was charged, relief funds were being used to support the FERA school in New York City where "Communism and Revolution are openly taught to Americans." A short time later, Senator Schall was happy to oblige the Seventy-Six League by inserting in the *Congressional Record* excerpts from its publication, *The Minute Man*, which insisted that Roosevelt's proposal for establishment of a permanent National Resources Board sounded like the first step toward a Russian-style five-year plan. The New Deal, the article continued, was "a menace to democracy"; men "high in the councils of American Government" had already "planted the seed of communism. . . ."[30]

About the same time, Schall startled his Senate colleagues with another interesting charge. According to Schall, the Russian press, prior to the election of 1932, had carried pictures of Franklin Roosevelt, describing him in the captions as "the first communistic President of the United States."

Schall had gotten this from another of True's *Industrial Control Reports* (No. 102, June 15, 1935) which he very promptly entered in the *Congressional Record*. This report was largely devoted to comments about the recent Grass Roots Convention of Republicans in Springfield, Illinois, a meeting attended by 8,666 delegates from ten states. The speeches and resolutions at that convention critical of the New Deal, said True, were a vindication of what he and people like him had for months been telling the public through "millions of letters, books, pamphlets, small periodicals, booklets" despite the fact that thousands of these pieces "have been stolen from the mails by 'new dealers' in the Postal Service." Singling out Elizabeth Dilling, Gerald Winrod, Harry Jung, Colonel Edwin Hadley, Robert Edmondson, Colonel Sanctuary, and John B. Trevor for special commendation, True claimed that they ("and many others") had, "at great personal sacrifice," been responsible for exposing "the communistic fallacies of the administration and the sinister international influence [i.e., the Jews] behind Roosevelt."[31]

Senator Frederick Hale of Maine thought it important to bring to the attention of the House a pamphlet issued by the League for Constitutional Government of New York City (consisting of four parallel columns, one headed Communist International, another Communist Party of America, then Socialist Party and, finally, New Deal), the purpose of which was to demonstrate that the New Deal was merely an adaptation. For the Democratic platform of 1932 the program of the Communist International

Love at First Sight. *Reprinted with permission of Hearst Newspapers. Cartoon by Swinnerton.*

in substance (as interpreted by the Communist Party in America and the Socialist Party) had been substituted. "Is this," the League wanted to know, "a part of a world conspiracy?" In another of its publications the League undertook to analyze the history of the New Deal, an heroic effort which began with the Devil Worshipers of Arabia, the Satanists and Luciferians, and ended with the Stalinists of Russia. The conclusion was not hard to predict: "The program of the 'New Deal' is the program of socialism and communism. Let there be no mistake about that."[32]

The Industrial Defense Association, a source of embarrassment to Bostonians, distributed a pamphlet in the summer of 1935 that came right to the point in the first sentence. "President Roosevelt is a Socialist Pure and Simple," it began. And then, with a knowing wink at the reader, added, "but perhaps not so pure and not so simple as appears on the surface," a bit of heavy-handed wit which Roosevelt did not think was very funny. "Try to find out who is paying for this. F.D.R" read the memorandum attached to the pamphlet that was sent on to Attorney-General Homer Cummings. In June, Congressman William Henry Wilson of Pennsylvania felt compelled to enter in the *Congressional Record* a roster of ranking New Deal officials with a summary of their alleged socialistic and communistic connections. When pressed, Wilson conceded that his information came from Dilling's *The Red Network*, which Wilson described as being "incontrovertible facts."[33]

And John Henry Kirby, speaking for his Southern Committee to Uphold the Constitution, told a group of newsmen in New York that his organization had enrolled some fifty thousand southern Democrats who would vote against "that apostate," Roosevelt, and his socialistic New Deal policies which he had assembled "from the garbage cans of Europe."[34]

Among the southerners who Kirby predicted would vote against Roosevelt was one of singular prominence, the governor of Georgia, Eugene Talmadge. Talmadge, with his red galluses, owlish eyes behind horn-rimmed glasses, a black cigar protruding from some remote corner of his jaw, and a shock of black hair hanging over his forehead, seemed like a character out of *Tobacco Road*. "Our Gene" had a mind like a steel trap to go with his law degree from the University of Georgia. But he played the role of the country yokel. With his thumbs hung in his galluses, he recited the catechism of poor-white, redneck prejudices all over the state, a performance which put him in the governor's mansion in Ansley Park the same year that Roosevelt moved into the White House. In that first election, Talmadge liked to boast, he had not carried a single county in Georgia in which there was a streetcar track.[35]

Talmadge developed an early intense dislike toward the New Deal. He despised the NRA, WPA, AAA, and TVA; and he did not like New Dealers any better than he liked their programs. His fights with Hugh Johnson, with Harry Hopkins and with Harold Ickes were amusingly raucous. But his malicious contempt for Roosevelt was not very funny. In April, 1935, Talmadge (who referred to the President as "that cripple in the White House") told a radio audience that "the greatest calamity" to the country was that Roosevelt "can't walk around and hunt up people to talk to." The next President, he said, should be one who was "able to walk a two-by-four plank. . . ." For this uninvited cruelty he was censured by the Georgia Federation of Labor; and Congressman O'Connor of New York remarked that any man who would say such a thing about the President was "unfit to be elected a dogcatcher, let alone Governor. . . ."[36]

In the spring of 1935, Talmadge began a frontal assault with the slogan, "Americans, Wake Up!"; the purpose of which, he announced publicly, was to prevent the renomination of Roosevelt. Talmadge did not beat the devil around the stump: Roosevelt was a Communist. Major New Deal programs were also communistic, he said. "They are in the Russian primer," he told the New York Board of Trade, and Roosevelt "has made the statement that he has read it twelve times." When it was brought to his attention that Communists were branding Roosevelt a Fascist, Talmadge insisted it was part of a deal. "They have a tacit understanding between themselves," he warned, "to fight on the surface." His talk about New Deal communism and the thought that perhaps the only way to save Georgia from it might be secession cost him the invaluable support of Clark Howell, editor of the Atlanta *Constitution*, who was "amazed" by such irresponsible statements.[37] Talmadge did not relent. Through the summer of 1935, he continued to wage war on New Deal communism.

At some point along the way, Talmadge had seen a vision. During 1935, he maintained friendly liaison with Huey Long and the Share-Our-Wealth crowd, not because he particularly approved of the wealth-sharing nostrum but because it seemed to offer possibilities of stopping Roosevelt while advancing his own political fortunes. When Long was assassinated in September, 1935, it seemed like fate was taking a hand. Perhaps Talmadge was after all a man of destiny. But if he were not a man of destiny he at least began sounding like a man who would like to be President.

In the fall he toured the South, a tour in which he found "a tremendous revolt against Franklin D. Roosevelt." "There is," he added meaningfully, "a great demand for an old-fashioned Democrat." His presidential dreams received aid and comfort from an unexpected source when Mayor William McNair of Pittsburgh announced he would support Talmadge for reasons that were not entirely clear, and would see that his name was on the ballot in the Pennsylvania primary. And he was feeling cocky enough to file a petition on his own in U.S. district court to test the validity of the Bankhead Cotton Control Act. When, late in November, Roosevelt came to Atlanta for a speaking engagement the Governor refused to see him, telephoning from his Telfair County farm that he planned to spend the day hunting—"hunting something to plant that there's not any processing tax on."[38]

Likewise waiting to give Talmadge a helping hand was Kirby. Kirby, an incorrigible supporter of patriotic causes, who had made and lost fortunes in Texas oil and lumber, was willing to put his Southern Committee to Uphold the Constitution at Talmadge's disposal to fight the New Deal and to launch the Talmadge presidential boom.

In January, 1936, the Talmadge-Kirby tandem produced a Grass Roots Convention of Jeffersonian-styled Democrats in Macon, Georgia. But a seven-thousand-seat auditorium less than half full was mute testimony that the boom was a bust. Talmadge's gospel of racism and anti-communism preached in a setting of Confederate flags and choruses of "Dixie" made few converts. As if to add insult to injury, Gerald L. K. Smith stole the show from the star performer.

In June, 1936, his candidacy in shambles, Talmadge withdrew from the Georgia primary showdown with Roosevelt; and, in September, he was trounced by a 2-to-1 margin by Richard Russell in the Senate primary race. What had started as a crusade to stop that "damned Communist" Roosevelt ended in November with Talmadge cancelling his hotel reservation and refusing to attend the Democratic National Convention in Philadelphia.[39]

It was also in 1935 that the Communist charge was leveled against Roosevelt from even more unlikely quarters. It came as a real surprise to most people to learn that a man like Percy Crosby, the creator of the lovable comic-strip character "Skippy," even thought about politics. But he did. And when he did, he thought about plots, conspiracies, and Red subversion.

Crosby loathed Roosevelt and made no effort to conceal it. The viciousness of his attacks on the President was a source of joyful amazement even to the severest critics of the Administration. In 1935, Crosby was referring sarcastically to Roosevelt as "the good President," "that great American," with "face-squeezing joviality" and "pince-nez smile." "It is like losing one's individuality in the rays of the sun," Crosby wrote.

All this led up to his insisting that Roosevelt was a dictator, a subversive who, said Crosby, could be expected to ask Congress for a law renaming the Washington Mounment in honor of Benedict Arnold. His contribution during the election year was an incredible five-hundred-page diatribe entitled *Three Cheers for the Red, Red and Red.* The point of the whole business was contained in the title—Roosevelt was a Communist.[40]

The further he went the more intemperate he became. By 1937, he was talking about Roosevelt's "mental putty box" which was "molded to a model of Karl Marx" and the New Deal's Communist Manifesto formula which Roosevelt had "polished to oily smoothness." The President's second inaugural address was "vapor of professors' minds, swooned on the air in puffs of Marxian coffin dust." "When swept of powdered phrase . . . ," Crosby mocked, "the speech conforms to the exact proportions of a Columbus Circle soap-box."[41]

By 1938, his attacks had become so violent that they alarmed even the Secret Service. It is little wonder. Crosby wrote and paid for full-page advertisements entitled "Machine Gunning for Peace," a scathing indictment of Roosevelt in which he twice admonished his readers: "Never wound a snake, but kill it."

Crosby never looked back. He was still talking about killing snakes a short time later in *Would Communism Work Out in America?*, a book in which Roosevelt became a "usurper," a "power-crazed robot," "Moscow's mouthpiece." Even so, there was still hope. Crosby doubted that communism would work in America "even if Roosevelt does succeed in carrying out Moscow's orders."[42]

VI

With some of Roosevelt's critics any time was a good time to brand him and his New Deal communistic; an election year was even better. In an election year, readers and listeners were not just people, they were voters, voters who could translate the dream of the demagogue; turn it into something moral, endow it with divine sanction. The majority could do no wrong; it could unhorse Roosevelt if it would. The prospects of shaping that majority, of perhaps directing it, of claiming credit for it were intoxicating; it moved some to superhuman efforts.

Coughlin for one. In his vendetta with Roosevelt, Coughlin started early on what he called the atheists, the "red and pink Communists" and the "frankfurters of destruction" who surrounded the President. Eighty thousand people at Chicago's Soldiers Field in September, 1936, heard his violent attack on those close to the President—on Henry Morgenthau ("the lover of the international bankers"), Rexford Tugwell ("the hand-shaker with Russia"), Mordecai Ezekiel ("the modern Margaret Sanger of the pigs"), and Frances Perkins ("with her three-corner hat . . . one for communism, one for socialism and one for Americanism").[43]

But before the campaign of 1936 was over, Coughlin discarded the subtlety of damning Roosevelt by association. The New Deal, said the Detroit priest, even while "its golden head" babbled about Christian justice, had its feet of clay mired, "one in the Red mud of Soviet communism, and the other, in the stinking cesspool of pagan plutocracy." The issue, he told his radio audience near the end of the campaign, was not Roosevelt or Landon or Lemke; "it is Christianity or chaos; Americanism or Communism." For Coughlin it had become just that simple.[44]

Coughlin's allies in the election year, Gerald L. K. Smith and Francis Townsend, both loudly echoed the refrain that Roosevelt was a Communist. With Smith, Roosevelt was some other things, too. In January he was telling the sparse crowd at the Talmadge Convention that Roosevelt was the most despised President in history and solicited their help in driving "that cripple out of the White House." At other times he raged about the dictatorship in Washington and the "damnable tyranny" of that "sick man."[45]

But as Smith saw it the real issue in the election year was New Deal communism. He liked to quote a statement attributed to George Bernard Shaw upon Shaw's arrival in Havana in February, 1936. "President Roosevelt," the famous English author had allegedly said, "is a Communist but does not know it." Only Smith was convinced that Roosevelt did know it, which explained why he had surrounded himself with a "pink, bureaucratic, socialistic, pro-communist clique," a "slimy group of men culled from the pink campuses of America with friendly gaze fixed on Russia . . . beginning with Frankfurter and all the little frankfurters." The first clue of what was in store for the American people was the recognition of the Soviet Union, "where two million Christians had been butchered and the churches were still burning."[46]

As the election approached, Smith became increasingly reckless. If the Reds had their way, and the American people did not wake up, and soon, they would "never know what hit them." He confronted the country with the simplest of alternatives: Would the country act, or would it stand idly by "and merely wait for the savage Communist and the Christ-hating tyrant to draw a razor blade across our throat or drive a bloody dagger into our backs?" In September, he revealed that the real plan of the Communists, a plan to assassinate the twenty leading citizens of every town in America and burn the public buildings, was imminent. Roosevelt could not stop it even if he wanted to; "they've Kerenskyized him, he's so flabby—and he's greased for the pole." In late October, Smith expressed the opinion that if he had to choose, on election day, between Roosevelt and Norman Thomas he would prefer Thomas.[47]

It was clear to Smith by this time, as it was to most people, that Roosevelt would be re-elected. The Lemke cause was hopeless and Smith deserted Lemke, the Union Party, and his allies to form a new nationalist organization, the Christian Nationalists (just "old-time Americanism," according to Smith), to combat the New Deal and the Red menace.

The parting was mutual. When Townsend and Lemke heard of Smith's plans, they announced they were severing all connections with him. It was not so much that Lemke and Townsend disagreed with Smith regarding the menace of the New Deal. Lemke, himself, had said early in October that he regarded Roosevelt as "the bewildered Kerensky of a provisional government." And the quaint doctor from California had been heading toward the deep end for some time.[48]

Townsend's hostility toward Roosevelt apparently began with a personal slight in late 1934, when he was denied an interview with the President. At the time, the Townsendite official publication made much of the snub ("President Roosevelt even refused to meet Dr. Townsend. . . . We have aristocracy in the White House—not democracy"), and Townsend often alluded to it.[49]

After conversations with Townsend in Los Angeles in the summer of 1935, Stanley High reported to Stephen Early that the old gentleman had "let fly an amazing—for him—broadside against Roosevelt" because he had been "rebuffed by the White House staff" when he had sought an audience with the President. High thought Townsend might be placated if Early would arrange a meeting during Roosevelt's next trip to the West Coast. It was politically dangerous, High warned, to disregard this simple bit of fence-mending ("the biggest 1936 political mistake is going to be made by the people who try to laugh off the Townsend out-fit," High cautioned).[50]

Some Democrats with divided loyalties, like Congressman Martin F. Smith of Washington, who was temporary chairman of the Townsend Convention in 1935, were likewise uneasy and disturbed by the situation. Smith wrote James Farley, remarking on the snub Townsend had re-ceived from the White House. Smith wanted to be able to tell the convention that Roosevelt would see Townsend. "We cannot afford to ignore a man who has millions of loyal followers," Smith wrote. In mid-January, 1936, J. F. T. O'Connor, the Comptroller of the Treasury, also wrote a brief note to Roosevelt urging upon him an immediate meeting with Townsend.[51]

Roosevelt's public silence regarding Townsend's scheme and the passage of the Social Security legislation were taken as additional evidence of the President's hostility. But the final indignity was a congressional investigation into the Townsend movement in the spring of 1936, with the strong implications that the whole thing was a promotional scheme. Townsend, deeply resenting what he regarded a slanderous attack upon his integrity, stalked out of the hearings, a display of temper for which he was cited for contempt of Congress. The dissemination of "vicious and shameless gossip" by an "inquisitorial committee" Townsend believed had been inspired by Roosevelt.[52]

Hurt feelings now became active hatred, and hatred drove Townsend into the arms of Gerald L. K. Smith, literally. Looking for a place to light after the death of Huey Long and the collapse of the Talmadge boom, Smith found it in the old age pension movement. The day Townsend bolted the committee hearing, Smith was there with a Rebel yell to grasp him by the hand and lead him from the room. He had not met Townsend up to that moment. But now Smith became his most intimate associate and advisor, and soon after announced they were combining forces to defeat Roosevelt, combining to present "a common front against the dictatorship in Washington." On Townsend's authority, Smith became a member of the movement's board of directors and took over leadership of the political activities of the organization.[53]

With the Townsend Movement making only modest headway with the major parties, it was not surprising that Townsend and Smith agreed to pool their resources with Coughlin and embarked upon a third-party enterprise, the Union Party of William Lemke.

The decision to support Lemke badly split the Townsendites, many of whom thought the organization should remain nonpartisan and feared that the third party could only lead up a blind alley. At least one, Gomer Smith, a vice-president of the Townsend Movement and later a Democratic congressman from Oklahoma ("Farley's man," Townsend had called him, disgustedly), believed the third party was little less than a betrayal engineered with Republican money to neutralize the potential power of the Townsend crowd which might normally be expected to vote Democratic. Townsend's appeals to his followers that they vote for Landon in those states where Lemke was not on the ballot offers no solid clues regarding possible Republican support; by this time it seems it was a matter of voting for Landon as a lesser of two evils.[54]

As the 1936 campaign waxed hotter, Townsend, probably egged on by his allies, became more extravagant in his criticism of Roosevelt. Roosevelt was taxing the country into bankruptcy (although the Townsend Plan would have required the most colossal tax measures in history); Roosevelt was a spendthrift (those who would require, by law, that millions spend two hundred dollars a month each ought to know); Roosevelt was a dangerous atheist (Townsend was an admitted atheist, but not dangerous it would seem); Roosevelt was a Communist (unlike Townsend, who simply wanted to license every farmer and businessman and to make the record of every business transaction subject to government review). "Now, wait a minute, what did you want to ask me?" inquired Dr. Townsend. The reporters' questions confused and bewildered him. "Roosevelt? He's just a soft, vacillating politician who is being used by Tugwell and the other Reds. I'd rather see Norman Thomas in the White House."[55]

VII

Before mid-summer, 1936, Elizabeth Dilling rejoined the extremist circus. As a companion piece to her *The Red Network*, she added *The Roosevelt Red Record* as her contribution to the presidential campaign.[56]

Shrill, gaudy, and middle-aged, the wife of a minor official in the Chicago Department of Sanitation, she rose to fame through a simple but dangerous technique. She insisted that everything and everybody, from Jane Addams to the YMCA, was communistic. With the fervor of a Joan of Arc and the indifference to ridicule of a suffragette, Elizabeth Dilling spread the alarm. Her beloved land, cried the Super-Expert-Patriot (an appellative of her own choosing), was being ravished by Communists. No one escaped her accusing finger. No one. From the lecture platform and in her books (the "index expurgatorius," *The New York Times* called them), she named them all . . . Albert Einstein . . . Newton D. Baker . . . Fannie Hurst . . . William E. Borah . . . Louis Brandeis . . . Dr. Harry Emerson Fosdick . . . the University of Chicago . . . Mahatma Gandhi . . . Vincent Astor . . . William Allen White . . . Eamon de Valera. Henry L. Mencken was a Communist. Dr. Glenn Frank, chairman of the Republican Party Policy Committee, was a Communist. So was Chief Justice Charles Evans Hughes. The Federal Council of Churches, the Methodist Federation, and the American Federation of Labor were little better than Communist fronts. The famed conductor, Leopold Stokowski, was a Communist for including *Ode to Lenin* on a symphonic program. Somewhere in his long, brilliant career in business, Walter A. Gifford, president of the American Telephone and Telegraph Company, had taken a wrong turn and landed on her list. In some ways the most interesting name to appear was that of Gilbert Seldes, well-known writer and literary critic, who had accomplished the rare feat of being "a radical columnist for the Hearst papers."[57]

Such infantile nonsense found its way into libraries and onto bibliographies across the country. Advertising herself as an expert, an authority, a close student of radicalism, she spoke everywhere—in schools, churches, patriotic societies, American Legion posts. She could boast that her first book, *The Red Network*, had been recommended by "the Army and Navy Register, the American Coalition of Patriotic Societies, the National Sojourners, the National Americanism Chairman of the American Legion, and countless patriotic leaders."[58]

She had been claiming all the time that the New Deal was communistic, that New Deal officials from the President to the lowest paid National Park ranger were little better than agents of Moscow. In 1936, *The Roosevelt Red Record* was her proof that Roosevelt (and his wife) were the willing tools of "the Red ruling clique running him and the Government with his full approval and cooperation. . . ." The President, she wrote, was merely "an ambitious rich man's son, eager for honors. . . . The program goes on with or without him."[59]

Page after page, and chapter after chapter, she ranged far and wide in an interminable recital of the most incredible flummery. Her format was to extract some statement by Marx or some Marxian principle, and, by example, show how it was being carried out by Roosevelt and the New Deal. Thus, Marx and Engel's first rule for destroying capitalism: "Abolition of all property in land and application of all rents of land to public purposes." Proof that this was being accomplished by Roosevelt was not hard to find. Look at the Home Owners' Loan Corporation plan, she urged, or the Reconstruction Finance Corporation (which she failed to mention was a Hoover measure), or the Agricultural Adjustment Act, the villain of which turned out to be "Dr." Rexford Guy Tugwell (Rex meaning "King," she reminded her readers) whose title stood for Doctor of Marxian Foolosophy. Four hundred and thirty-nine pages of this and similar conclusive proof, mounting evidence based on smoking, drinking, divorce, reckless driving, and other Rooseveltian manifestations of Communist malfeasance, enabled Mrs. Dilling to emerge where she had begun: "That Roosevelt is following Marx nicely will be evident. . . ."[60]

Colonel Sanctuary's contribution to the mounting total of extremist campaign literature was a pamphlet entitled *Is the New Deal Communistic?*, which looked much like a digest version of Dilling's book. In it he listed thirty-five objectives of Karl Marx's "1848 Program," comparing it to a similar number of New Deal programs. The similarities spoke for themselves, he said. To make sure no one missed the point, Sanctuary included an editorial from the Princeton, West Virginia, newspaper describing the town of Norris, Tennessee, one of the communities that was created as part of the TVA project. Norris was "a complete Soviet town" peopled by those "carefully selected with the idea that he would fit into a Communistic settlement." But that was not the worst of it. "One sees no churches in Norris," said the editorial, because with New

Deal planners " 'superstitions' such as God and religion are forgotten."
TVA bothered Sanctuary. In one of his many letters, Sanctuary began his
explanation of "what's back of the man in the White House" by saying that
Roosevelt was "the bellwether of the real gang trying to establish socialism
in this country"; the proof was that his whole TVA program had been
borrowed from Lenin's rural electrification plan for Russia.[61]

During the campaign Sanctuary also circulated two other choice items,
one of which literally placed Roosevelt alongside the great heroes of the
Communist movement. The Communist technique for achieving power,
wrote Sanctuary, the technique outlined by Marx "and improved by Lenin,
Trotsky, Stalin, Blum, Frankfurter and Roosevelt and the Komintern,
may be briefly summarized as follows: 1) Deception; 2) Confusion;
3) Collapse; 4) Dictatorship."[62]

The other item was a letter from Carveth Wells, a well-known African
explorer and fellow of both the Royal and American Geographical Societies. Wells related how, during a trip to Russia in 1932, he had seen
"flattering" pictures of Roosevelt heralding him "The Next Communist
President of the United States." His guides, Wells related, had asked him
when "Comrade" Tugwell was going to have Russia recognized, and had
indicated that when recognition was extended "Comrade" Bullitt would
be the first ambassador. "Future events," Wells wrote to Sanctuary,
"showed that the young communists of Russia knew more about American
politics than I did."[63]

VIII

Democracy was doomed, Father Coughlin had said during the campaign
of 1936; this would be the last national election in the United States, an
election in which the choice was fascism or the communism of the New
Deal. Coughlin made his choice ("I take the road to fascism," he said,
unashamedly); and he urged others to make the same choice. Most of the
extremists had already made their choice, even the German-American
Bund, which usually took little direct part in political campaigns. After
having spoken intermittently on behalf of Lemke and the Union Party, the
Bund leader, Fritz Kuhn, switched his support to Alf Landon and the
Republican Party. Landon, he said, represented a better chance than
Lemke of turning back Roosevelt, whose support in 1936 by Earl Browder
and the Communists was proof of what the New Deal was.[64]

Coughlin's prediction, of course, did not come true; other elections were
held on schedule, the Kremlin opened no branch offices in Washington,
the Republic survived. But to heed the extremists during Roosevelt's
second term one might have been led to believe that the Red flag with
hammer and sickle was about to be unfurled any day above 1600 Pennsylvania Avenue.

The Roosevelt court plan, for example, set William Dudley Pelley to palpitating about "pro-Soviet policies," about a President who served the interests of "godless foreign schemers," about a Chief Executive whom Jewish Communists could claim "is one of them," about a man who practiced a "Red variety of democracy that at its best is diluted Judaism." Pelley pled in 1937 that there was still hope if the Congress would impeach Roosevelt for treason, remove him from office, and make John Nance Garner President in his place. It perhaps did not occur to Pelley that if, as he suggested, it were still possible for this constitutional procedure to be carried out, things were not so bad as he was letting on.[65]

Nor were people likely to be stirred to action when Pelley revealed a whole new area of New Deal subversion, the communizing of the American Indians, specifically the eastern Cherokees in North Carolina. In urging that something be done to save the Indians from a fate worse than death, Pelley managed to brand as Communists both John Collier, chief of the Indian Bureau, and his boss, Harold Ickes, Secretary of Interior. Pelley thought the country owed the Indian more "than the red flag of Soviet Russia flying over Indian Territory."[66]

The matter of Stalinizing the noble savages eventually came to the attention of Martin Dies and the House Committee on Un-American Activities where it died after making the usual headlines. The Charlotte (North Carolina) News wrote the obituary. "Alice Lee [Alice Lee Jamison, a lobbyist for the American Indian Federation, who had brought the matter to the attention of the committee] and Mr. Dies—let us never overlook Mr. Dies—deserve a roar of thanks for having unearthed such nefarious doings in high places."[67]

But Pelley kept up his crusade against "this American Communist New Deal," foisted on the country by "Communist experts which Central Europe has discarded"; against New Dealers being paid salaries by the government "that would stagger you if you knew what they take out of your pockets every month"; against a philosophy which Karl Marx called "Scientific Socialism" but which "came to America under the guise of a 'New Deal'" (the word "communism," explained Pelley, "was not adapted to Americans on account of the ill repute it had attained on the continent of Europe").[68]

All of the time of the Dies Committee was not spent listening to tales of Russianization of the reservation. Nor was it spent in slapstick comedy, as when Congressman Starnes of Alabama wondered aloud if Christopher Marlowe were not a Communist, an hilarious insight into congressional frailties which reminded the editorial writer of the Denver Rocky Mountain News of the lady of literary pretensions who considered Scott's Emulsion the best thing he ever wrote.[69]

By the time Dies submitted the first report of his committee early in 1939, he had heard enough to convince him that the New Deal was riddled by communism, from Mrs. Roosevelt on down, a thesis which he developed at considerable length in a book, *The Trojan Horse in America*.[70]

Whether or not Dies intended it that way or preferred it that way is of little concern, an important consequence of the Dies Committee was that the extremists had a new champion, someone of an official nature, high up in government, unimpeachable, and a Democrat to boot, who seemed to be agreeing with them. This is what the Christian American Patriots from their Denver headquarters (and with their inflated membership rolls of two and a half million) told Roosevelt when they wrote him demanding his resignation. This is what the Christian American Crusade put in its literature which it mailed out from Los Angeles. The Dies investigation, they insisted, "TRACED THE ROOT OF THE COMMUNIST PROGRAM TO THE DOOR OF THE WHITE HOUSE." This is what Joseph McWilliams, the leader of the Christian Mobilizers, was twisting to his own purposes when he told a rally in New York City in September, 1939 (at which both George Deatherage and Fritz Kuhn also spoke): "We must learn to hate all Roosevelts and LaGuardias because they represent the interests of internationalism and communism, and these are to us synonymous with world Jewry."[71]

Dies' Trojan Horse idea ran through the book *Riding High* by David Milton Proctor, a former Missouri state senator and contemporary of Roosevelt's at Columbia University. Proctor's earlier book, *Pay Day*, a vigorous indictment of the Roosevelt Administration, had received wholesale distribution during the 1936 campaign, one million, three hundred thousand copies according to one estimate. In *Riding High*, an imaginary citizen was writing to an equally imaginary United States senator about "Roosevelt Communists and New Deal Congressmen." After a long recital of New Deal sins and treachery, the writer expressed the hope that the senator would have the courage of his convictions and, along with his patriotic colleagues, call a halt to the betrayal. If he would do that, the New Deal could be voted out of office in 1940. The writer was optimistic. "I have an abiding faith," he told his senator, "that we will go over the top in our battle against the entrenched New Dealers. I believe history will chisel this inscription on the little white tablet of the New Deal:

> Here lies the New Deal
> 1933–1941
> Its last words: Retreating to Moscow."[72]

IX

Sooner or later, with so many people doing so much talking about Jewish conspiracies and Communist plots, it was perhaps inevitable that some of them would get around to talking a little treason of their own. And apparently they did. Who can say how often they drank the heady wine of glorious insurrection? Or dreamed their dreams of bursting into the Executive office, pointing the accusing finger at the President, and ordering their loyal retainers to lead the traitor away? What exhilarating thoughts these must have been! Monstrous rallies . . . riding in the back of big black automobiles . . . through streets lined with cheering, adoring throngs . . . stirring ceremonialism . . . thrilling band music . . . good food . . . good drink . . . the good life . . . awe . . . splendor . . . applause . . . bouquets tied with ribbons, proffered by shy, bashful little girls. But above all, the enormous satisfaction of knowing that their beloved land had, at long last, been made safe and secure from Jews . . . Communists . . . all its enemies. With all that at stake who would not feel compelled to talk a little treason?

While talking treason was one thing, putting it in writing was quite another. George Deatherage, leader of the Knights of the White Camellia, was one who made the mistake of committing his vague plans to paper. Even the Dies Committee paid attention when it learned that Deatherage had written to James E. Campbell of Owensboro, Kentucky, another practicing patriot: "Please rest assured that our time is coming and that within the next twelve months those that have borne the heartbreaking load of carrying on the fight will come into their own." To Campbell, Deatherage was promising a conspicuous place in the "inner circle" of the new revolutionary government when it took power, a reward for the sacrifices he had made for the cause. Campbell was himself a very busy man, the Dies Committee learned, preparing a plan of his own, a counterattack that would frustrate a Communist uprising to take the government by force scheduled, according to Campbell's information, for August, 1939.[73]

For someone to lead his putsch (". . . the plan is to do this job peacefully, and by force only if it becomes necessary" Deatherage told Campbell), he had chosen unwisely. Major General George Van Horn Moseley, forty-three years of distinguished Army service behind him, handsome, tall, erect, belying his sixty-four years, was Deatherage's candidate. Moseley, who thought he deserved to be Chief of Staff before he retired, was a bitter man. Intemperate of speech, suspicious by nature, and overly susceptible to flattery, Moseley was easily convinced by dreadful people like Deatherage that mischief was on the march, that the country was in awful danger.[74]

If Moseley entertained any ambitions to be an American-style Hitler, he apparently did not expect to reach his goal solely with the support of Deatherage. In fact, it appears that the plan may have existed only in the mind of Deatherage who told Campbell that "we have to educate him [Moseley] to what this is all about without his getting the idea that we are trying to influence him. . . . I see now that we cannot give him all this in one dose without upsetting him." To add to the delightful excitement of conspiracy, Deatherage suggested to Campbell that in their future correspondence they refer to General Moseley as "the Boss"; the reason for this naughty-little-boy approach, Deatherage explained, was "in case Mr. Farley is interested."[75]

Moseley spent five stormy hours before the Dies Committee, attended by a small battalion of lawyers and Congressman Thorkelson of Montana who, only recently, had been described in Pelley's *Liberation* as "a new statesman rearing high above this miasma of skullduggery." Between skirmishes over whether or not he would be allowed to read into the record the mountain of material on the desk before him, Moseley made it clear where his heart lay. With a flourish, he insisted that "the Jew is an internationalist first . . . a patriot at home second." Protesting that he harbored no anti-Semitic feelings, Moseley proceeded to warn the committee that the country was about to be overwhelmed by "a Jewish-led Communist revolution." Organizations like that of Deatherage's and the others Moseley thought were good things; they were, he said, "an antitoxin for the disease of Communism." He even spoke a good word for the German-American Bund, describing its purpose as that of seeing to it that the Communists "don't take over the country."[76]

Moseley was no Hitler. This much was apparent the moment he opened his mouth. The Deatherages of this world would have to look elsewhere for a fuhrer. Since 1933 they had talked much about Jews and Communists, had attacked the Roosevelt Administration, much of the time with unbelievable ferocity, had spread vicious rumors, had held parades, sold shirts, sponsored rallies, incited to riot, gone to jail, testified before committees. But up to 1939 there had been not a single overt act of real mischief, not even a respectable assault on a beerhall. They lacked a leader, a messiah among messiahs.

Meanwhile, until their time came, as Deatherage had written, they could do what Thorkelson did—continue to rail against the Roosevelt-New Deal Communist betrayal. Moseley's appearance before the Dies Committee had dissolved in confusion, name-calling, and threats to have Moseley court-martialed. On the floor of the House of Representatives, Thorkelson dared the adversary to court-martial the general. Nothing, he jeered, was said about impeachment when President Roosevelt "dressed the Court in pink and red." "No one is going to court-martial General Moseley," Thorkelson taunted; to do so "would lift the scarlet cloak of the New Deal and expose the most criminal attempt to convert our country into a proletarian communistic despotism."[77]

And it must have sent every extremist in the land back to the fray with renewed spirit when Thorkelson added, "I know the boys out West . . . it will be found that they can do their own cleaning when the proper time comes."[78]

PART III

Up One Side, Down the Other

WHILE the fuhrers of native fascism strutted and goose-stepped through their burlesque of patriotism, a few Americans, embittered and rootless, crushed by the Depression, impatient for change, looked to the Left for simple solutions and easy answers. And there were more than enough to go around—solutions offered by Communists, Socialists, Progressives, and by an odd assortment of priests, preachers, physicians, and politicians, all peddling patent economic elixirs compounded of one part hope, one part ignorance, and one part hogwash.

Communists and non-Communist radicals alike agreed that New Deal efforts to cure the nation's economic ills were, as Norman Thomas put it, like "trying to cure tuberculosis with cough-drops"; but they disagreed in reaction and remedy. To Communists (at least until mid-1935) Roosevelt was a Fascist and the New Deal a dictatorship designed to gut the worker and betray the masses; only radical surgery could remove the diseased organs of government. To non-Communist radicals Roosevelt was a decent, well-meaning though halfhearted liberal and the New Deal a mass of halfway piecemeal legislation offering a palliative of relief—not enough to do any real good, just enough, they feared, to still the voices of political and social protest.

Communist criticism was based on hatred of the existing system, radical criticism on regret for its lost opportunities. Communists feared and despised a capitalist future; radicals were frustrated by dreams of what the future could be. They criticized the New Deal, not out of hatred, but in terms that reflected their alternate hopes and fears. Communists touted a solution rooted in emotion and nourished on a faith foreign to American traditions; radicals made a sincere effort to think through America's economic problems. Their solutions, however drastic and erroneous, were grounded in rational analysis.

For all its bluster, left-wing criticism of the New Deal was largely ineffectual, all but impotent. A multiplicity of radical organizations, agreeing on essentials, disagreeing on details, divided by factionalism, torn by jealousy, produced only confusion, a tragicomic clamor of radicals rushing toward common goals at different speeds and in different directions. If socialism could be identified with increased state regulation of economic affairs, or even with giant steps toward the establishment of a welfare state, the decade of the New Deal could be regarded by radicals as a decade of unprecedented progress. But the New Deal was also a period in which radical movements shrank almost to the point of invisibility. Socialist party membership, for example, declined from a peak of 23,000 in 1934 to fewer than 7,000 by 1938. It is an historic irony that during capitalism's worst crisis the Socialist Party, while loudly predicting the death of capitalism, itself died—with alarums on its lips.

While radicals were attacking Roosevelt for doing too little too slowly for too few, other dissident groups opened fire. By the winter of 1933–34 Roosevelt and his New Deal were being raked up one side and down the other. Impatient farmers protested meager AAA benefits; promised bread they were being handed stones. From their miserable shanties along roadsides and railroad embankments embittered sharecroppers and farm-hands blasted the AAA and its crop-reduction policies for driving them off their wornout land. Labor leaders objected to the NRA, objected because it had been seduced by big business, objected because Roosevelt was unable—or unwilling—to enforce Section 7a.

Business leaders sensed that Roosevelt did not define "recovery" as they did, that he did not mean to reestablish the old order, did not intend to return business to the head of the line. The fast and furious reform and recovery measures of that first spring would continue; they would not be let alone. Roosevelt was about to make them the whipping boy of the Depression. Their cries, rising from the concrete canyons of Wall Street, echoed across the land, by ticker, by telephone, by word of mouth—great lamentations against broken promises, extravagant spending, experimentation, socialism, against Tugwell and Frankfurter and Cohen, against TVA, increased taxes, bureaucracy, regimentation, against inconsistency, vacillation and unpredictability in national planning. They objected not so much to business regulation, for business had been regulated in the past. The thing that galled them, made them see red, was the personal nature of the regulation, the feeling that it was Roosevelt's personal will and personal capriciousness at work, and they could not control him. They grew sick and tired of His voice, His grin, His cocksure manner, His cheerful deceits.

So businessmen organized and criticized and printed pamphlets and sponsored meetings and bellyached. Their cries fell on sympathetic ears in the conservative press; editors listened, but hardly anyone else did. Not even when editors spoke.

CHAPTER V

The Devoted Wall Street Lackey

Is not this trickery the hallmark of this Wall Street tool, this President who always stabs in the back while he embraces? How unctuous is his empty solicitude for the ragged, hungry children . . . with the ruthlessness of a devoted Wall Street lackey spending billions for war and profits, and trampling on the faces of the poor. —Communist *Daily Worker, 1934*

> *Mr. Roosevelt won't you please run again*
> *For we want you to do it*
> *You've got to go through it*
> *Again.* —Communist *Daily Worker, 1939*

Mr. Roosevelt did not carry out the Socialist platform, unless he carried it out on a stretcher. —*Norman Thomas*

Failure is a hard word. . . . Yet we believe the record indicates that nothing but failure can be expected from the New Deal.
—Common Sense
September 1934

I T was the spring of 1935, and Roosevelt was angry. His blue eagle was dead, vanquished by a sick chicken. The Supreme Court decision in *Schechter* vs. *U.S.* (the "Dred Schechter" case, to use one of Mencken's humorous figures) had endangered his entire recovery effort. Publicly Roosevelt criticized the Court for turning the Constitution back to "horse and buggy" days. And publicly he smiled (a little bitterly perhaps as he noted a comment from the Hearst press that the death of the NRA had restored the rule of Christ).

But Roosevelt was angry. In private he was more irritable than he had been since entering the White House. At one luncheon however, while the President verbally raked the Court over the coals, an old friend succeeded in changing the temper of the conversation by changing the subject. "Governor," he ventured, "did you see this morning's *Times*? You don't have a thing to worry about. The Communist Party has decided to pat you on the head."[1]

The President, with a characteristic gesture, threw back his head and roared with laughter at the thought of friendly Communists. And he had a right to laugh. The serpentine party line had just reversed itself; friendliness to Roosevelt was a new guise for the Communists.

II

At the outset the Communists had denounced the New Deal and Roosevelt with unremitting hostility. "Mr. Roosevelt," wrote William Z. Foster, one of America's top Communists, in 1932, "is nothing more or less than a lightning rod for capitalism to protect it from danger. . . . He offers to the workers and the poor farmers and the starving masses of this country the opportunity of jumping out of the Hoover frying pan into the Roosevelt fire."[2]

Communist hostility to the New Deal was not the result of homegrown Communist policy, nor had it sprung fullgrown in 1932 from the brows of American Communist leaders. It was simply the continuation of a worldwide party line set by the Sixth World Congress of the Communist International Organization. In 1928 the Comintern, meeting in Moscow, prescribed a policy of muscle and iron, of uncompromising revolutionary militancy. The new line defined liberals and progressives, Social Democrats and trade unionists—in fact virtually everyone who was neither a card-carrying Communist nor jack-booted Nazi—as "social fascists," political hypocrites who blocked real change by offering tongue-in-cheek economic and social reforms.

Even in Germany where Nazi power was increasing alarmingly, the party line forced German Communists to direct their main fire against Social Democrats, not against the hoodlums in storm trooper uniforms. The brutalities of Hitlerism went unchallenged; the Communists dared not deviate from Comintern instructions. Shortly after Hitler seized power a Comintern document, reprinted in the *Daily Worker*, insisted that the "task of the Communist Party remains, as before—to direct the chief blow . . . against Social Democracy."[3]

The American Communist Party, led by its Kansas-born general secretary, Earl Browder, applied this directive against Roosevelt and the New Deal with all the fervor of religious fanatics. In Europe the policy brought high tragedy; in America it resulted in low comedy. For the Communist picture of America to coincide with Comintern line, American Communists had to profess belief in the immediacy of a "final conflict" in the United States, a confrontation between the masses under Communist leadership and the bourgeois social Fascists. Although it was hardly necessary to exaggerate the ills of American society, this new position required that the Communists create a picture of capitalism much worse than it was.

Roosevelt, to the shrilly hostile Communist *Daily Worker*, was the prince of social Fascists. The New Deal, according to Browder in the summer of 1933, was "a policy of slashing the living standards"; Roosevelt was "carrying out more thoroughly and brutally than even Hoover the capitalist attack against the masses." There was nothing about Roosevelt, his Administration, his family, or his policies that Communists found to their liking. The Roosevelt name was synonymous with "smiling India rubber liberal in the White House," "fascist . . . financial dictator . . . imperialist," "skilled demagogue"; his New Deal meant "drastic attacks upon the living standards of the masses" . . . "the terrorization of the Negro" . . . "the systematic denial of civil rights." He was described as "a rich cotton planter" itching to make money out of the destruction of cotton. "Is not this trickery," asked the Communist *Worker*, "the hallmark of this Wall Street tool, this President who always stabs in the back while he embraces? How unctuous is his empty solicitude for the ragged, hungry children . . . with the ruthlessness of a devoted Wall Street lackey spending billions for war and profits, and trampling on the faces of the poor."[4]

III

"No new social order," commented world-renowned economist Harold J. Laski, non-Communist member of the British Labour Party, "has so far come into being without a violent birth."[5]

This simple proposition was the foundation of radical left-wing hostility toward the New Deal. Since neither Marx nor Engels had given the slightest consideration to a reformed capitalism, Marxists totally rejected the idea that American society could be patched up. According to Marx's "scientific" laws of history, a series of increasingly severe business crises climaxed by a profound depression would be the historical moment for the Socialist revolution. Thus Marxists argued that what was needed (and what would inevitably come) was not a new patch but a whole new garment, that evolution was futile, that revolutionary change was the only solution to the contradictions of capitalism.

Since revolution was essential, the Roosevelt efforts to shore up the crumbling structure of capital, they contended, were worse than useless, they were dangerous. "Roosevelt, like Hoover," said leftist writer Anna Rochester, "has acted to protect the capitalists. . . . The 'New Deal' uses the same old cards and continues the same old game. . . . His program [is] an elaborate apparatus to fool the workers into believing that they are his chief concern." Efforts to reform capitalism reminded the authors of a wittily written Marxist analysis of the New Deal of the efforts of a Russian peasant to patch up the seat of his trousers by cutting a piece of cloth from the front, and then a piece from the leg to patch the new hole. "After repeating this operation a dozen times he wound up, very much like the New Deal, with his pants all in patches and the migratory hole still there." "There is nothing," they concluded, "the New Deal has so far done that could not have been done better by an earthquake." An earthquake, they said, would have established scarcity and provided jobs with far more speed and far less noise than the New Deal.[6]

Israel Amter, a Communist leader, agreed. "The New Deal," he commented, "is the rawest deal that the workers have ever received. . . . Industrial slavery stares us in the face from the hands of that great demagogue, Franklin D. Roosevelt, the new Messiah, the great savior— the dictator." Browder (who once charged that Roosevelt had turned the public treasury into a "huge trough where the big capitalists eat their fill") defined the program of the New Deal as "the same as that of finance capital the world over." It was, he insisted, essentially "the same as Hitler's program," a program of "hunger, fascization and imperialist war," differing only "in the forms of its unprecedented ballyhoo, of demagogic promises, for the creation of mass illusions of a saviour who has found a way out."[7]

In the National Industrial Recovery Act the Communists saw a particularly odious form of Wall Street oppression. "The claws of the Blue Eagle," said Gil Green, spokesman for the Young Communist League, "are the grasping hands of the parasitic rich." "The victims," he continued, "are you and I . . . the working people." The public, he said, had been hypnotized into believing that the NRA Blue Eagle ("this vulture" whose sharp talons "have been hidden behind a veil of promises") had "suddenly become a dove of peace."[8]

In August, 1933, the Communist Party sponsored an anti-NRA conference in Cleveland, Ohio. The brochure publicizing this "Opposition Labor Conference Against Industrial Recovery Bill" declared that the New Deal, particularly the National Industrial Recovery Act (which, they said, should be properly called the "Industrial Slavery Act") was "from beginning to end an enormous looting of the government treasury, a further robbery of the workers and toilers generally for the benefit . . . of Wall Street."[9]

The real fear of the Communists was not that the New Deal was thinly disguised fascism. What terrified them, what evoked from them exaggerated invective was the fear that the New Deal recovery and reform measures would be successful. Their recurring plea was that the New Deal must not be permitted "to lull the masses into a sense of security, flabby optimism, and passivity." Workers must "arouse themselves, [and] refuse to be duped by rosy dreams."[10]

When it became evident that the NRA might actually bring about some improvement in the Depression, the Communist Party became almost desperate in its attempts to maintain the revolutionary fervor of its members. It has already demonstrated, wrote Alex Bittelman, Communist theoretician, in January, 1934, "that the so-called concessions of the NRA . . . are nothing else but a snare and a delusion." Not only was the NRA failing to help the American worker, he charged, it actually reduced his standard of living by permitting its proposed minimum wages to become maximum wages. "The unemployed," declared Abe Bluestein, another leftist writer, "must not suffer from any illusions of genuine relief from their heavy burdens under capitalism." To settle for anything short of total success, for "partial victories after valiant struggle," might shatter their morale.[11]

Section 7a of the NRA, which guaranteed workers the right to organize and to bargain collectively was more violently attacked than perhaps any other measure of the Roosevelt Administration. Bittelman considered the collective bargaining clause as nothing more than a paper provision designed to prevent strikes and free trade union organization which had only weakened labor's bargaining power. The NRA, declared Israel Amter, is "a huge fraud." The workers, he contended, were being "pressed into company unions" and "herded into jails" instead of being permitted to organize freely and bargain collectively.[12]

In the closed corporation of Communist thought where compromise was the mortal sin the New Deal represented an attempt, clumsily ignorant or cunningly diabolical, to interfere with the natural birth of world socialism; to endorse such a program would be to snatch defeat from the jaws of victory.

If Communists could not approve the New Deal in principle neither could they approve it in specifics. In their condemnation of early New Deal policies, only a Gilbert and Sullivan could have done justice to the comic exaggeration of Communist reaction, a reaction in which the singing of the national anthem at a Socialist Party meeting became "unparallelled treachery," and even the Boy Scouts and baseball were called weapons against the workers.[13]

The Communist elaborate protestations of fascism and government-sponsored terror would have appeared even more farcical had not American society itself been disordered. They balanced absurdities with an equal number of verities, which one did not have to be a Communist to recognize. Millions *were* unemployed, as the Communists said. People *were* hungry; men *did* feel helplessly and hopelessly caught in a trap not of their making; there *was* much talk of an imminent American revolution; children in rags; men idling in public parks or selling apples on street corners or shuffling in soup lines *had* become a familiar and almost accepted part of American life.

And the Communists made the most of it. The Roosevelt Administration, they reiterated, was not a new deal for the downtrodden workers and farmers; it was designed to save Wall Street and the fat-bellied moneymongers. The contradictions of capitalism, they insisted, could not be resolved by the oppressive measures of Roosevelt. Fascism had found a strong advocate in "that skilled demagogue" in the White House.

IV

The anti-Roosevelt, anti-New Deal line continued unabated until late 1935 when Comrade Browder returned from the Seventh Moscow Comintern revival bearing a new gospel.

Again the message was not addressed exclusively to American Communists, but was another attempt at worldwide evangelism. The Social Democrats in Germany, Leon Blum in France, and Franklin Roosevelt in the United States, who only yesterday had been social Fascists, were now ardently courted by the Communists. The new doctrine redefined Communist goals; the party line made another 180-degree turn.

The image that the 1936 Communist attempted to paint of himself and the image that he held of the New Deal both underwent radical transformations. From the bewhiskered, bomb-carrying, sinister figure in a threadbare coat shouting revolutionary slogans and accusing liberals and moderates alike of fascism, the new Communist became the cleancut all-American boy, reasonable and self-effacing, calling for a United Front against a common foe. In addition to the Communists the new entente in the United States, it was hoped, would include New Dealers, Socialists, Farmer-Laborites, the various radical and progressive groups—everyone in short who somehow had been miraculously converted by Communist magic from social fascism to anti-fascism.

Whatever else it may have implied the miracle performed by the Seventh World Congress of the Communist International recognized that the Soviet Union would need all the allies it could muster against the rising threat of Hitler. But in the United States Communist leaders could argue (and did) that reversal of Communist policy toward the New Deal was not kowtowing to Russian needs and the orders of the Comintern. American Communism, they blandly explained, was revising its position in response to a leftward shift by the New Deal.

The New Deal did appear to be moving to the left. And there was just enough in the first New Deal that looked like fascism (the NRA was probably the best example) to lend plausibility to the new Communist line. They had opposed the Fascist trends in the early New Deal; they changed their position only when the character of the New Deal itself changed. When critics continued to insist that the new party line was a contradiction, Earl Browder innocently replied that Communist policy "represents a constant struggle to meet more adequately the problems of a rapidly changing world. Every step we make in this direction is a 'contradiction' of the position from which we stepped." "It is true," he confessed, "that, prior to the Seventh World Congress, we Communists of America were not fully conscious of the possibilities and necessity for the anti-fascist People's Front."[14]

The argument that the change in party line was only a response to changes in the domestic policy of the United States had obvious flaws. Had American Communist leaders been independent enough and flexible enough to formulate their own response to the New Deal, it is unlikely they would have found absolutely nothing in it to merit support. Nor is it likely they could have found it necessary to damn virtually all New Deal measures as Fascist or to call Roosevelt an unprincipled dictator. To believe that the new Communist approach was domestically formulated took a lot of believing. It meant believing that a fantastic coincidence had occurred, one in which the Communist parties of all nations decided to change their positions at exactly the same moment, in exactly the same direction, and in response to exactly the same changes in their own national governments.

Regardless of how the change was made and on whose orders, the fact remained that the Communist attitude toward Roosevelt was reversed in late 1935. Through the sudden chemistry of Communist reaction, Roosevelt was metamorphosized into a friend, an ally against nascent fascism. Nor was Roosevelt alone in the ranks of the Communists' newly acquired friends. Brewed in the same Communist pot of instant friendship were virtually all former "social fascists," the left-of-center groups, Progressives of the East and radicals of the Midwest, who only recently had been castigated as betrayers of the working class. The proponents of "twentieth-century democracy," as the Communists now liked to identify themselves, urged all "anti-fascists" to join them in a holy crusade against national socialism.

Except when relief appropriations were cut and when an embargo was imposed against Loyalist Spain, little Communist criticism of Roosevelt appeared from 1936 to 1939. The Communists became especially friendly toward the President after his "Quarantine the Aggressor" speech in Chicago in October, 1937. Occasionally the *Daily Worker* implied that Roosevelt was almost as great as Earl Browder. In 1939 when the Communists were supporting a third term for Roosevelt, the *Daily Worker* added this ditty to the campaign:

> Mr. Roosevelt won't you please run again
> For we want you to do it
> You've got to go through it
> *Again.*[15]

V

In 1928 the wife of the Socialist candidate for governor of New York, Louis Waldman, after meeting the Democratic candidate, told her husband, "Roosevelt is the most formidable opponent that the Socialist Party will ever have in the United States."[16]

Her remark was prophetic. Five years later the Socialists found themselves in a fight for their lives with Mrs. Waldman's "formidable opponent," who was now the new occupant of the White House.

Although the Socialist Party polled nearly 900,000 votes in the 1932 presidential election, it had a total membership of only 15,000; and this small band was further weakened by internal dissension. But the party showed signs of life; it was growing. From less than 8,000 in 1928 the membership increased to almost 23,000 by September 1934. The Depression and the charm of a new leader, Norman Thomas, was infusing new blood into the party.[17]

The new group, calling itself the Militants, was eager, impatient, and full of fight. The Old Guard, Marxist in its avowed philosophy but lacking the will to translate it into radical action, was wary of the upstarts. The Young Turks, who, at the extreme left were hardly distinguishable from Communists, would destroy the Socialist movement in the United States, they feared, by brash and ill-considered action.[18]

The Old Guard was opposed by still another faction, an ill-defined group which might be called the Progressives. The Progressives, loosely organized and representing many degrees of Socialist belief, consisted of party members who were dissatisfied with the inactivity of the Old Guard but fearful of the Militants. They were not doctrinaire Marxists. Their goal was simply the realignment of American politics to give better representation to laborers and farm workers. In September, 1929, some of the leading members of this group—Norman Thomas, Paul Blanshard, Harry W. Laidler, and Reinhold Niebuhr—had joined with leading non-Socialists to organize the League for Independent Political Action.[19]

By 1935 Socialist Party factionalism and an infusion of ex-Communists resulted in mass exodus from the party—seven thousand members, nearly a third of the total membership, by the end of the year. The problems which bedeviled the Socialist Party elicited from *Common Sense*, the organ of the League for Independent Political Action, a cry of despair: "The Left Wing leans to the side of revolution, the pacifists withdraw from the idea of violence, the Westerners get distrustful of the New York Jewish legal crowd, the trade unions resent the highbrows."[20]

Internal dissension was a serious matter; more serious however was the formidable threat confronting the Socialists from the outside, from the

New Deal. Roosevelt's efforts to reform capitalism, to restore it to health, and to relieve the suffering brought about by its apparent failures cut deep into Socialist support. Decline of the Socialist Party in membership and influence was in inverse proportion to the success and popularity of the New Deal. "What cut the ground out pretty completely from under us," said Norman Thomas later, "was Roosevelt in a word. You don't need anything more."[21]

Although many Roosevelt critics from the right accused the New Deal of being out-and-out socialism, Thomas, Mr. Socialism himself, disagreed. He admitted that much of the public identified the New Deal with socialism; but Roosevelt, he said, "did not carry out the Socialist platform, unless he carried it out on a stretcher." One reason people confused the New Deal with socialism, Thomas said, was because they had been told it was socialism "in various accounts by Mr. David Lawrence, Mr. Alfred Emanuel Smith, and Mr. James P. Warburg." The identification of socialism and the Roosevelt program was, perhaps, one of the reasons Socialists found it necessary to attack the New Deal so vigorously.[22]

The need to establish clearly a separate identity may have added fuel to their attacks. But the Socialists were honest; they criticized the New Deal for not being precisely what the right-wing swore it was, Socialist. In 1934 at an Independence Day rally in New York, the Socialist candidate for governor, Charles Solomon, spoke scornfully of those who saw any organic resemblance between the New Deal and socialism. "There is none," he insisted. Thomas emphatically agreed. He told a convention of school administrators in St. Louis that the New Deal which had been falsely attacked as socialism by the Republicans had "temporarily saved capitalism better than the old deal did." During the 1936 campaign Thomas ridiculed New Deal programs as attempts "to cure tuberculosis with cough-drops." Roosevelt, Thomas conceded, had borrowed some ideas from the Socialists. But what happened to Socialist ideas in the wrong hands, Thomas wrote sarcastically, "merely illustrated the principle that if you want a child brought up right you had better leave the child with his parents and not farm him out to strangers."[23]

Socialist efforts to maintain an identity as a separate political party and to promote a positive economic philosophy led not only to denying that the New Deal was socialism. It also meant accusing Roosevelt of leading the nation in the direction of "State capitalism." Thomas, in his book *The Choice Before Us*, described the New Deal as "essentially State capitalism," which was only one step removed from fascism—and not a long step either. In June, 1933, in answer to the question "Is the New Deal Socialism?", *The New York Times* quoted Thomas as saying, "Mr. Roosevelt's revolutionary achievement is emphatically in the direction of State capitalism and not socialism." And, he warned, "we shall not long have the economics of fascism without a considerable dose of its politics." In 1935 Thomas repeated that Roosevelt was no Socialist; his economic ideas, he said, were similar to those of Hitler and Mussolini.[24]

Thomas' fear was not that Roosevelt himself would lead America to fascism. Roosevelt was personally harmless, an amiable sort, "in the best sense of the word an aristocrat." In their lighter moments Socialists could assert that Roosevelt's accent alone disqualified him as a potential Fascist leader.[25]

It was the New Deal that was dangerous, that filled them with foreboding. The New Deal's "capitalistic collectivism" could set the stage for fascism. But what made the New Deal doubly dangerous, according to the Socialists, was its lack of awareness, its lack of self-consciousness. While its tendency was toward state capitalism, there was no assurance that it would arrive there; or if it did that it would stop there. "The greatest fraud among all utopias," said Socialist Militant D. P. Berenberg, "is the 'New Deal.' Based on no philosophy, it is the apotheosis of opportunism." "They rather exult," wrote Thomas, "in a pragmatism of an opportunistic sort." Agreeing that there was "some truth" to the *Saturday Evening Post*'s criticism that the New Deal was "a hodge-podge of opportunistic laws contradictory one to the other," Thomas attacked the experimental aspects of New Deal legislation and Roosevelt's comparison of himself to a "quarter-back who has to try different plays." "Some of us," he declared, "would not mind his trying plays if we were sure he might not, as happened in a famous game in California, score a touchdown behind the wrong goal!"[26]

Socialists did more than criticize the philosophy of the New Deal, or its lack of a philosophy; while they attacked it in general they also attacked its particulars. Few measures of the New Deal program escaped; but two of them, the National Industrial Recovery Act and the Agricultural Adjustment Act, received the brunt of the attack. Although Roosevelt was "no Mussolini," Thomas told a New Jersey convention of the Continental Congress on Economic Reconstruction in June, 1933, his economic policy was "extraordinarily like the Italian program." The NRA, Thomas thought, had put the "money changers back in the temple singing in the choir praises to Roosevelt." In 1934 he charged that the NRA was permitting widespread chiseling by "great employers" who were managing to circumvent its codes, that its minimum wages were becoming maximum, and that consumers' interests were being largely neglected. The NRA, he said, was "another illustration of the fact that capitalism and desirable social planning, or indeed any effective social planning, are incompatible."[27]

It was in the NRA that Socialists saw the most ominous signs of Fascist tendencies. "The President," wrote Thomas, "has now bargained with industry for a semi-dictatorial control . . . which Mussolini might honestly applaud." A resolution adopted by the Socialists in their 1934 convention in Detroit stated that while the NRA was not fascism, it has "the potentialities of fascism."[28]

A year earlier the party's National Executive Committee had said that the NRA was "an official admission that capitalism" could make "no recovery without government supervision." There was a danger; the statement continued, that fascism would "be the next step if labor failed to organize fully under Section 7a." While the statement did not claim that the NRA was Fascist, it did point out its similarity to the European cartel system and the Italian corporate state, declaring "it can easily be made into Fascism."[29]

Thomas, joining the either-or camp containing so many of Roosevelt's critics, concluded "sooner or later we shall swerve sharply to a Fascist right or to a Socialist left." "We are," Thomas wrote concerning the NRA in 1934, "making fast headway in America to the labor serfdom which Fascist countries have set up." "We are at a crossroads," he had said earlier, "the open roads are State capitalism, almost inevitably of the Fascist brand, and ruthless Communism."[30]

While Socialist criticism of the NRA had little or no effect on national policy, criticism of New Deal agricultural measures fared somewhat better. At a time when the economic aspects of agriculture were the overriding concern, Socialists raised a serious moral and social issue; one that Roosevelt could not safely ignore indefinitely.

More than once Norman Thomas was the voice of the American conscience during those days when matters of conscience were often ignored or sacrificed to the pragmatic or the expedient. Despite all the talk about the "forgotten man," many men were still forgotten. But Thomas remembered them. If men would not vote for him, they at least applauded him for his consistent concern and for his constant reminders that the individual was being overlooked in the onrush of politics and experimental economic schemes.

Thomas sharply criticized the New Deal farm programs, particularly the AAA, its seeming indifference to such forgotten men as Negroes, sharecroppers, and tenant farmers, just as he shamed the NRA for its record of social injustice in parts of the country where the initials apparently stood for "Negro Removal Act." Farm laborers, sharecroppers, tenant farmers, little people who had been particularly hard hit by the Depression, were struck another blow by the AAA. Although the law provided that benefit payments to farmers for not growing certain crops were to be shared with tenants, no plan was worked out to see that they were. In many cases the landlord kept the entire payment, often using it to purchase farm machinery which in turn eliminated the need for tenants and farm hands altogether. The AAA, wrote Thomas in 1934, works to drive out "as homeless wanderers" the "miserably poor cropsharers of the South chronically held in serfdom to the landlords by their debts." Thomas thought it perfectly obvious that any law reducing acreage and paying the landlord for it could have no other effect.[31]

His efforts to get the New Deal to remedy this injustice led him to Henry Wallace, Secretary of Agriculture. In a letter to Wallace in 1934, Thomas raised two questions: "What about the share-croppers driven from the land under any system of limitations? Will the Bankhead bill or any other legislation see that the rewards of *not* planting cotton are passed on to the men who have been forced to stop planting cotton?" Wallace, in a polite but noncommittal reply, denied that the problem was serious enough to demand remedy. Having failed to obtain Wallace's interest in the plight of farm workers, Thomas took the problem directly to Roosevelt, who admitted the existence of the problem but could see nothing that his Administration could do to solve it. "Norman," he said, "I'm a damn sight better politician than you." "Certainly, Mr. President," Thomas replied. "You're on that side of the desk and I'm on this."[32]

If Roosevelt and Wallace would not listen, perhaps the people would. On February 27, 1935, over network radio Thomas went to the people with a poignant story of tenant farmers. There was more and worse restriction under the New Deal than there had ever been under the Hoover Administration, he told the country. The Department of Agriculture, he charged, had made itself "the ally of the plantation system and the planters to an unprecedented degree." "I think it is about time," he challenged, "to call this New Deal bluff." Thomas undertook to practice what he preached and played an important role in organizing the Southern Tenant Farmers' Union.[33]

For several decades the plight of the sharecropper and the tenant farmer had been the shame of the South. Under AAA policies it became almost a national scandal. The local administration of AAA was dominated by plantation owners, who let little federal money filter through to those most directly injured by AAA crop-reduction programs. As share-croppers lost their crops, farm workers lost their jobs, and tenant farmers lost their farms, a new emotion came to the South—an emotion born of despair and desperation, an emotion calling for unity and militance to secure relief for the tenant farmer.

This emotion found positive expression in July, 1934, when two young Socialists from eastern Arkansas, Harry L. Mitchell and Clay East, organized the Southern Tenant Farmers' Union. The union, wrote Mitchell, was "born out of the suffering of the multitude of tenants who were evicted from their lands in consequence of the forty per cent acreage reduction in 1934." The union's objective, he stated, "was to oppose an extension of these trends, and to secure administrative and legal enforcement of the labor sections of the contracts." Almost immediately the union aroused determined opposition from plantation interests. There were mass evictions of union members; union meetings were broken up by landlords assisted by law enforcement officers; union members were flogged, shot, arrested, and jailed. Despite the campaign waged against it, union membership increased, to over 25,000 by 1936.

In 1935, H. L. Mitchell reviewed the union's first year for *The Nation*. We have disclosed, he wrote, "the complete failure of the 'New Deal' to benefit the men and women who do the work in the fields." The union, he charged, had exposed "the essential dishonesty of the labor sections of the cotton acreage-reduction contracts" and Washington's refusal "to combat abuses or construct any effective agency for enforcement."[34]

In 1936 the southern tenant farmers' plight had improved little if any. J. R. Butler, president of the union, repeated the charge: "The Roosevelt New Deal paid thousands of dollars in AAA benefits to the plantation owners for plowing under cotton, but not a cent went to the sharecroppers. Instead, many of us lost our one means of support."[35]

Socialists joined other critics in condemning the paradox that was the AAA—a program of killing pigs, plowing up cotton, and destroying agricultural products. Solving poverty in the midst of plenty by eliminating surpluses, by paying bonuses to farmers to plow up and plant less in a naked and hungry world was a crowning irony. The AAA, Thomas thought, was "the greatest satire that could be penned on the civilization that was alleged to make it necessary," because it attempted to "re-create artificially a scarcity which centuries of struggle had at last taught man to conquer." Like most of the New Deal, Thomas insisted, the AAA was the product of a "cruel and lunatic order of society." With this verdict even critics of a less radical persuasion could concur.[36]

VI

Although some people mistakenly identified Roosevelt as a Communist or a Socialist, they were usually people who could not have recognized a Communist or a Socialist had they met one in the street. Communists and Socialists never mistook Roosevelt for one of their own. In fact, Roosevelt was so unconvincing a liberal, his New Deal program for all its theatrics seemed so uninspired, that even liberals refused to claim him.

"All gods are dead," declared one of novelist Scott Fitzgerald's characters. And so it seemed in the fashionable disenchantment of the post-World War I decade. The collapse of values, the moral chaos, and the preoccupation with the marketplace all but annihilated liberal impulses; the voice of political protest was barely audible in the land. In those years, liberals had no one to listen to them, no place to go. In 1924, they followed La Follette without enthusiasm, without much hope. By 1928, urban liberals had enlisted under the banner of the New York Governor Alfred E. Smith, mistaking for liberalism his humanitarianism, his genuine concern for the underdog, and his forthright stand on Prohibition. Rural progressives, with their congenital fear of the Big City, decided to take a chance with Herbert Hoover. But Smith lost, and it was soon apparent that Hoover meant to change nothing. It took the Great Depression and recognition that Hoover had no adequate program to counteract it to revive these stilled voices, to put the liberals back in business.

The first consolidated left-wing movement of the thirties, the League for Independent Political Action, was organized in September, 1929, with a list of officers reading like a "Who's Who" of liberalism—John Dewey, Paul H. Douglas, Oswald Garrison Villard, Nathan Fine, Paul Blanshard, Harry N. Laidler, Reinhold Niebuhr, Stuart Chase, John Haynes Holmes, and W. E. B. DuBois.[37]

What these men espoused was vigorous, positive Progressivism; not the progressivism that depended on persuasion and education to root out favoritism and vested interest in government, not the Jeffersonian-type umpire state that feared big government, but rather the intellectual progressivism of the twenties, a progressivism anchored to a strong middle-class and national economic planning developed by such men as Dewey, Veblen, Lippmann, and Croly. For them, capitalism, he-man style, was doomed; but at the same time they insisted that a new society built on the proletariat, Marxist style, was a cruel hoax.

Toward the New Deal the LIPA adopted a "wait-and-see" attitude. Failure by the Democratic Party to pass adequate legislation, they warned, would force them to reconsider the question of political alignment, might in fact result in the formation of a third party, a new party dedicated to liberalism. It did not take the league long to decide the New Deal was failing. In September, 1933, after only six months of waiting and seeing, the League issued a call to farm and labor leaders to meet in Chicago. In a major address to the conference, Thomas Amlie, Wisconsin Progressive and former congressman, declared that Roosevelt had failed to propose the only measure which might have saved capitalism—a twenty-billion-dollar public works program. But even had Roosevelt proposed such a program, it would not have mattered. Capitalism, Amlie contended, was "not worth saving." Nor could it be reformed; between capitalism and socialism in some form, argued *The New Republic*, "there is no longer a feasible middle course."[38]

"Even as we go to press," the call to the conference had stated, "there are signs that a collapse may be right ahead. . . . *We are living on top of a volcano.*" The radicals' hope was that the American economic system could be totally revised from production-for-profit to production-for-use. Disintegration was just around the corner, leaders of the league feared; and the conference was called for the urgent purpose of setting up a third party that could be ready to step into the breach. "Unless we have an organization . . . ," Amlie said, "it is clear that a movement . . . will come from the right, and this is what we have come to know as 'fascism.' "[39]

Conceived in genuine fear, the Chicago conference adjourned in futility. The tangible result was not a new national party as planned but a sister organization to the LIPA, the Farmer-Labor Political Federation, which league leaders hoped would have broader appeal among farmers, laborers, and intellectuals.[40]

Both the LIPA and the FLPF excoriated the New Deal, Roosevelt's vacillation, and the inadequacies of his programs. In a series of forums sponsored by the FLPF such top-level leaders as A. F. Whitney, president of the Brotherhood of Railway Trainmen, and Milo Reno, head of the Farmers' Holiday Association, continued the assault upon the New Deal and urged formation of a genuinely liberal party before it was too late.

Alfred Bingham, co-editor with Selden Rodman of *Common Sense*, a new spokesman of liberalism (it was founded in December, 1932), in an "Open Letter to President Roosevelt," accused the President of "money juggling" instead of facing squarely the need for a sound system of money and credit. The letter indicted the New Deal for failing even to attempt enactment of an unemployment insurance or social security measure. Bingham commended the President for displaying some understanding that "the old days of laissez-faire capitalism were over," but, continued Bingham, Roosevelt's hopes for a controlled capitalism were headed for disaster. Already the result was "more monopoly than ever." The New Deal farm program, with its "billion dollars in bribes to farmers to pacify their resentment" and with its absurd and inhumane goal of cutting production while many were hungry "is not the way out," Bingham told the President.[41]

Bingham and Rodman spoke often and disparagingly of futile Rooseveltian "liberalism"—with liberalism always in quotation marks. The New Deal was "whirligig reform" concocted by a leader "more renowned for his artistic juggling than for robust resolution." The steady theme in *Common Sense* was that the New Deal, despite its apparent humanitarianism, was "a fraud and a sham." "When an egg is rotten," Bingham wrote, "painting it pretty colors won't improve it." Whatever else it may have been the New Deal was a hopeless attempt to make capitalism work. "And since it is impossible today to make capitalism work for long," wrote Bingham, "the New Deal is doomed to failure. With this in mind no intelligent or courageous radical can support Roosevelt." The native radicals rested their case on the grounds that Roosevelt had not gone far enough. And the longer he dallied the more certain was the inevitability of fascism.[42]

In September, 1934, *Common Sense* expressed its opinion of the New Deal even more directly: "Among radicals, liberals, embittered and disillusioned rank and file labor, desperate farmers," it declared, there is "full awareness of the devious role the President is playing." His formula, said the writer, recalling memories of an earlier Roosevelt, could be summed up in a few words—"Talk tough, tread softly." "Failure is a hard word," *Common Sense* editorialized. "Yet we believe the record indicates that nothing but failure can be expected from the New Deal."[43]

VII

FLPF did more than preach and editorialize. It played an influential role in organizing the Iowa Farmer-Labor Party, the South Dakota Farmer-Labor Economic Federation, and, more importantly, the Wisconsin Progressive Party.

Organized in 1934 around a core of Progressive Republicans led by Thomas Amlie, Philip La Follette, and Robert La Follette, Jr., the Wisconsin Progressive Party denounced the "cruelty and stupidity" of the nation's economic system and called for a "new order of security and plenty" for America. In 1934 the Progressives elected seven of Wisconsin's ten U.S. congressmen, including Thomas Amlie. Robert La Follette, Jr., was reelected United States senator, and Philip La Follette regained the governorship. As leadership of the party slipped from Amlie to the La Follettes it became perceptibly less critical of Roosevelt's program and even supported some of the more liberal features.[44]

At the same time it was achieving partial success in Wisconsin, the Farmer Labor Political Federation was attempting to influence the program of the Minnesota Farmer-Labor Party. By convincing party leaders that the Depression could be stopped only by bolder, more radical measures than the New Deal was willing to attempt, the FLPF hoped to turn the party's 1934 political platform into an uncompromising declaration of radical doctrine.

Minnesota's Governor Floyd Olson endorsed the plan; for Olson, who had learned his radicalism on the Seattle waterfront as a longshoreman member of the Industrial Workers of the World, "liberal" was too mild a term. "I am what I want to be—I am a radical," he declared, a radical who wants "a definite change in the system," who is fed up "with tinkering . . . with patching . . . with hanging a laurel wreath on burglars and thieves and pirates and calling them code authorities or something else." "You bet I'm radical," he is reported to have said to an interviewer; "you might say I'm radical as hell."[45]

In December, 1934, speaking to an FLPF conference held in St. Paul, Olson commended the federation for aiming at a "new deck," not just a new deal. To obtain this "new deck" the conference called upon the various state Farmer-Labor parties and federations and the Wisconsin Progressive Party to sponsor a call for a national third-party convention.

The conference call, sent out in June, 1935, over the signatures of five congressmen (Wisconsin Progressives Thomas Amlie and George Schneider, Progressive Republicans Vito Marcantonio of New York and Byron Scott of California, and Minnesota Farmer-Laborite Ernest Lundeen) invited participation in a conference to discuss the following principles:

1. That the old order is breaking down and must be replaced by an economic system which will substitute planning for chaos, service for profit, and abundance for poverty.

2. That the present national leadership of the old parties offers no hope to the people of the United States.

3. That united action of all the forces working for political and economic democracy is urgent in the present crisis.

4. That any action must be based upon a fundamental program striking at the roots of the profit system.

The delegates to the conference, meeting in Chicago on July 5 and 6, formed a new party for the 1936 elections, the American Commonwealth Political Federation.[46]

Hopes ran high early in 1936 that the American Commonwealth Political Federation might be the nucleus around which a genuinely liberal movement might rally to dislodge Roosevelt. "We must have a new national third party," wrote Governor Olson. "1936 Is The Time!" was the clarion call of *Common Sense* as late as April.[47]

The dream of a third party faded when the leaders of the ACPC took a long, hard look at Main Street. Should they, in the interests of what they regarded as a genuine liberalism, organize a third party which, if it got any substantial support, could only deliver the country to conservatives and reactionaries; or, as Olson put it, for the less fastidious, elect a "Fascist Republican?" The dilemma was so frustrating it made Rodman weep. But a choice had to be made, and a *Common Sense* poll of its people indicated that 50 per cent were going to vote for Roosevelt, 44 per cent for Norman Thomas, 4 per cent for Lemke, and the others scattered. Even Bingham, the conscience of the native radical movement and executive secretary of the American Commonwealth Federation, capitulated, announcing that he would give Roosevelt "a support limited only to the next few weeks, and withdrawn the day after Election Day." For all his blustering, Governor Olson confided to Harry Hopkins that he also planned to support Roosevelt in 1936.[48]

Most liberals agreed with Bingham and Olson and jumped on the Roosevelt bandwagon. Roosevelt could not be all bad, they told themselves, if big business and the American Liberty League opposed the President with such intensity. His apparent swing to the left and the Supreme Court attack on New Deal legislation brought progressives rallying to his support.

With wholesale desertions from third-party movements, the day after election found liberals even more disorganized than in 1932. But disorganization in 1936 was not so serious. Roosevelt was almost all Farmer-Labor groups and Commonwealth members could expect. The New Deal began to look very much like a third party—a coalition of independents, progressives, and labor unions—formed within the framework of the Democratic Party. Many progressives felt they could rely on Roosevelt to push their programs for a planned economy and that they could be more effective working inside the Democratic Party than in splinter movements. By 1938, *Common Sense* could declare it would not only support a third term for Roosevelt but would support any party he wished to lead.[49]

Not all progressives agreed. Third-party sentiment was still very much alive. Farmer-Labor and Progressive leaders had scored impressive victories in Minnesota where Farmer-Laborite Elmer Benson had won the governor's seat with a record-breaking plurality and in Wisconsin where Progressive Philip La Follette was reelected governor by polling almost 600,000 votes.

Common Sense reported that some progressives thought that these victories indicated a bright future for Farmer-Labor and Progressive movements. Governor La Follette predicted the establishment of a national organization as the next step toward a new third party. The American Labor Party, formed in 1936 in New York through the cooperation of Labor's Nonpartisan League and the Social Democratic Federation, predicted a national Farmer-Labor party by 1940.[50]

The ALP had made impressive showings in its first efforts at the polls: five of its members were elected to the New York City Council, and it had contributed almost half a million votes—the margin of victory—to Mayor Fiorello La Guardia's 1937 victory.

By mid-1937 the third-party idea began gaining ground. Changes in the New Deal seemed to indicate a swing back to the right. Economy measures which sharply reduced the number of public works employees and relief recipients disappointed many liberal supporters. Roosevelt's strong congressional opposition in 1937 and early 1938 which defeated or delayed many of his legislative proposals—executive and judicial reorganization, slum-clearance, crop control, and wages-and-hours—led many progressives to believe that he had lost control of Congress. The recession of 1937 and 1938 and Roosevelt's demand for increased armament expenditures added fuel to dissident fires.

In April, 1938, Philip La Follette called a convention to establish a new national progressive party. On April 28, La Follette's third party, the National Progressives of America, was launched. Despite Governor La Follette's declaration that "this is NOT a *third* party . . . [but] THE party of our time," liberals were not enthusiastic. *Common Sense* advised progressives to ignore this new party and to continue their support of the New Deal. The National Progressives went on the ballot in Iowa and California and were soundly trounced. To cap it off, La Follette was defeated in his bid for reelection as governor in November 1938. La Follette's defeat signalled the end of the National Progressives and of progressivism as a third-party threat.[51]

VIII

If third-party movements failed to enlist the unqualified support of progressives, they failed even more decisively to obtain the vote of labor. By 1936 the New Deal, through the Wagner Act and NRA, had given labor a shot in the arm. Labor recognized that perhaps for the first time it had a real friend in the White House, and it determined to keep him there. As one worker put it, "Mr. Roosevelt is the only man we ever had in the White House who would understand that my boss is a sonofabitch."[52]

Labor went all out for Roosevelt, and for the first time became a potent force in national politics. To mobilize the labor vote John L. Lewis, the bushy-browed boss of the United Mine Workers, Sidney Hillman, the astute president of the Amalgamated Clothing Workers, and George L. Berry, leader of the A. F. of L. Printing Pressmen, formed Labor's Non-partisan League in April, 1936, for the express purpose of reelecting Roosevelt. "Labor owes him a debt of gratitude," Lewis said, "that can be liquidated only by casting its solid vote for him at the coming election." "The defeat of the Roosevelt Administration," added Hillman, "means no labor legislation for decades to come."[53]

Though labor's Nonpartisan League built a nation-wide movement, with regional and even precinct organizations, its greatest contribution was money. Lewis contributed almost $500,000 to Roosevelt's campaign from the United Mine Workers' treasury. For this donation and for his influence in the consolidation of labor's support behind New Deal candidates, Lewis expected Roosevelt to treat him as his chief labor adviser. "Is anyone fool enough to believe for one minute," he asked later, "that we gave this money to Roosevelt because we were spellbound by his voice?"[54]

All this activity and financial support, however, did little to make Roosevelt more willing to listen to Lewis. For one thing the size of Roosevelt's landslide election made it clear that the Democrats would have won handily even without either the help from the League or Lewis' contribution. Moreover most of the New Deal's labor legislation had been enacted in Roosevelt's first term.

Bad blood between Roosevelt and Lewis ("Frankie and Johnny" as *The*

New Republic appropriately called them) began when the President failed to respond to labor's demands as Lewis thought he should. Lewis, taking credit for Roosevelt's labor vote, fully expected Roosevelt to repay labor for its political and financial support. In 1937 at the peak of a labor-management dispute in General Motors plants, Lewis demanded that the President support General Motors workers against the same "economic royalists" who had "contributed their money and used their energy to drive the administration out of power."[55]

Roosevelt, embarrassed and antagonized by Lewis' ill-advised statement on one hand and attacked by the press for giving labor preferential treatment on the other, replied "a plague o' both of your houses." Lewis, angered by the rejoinder, turned on Roosevelt like a woman scorned: "It ill behooves one who has supped at labor's table and who has been sheltered in labor's house to curse with equal fervor and fine impartiality both labor and its adversaries when they become locked in deadly embrace."[56]

Roosevelt was by no means the only Administration target at whom Lewis aimed verbal brickbats. In the first week of August, 1939, Lewis spoke at a House Labor Committee hearing on revision of the Wage-Hour Law. With ashtrays rattling as he struck the table with his fists, Lewis' organ-like voice swelled as he denounced the Vice-President, John N. "Cactus Jack" Garner:

The genesis of this campaign against labor in the House of Representatives is not hard to find. . . . It runs across to the Senate and emanates from a labor-baiting, poker-playing, whiskey-drinking, evil old man whose name is Garner. . . . I make a personal attack on Mr. Garner for what he is doing, because Garner's knife is searching for the quivering, pulsating heart of labor.

"And" he added somewhat superfluously, "I am against him."[57]

If this break between Lewis and the New Deal was not complete enough, a more dramatic one would come during Roosevelt's third presidential campaign. According to E. L. Dayton, in *Walter Reuther, The Autocrat of the Bargaining Table,* Lewis was summoned to the White House on the morning of October 17, two weeks before the 1940 election. During his conversation with Roosevelt, Lewis accused the President of having his telephones tapped by the FBI. "That's a damn lie," Roosevelt retorted. Lewis turned his back on the President and stalked from the room, saying "Nobody can call John Lewis a liar and least of all Franklin Delano Roosevelt."[58]

About a week later, Lewis would take to the radio to denounce Roosevelt and his bid for a third term. His rich rhetoric, which for so long had moved and persuaded his followers, betrayed his bitterness:

The present concentration of power in the office of the President has never before been equaled. The suggestion of a Third Term is less than wholesome or healthy. Personal craving for power, the overweening abnormal and selfish craving for power, is a thing to alarm and dismay. His motivation and objective is war. Are we to yield to a man who plays with the lives of human beings for a pastime?[59]

For all his blustering, however, Lewis as a powerful influence in politics was a failure. His effect on the votes of labor was as little felt as his influence on the President. Unlike Lewis, rank and file union members had interests outside their labor activities. Gallup polls indicated that in 1936 80 per cent of the union members and 85 per cent of Lewis' followers were Democrats who probably would have voted the New Deal ticket with or without Lewis. In 1940, after the labor difficulties and the economic recession of 1937 and 1938 and after Lewis' break with Roosevelt and his return to the Republican Party, 79 per cent of CIO members still stated that they were Democrats.[60]

Labor's criticism of the New Deal was always minor, for it was convinced that, however it might differ with the President on specifics, Roosevelt was the best friend labor had ever had in the White House. And, like Roosevelt, labor was wedded to the existing economic order and felt that any improvement would have to be made within the framework of capitalism.

IX

Maybe agrarian and labor liberals were committed to Roosevelt and the New Deal, but the real radicals of the country were not. Communists were not (though they paid it lip-service after 1935—expedience demanded it), Socialists were not (though Roosevelt cut deep into their membership), radicals were not (though Roosevelt captured 50 per cent of their votes in 1936 and killed their plans for an effective third party). To the Communists, Socialists, and other radical left-wingers, Roosevelt was on the wrong track. "The essential logic of the New Deal," wrote Max Lerner in 1936, was "increasingly the naked fist of the capitalist state." And when they were really being honest with themselves, radicals never doubted it. And they agreed just as strongly with Tom Amlie that capitalism was "not worth saving." It was the system itself that was at fault, and improvement would come only when the system was changed, really changed, not just adjusted, not just tampered with or patched up but really changed—changed from top to bottom.[61]

To proponents of either political extreme in the 1930's, left-wing radicalism or right-wing reaction, the question of national ideology resolved itself neatly into black or white, either-or. Either the system was to be socialism in some form, or it was to remain capitalism. And capitalism, at least to the political left, meant fascism; "if we maintain the capitalist system," wrote John Strachey, the British Marxist, "there is no other possibility."[62]

In general the political right also agreed there was no middle ground. But they feared the battle had already been lost; New Deal reformed capitalism was socialism, and socialism meant communism.

CHAPTER VI

A Traitor to His Class

Private fulminations and public carpings against the New Deal have become almost a routine of the business day. —Time, September 24, 1934

Regardless of party and regardless of region, today, with few exceptions, members of the so-called Upper Class frankly hate Franklin Roosevelt.
—Time, April 27, 1936

Never before in all history have these forces been so united against one candidate as they stand today. They are unanimous in their hatred for me— and I welcome their hatred. —Franklin D. Roosevelt, 1936

T HE Wirt affair in 1934 gave the nation its first bellylaugh of the New Deal. The spectacle of a scared old man pouring out a frightening tale of intrigue and subversion to a congressional committee was a rare absurdity in the early days of the New Deal. Though others would soon pick up the tattered ends of this tale of Red terror and embroider it with their own peculiar brand of nonsense, the first year of the New Deal witnessed a unanimity almost unparalleled in the history of American politics.

From the money baron on Wall Street to the haberdasher on Main Street, Roosevelt was the man of the hour, the nation's deliverer, who would rescue rich and poor alike. The editors of *Fortune* magazine wrote glowingly of how Roosevelt had proved it was "possible for a democratic government . . . to act more rapidly and decisively than either Hitler or Lenin was able to act in the moment of assuming power." In April, 1933, General Motors executive and former chairman of the Democratic National Committee, John J. Raskob, wrote Roosevelt: "Except in war time, few Presidents have accomplished as much in a whole term as you have in a single month." "Roosevelt is the greatest leader since Jesus Christ," a prominent businessman told John T. Flynn; "I hope God will forgive me for voting for Hoover." James W. Gerard, millionaire industrialist who was Wilson's ambassador to Germany, credited Roosevelt with saving the country. America, he said, was "on the brink of a precipice" in March, 1933, but Roosevelt's bold action was the turning point. "If we continue to stand behind President Roosevelt he will pull us through."[1]

But a year later, "standing behind Roosevelt" was a position in which businessmen and the well-to-do were rarely found. By the end of 1933 the wonderful euphoria of the spring was gone; by mid-1934 the honeymoon was over; in September, 1934, *Time* magazine could report that "private fulminations and public carpings against the New Deal have become almost a routine of the business day."[2]

The NRA which had given so much enthusiasm and momentum to the New Deal was slowing down; businessmen, the whole country for that matter, were beginning to listen somewhat more skeptically to the President's smiling optimism and Hugh Johnson's ballyhoo and tub-thumping. The Federal Reserve Board's Adjusted Index of Industrial Production which had risen from 59 in March, 1933, to 100 in July had, by November, slipped back to 72. The spirit of the National Industrial Recovery Act was being frustrated and its codes were being evaded both openly and in secret.[3]

But on the whole, business conditions by 1934 were much improved, and the economic outlook was brighter than it had been since 1929. Arthur Krock, writing in *The New York Times*, reported that over 14,300 banks had failed between 1930 and 1933, while only 179 closed in 1933 and 56 in 1934. In 1934, General Motors sales netted almost 50 per cent more than in 1933; Sears-Roebuck reported their best year since 1929; automobile production was 90 per cent above 1932. Federal Reserve Board figures comparing 1933 with 1934 showed industrial profits up 70 per cent, store sales up 13 per cent, wages up 25 per cent. By the end of 1934, savings deposits in the United States were up 3½ percent, according to the American Bankers Association, the first increase since 1930.[4]

As business conditions improved it seemed reasonable to expect that approval of Roosevelt within the business community would spread. Perhaps that approval would not be so uncritical as at the outset, perhaps it would be a little more restrained, a little less unqualified. But that Roosevelt would enjoy the confidence of most businessmen seemed beyond doubt.

That was not what happened. As fear of depression subsided, businessmen and wealthy property owners took a closer look at Roosevelt; and what they saw frightened them, made them indignant. Senator Tom Connally of Texas was describing their reaction more than he was explaining it when he told his Senate colleagues: "As soon as the businessman sees a slight improvement he keeps shouting 'the government must get out of business.' Businessmen do nothing but belly-ache."[5]

They thought they had good cause to bellyache. The Roosevelt whom they had at first hailed as their deliverer had become, they thought, a traitor to his class. He talked of a national recovery; but it was apparent they were not to get the kind of recovery they had expected, because Roosevelt did not define "recovery" as they did. He was not attempting a recovery of things as they had been in 1929; he actually wanted to change the old order.

It was an easy matter, after they had gotten their second wind, to forget there had been anything wrong with the country before 1933. The business community and the well-to-do had said little in 1933 when they had nothing to lose; but as soon as profits were restored and they once again had a status quo worth protecting, they resented all hint of change. In an atmosphere supercharged with changing attitudes and institutions they became very bitter indeed—bitter against the increasing militancy of organized labor, against expanding bureaucracy, against visionaries and absent-minded professors in government, in short against Roosevelt and the New Deal.

The psychology of business reaction to Roosevelt was (in a simile once used by Governor Philip La Follette of Wisconsin) like that of a drunk picked up from the gutter. Ever after, the drunk bears resentment toward the man who picked him up, because the good Samaritan had seen him in such a degrading position. Roosevelt had seen businessmen in the economic gutter, had picked them up, had set them on their feet. They resented having been saved; they burned with shame at having been so submissive to "that man in the White House," as they were now beginning to call him. Most of all they resented Roosevelt and the New Deal for refuting the notion that wisdom and making money were the same thing, for dissociating the concept of wealth from the concept of virtue, for toppling the divine right theory of the bank account, for exposing them as mere mortals.[6]

Part of the early indignation on the part of businessmen toward Roosevelt was therefore motivated by a desire to save face. It took the form of setting up straw men for the sake of knocking them flat. One active participant in this endeavor was ex-President Herbert Hoover. "The New Deal," said Hoover, "is a veritable fountain of fear." Yet less than a month later the New Deal "fountain of fear" was producing headlines such as the one in the Washington *Daily News*: BUSINESS APPROACHES PROSPERITY LEVELS OF 1929; REMARKABLE GAINS REPORTED IN FIRST QUARTER OF THIS YEAR. Nor did the headlines appearing in *The New York Times* support Hoover's melancholia: SAVINGS BANKS SEE THRIFT INCREASING; DEPOSITORS NUMBER ABOUT . . . 2,000,000 MORE THAN IN 1929; NATION TESTIFIES TO TRADE REVIVAL; STOCK PRICES ROSE BY A THIRD IN 1935.

In 1935, the *Times* reported a slashing attack on Administration policies by Alfred P. Sloan: SLOAN IN ATTACK ON NEW DEAL, SAYS IT RETARDS REVIVAL; GENERAL MOTORS HEAD ASSAILS EXPERIMENTS IN ECONOMICS. The ink was barely dry on the Sloan story before new headlines appeared: 7-YEAR RECORD SET BY GENERAL MOTORS; FIRST QUARTER'S NET PROFIT . . . HIGHEST FOR PERIOD SINCE 1929. In March, 1936, Henry P. Fletcher, chairman of the Republican National Committee, was sounding like the chairman of the opposition party when he declared in a press statement, "To date the Roosevelt administration has merely deepened the depression." The same month the New York Stock Exchange reported the total market value of listed stocks was up better than 250 per cent since March, 1933.[7]

II

By 1934, the reaction of embarrassment coupled with a genuine concern regarding trends in the New Deal produced in the business community a coalition of discontent that was truly formidable.

The earliest, the most readily discernible danger in the New Deal was abandonment of traditional American economic policies. The lament over economic changes consisted of several elegiac movements: the government was violating natural law by fixing prices and ignoring the law of supply and demand; the government was interfering with private enterprise; the government was depriving business management of its discretionary authority; the government was declaring itself anti-business by branding the profit motive anti-social, thereby undermining business confidence and initiative. The government's next step, the final, inexorable step, would be socialization of all property.[8]

The experimental nature of some New Deal recovery measures evoked widespread mutterings about the "rather heavy strain of Alice in Wonderland economics." "I think the New Deal," wrote Glenn Frank, former president of the University of Wisconsin, "despite its protestations to the contrary, is playing fast and loose with the values of private initiative, permitting the sins of its practitioners to obscure the productive virtues of the principle itself." Virgil Jordan, president of the National Industrial Conference Board, agreed with Frank. The capriciousness of New Deal policies ("crippling of individual initiative and enterprise through the control of bureaucratic agencies") would, over the long haul, lower production, restrict opportunities for employment and reduce the standard of living.[9]

Businessmen likewise feared the New Deal had placed the reins of government in the inexperienced hands of a group of "third rate college professors," a "coterie of visionaries," who were attempting to turn the country into a laboratory for economic experiments "that bid fair to result in an explosion and a stink." "Business is the Administration's guinea pig," complained Colby M. Chester of General Foods to the Sales Executive Club of New York. "American business is chloroformed with fear and then experimented upon by gleeful theorists who developed their economic and merchandising dreams behind ivy-covered college walls, but do not know if they'll work because no one had attempted to find out. . . ."[10]

Before a meeting of the American Iron and Steel Institute, Senator Millard E. Tydings of Maryland likewise attacked the economic policies of the New Deal, the "reckless government spending," the "excessive taxation and efforts to destroy business." "The men who advocate spending one's self out of debt," he declared, "are the ones who advocate drinking one's self sober. . . ."[11]

Businessmen warned that one certain, one inevitable result of such policies was destruction of business confidence. "Where political uncertainty is the rule," declared Merle Thorpe, editor of *Nation's Business*, "businessmen cannot make long term contracts; they cannot plan ahead; they cannot expand." "Uncertainty of the Administration's next move," wrote John E. Dowsing, author of *The New Deal—Shadow or Substance*, "what new experiments will be resorted to, what noxious nostrums some of the quack doctors will prescribe and cockeyed statutes force down the patients' throats, breed distrust."[12]

III

Arthur M. Hyde was Secretary of Agriculture in the Hoover Cabinet. When the going was tough and all the news was bad, Hyde never lost faith in his chief. When, in 1934, he told a Lincoln Day dinner audience in New York that only Hoover had recognized the dangers in the philosophy of the New Deal he meant it. Only Hoover, he said, "had stood upon the lookout tower of the nation . . . and warned." Hyde was asserting much more than he could prove. But it was true, in a way. Hoover had, like a modern Paul Revere, shouted to an inattentive and disinterested citizenry that the Communists were coming. In his book, *The Challenge to Liberty*, Hoover described the New Deal as "the most stupendous invasion of the whole spirit of Liberty that the nation has witnessed since the days of Colonial America."[13]

Hoover was not, as Hyde claimed, alone in spreading the alarm. But he was among the first of a long list of conservative New Deal critics to sound the tocsin in print. Despite jokes about the literary fecundity of New Dealers, it was representatives of business, industry and their allies, people like James P. Warburg, Ogden L. Mills, Isaac Lippincott, Ralph West Robey, Raoul Desvernine, who, as part of their propaganda campaign against Roosevelt, led the political book parade. They spent a king's ransom trying to beat Roosevelt with the printed page.

James P. Warburg, banker and a Roosevelt economic adviser until November, 1933, published *The Money Muddle* within a year of his break with the New Deal over monetary policies, the first of a trilogy of anti-New Deal books in which he deplored Roosevelt's dalliance with policies such as the commodity dollar and securities regulation. In 1935, his *Hell Bent for Election* continued the attack on Roosevelt's handling of the money question. Roosevelt, Warburg reported, seemed alternately bored and fascinated by discussions of monetary policy. "You were up against a compulsive drive to do something in this area," Warburg wrote, his dismay still evident in his words, "without ever being able to pin the man down so that he would really think about it—a very odd experience." In 1936, Warburg returned to the attack with a sequel, *Still Hell Bent*, a hastily conceived campaign document in which the principal preoccupation was with defeating Roosevelt for reelection. In it Warburg struck out wildly in many directions, at the "orgy of wild spending," at making "a laughing stock of the sanctity of our national promises," at "leading this nation upon the heels of Russia, Germany, Austria and Italy . . . toward dictatorship."[14]

In 1934 Ralph Robey, member of the banking faculty of Columbia University and journalist who wrote for the New York *Post* and Washington *Post*, published *Roosevelt vs. Recovery*. His was an oversimplified thesis: Roosevelt had, by unbridled spending, led the nation to a point where more and more money would have to be poured into public works lest the entire jerry-built New Deal economic structure topple. His remedy was equally oversimplified: Scrap the New Deal, stop spending, pay homage to that sacred cow, the balanced budget, return to the policies of Hoover—deflation and budget-balancing to the bitter end—return to methods pursued by American business and finance since the days of Harding.[15]

Among the more lucid statements of the conservative businessman's position was that contained in the three books by Ogden Livingston Mills—*What of Tomorrow?*, *Liberalism Fights On*, and *The Seventeen Millions*—all published between 1935 and 1937. Mills, Hoover's Secretary of the Treasury, developed two major themes. The one was a refutation of the New Deal by explaining what should have been done during the Depression crisis. The other was the redefining of the conservative political philosophy for the seventeen million voters who, in 1936, "recorded their opposition to the direction (i.e., collectivism) in which the United States is traveling."[16]

Reduced to simplest terms his argument was for individualism as opposed to collectivism, for maximum freedom from governmental control as opposed to the doctrine of state capitalism. The New Deal ("a mixture of idealistic aims, false economics, impractical experiments and revolutionary dogma dressed up in the language of social reform") was therefore wholly inconsistent with "the principles underlying our American civilization"; it was the American version of what Mills called "the New

Movement"; by which he meant the all-pervasive state "exemplified in Europe by the Nazi Government in Germany, the Fascist Government of Italy, and the Communist Government of Russia."[17]

Howard E. Kershner's *The Menace of Roosevelt and His Policies,* though judiciously crediting Roosevelt with "the highest motives and the greatest devotion," slashed at the President's "destructive and vicious" policies. William MacDonald in *The Menace of Recovery* considered the economic program of the New Deal disastrous. In the pursuit of economic recovery "the Administration has become a dictatorship, the public debt has been swollen to unprecedented peace-time proportions, the gold standard has been abandoned, and the dollar has been left to find its own level in the shifting sands of commodity prices." "There is no dictionary," he insisted, "that defines 'recovery' in such terms."[18]

IV

The presidential election year, 1936, produced a bumper crop of anti-New Deal books which *The New York Times* classified into four types: the "Deadly-Earnest, America-at-the-Crossroads, Leveled-Finger"; the "Jocose, Quasi-Literary"; the "Baffling, Mystical"; and the "Catechismal, Semi-Irrelevant."[19]

Books in the first category, usually written by a professor of economics or a literate lawyer, customarily opened with a claim of nonpartisanship, then moved quickly to "the fundamental issue" amid much somber prose about how the country was confronted with the most critical days since 1776. Included in this type were Isaac Lippincott's *Sold Out* and Raoul Desvernine's *Democratic Despotism.* For Lippincott the fundamental issue was not one of economics but of morals: "The morality of the Fathers has gone into discard, and thereby hangs the story of our woes." The New Deal, he insisted, "smacks of Marxian socialism." Raoul Desvernine, attorney and president of Crucible Steel Company, accused the New Deal of being a New Despotism. Nothing remained to the New Deal, he wrote, but to "destroy the 'two-party' system in order to attain the perfection of the New Despotisms," meaning the new regimes in Italy, Germany, and Russia. "The merry makers at our banquet," he wrote, "have whiffed the aroma of Marxian champagne. They are giddy, and the spirit of Marx hovers over them."

Desvernine's book was one of the more serious efforts to link the New Deal with the programs of the "new despots"; but it strained the credulity of even the most ultra-conservative by suggesting there was ominous significance in the seeming addiction of New Dealers and European dictators to the number three. Stalin, Desvernine pointed out, had his Third International, Hitler his Third Reich, Mussolini his tripartite corporate system. Among New Dealers, Rexford Tugwell spoke of a Third Economy and Henry Wallace advocated an emblem of three spheres in a circle as the symbol of the New Deal. Adapting what he called "an historic utterance," Desvernine concluded his attack with the question (in bold-face type): "Delano, Quo Vadis?"[20]

Another of the crisis, America-at-the-crossroads variety was a mean little volume by Colonel Frank Knox, Chicago newspaper publisher and Republican candidate for Vice-President in 1936. In *We Planned It That Way* Colonel Knox accused Roosevelt of attempting to "slip over legislation depriving the people of . . . their rights." The purpose of this "rape of democracy," he declared, was "to arouse suspicion against the business men . . . ; to destroy confidence in business management . . . ; and by search and seizure and demagogic appeal, to arouse labor against capital." To carry out his attack against democracy, Roosevelt had set up a New Deal propaganda machine, Knox charged, which was "the equal, if not the superior, of the machines set up to praise Stalin, Hitler, and Mussolini."[21]

Howard Wolf's *Greener Pastures* (dedicated to Marc Connelly, Roark Bradford, and the Forgotten Man) was an example of the jocose, quasi-literary variety. It took nineteen scenes to introduce such characters as The Lord Chief Executive, General Jim, Moley the Brain, Eleanor, Angel Astor, and Pharaoh Morgan. "In the beginning," chanted the Professor in *Greener Pastures*, "Franklin created the AAA and the NRA. And the NRA was without form, and void; and the Astor yacht was upon the face of the deep."[22]

Another of this type was a small volume that appeared in 1934, entitled *Frankie in Wonderland*. Although this parody on *Alice in Wonderland* was written by an anonymous author who signed himself "A Tory," it was published by the well-known firm of E. P. Dutton and was dedicated by the author to "The American Eagle, that noble bird before it was painted blue and turned into a Soviet Duck . . ." with "apologies to Lewis Carroll, the originator and pre-historian of the New Deal." Sample verses lumped heterogeneously and somewhat incongruously together Justice Brandeis, Henry Wallace, Harold Ickes, Frances Perkins, Donald Richberg and Felix Frankfurter:

> 'Twas brandeis and the brainy coves
> Did slyly wallace in the wave,
> All ickes were the laborgoves
> And the perkins outgave.
>   One, Two! One, Two! And through & through
>   The richberg blade went snicker-snack!
>   He left it dead and with its head
>   He came frankfurting back.[23]

The baffling, mystical variety, usually privately printed in limited editions, were not always easy to come by. Typical was the anonymous *Re-*

Birth of the Nation; or, What's to Become of Us, a confused and confusing little volume which asserted that national leaders in horse-and-buggy days were smart enough "to lay the foundations of a national economic system workable within the limitations of the Constitution of the United States, without the assistance of Carl [sic] Marx." It denounced the New Deal for violating the Constitution which was founded "on the unwritten Supreme law of the constitutional government of all creation, called Nature, as well as upon the written laws of Revealed Truth, which Supreme laws are the immutable decrees of the Omnipotent Creator of the Universe."[24]

An example of the catechismal semi-irrelevant variety, was Russell Moore's *Roosevelt Riddles.* According to the dustjacket the book contained 383 "embarrassing questions and answers," although from the questions and answers it was difficult to guess who was supposed to be embarrassed: "Q.—To whom did G. W. Dyer of Vanderbilt University refer as the 'Little Dictator'? A.—Henry A. Wallace, Secretary of Agriculture." "Q.—What wages are paid unskilled labor in China and Japan? A.—15 cents and 35 cents per day." "Q.—How much is the federal tax on a package of cigarettes? A.—Specific tax, 6 cents; indirect tax, 1 cent. This more than doubles the cost." "Q.—May more than one person in a family work for the WPA? A.—Three members of the family of Joseph Crozier, Philadelphia, were receiving a total of $260 a month." "Q.—How far is up? A.—Who wants to know?"[25]

Almost as inane was another of the question-and-answer books, John C. Bell's *What Do You Know About the New Deal?*: "Q.—What well-known writer expressed the general feeling when he said that the theory that a body of people who are too poor to buy food and clothing at low prices will find it easier to buy them at much higher prices is beyond the ordinary understanding? A.—Westbrook Pegler." "Q.—Of whom is it said 'He found want in the midst of plenty and destroyed the plenty'? A.—President Roosevelt."[26]

To many authors of anti-New Deal books there was little doubt the philosophy of the Roosevelt Administration stemmed from other than American ideals. And, although there was no unanimous agreement concerning the origin of such an un-American philosophy, the consensus was that it was socialistic, that it violated not only American ideals but the Constitution as well.

In 1935 David Lawrence, editor of *United States News,* produced *Stumbling into Socialism,* in which he combined an anti-Roosevelt attack with a call for formation of a new Constitutional Party. In a tangle of loose assertions and confused definitions, Lawrence had but one thesis: "The main issue which supersedes all others is whether we shall change our form of government."[27]

A similar theme ran through other anti-New Deal books like Earl Reeve's *The Truth About the New Deal,* published in time for the 1936 campaign ("The present administration now stands four square upon thirty planks of the Socialist Party platform of 1932 . . . continuing expansion of government competition with private enterprise portends further governmental displacement of private business . . . no such Communistic policy has ever been authorized by the American people. . . . New Deal leaders have adventured into Socialism without Authority"); Clayton Rand's campaign contribution, ABRACADABRA (". . . the 'New Steal' was in reality an act of piracy—snitching the Socialist Party's platform complete"); and Fools Gold by Fred R. Marvin, who signed himself the "Senator from Alaska" ("The philosophy [of the New Deal] . . . is unAmerican, unethical, anti-religious and economically unsound. . . . It is best known today as socialism and communism."). Occasionally the message was delivered with a spark of genuine humor as when George Harrington, in his Horse and Buggy Days Are Here Again, declared, "Marx inspires this administration—whether Karl or Harpo requires an explanation."[28]

<h1 style="text-align:center">V</h1>

At every opportunity important and responsible members of the business community were saying these same things, and more. What was being said of Roosevelt in books was being repeated by businessmen and their allies in speeches, in statements for the press and magazines, in public letters, in stockholders' meetings, from every form of public forum—grim-faced, deadly serious accusations of corruption and subversion in high places. Many New Deal critics, having demonstrated (to themselves at least) that Wirt's charges were true, that the Roosevelt Administration was a monstrous usurpation of democracy and an offense against good taste, common decency, and American ideals, turned their attention to discovering the cause of the malignancy, outlining its prognosis, and recommending a cure. The cause was easy to find; the prognosis clearly evident; but the cure—as was to be driven home particularly hard in 1936—was entirely a different matter.

The cause, as any observant right-winger was quick to tell you, was that government had been turned over—lock, stock, and barrel—into the hands of "third-rate college professors and unsuccessful welfare workers . . . Humanists . . . Liberals . . . Socialists . . . Internationalists . . . Communists." Businessmen took comfort in quoting the Saturday Evening Post's solemn declaration that if Brain Trusters were competent to plan and run the business of the country "then practical experience and training in industry have lost their meaning." They repeated Hugh Johnson's description of the takeover of the government by the Brain Trust as if it were a campfire ghost story: "Shortly after the election there began to occur one of the cleverest infiltrations in the history of our Government. There was no noise about it. The professor [Frankfurter] himself has refused every official connection. His comings and goings are almost surreptitious. Yet he is the *most influential single individual in the United States*. His 'boys' have been insinuated into obscure but key positions in every vital department—wardens of the marches, inconspicuous but powerful." And they chuckled time and again at Arthur Hyde's clever thrust at the Brain Trust in a speech at the Lincoln Day dinner in New York in 1934. "Let us be thankful," Hyde said, "that Rasputin is dead and that Svengali never lived."[29]

Not all would have agreed with Hyde that Rasputin was dead; his sinister spirit was very much alive, they believed, in Felix Frankfurter, in Rexford Tugwell and company. Many agreed with George Moses, Republican senator from New Hampshire, that the country "is going to hell in a hack," and "cannot continue to exist half Roosevelt and half Frankfurter." Even God's assistance against those "impractical and claptrap theorists" was solicited: "Save us," prayed Cardinal Dougherty at a Columbus Day observance in 1934, "from the theorists who change our fundamental laws. Save us from the anarchists who undermine our form of government." All of which elicited from Donald Richberg, counsel to the NRA and later its chairman, a wistful thought: "When any man ventures to scoff at the use of brains in government he should be asked to explain by what part of the anatomy he believes human affairs should be conducted."[30]

College professors, these "Utopian minnesingers," these "visionaries and dreamers," this "esoteric profession of crystal gazing," was only one part of what was wrong with the New Deal. According to the economist Roger Babson, another serious danger in the New Deal (the "New Dilemma," Babson called it) was the development of bureaucratic "capitolism." Bureaucracy and the concentration of power in Washington, said Babson, was the other face of a Janus-like administration. As early as October, 1933, Alfred E. Smith, who was already drifting into the open arms of the General Motors-DuPont-Sun Oil Company people, denounced the Administration as "bureaucratic." By 1936, when he was the star performer of the American Liberty League, Smith was still singing the same refrain. The New Deal, he said, was "government by bureaucracy instead of what we have been taught to look to: government by law." According to Virgil Jordan, American business was faced with nothing less than a "centralized bureaucratic dictation of industrial management." Herbert Hoover proclaimed loudly and often that the New Deal was "regimentation of people directly into a bureaucracy." And the President's distant cousin, Colonel Theodore Roosevelt, Jr., son of a former President, insisted the New Deal was simply an attempt to make the American people "submissive to the dictates of . . . a single individual at the head of a vast bureaucracy." The colonel was getting close to what would become the most serious charge leveled at the Administration by a large majority of the business elite.[31]

Having discovered that the cause of this American malignancy, the New Deal, was the twin tumors of addlepated academicians and burgeoning bureaucracy, right-wing partisans set about to prognose the course of the disease. Perhaps its most serious complication, they decided, was that it would lead to the establishment of a vindictive personal government. Brain Trusters could make veins stand out on the foreheads of businessmen. Bureaucrats could harass and frustrate businessmen. But the real threat was dictatorship. Roosevelt was a dictator. After several false starts and some early confusion as to what kind (some thought him a Fascist), the threat became perfectly clear. Roosevelt was a Socialist (maybe even Communist) dictator.

The New Deal had become a "maelstrom of centralized order-giving," according to David Lawrence, editor of *United States News*, which "more strongly resembles the dictatorship of the Fascistic and Communistic states of Europe than it does the American system." Business was fast approaching "the gravest danger," warned Virgil Jordan, that ever confronted the country, the "danger of destruction . . . by political dictatorship." After a trip to the United States in 1936, Carl Jung, the eminent Austrian psychologist, told reporters: "I have just come from America where I saw Roosevelt. Make no mistake, he has the most amazing power complex, the Mussolini substance, the stuff of a dictator absolutely."[32]

"By means of taxation and spending, by indefinite extension of bureaucracy, and by political control of the courts . . . ," declared the *National Republic*, "a Socialistic-Communistic state has the machinery . . . to perpetuate its own political power." "Those responsible for the so-called New Deal," the *National Republic* charged, "are engaged in an effort to substitute an alien system the ultimate and inevitable purpose of which must be to destroy the Republic." Recovery is only partially the aim of the New Deal, Bainbridge Colby told the New York Economics Club in 1934; "a great part of its interest has been in radical institutional overthrow . . . of the State." In 1935, Colby told the Bureau of Advertising of the American Newspaper Publishers Association, that Roosevelt had, in less than two years, converted the republic into something "too closely approaching a Socialist State. . . ." At this point he paused and asked the audience if he spoke "too strongly." His listeners responded with a roar, "NO!" Roosevelt, Colby declared in 1936, had gone "hook, line, and sinker to the Communists and Socialists by whom he is surrounded" and was well on his way toward setting up all over the land "a collectivist tyranny patterned upon the degraded Soviet Regime which prevails in Washington."[33]

The New Deal, asserted Merle Thorpe, whose articles appeared regularly in the best business publications, "is headed down the same road as Communism." The country, he said, "was concerned about Communist agitators with whiskers and bombs but was in reality accepting their program under the brand of a new order guaranteed on the label to save democracy." "We have," Thorpe wrote, "given legislative status, either in whole or in part, to eight of the ten points of the *Communist Manifesto* of 1848." Even such a moderate conservative as Lewis Douglas, Director of the Budget until September, 1934, was convinced that the New Deal was headed toward communism. "The present pseudo-planned economy," he declared, "leads relentlessly into the complete autocracy and tyranny of the Collective State."[34]

Although many critics expressed the general fear that the New Deal was becoming a Communist tyranny through socialistic legislation and increasing control of business, only a few entertained the more specific fear of armed revolution. These few believed—or said they believed—the Administration planned to use the unemployed or the veterans or the CCC or any one of a number of such groups as the core around which to organize an armed revolutionary force to take over the government. "To the embittered army of the unemployed," wrote a member of the National Committee to Uphold Constitutional Government, "the New Dealers would look for the shock troops of the revolution." He did not bother, of course, to explain why it was necessary for Roosevelt to use such tactics if he were indeed a dictator as they charged.[35]

In April, 1935, after returning from a transcontinental trip, Roger Babson had a lot on his mind when he spoke before the New York Babson Institute Alumni Association. "The C.C.C. camps," he reported, "are becoming hotbeds of radicalism." If the men are not absorbed quickly into industry "they will become a revolutionary army."[36]

Even some members of Roosevelt's cabinet had opposed establishment of the Civilian Conservation Corps, fearing it might be dangerous to assemble large numbers of unemployed and resentful men in the woods. An unfortunate choice of phrasing by Harry H. Woodring, Assistant Secretary of War, seemed to add credence to the fear. The CCC, he had once stated, "should be expanded and put under the control of the Army," adding that the Army was prepared to organize the CCC, World War veterans, and people on relief into a system of "economic storm troopers." To make matters worse, a major general, in an article in a CCC bulletin, had argued in favor of making the CCC a combination conscript army and economic army (like Hitler's labor conscripts), and making it compulsory to all youths eighteen years old and over.[37]

Within a year after Roosevelt took office, spokesmen for business saw socialism in every reform measure, however mild, labeled as Socialist every New Deal liberal, however timid. TVA, PWA, CCC, social security, unemployment relief were branded as giant strides toward the collectivist state. Even the mild tax bill, introduced in the summer of 1935, was described in the monthly bank letter of the National City Bank as "based upon the principles of Karl Marx and the *Communist Manifesto*."[38]

VI

After describing the cause and symptoms of the New Deal disease and prognosticating the course of its deterioration, businessmen set out to prescribe a cure. For the most part recommended remedies were so innocuous they did not call even for the establishment of new organizations.

Criticism of Roosevelt and the New Deal, businessmen decided, should not consist merely of isolated shots in the dark, of random, unrelated guerrilla attacks by prominent people. Businessmen, for all their alleged political obtuseness, were too bright for that. It was inevitable that they would soon bring into play the powerful machinery at their disposal with which they had customarily pressured government and administrations in the past.

The signal that it was time to begin playing rough may have come from Edward F. Hutton, chairman of the board of General Foods. In 1935, in *The Public Utilities Fortnightly*, Hutton suggested that the only way to combat "the plans so carefully drafted by the radical Socialists" was to "gang up." By "gang up," he explained later, he meant only "get together." From 1934 and after, businessmen did a lot of "getting together" to discuss the New Deal menace.[39]

In 1933, with the special session of Congress still drafting the first steps of Roosevelt's recovery plan, the twenty-first annual meeting of the United States Chamber of Commerce had assembled only a stone's throw from the White House. In keeping with the seriousness of the national crisis, there was more than the usual amount of resolving that goes on at those normally dull affairs. In general the Chamber urged renewed confidence in "the permissive right of self-regulation" for business; but, in a shortlived spirit of cooperation, it swallowed the New Deal NRA and AAA pills and praised the medicine.[40]

By 1934 the Chamber was beginning to gag on the stronger doses of direct relief, the Security Act, the National Emergency Council, and the Federal Works programs. Silas Strawn, Chicago lawyer and former president of the Chamber, thought the time had come for an official announcement that the emergency was over and for a budget-balancing reduction in government spending. In rebuttal President Roosevelt sent a message chiding the Chamber for its testy attitude. "It is time," he said, "to stop crying 'wolf' and to cooperate in working for recovery. . . . I confidently count on the loyalty and continued support of the Chamber of Commerce of the United States." If the President really expected continued support from the Chamber it was a false hope. By the time of the next annual meeting the Chamber was red in the face and choking on what it considered a surfeit of New Deal nostrums.[41]

On April 28, 1935, just thirty-six hours before the Chamber convened, President Roosevelt offered the nation a blanket invitation in his fireside chat. "Feel free to criticize," he had said. The Chamber took him at his word. Again Silas Strawn, counsel for the National Association of Manufacturers, showed the way: "We have floundered along for two years. . . . We have a right to know where we are going." For three days, in round table conferences, in committee meetings, at plenary sessions, in luncheon speeches, the Administration caught it from all sides. And the Chamber was just getting warmed up.

On the fourth day at the closing session the Chamber approved overwhelmingly a series of anti-New Deal resolutions: social security legislation ("doubt the propriety as well as constitutionality"); NRA ("must be allowed to expire in June"); Public Utilities Holding Company Act ("would mean violation of fundamental principles"); Banking Act ("would amount to little short of political dictatorship"); Wagner Act ("encroachment on right of contract"); AAA ("would inevitably react to the disadvantage of the country").[42]

In September, 1935, the directors polled the fifteen hundred member organizations asking their opinions on the trend of New Deal legislation. Judicious wording of the questions left little doubt what answers were wanted and expected; it was hardly surprising that the results of the poll ran 35 to 1 against the Administration's policies. As if to emphasize their outrage at Roosevelt's policies, a two-page leaflet published by the New York Chamber was widely circulated, deploring the "billions of dollars of the people's money" which Congress had entrusted to "the political accident in the White House" for him "to juggle with as suits his whims." And they warmly applauded Alfred P. Sloan when he told the Michigan Chamber of Commerce, "We are not going to tolerate further interference in recovery. . . . [We] must liquidate the panaceas and discard quack theories."[43]

By 1936 Chamber opposition to the New Deal had set as hard as concrete. The most admirable achievement at the annual conventions during the remaining years of the 1930's was the ingenuity displayed by speakers in discovering new ways of repeating the same things. The theme of each succeeding convention was virtually a repetition of the preceding one, a theme that covered all New Deal sins under one blanket indictment: "Too long have we remained silent while demagogs attack unfairly the integrity of our business institutions. . . . Too long have we introduced carelessly into the stream of our national life alien philosophies of government control and foreign ideas of repression of the individual that have no place in this land of freedom."[44]

Other national business organizations, in their meetings, their resolutions, their speeches and publications, assumed virtually the same stance against the New Deal taken by the Chamber. The New Deal, declared the American Management Association in 1934, consists of a "planless mess" of "punitive legislation" and a "new crop of radical inflationary proposals." There was much nodding in agreement at the meeting of the Congress of American Industry in 1934, when Virgil Jordan charged that "government is in the hands of an organized mob"; that gestures in the direction of national economic planning were "only a new name for State capitalism under central dictatorship."[45]

Clinton L. Bardo, president of the National Association of Manufacturers, had fighting words for the association at its annual meeting in 1935. Industry was "now in politics," he said menacingly, "to rid the United States of the New Deal." There was no other choice, he insisted; it was either take this position "or be destroyed . . . by a deliberate and well-timed rapid-fire and devastating attack by economic crack-pots, social reformers, labor demagogues and political racketeers." The National Industrial Council, meeting jointly with the National Association of Manufacturers, ridiculed Roosevelt, demanding an uncompromising repeal of that "obstacle to recovery," the New Deal. The country, said Council spokesmen, must turn away from this "alien importation," this "oriental philosophy," from treacherous "invisible government" and return to the "American System." Business must step up its attack on the New Deal, which had, in the words of the New York National City Bank, made a "declaration of war upon so-called capitalism."[46]

If Roosevelt were declaring war on capitalism, as they now believed, businessmen and their allies should stop writing and talking a good fight. They should declare a war of their own. Not a defensive war, not a mere holding action. But a holy crusade to rid the land of the enemy, the New Deal.

And they did. In a superficial spirit of getting together in common cause, business organizations flourished. But as memberships and budgets increased there was no corresponding increase in the ability of the organizations to influence New Deal legislation or policies. Criticism from organizations in which businessmen spoke only to businessmen was largely ineffectual. This impotence was, in part, the result of the diversity of interests among members. Big business criticized the Chamber of Commerce for representing only small commercial enterprises, and small business criticized the National Association of Manufacturers for representing only big industry. Only in their hatred of Roosevelt was business united, and even here business solidarity was largely an illusion. Only in answer to the broadest questions about New Deal policy was there unanimity. More often than not the legislative interests of one company or of one industry were in direct conflict with those of several others.

Not only were there occasional conflicts and competition among business organizations, but within any one organization there were likely to be differences of opinion concerning what position to take on New Deal policies. The Chamber of Commerce's seemingly violent anti-New Deal position was tempered by the views of some of its more powerful members. In 1936, for example, Chamber President Harper Sibley disagreed with the vehemence of the Chamber's position, and urged a more conciliatory approach: "If the American people have given ear to false prophecies, they are not to be herded back to the right path by denunciation and abuse. . . . It is a task for both business management and political management." Eastman Kodak treasurer Marion B. Folsom argued against the Chamber resolution on the Social Security Act, urging business cooperation to improve the act. "Employers must realize that the country is facing an old age and an unemployment problem," Folsom said, "and that legislation to meet these problems is inevitable." In 1935 a member organization of the Chamber of Commerce, the National Association of Textiles, rebelled, stating that the Chamber was being used "as a catspaw" by a small but aggressive minority "with selfish political and business interests who seek to accomplish through the Chamber purposes which they cannot attain alone."[47]

In May, 1935, the Business Advisory Board of the Department of Commerce issued a report which took much of the sting from Chamber of Commerce criticism of the New Deal. Members of the board—including Henry Harriman, the outgoing president of the Chamber of Commerce; Gerard Swope of General Electric; and Winthrop Aldrich of New York's Chase National Bank—disapproved the Chamber's platform, approved at least in general terms the Social Security Act, and recommended a two-year extension of the NRA. "Certain of our members," said the Advisory Board report, "are also members of the United States Chamber of Commerce, but we are not spokesmen of the Chamber or of any other organization. We are here to uphold [the President's] hand in the fight against the depression."[48]

For the first two years of the New Deal, businessmen had tried to follow Edward Hutton's advice to "get together," with little to show for their efforts. Despite the obvious fact that recovery was by no means a *fait accompli*, business criticism was having little, if any, effect on the course of the New Deal. The ineffectiveness of criticism by businessmen and their organizations was in part because of dissension and conflicting interests. They spent too much time contradicting each other. More important was the fact that business organizations did not represent all segments of conservative opposition to the New Deal. What was needed was some kind of organization with a broader base, an organization which could bridge the gap between economics and politics yet maintain a posture of bi-partisanship. In August, 1934, when Jouett Shouse, former executive chairman

of the Democratic National Committee, held a press conference to announce formation of the American Liberty League, a new organization "to
defend and uphold the Constitution," businessmen were certain they had
found what they were looking for.[49]

VII

The American Liberty League, Shouse assured the press, was "not
inimical to the national administration," was "definitely not anti-Roosevelt," "would not actually participate in elections," and, he added
solemnly, the League was "a non-partisan organization."

It was nonpartisan, structurally at least. To provide a proper neutral
flavor its six organizers were conservatives from both the Democratic
and Republican parties: John W. Davis, corporation lawyer and 1924
Democratic presidential nominee; Nathan L. Miller, former Republican
governor of New York; Alfred E. Smith, Democratic presidential nominee
in 1928; Irénée du Pont, former Republican, who had voted for both
Smith and Roosevelt; and James W. Wadsworth, Republican representative and former United States senator from New York.[50]

Reaction to the new organization of liberty-lovers and Constitution-
defenders was varied. At his next regular Friday morning press conference,
President Roosevelt discussed the League with high good humor. The
League organizers, he said, were "lovers of property." He compared the
League to a mythical organization formed to uphold strongly two, and
only two, of the ten commandments. To at least one newspaper reporter
the President seemed to be "praising the League with faint damns."

Roosevelt told the newsmen he had laughed for ten minutes over an
item in the "Topics in Wall Street" feature of *The New York Times*,
which read: "Talk in Wall Street yesterday indicated that the announcement of the new American Liberty League was little short of an answer to
a prayer." Most loyal New Dealers, following the lead of the President,
also scoffed. The Liberty League for "right-thinking" people, said Harry
L. Hopkins, Federal Relief Administrator, "is so far to the right no one
will ever find it."[51]

Even conservatives occasionally fell victim to strange lapses when dealing with such subjects as radicalism and the American Liberty League.
Dr. Theodore Graebner, professor at Concordia Theological Seminary and
editor of the *Lutheran Witness*, in a 1936 speech entitled "Termites in
the Temple Gates," committed the fantastic blunder of charging that the
American Liberty League was one of the "principal Russian communistic
organizations in this country."[52]

While this error was unique, no one, whatever his political persuasion,
was fooled by the nonpartisan claims of the League. One of the organizers,

Irénée du Pont, lacking Shouse's political experience, almost shattered such claims the day after Shouse's public announcement. "The necessity for this association," said du Pont, "has become apparent in the continual gnawing at the vitals of the Constitution, both by change of its interpretation and by giving fictitious names to unconstitutional acts so as to make them appear constitutional." The League, he declared, "would not condone any unconstitutional act regardless of the politics of the transgressor." The New Deal, he stated, had done much harm to a large part of American business; the NRA, a serious affront to private property rights, should be repealed. Almost as an afterthought he added, "of course the association is strictly non-partisan."[53]

The Liberty League quickly became the most important anti-Roosevelt organization in the country. Although it was never able to rally a significant grass roots membership, its rolls read like a Who's Who of American business leadership: Detroit industrialists like Alfred P. Sloan, Jr., Alvan Macauley and Henry B. Joy; Sewell L. Avery of Montgomery Ward; E. T. Weir of Weirton Steel; bankers, financiers, and lawyers, including W. R. Perkins, Frederic R. Coudert, Jr., and Raoul Desvernine; Edward F. Hutton, chairman of the board of General Foods Corporation; Frank C. Rand of Industrial Shoe Company; at least one prominent member of the motion picture industry, Hal E. Roach; and a seemingly inexhaustible supply of du Ponts and Pews.

It had almost unlimited financial resources, most of it from the du Pont family. From September, 1934, until November, 1936, the League spent over a million dollars in an attempt to destroy the New Deal. Money that was not spent on salaries and organizational work went into one of the most extensive propaganda campaigns of the twentieth century. The publication program of the Liberty League rivalled that of the country's largest publishers. Between August, 1934, and September, 1936, the League issued 177 separate titles and distributed over 5,000,000 copies. The potential audience far exceeded the number of copies distributed, for copies went to newspaper editors, press associations, radio stations, and libraries. In addition to its regular publishing program the League also provided canned editorials and news stories to approximately 1600 newspapers in fourteen western, midwestern, and southern states.[54]

Shortly after the 1934 elections the Liberty League campaign against Roosevelt and the New Deal began in earnest. Its literature pictured the United States on the brink of chaos, threatened by bankruptcy, socialism, dictatorship, and tyranny. Few New Deal measures escaped its fire. The AAA was "economic and political quackery," a "legislative monstrosity," a "trend toward Fascist control of agriculture"; the Public Utility Holding Company Act was "a calamitous blow"; the Potato Control Act, "another step toward Socialism"; the NRA had pushed the nation into a "quicksand of visionary experimentation"; social security and relief were "an end of democracy"; the Bankhead farmers' home bill "would produce a government-sustained peasantry."[55]

By the time the Liberty League had finished telling its story it had said, and said well, what businessmen had been unable to say for themselves. Roosevelt had to be defeated in 1936 because: (1) New Deal measures endangered the Constitution; (2) centralization of power tended toward tyranny and dictatorship; (3) the New Deal was predicated upon coercion rather than voluntary cooperation; (4) all the various manifestations of New Deal economic planning were dangerous and deceitful; (5) government regulation of business was based on false economic theories; (6) New Deal measures in the name of reform had retarded a natural recovery; (7) regimentation of agriculture was a cure worse than the disease; (8) most New Deal measures were socialistic or fascistic, or both; (9) New Deal tax policies were damaging to private enterprise; (10) New Deal spending and unbalanced budgets were threatening a disastrous inflation; (11) banking policies were designed to subject the banking community to political control; (12) monetary policy impaired the credit of the United States and endangered the national currency.[56]

By late 1935, with total membership at only 75,000, it was apparent to even the most optimistic that the Liberty League campaign was generating little popular support. As 1936 and the presidential election approached, the League grew more desperate in its attempts to win public approval for its program. For its supreme effort the League called from retirement the Happy Warrior, Alfred Emanuel Smith.

It was a long way from the Lower East Side of New York to the

Shot in the Arm for Ailing Business—and Then What?

Reprinted with permission from the Washington Star. *Cartoon by Jim Berryman.*

Mayflower Hotel in Washington, and even farther from liberalism to reaction. Smith made both trips in four years. In 1928, he lost a bitter
campaign to Herbert Hoover. He expected to lose. More bitter was the loss
of the nomination in 1932 and the certain knowledge that whoever was
the Democratic nominee was bound to become President. Smith was
unable to hide the feeling that Roosevelt had denied him a second
chance, had stolen the nomination from him, something that was right-
fully his. Although he campaigned for Roosevelt his bitterness grew, and
he turned his back on his liberal past. In July, 1933, as editor of the
New Outlook, Smith wrote, "It may well be that we have reached a new
era in which the government must run everything, but I hope not. . . .
If that should happen, we shall have sold our American birthright for a
mess of Communistic pottage." Smith's growing hostility to Roosevelt
and the New Deal was revealed again in December, 1933, in an open letter

For That Depressed Feeling

Reprinted with permission from the Detroit News. *Cartoon by Bert
Thomas.*

to the Chamber of Commerce of the state of New York: "If I must choose between the leaders of the past . . . and the inexperienced young college professors . . . who are ready to turn 130,000,000 Americans into guinea pigs for experimentation, I am going to be for the people who have made this country what it is."[57]

From the editorial columns of the *New Outlook* his comments on the New Deal became progressively more critical. Roosevelt monetary policies, he said, produced "baloney dollars." He ridiculed the increasing number of New Deal agencies as "alphabet soup." But his most complete break with his Progressivist past came when he joined Bourbon Democrats and Conservative Republicans in the American Liberty League.

On the night of January 25, 1936, Smith, resplendent in tails, white

Women of America, Wake Up!

We housewives, more than a million strong, demanded that our Senators and Representatives oppose further "Pump Priming," reduce government expenses, keep our children's future unmortgaged and give us all a chance to SAVE OURSELVES.

How did our hired men answer this demand?

They answered it when they added a billion dollars to the "Pump Priming" bill, voted down every amendment to keep them from using relief money to buy votes, then gaily left for home to build up their political fences with our money.

We can't escape the mortgage of twenty billion dollars which the New Deal Congressmen hung around our necks in the last five years.

We can't escape paying $2.10 in taxes every time we spend $5.

But we CAN return to private life the men who spent our money so wastefully.

Let them learn how much harder it is to earn a dollar than to spend a dollar.

How much harder to pay taxes than to spend taxes.

The Housewives of America can force the New Deal hired men to share this tax burden they have saddled on us.

Then, too, if we bring them back home they can also share the evil effects of the laws they passed — often without reading them — on the homes and lives of the American people.

Wouldn't you like to see the men who voted for the Social Security Law hunting up their birth certificate, applying for a number, sweating over the graveyard questionnaire and having a slice of each pay check taken from them.

We women still have our votes. Let us use them before they are taken from us. Use them to send the wasters back home before they bankrupt our country.

Don't forget they are spending our money to keep themselves in Washington.

We women have the power to elect Senators and Representatives who will practice ECONOMY and protect our Constitution.

If we organize we can defeat all the men who sold us out to the New Deal. We must pledge ourselves to vote for or against men and not for or against party.

For these spenders run under both the Republican and Democratic Label. Their real label should be NEW DEAL SPENDERS.

If you write us we will send a record of how your Senators and Representatives voted, so you can tell the New Deal Spenders from the Democratic and Republican ECONOMIZERS.

Women! Save this Country for your children!

WOMEN'S REBELLION
SARAH OLIVER HULSWIT, Housewife,
Chairman.

Suffern, N. Y., July 1938

tie and high stiff collar, faced two thousand dinner guests of the Liberty League at Washington's Mayflower Hotel. A large part of the country's wealth ("the largest collection of millionaires ever assembled under the same roof," according to one reporter) applauded vigorously as Borden Burr, Birmingham lawyer, introduced the speaker as "Al Smith of America."

For nearly an hour his sharp tongue and raucous voice lashed the policies of the President. During the entire speech he did not mention Roosevelt by name, did not attempt to argue the philosophy of the New Deal. He hacked and sliced with what his wealthy friends would call an appeal to principle and New Dealers an appeal to prejudice. "I'm going to let you in on something," he confided. "How do you suppose this happened? This is the way . . . : The young brain-trusters caught the Socialists in swimming and they ran away with their clothes. Now, it is all right with me, if they want to disguise themselves as Karl Marx or Lenin or any of the rest of that bunch, but I won't stand for their allowing them to march under the banner of Jefferson or Jackson or Cleveland."

Al Smith had seen red, and, mounted on his strange new charger, he

"Gawd, how I hate his guts." *Reprinted with permission of the artist,* C. D. Batchelor.

sounded the alarm. "There can be only one capital," he solemnly concluded, "Washington or Moscow. There can be only the clear, pure, fresh air of free America, or the foul breath of communistic Russia. There can be only one flag, the Stars and Stripes, or the flag of the godless Union of the Soviets. There can be only one national anthem, The Star-Spangled Banner or the Internationale."[58]

Smith's speech started a whirlwind of reaction. But after the dust settled it was apparent it had done the New Deal more good than harm. The resurgence of Roosevelt's popularity in 1936 was dated by Arthur Krock in *The New York Times* from the Liberty League dinner.[59]

VIII

Liberty League support was not always limited to speakers with Smith's impressive credentials. Some Liberty Leaguers at least were willing to support that strange ménage of rabble-rousers at Talmadge's grass roots convention.

Talmadge, who had ambitions to become the kingfish after the assassination of Huey Long, had never been reticent about his opposition to the New Deal and to "that cripple in the White House," as he occasionally referred to Roosevelt. The co-sponsor, John Henry Kirby's Southern Committee to Uphold the Constitution, was only slightly less critical.[60] In a letter to its members in September, 1935, the Southern Committee stated its purpose was "to combat encroachment against American liberties by the New Deal. . . . Every informed American knows that if Mr. Roosevelt is re-elected in 1936, the sovereign rights of the states will be completely demolished. . . ." According to Kirby the membership of the Southern Committee to Uphold the Constitution was "drawn up from the Flower of Southern Democracy and is composed of men and women who refuse to stand idly by while the form of government, which has made America the greatest country on earth, is surrendered to a dictator without a struggle."[61]

With such liberty-loving, Constitution-defending Americans as sponsors, it is hardly surprising that the keynote of this extraordinary political spectacle was, "Put the Communist out of the White House and never let him return!" One of the most distinguished speakers at this meeting of "Goober Democrats," as they came to be known, was North Carolina's novelist Thomas Dixon. Speaking under the shadow of a huge Confederate flag, Dixon denounced the New Deal for the Wagner-Costigan anti-lynching bill, "the most brazen attempt to outrage states' rights by placing Federal bayonets at our backs."

After Dixon had blasted Mrs. Roosevelt for encouraging the southern "Niggah" to embrace a collectivist philosophy, the Reverend Gerald Lyman Kenneth Smith of Shreveport, Louisiana, a lieutenant of the late

Senator Long, rose to deliver the top tirade of the day. "Roosevelt," bellowed this pious faker, "is rapidly becoming the most despised President in the history of the country. . . . He gave us the Russian primer and cursed the Bible. . . . He and his gang are in the death rattle. We have only to put the cloth of the ballot over his dead mouth!"

With the Georgia crackers shouting "Give it to 'em, brother!" Governor Talmadge began his speech. But following such vituperative outpourings as Smith's, his talk seemed almost temperate. He confined his remarks to referring to the Roosevelt Administration as a collection of "cheats, racketeers, and madmen."[62]

But for all its volley and thunder the Macon Grass Roots Convention was no more effective in wounding the New Deal than Al Smith had been in Washington. Summarily dismissing the "Goober Democrats," the Charleston (Mississippi) *Sun* stated, "The malcontents and mutton heads who met in Macon to cheer Georgia's insurgent Governor in his invectives . . . no more represent the South than the Liberty League represents America."[63]

From the financial cornucopia that poured money into the Liberty League came economic nourishment for the Southern Committee to Uphold the Constitution and the multitude of other organizations with similar aims. Though there was no complete unanimity among the organizations and no formal organizational connections, their opinions and tactics coincided, they received funds from many of the same pockets, and many had interlocking leaderships.

John J. Raskob and Pierre du Pont had each given five thousand dollars because they "believed in the principles" of those backing the Macon meeting. Other contributors included prominent Liberty Leaguers like Lammot du Pont, Henry B. du Pont, Irénée du Pont, Alfred P. Sloan, and Alvan Macauley of Packard Motor Company. Other Liberty Leaguers of similar caliber also poured their money into a variety of lesser known organizations all dedicated to saving something or other, served on their boards and committees, made speeches on their behalf, wrote articles, distributed their literature, and used their influence to recruit other businessmen to the cause of such anti-Roosevelt organizations as the Crusaders, Sentinels of the Republic, American Taxpayers' League, Farmers' Independence Council, American Federation of Utility Investors, National Committee on Monetary Policy, League for Industrial Rights, Minute Men and Women of Today, National Economy League, Women Investors of America, and others.

IX

Despite the organized opposition of business through such high-powered machinery as the Chamber of Commerce, the National Association of

Manufacturers, and the American Bankers Association; despite (and maybe, in part, because of) the American Liberty League and a multitude of other well-heeled organizations like the League, the people spoke for Roosevelt on November 3, 1936.

And how they spoke! Never before had there been such a victory. Roosevelt won with the largest presidential vote in history, the largest plurality, the largest percentage of electoral votes since 1820, the largest majority in the House since 1855, and the largest in the Senate since 1869.[64]

Most of the business-backed conservative flag-waving organizations died in the wake of that victory—partly from shock, partly from embarrassment over their own anachronistic existence; died, except for two enfeebled heartbeats: in 1937, in response to Roosevelt's attempt to reorganize the Judiciary, and again in 1938, with the Executive reorganization plan.

In February, 1937, at the time of the court fight, Frank E. Gannett, publisher of a chain of ultra-respectable newspapers in New York state, became founder, chairman and treasurer of an organization with a familiar-sounding name, the National Committee to Uphold Constitutional Government. The object of this new committee was, according to its founder, to "help mobilize and coordinate individual and mass protests against the proposed undermining of our independent judiciary." Though Gannett vigorously opposed Roosevelt's so-called court-packing plan (he was "panic stricken over the outlook for America"), the main effort of his committee was directed against the reorganization plan of 1938, a plan to streamline the Executive branch of government.[65]

Gannett addressed an open letter "To Wide-Awake Citizens, Everywhere," stating that the "alarmingly dangerous" reorganization bill, another of the "ceaseless stream of half-baked reform bills written by the Corcorans and Cohens," was "designed to undermine democratic government and substitute centralized one-man power—inevitable forerunner of dictatorship."[66]

In March, 1938, the National Committee, playing the familiar old song, issued an official statement: "In our opinion the time has come when the country should clearly realize that the President is deliberately trying to liquidate our democratic institutions, and set up in their place . . . a political and economic dictatorship."[67]

Not to be outdone by their husbands, women also organized to uphold the Constitution and to save American liberty. In 1936 the first Finance Congress of Women was held in Chicago's Palmer House under the sponsorship of the Women Investors of America, Inc. From eighteen states four thousand distaff capitalists gathered to extol the rights of property and to exhort each other to defend their stocks and bonds as they would their children and homes. Catherine Curtis, a notorious professional patriot of the Elizabeth Dilling variety and director of Women Investors, keynoted the congress: "Have we been blinded by demagogs? Have we been lulled to a state of catalepsy by political pap, or have we been too lazy to assert and demand our sovereign rights . . . ? Woman . . . is the greatest capitalist in the world. We mobilize to save this capitalism!"

The slogan of the organization was a real mouthful: "One Woman Can Be Forceful; One Hundred Women Can Be Helpful; One Thousand Women Can Be Powerful, BUT ONE MILLION WOMEN—UNITED—ARE INVINCIBLE! LET'S GO!" And go they did. "The state at which we have arrived," warned Mrs. Grace H. Brosseau, former president of the Daughters of the American Republic, "did not spring up in a night. It dates back to the Secret Order of the Illuminati, which was organized in 1776 by Adam Weishaupt of Bavaria. . . ." From Weishaupt she quickly traced the deterioration through Karl Marx, and from Marx it was only a short step to the New Deal. "Let us work together," she implored her audience, "to keep the Constitution on the upper level and the American flag floating."[68]

Other organizations of female flag-floaters, the counterparts to the American Liberty League and company, included the Women's Rebellion, American Women Against Communism, the SOS (Save Our American System), and the Independent Coalition of American Women. Aside from the corporate connections of their husbands the members of these organizations had one common interest, hatred of President Roosevelt and of the social and economic reforms of the New Deal.

They expressed grave concern about "pump-priming," about taxes and New Deal extravagance; ". . . and your husband is the fellow who pays for them" (Independent Coalition of American Women). "We housewives, more than a million strong [demand], that our Senators and Representatives oppose further 'Pump Priming' . . . reduce government expenses . . . keep our children's future unmortgaged . . . give us all a chance to SAVE OURSELVES" (Women's Rebellion). [We are] "distressed at the moral as well as the economic depth to which the country has sunk after five years of government waste and extravagance, ruinous taxes and class conflict" (Save Our American System).

One of the specific objectives of the Women's Rebellion urged by the founder of the organization, Mrs. Sarah Oliver Hulswit of Suffern, New York, was the disfranchisement of all relief recipients and WPA workers: "The New Deal has made millions of paupers deliberately and maliciously. As long as they can keep themselves in power by keeping millions of citizens on relief they will do so."[69]

The American Women Against Communism had but one objective, to lay bare a New Deal plot to "carve out of the federal territory a NEGRO REPUBLIC." Anti-Negro attacks of this kind on the Administration were by no means uncommon among the female critics. In 1936 a letter signed by Mrs. Lowell F. Hobart, former president-general of the Daughters of the American Republic, was distributed to Democratic women in many parts of the South. Addressed to "My Friends in the Southland," the letter asked: "Do you realize the activities of Mr. and Mrs. Roosevelt in spreading Communism in your beloved Southland? They are deeply involved in the many Negro organizations such as: The Struggle for Negro Rights, the Scottsboro Case, the ANGELO HERNDON PETITION COMMITTEE (All advocating equality with whites, even marriage) and Communistic Plans for a Negro Soviet South (The Bible Belt). Mrs. Roosevelt's picture appears many times at their meetings, or receiving with them, also at the White House. . . ."[70]

Such loose and inflammatory talk, whether they knew it or not, meant they were treading dangerously close to the native Fascist camp where such racist tales of plots and intrigue were staples. It appears most unlikely any of the ladies ever thought seriously of a Fascist solution to the New Deal threat. But apparently some of their husbands did. At least a few. In September, 1932, Frederic A. Ogg, editor of the *American Political Science Review*, reported in *Current History*:

For a good while certain powerful elements have been toying with the idea that the way out of our troubles lies through the establishment of some form of economic and political dictatorship, and meetings of important personages are known to have been held in New York and Chicago, at which sentiment was tested out and possibilities discussed. It does not appear that anything more startling came out of these conferences than a more or less general consensus in favor of a coalition super-cabinet of bankers and industrialists. But in other quarters there has been less moderation.[71]

In 1933, with the New Deal hardly under way, with most of its more dramatic reforms still to come, a small minority of the more adventurous members of the business community were still apparently toying with the idea of such a remedy. This, at least, was the verdict of the McCormack-Dickstein Committee, later to become the House Un-American Activities Committee.

The most spectacular inquiry of the Committee, in the fall of 1934, was into a story by the retired Marine Corps Major General Smedley D. Butler that he had been approached to head a Fascist coup financed by bankers and businessmen. Witnesses called before the Committee to answer Butler's charges denied the entire story.[72] And that, as far as the printed hearings were concerned, was that. No one knew just what to make of the Butler affair. But the nation had just finished its laugh over Dr. Wirt's great Red scare, and this balanced it off perfectly; 1934 was, it seems, a year for fantasy.

But the Butler incident was only one part, a dramatic part, of a broader investigation into Fascist activities in the United States, an investigation that led the committee to write, in its final report in 1935: "Evidence was obtained showing that certain persons had made an attempt to establish a fascist organization in this country. There is no question but that these attempts were discussed, were planned, and might have been placed in execution when and if the financial backers deemed it expedient."[73]

The Committee did not identify "the financial backers"; it would probably have served no useful purpose and might have sown wider the seeds of suspicion and distrust. There was quite enough evidence from other sources indicating that a few business leaders, a very few fortunately, were so opposed to Roosevelt they listened to extremists, supported extremists, accepted without due caution any ally in the fight against the New Deal.

X

In their duel with Roosevelt and the New Deal, businessmen failed. Despite their criticism, their multitude of organizations, their limitless funds, they failed. Roosevelt was to be, as they feared, "President for life." Their plans, their pleas, their alarms went for nothing. They stood alone. They had underestimated the intelligence of the average American, and they had lost.

But if businessmen had little influence on the New Deal, on what it was and what it was to become, another segment of American conservatism, an old friend and partner, had even less. The press, proud of its freedom and certain of its power, considered itself the great molder of public opinion. Almost no one doubted that the voice of the Fourth Estate was the voice of the people—almost no one, that is, before 1936. In the 1930's the news-publishing industry, arrogantly and overwhelmingly anti-Roosevelt, met its match. People would buy newspapers and they would read newspapers. But they would not believe newspapers—not where Roosevelt and the New Deal were concerned. In 1936 Americans discovered (and the discovery was corroborated in 1940 and 1944 and again in 1948) that the press had as little to do with forming or even reflecting public opinion as Mrs. Hulswit's Rebellion.

CHAPTER VII

All the News That's Fit to Print

"It has been necessary . . . to place before the electors the perilous tendencies of some Roosevelt policies. It has been in accord with sound political practice to exaggerate a little. . . ."
—Editor and Publisher

"This may be truthfully called one of the most slanderous campaigns in the entire history of American journalism."
—The New Republic

"Do you know that thousands, probably millions, of the ballots which American citizens thrust into boxes carried not only a vote for Mr. Roosevelt but an equally discernible vote against you?" —An Open Letter to Publishers
The Christian Century

T H E weather was frightful. December weather was usually frightful in Washington. But it was warm and pleasant in the banquet hall of the Willard Hotel where the Gridiron Club dinner of 1934 was drawing to an end. Four hundred guests, after much rich food and strong drink, had enjoyed two hours of skits lampooning Roosevelt and his Administration.

The dinner was an annual rite, a time when the working press was free to pan Presidents, a time when stuffed-shirts got unstuffed, when public figures paid for their frailties, and woe to the man with thin skin. It was great sport; two hours of hazing, of wickedly funny songs, parodies, and skits. The final skit of the evening had pictured the New Deal as a train wreck blocking the tracks of "Prosperity Unlimited"; and the irrepressible H. L. Mencken, the Sage of Baltimore, had just completed a speech in which he accused Roosevelt of violating all the articles of the Bill of Rights but one: no troops had yet been quartered in anyone's home without his consent.

Now it was Roosevelt's turn. As he wheeled to the speaker's stand it was evident that he was not at all ruffled by the evening's entertainment. Turning on his famous smile, he began by referring affably to "my old friend, Henry Mencken." But the President was not making the genial and humorous retort everyone had expected. Roosevelt's smile had disappeared and with his jaw set he launched into a scathing attack on the

American press. "The evils that continue to beset American journalism," he said, are due to the "stupidity, cowardice and Philistinism of working newspapermen." These "cheap, trashy, stupid and corrupt" journalists are managed by editors "who have never heard of Kant or Johannes Muller and never read the Constitution of the United States; there are city editors who do not know what a symphony is, or a streptococcus, or the Statute of Frauds; there are reporters by the thousand who could not pass an entrance examination for Harvard or Tuskegee, or even Yale."[1]

As Roosevelt continued his attack on the press its "vast and militant ignorance," "its wide-spread and fathomless prejudice against intelligence," the audience slowly caught on. This was not a presidential philippic; it was a long quotation from Mencken's 1927 "Journalism in America," the first essay in his book, *Prejudices: Sixth Series*. All eyes turned toward Mencken, now the color of an overripe tomato. Realizing what Roosevelt was doing, Mencken leaned toward his dinner companion, Governor Albert Ritchie of Maryland, and whispered, "I'll get the son-of-a-bitch; I'll dig skeletons out of his closet."[2]

II

Mencken had been the gadfly of the boom era. Through his essays and his editorial columns in the Baltimore *Sun* and the *American Mercury* he had tremendous influence on the articulate and literate youth of the 1920's. To his followers he was the archenemy of Puritanism and champion of heterodoxy. But his disciples often failed to recognize that the "censor-baiting, freedom-roaring Mencken" (as Malcolm Cowley called him) was no economic or political liberal.

He had supported Roosevelt in 1932, but with misgivings. In a letter to Louis Untermeyer after the election, Mencken wrote, "I voted for Roosevelt yesterday and now feel almost ashamed, for he is the first candidate of my choice ever to win." Later that month he wrote to Ezra Pound, "Roosevelt is a weak sister, but he is better than Hoover. I look for a circus during the next year or two."[3]

Mencken's mild support was short-lived, had never been based on much more than the hint that Roosevelt favored repeal. Otherwise, he could see little to distinguish Roosevelt from Coolidge or Hoover ("the fat Coolidge," Mencken called him). "I hear that Roosevelt likes his martinis," Mencken once said, "and that is a very high recommendation. Coolidge used to drink cold tea, and Hoover drinks cocoa, not too strong."[4]

In a moment of uncommon enthusiasm soon after the bank holiday, Mencken proposed that Roosevelt be made king, an endorsement that did not long remain unqualified. "The republic proceeds toward hell at a rapidly accelerating tempo," he wrote to Albert Jay Nock in June, 1933.

"I am advocating making him a king in order that we may behead him in case he goes too far beyond the limits of the endurable. A President, it appears, cannot be beheaded, but kings have been subjected to the operation from ancient times." After the Gridiron Club dinner in 1934 the next order of business for Mencken was to get on with the beheading.[5]

Mencken had never before supported a President in office. And Roosevelt had little to recommend him as the one to break this record. Roosevelt's willingness to spend was, in itself, alarming to Mencken; but even more distressing to his Nietzschean philosophy was Roosevelt's willingness to spend to relieve the plight of the indigent and unemployed. This, wrote Mencken, was "the beginning of the end." "The country of Jefferson," he contended, "has become the country of lackeys and mendicants." He regarded most New Deal projects as forms of inane charity for the "congenitally worthless and unemployable," which had but one effect, "to degrade and vulgarize the country." "The best thing that could happen," he said, would be for "all those who suck at the public teat now, thanks to FDR . . . to . . . die off. They are of no value to themselves, and a drain upon the nation." In his determination to "get that son-of-a-bitch," Mencken declared that Roosevelt's concept of government was that of a "milch cow with 125,000,000 teats." There was, he said, "only one intelligible idea in the whole More Abundant Life rumble-bumble, and that is the idea that whatever A earns really belongs to B. A is any honest and industrious man or woman; B is any drone or jackass." The benefits of government, such as they are, Mencken reported, "have gone in the main, not to honest and industrious men caught in a universal misfortune, but to rogues and vagrants to whom a universal misfortune is only a new excuse for avoiding work."[6]

III

Throughout the New Deal years Roosevelt maintained remarkably friendly relations with the working newspaper people. After the barren years of Coolidge and Hoover they welcomed the easy give-and-take, the quips, the banter of Roosevelt's frequent press conferences. The whiskey, black coffee, and pad-and-pencil newsmen liked him. He made their jobs easier; he was good copy.

It was columnists and editorialists, people like Mencken, who made life miserable for Roosevelt. Mencken's project of beheading Roosevelt was no one-man show. The woods were full of Menckens. He had help, lots of it, from that special breed of journalists who had their own byline (and maybe their picture) on the editorial page, men of divine inspiration who could resolve any problem of state in one column of newspaper type. Men like David Lawrence, editor of U. S. News; Frank Kent, columnist for the Baltimore Sun; Westbrook Pegler, syndicated columnist for Scripps-

Howard newspapers; Walter Lippmann, special writer for the New York *Herald Tribune*, all waged relentless war on the New Deal.

So did publishers. Early in the New Deal, publishers struck back at Roosevelt's attempt, through the National Recovery Act, to bring order to chaotic business conditions. Publishers balked when Hugh Johnson undertook to impose a code on newspapers, a code which would have clamped controls on newspapers similar to those already on other industries: minimum wages, maximum hours, and (this really galled) restrictions against employment of children. The government, they howled, was trying to regiment American youth. A confidential bulletin from the American Newspaper Publishers Association to its members, alerting them to the progress of the Child Labor amendment, referred to it as the "federal control of youth" amendment, a term apparently borrowed from the New York *Herald Tribune*. The Louisville *Courier-Journal* had its carriers deliver letters to all subscribers urging them to write Hugh Johnson, in protest because "reformers are attempting to prohibit . . . boys under eighteen from being gainfully employed."[7]

Enforcement of code restrictions, declared the publishers, would strike a blow at freedom of the press. Pro-New Dealers regarded this line of argument as insincere, a sham argument to protect not their freedom but their profits. Roosevelt, in answer to a question put by a reporter for the Chicago *Tribune*, said: "Tell Bertie McCormick that he's seeing things under the bed."[8]

Other editors were also "seeing things under the bed," but few were as incensed at what they saw there as S. W. Adams, editor of a small Texas newspaper, the Gladewater *Journal*. On July 17, 1933, in a letter addressed to "Mr. Franklin D. Roosevelt, Dictator of the United States," Adams challenged Roosevelt to stop dictating to small businessmen or to "boldly declare that democracy is dead" and shout "Long live fascism!" "There is," Adams stated, "no title inferior to that of dictator who . . . usurps dictatorial powers, and becomes a tool of greed. . . ." "I denounce you," he continued, "and your industrial act as the greatest scourge a free people ever suffered." Somewhat incongruously he closed the letter, "yours sincerely."[9]

Some publishers hinted broadly that, because of their influence, they expected preferential treatment or even exemption from the kind of codes enforced against other industries. William Randolph Hearst, who defined the NRA as "Nonsensical, Ridiculous, Asinine interference," instructed his editor of the New York *American*, Edmund D. Coblentz, to tell Roosevelt his code proposal for the press was "in direct violation of the Bill of Rights; . . . an abridgment of the freedom of the press" and that he was prepared to fight it "with every means at my command . . . even if it costs me every nickel I possess." When Coblentz delivered this message, Roosevelt replied that the code was a regulatory measure and would not interfere with freedom of the press. It was, he said, like fire department rules.

When fire department regulations were violated, he told Coblentz, "the Chief steps in and compels you to conform, does he not?" "Yes, Mr. President," Coblentz replied, "but he does not stop the presses."[10]

Besides the idea of a code for the industry, publishers looked askance at another section of the National Industrial Recovery Act. Section 7a guaranteed the right of collective bargaining and freedom of labor to organize. Because of this controversial section and, later, because of the Wagner Act and the National Labor Relations Board created by it, publishers were denied the right to dismiss journalists merely because they joined the Newspaper Guild. Publishers resisted Section 7a, and when the Wagner Act became law in July, 1935, it was immediately declared unconstitutional, not by the Supreme Court but by the American Newspaper Publishers Association. "Publishers from now on should flatly refuse to have anything to do with the NLRB," Elisha Hanson, attorney for the ANPA, instructed his clients "other than notify it that it is without power under the Constitution to interfere with their business. . . . No order of the Board . . . will . . . be upheld in the courts." Hanson, who was also legal counsel to William Randolph Hearst, assured them that "if the NLRB issued an order in this case, Mr. Hearst will not comply with it."[11]

Hanson was premature in declaring the Wagner Act unconstitutional. It was fitting that one of the decisive cases (*The Associated Press v. National Labor Relations Board*) involved the press. On April 12, 1937, the Supreme Court upheld the Wagner Act, ruling the Associated Press could not fire Morris Watson on grounds he helped organize the Newspaper Guild.[12]

IV

Fear that Roosevelt was intent on destroying freedom of the press was not based on concern over mere regulatory measures. Publishers feared the rapidly increasing number of government press agents, the growing effusion of official publicity, the flood of "government ballyhoo" that seemed to presage the nationalization of the press.

Early in the game, Roosevelt's implacable foe, Senator Schall, charged the President was planning to replace the three major commercial news services with a government press agency. In a telegraphed reply, Roosevelt challenged Schall to send him "such facts as you have," promising the charges would receive "immediate attention in order to make impossible the things you say will be done, because I am just as much opposed to them as you are." Schall only repeated the charges, adding that Roosevelt's telegram was part of a "constant effort to mislead and fool the public." For him to list all Administrative efforts "to throttle the press and free speech," wrote Schall, would be but "to recite incidents" with which Roosevelt was "entirely familiar."[13]

Since Schall refused to cite chapter-and-verse examples of Administration violations of press freedom, Roosevelt considered the incident closed. But he was mistaken. Schall, sensing he had struck a nerve, continued his tirades in the Senate. In January, 1935, the cry was taken up in the House. Congressman Martin Dies of Texas introduced House Resolution 52 requesting an investigation into charges made by Schall that the Administration was seeking to control the press "through a well-organized and highly developed plan of employing hundreds of newspapermen as press agents . . . and that the administration by other insidious and covert methods . . . is forcing the press to withhold from the public unfavorable facts."[14]

Nothing came of the Dies proposal. But the press needed no such inquiry to declare Roosevelt guilty. Samuel G. Blythe, writing in the *Saturday Evening Post*, admitted there had been "criticism, cavil, condemnation and discredit" of the New Deal by the press; but these attacks were "nothing compared to the vast Washington outpourings of self-praise and self-righteousness; . . . a thin trickle coming in compared to a Mississippi going out." New Dealers, Blythe continued, particularly the Brain Trusters, resembled "nothing so much as a company of ineffables sitting in a cave . . . in contemplation of their valorous and progressive and socialistic souls, and shouting hosannas over their vast accomplishments." The Administration, he warned, had better start paying attention to news coming in from the country instead of being so preoccupied with its "black sheets, propaganda, oratory, radio outpourings, special pleadings, ballyhoo, and general febrile maneuvering to send out news about itself." "One thing is clear about the 'New Deal,'" wrote Frank Kent, "if the American people do not swallow it whole, with all its strange tastes and queer flavors, it will not be because of any lack of effort to sugar-coat the dose." Elisha Hanson warned New York publishers that the "constantly growing propaganda machine" in Washington threatened "our democratic form of government." For Hanson, even official news releases seemed "to strike at the basic concepts of popular government." The torrent of "government ballyhoo," according to a *Saturday Evening Post* story, was encouraged by "Mr. Roosevelt [who] fully realized that he needed the aid of a good press to carry on his dictatorship." For others, the real motive behind troops of government press agents was to gloss over failures of the Administration, to conceal lack of planning, to excuse frequent changes in relief programs by impressing "a gullible public of their intrinsic worth."[15]

V

From the first days of the New Deal, public relief was a favorite object of ridicule by a substantial segment of the press. The Federal Emergency Relief Administration, established in the spring of 1933 to see that no citizen went hungry, triggered a public debate of the merits of the dole as opposed to work relief, the merits of federal programs versus local and private programs, a public debate in which the "Tory" press (as Roosevelt called his newspaper opponents) had plenty to say.

The dole system of FERA, a stopgap relief plan, was, they insisted, not only of dubious economic value, but it destroyed man's initiative and degraded his soul. In July, 1933, Bernarr Macfadden, health faddist editor of *Liberty* magazine, colorfully compared the dole to "a drug that dopes mind and body. The morale slowly disintegrates; the need to struggle no longer exists." Caught up in his own rhetoric, Macfadden described the horrible effects of the dole: "When a man who is accustomed to hard work finds himself on the dole, he becomes spiritless; loses ambition, enthusiasm, and he ultimately degenerates into a human clod." As though this alone were not enough to frighten even strong men, Macfadden continued, "Down, down you gradually descend in the scale of life until you join the oyster and the jelly fish—spineless, spiritless, without an atom of fight left in your personality."[16]

Colonel Robert R. McCormick, editor and publisher of the Chicago *Tribune*, restated the position of his paper on the matter of relief when he told a rally of the Sentinels of the Republic that the New Deal was wasting billions on "men who have been parasites their entire lives, have never produced anything and never intend to produce anything, who have always lived at the expense of others, and plot to live better than the others who support them." For social worker Evelyn Harvey, the most "sinister aspect of the question" was the "pauperization of many families" and the fear that among certain "classes" laziness was becoming a way of life. During seven years experience in relief work she had always found "a rapid change in the attitude" of those receiving relief, a change "from reluctant accepting to a belligerent demanding." The *Saturday Evening Post* commented snidely that "however saccharine . . . the content of the cane" in the Caribbean, the "real sugar bowl" was to be found in Washington, D.C., the home of "the sugar mama superlative."[17]

The deleterious effect of the dole on the soul received considerably more press attention than did the sustaining effect it had on the body. Although few presented the case as graphically as Macfadden, his general thesis appeared in numerous leading newspapers and magazines. However exaggerated were press claims that a dole weakened the moral fibre of the nation, the Administration admitted they contained an element of truth, enough truth that the temporary expedient of a direct dole soon was replaced by a variety of public work relief programs.

In the fall of 1933, the FERA gave way to a work relief program, the Civil Works Administration. The CWA at first escaped the kind of criticism heaped on the FERA, a fact for which Al Smith had an oversimplified explanation: "No sane local official who has hung up an empty stocking over the municipal fireplace is going to shoot Santa Claus just before a hard Christmas." As soon as the presents were distributed the sniping began, and with some justification. There was waste in the program, and some corruption. This was all the critics needed who opposed a work relief program anyway. When important Democrats, particularly southern Democrats, began warning that the budget could not stand the strain of such an expensive operation, Roosevelt wavered, then yielded.[18]

The Works Progress Administration, which replaced the CWA in 1935, was given a rough ride by the press. It was the newspapers that were largely responsible for spreading the numerous jokes, the broad stories and the cartoons ridiculing the WPA, for making "leaning-on-a-shovel" and the "WPA look" a part of the national patois. It was, according to Harry Hopkins, unfair "long range attacks, by newspapers in New York or Chicago" that were responsible for much of the mythology of the WPA, for tales that funds were being wasted in New England for malaria control when not a cent had been spent there for that purpose, or that a rat extermination project had cost the taxpayers $2.97 for each rat killed. WPA officials patiently explained that rat extermination was only a minor part of a public health program and that the charge was like "analyzing the costs of building a highway in terms of some specified amount per tree cut down in the process."[19]

Though much of the WPA mythology was phoney, there were enough projects that were trumped-up, half-baked absurdities, enough useless ditch-digging and leaf-raking, enough "boondoggling" nonsense to give the press critics plenty of room to navigate. And none took advantage of the opportunities more unfairly and uncompromisingly than Colonel McCormick's Chicago *Daily Tribune*. During one two-week period, when the *Tribune* concentrated its heaviest fire on Hopkins' agency, fourteen stories appeared with such headlines as GRAFT, FRAUDS, THEFT: WPA REEKS WITH CORRUPTION. Although it was the policy of the Administration to ignore such press tactics, the *Tribune* series was so serious in its implications that Howard O. Hunter, assistant WPA administrator, prepared a twenty-five page statement disproving and categorically denying each of the stories. The rebuttal was distributed to nineteen Chicago reporters. Not a word of it ever appeared in the *Tribune*.[20]

Few critics of the WPA had constructive alternatives to offer. The *Saturday Evening Post*, constant in its indictment of the relief program and consistent in its appeal for a balanced budget, recommended economy. In the midst of depression a balanced budget remained a sacred goal, inflation the overriding threat: "Delay in balancing [the Federal budget] . . . merely renders that much more difficult the attainment of favorable economic and social conditions in this country." "Thoughtful men and women," according to the *Post*, "constantly ask each other when Uncle Sam is to cease playing Santa Claus." The *Post* agreed with Lewis

Douglas, former Director of the Budget, when he raised the question, "which is more cruel, which is more inhuman, which entails the greatest destruction to individual self-respect—to continue a policy which must inevitably . . . plunge the people into the destructive effects of a collapsed currency, or to pursue a policy . . . predicated upon hard work and sacrifice?"[21] It was hardly surprising that the suggestion of sacrifice did not bring the eleven million unemployed Americans to their feet cheering.

Frequent changes in the relief programs provided another peg on which the press could hang its criticism. Even the liberal *New Republic* reported that the changes had confused the relief program, had clogged it with red tape. The *Saturday Evening Post* put it in stronger words: "Duplication, inconsistency and constant change of plan have characterized much of the spending policy." "Spending," the *Post* editorial continued, "cannot be other than prodigal when a government sets out to be the universal Santa Claus." "It is like a drunkard trying to drink himself sober," said publisher Frank Gannett, repeating one of the hoariest clichés of the New Deal years. Speaking to the National Republican Club in April, 1939, Gannett compared Roosevelt to the manager of a large industry: "If in any business a manager made such a great failure of his job, he would be fired without delay." How, he wanted to know, could prosperity emerge from deeper and recurring government debt?[22]

Criticism of New Deal extravagance was not confined to the richest and largest newspapers and publishers. Even ten-year-old Bruce "Buster" Hoefer, fifth grader of Sheboygan, Wisconsin, who published a six-inch by eight-inch twelve-page paper, the Sheboygan *Weekly*, got into the act. On a trip to New York in early April, 1936, he was reported to have said, "There is too much money being spent down in Washington."[23]

As late as 1939, Mencken, still trying to manipulate the guillotine, reported, "The essential fact is that the New Deal is a gigantic flop," myopically overlooking the 50 per cent rise in national income under Roosevelt, the 80 per cent increase in Dow-Jones industrial averages, the 50 per cent increase in company earnings, and Roosevelt's 98.5 per cent of the electoral vote in 1936. "The American people," he continued, "have been mulcted billions." Since no one, "not even the multitude of dolebirds" had gotten any good out of it, the money might just as well have been spent for "toy balloons and lollypops."[24]

Changes in relief programs led some critics to believe there were no plans. "In spite of all that comes in the way of big talk about the President's plans," wrote John T. Flynn in *The New Republic*, "it is as clear as ice that he has no plans."[25] In part Flynn was right. Errors were made; inconsistencies developed; agency piled upon agency, many with overlapping functions, some with contrasting goals. In general, the country agreed that bold action, even experimentation, was preferable to hesitation and calm deliberation.

The country agreed, but much of the press did not. Lawrence Dennis, author of *The Coming American Fascism*, accused the President of having "no integrated social thought." "So far," wrote Dennis, "Mr. Roosevelt has shown himself to be a master showman but not a master builder. To build, you need a plan." Mencken vigorously agreed with both Flynn and Dennis, critics who represented almost opposite ends of the political spectrum, agreed in characteristic Menckenese: "Planned? Then so is a dog fight planned. Of late . . . the spokesmen for the Brain Trust have begun to abate their tall talk about planning, and to speak of experiment instead. Experiment it is—in a dingy and unclean laboratory, with cobwebs choking the microscopes, and every test-tube leaking."[26]

Not all journalist critics thought the New Deal planless. Many believed it had been well planned, perhaps too well, but that the plan had originated in Moscow. Although the press attacked Roosevelt's program at all points, occasionally scoring direct hits on New Deal weaknesses of waste, inefficiency, and bureaucracy, its main assault was directed against the New Deal's most unassailable position, its motivation. With the single-mindedness of a trip hammer many daily newspapers—notably those of Hearst and McCormick—proclaimed the "crisis" of the imminent Communist revolution in the United States and portrayed Roosevelt and his Brain Trust as Reds.

VI

In 1934 Frank Kent, writing in the Baltimore *Sun*, stated that no President had been as free from "personal attack" as Roosevelt had been during his first year in office. *The New York Times*, commenting on Kent's statement, told a story that tells much of Roosevelt's political astuteness. To a friend who was congratulating him upon his exemption from personal abuse, Roosevelt quietly replied, "That will, of course, come later." And, of course, it did.[27]

Roosevelt's New York neighbor Howland Spencer, writing under the name "The Squire of Krum Elbow," penned some of the most vicious personal attacks. With implications not concealed by subtlety an editorial in Spencer's *Highland Post* pointed out that "lack of intelligence is probably prenatal . . . the flattery that fertilized of its purpose such a mind as our neighbor's can be traced to the cabal of Morgenthaus, Lehmans, Frankfurters, and Cohens." Many of Spencer's editorials were widely distributed in reprint form, "as the circulation of any weekly country newspaper is confined." The Squire evidently saw conspirators behind every tree. "The press of the country," he charged, "is controlled by the conspirators plotting to wreck America and liquidate you."[28]

Mencken, still smarting from his treatment at the hands of Roosevelt at the 1934 Gridiron Club dinner, continued his attack on "the Hon. Franklin D. Roosevelt, LL.D." Sketching his denunciation in red-hot ink, he depicted Roosevelt as "typical of the species" of "quacks . . . always friendly and ingratiating fellows and not infrequently . . . very amusing."[29]

It is an historic irony that the Mencken of the 1920's, an anathema to the Republicans, should in the 1930's become such an important part of the litany of Roosevelt hatred that the conservative Chicago *Journal of Commerce* bemoaned that he had said such unpleasant things in the past because "he really can be so convincing." Paraphrasing him, E. B. White summed up Mencken's reaction with this verse in the *Saturday Review of Literature:*

> Poetry, religion, and Franklin D.
> The three abominations be.
> Why mince words? I do not feel
> Kindly toward the Nouveau Deal
> Hopkins peddles quack elixir.
> Tugwell is a phony fixer.
> Another lapse
> For Homo saps
> Yahweh![30]

There was, according to Mencken, only one way to beat Roosevelt in 1936, and that was to attack him with "horse, foot, and dragoons, denouncing his montebankeries in a voice of brass and allowing him no virtue whatever." But the Mencken of the gaudy legend, the darling of the rebels, had all but disappeared. And the Mencken that was left flailed his arms, stuck out his tongue, and fired ineffectual spitballs. It was difficult to believe that ten years earlier Mencken had been a cannoneer to be feared. "They are all," he said of New Dealers, "flagrant and incurable asses, the higher their rank in the hierarchy of buncombe the more potent their asininity." And, to Mencken, the worst ass of all was Franklin Roosevelt. "The greatest President since Hoover," he charged, "has carried on his job with an ingratiating grin upon his face, like that of a snake-oil vender at a village carnival, and he had exhibited precisely the same sense of responsibility in morals and honor; no more." Roosevelt, Mencken thought, had advanced in the ranks of government service because he had no principles, had survived by a chameleon adaptability. "If he became convinced tomorrow that coming out for cannibalism would get him the votes he so sorely needs, he would begin fattening a missionary in the White House backyard come Wednesday."[31]

Others agreed. Mr. Roosevelt, stated a full-page Detroit *Free Press* advertisement in *The New York Times,* "gave his word of honor at Chicago [1932] that he would carry out the platform 100 percent. He did; he carried it out to the alley and dropped it into the ash can." Even the Canadian press was heard from. The Toronto *Globe and Empire* called Roosevelt "a Pied Piper of the air, fatuously fluting to rag time."[32]

Though Roosevelt caught the brunt of the press attack, the Brain Trust came in for its share of whipping-boy treatment. Members of the Brain Trust were charged with subscribing to practically all alien "isms" except cannibalism and of following virtually every foreign ruler except Haile Selassie. They were accused of every failing from simple ignorance and ineptitude to treason and communism.

The *Saturday Evening Post* called the Brain Trust a group of college boys tipsy on Russian vodka. "We are having," a *Post* editorial stated, "government by amateurs . . . who, having drunk deep, perhaps, of the Pierian Spring, have recently taken some hearty swigs of Russian vodka." A few journals were more direct in their attack on the Brain Trust. The Washington *Herald* stated, "public statements of Mr. Tugwell are infinitely more damaging, infinitely more Communistic, and infinitely more subversive of American ideals than anything alleged by Dr. Wirt. . . . Treason to American principles is revolution, and Mr. Tugwell's call to revolution is treason."[33]

Few newspapers or magazines went as far in their charges or in their use of intemperate language as the *Fellowship Forum* of Washington, D.C. In July, 1934, this magazine warned that "Catholics, Communists and Jews dominate the Roosevelt Administration and are in league to destroy the government." Under the heading "The New Dealers—God Save Us" the *Fellowship Forum* ran a list of names and commented, "the names read like a catalogue of radicals who are supplanting democracy with dictatorships in Europe. . . . The list is made up of alien-minded radicals. . . . Its spirit is that of Hitler and Mussolini and Dollfuss and Stalin."[34]

Mencken also despised the Brain Trust, that "Camorra of quarreling crackpots" with their "slimy false pretenses and idiotic contradictions." Few journalist critics were surprised, least of all Mencken, that the New Deal seemed headed nowhere when leadership was left to "the sorriest mob of mountebanks ever gathered together at one time. . . ." The best of the Brain Trusters, said Mencken, were only professional "uplifters and do-gooders," and from there they quickly ranged downward to "a miscellaneous rabble of vapid young pedagogs, out-of-work Y.M.C.A. secretaries, third-rate journalists, briefless lawyers, and soaring chicken-farmers."[35]

VII

The tidal wave of electoral votes that swept Roosevelt into his second term in the White House washed away more than Republican hopes. Amid the scattered wreckage following Election Day, 1936, lay the *Literary Digest*, its prestige permanently impaired after predicting a Landon victory; the black ties and starched shirts of Liberty Leaguers, men misled by the arrogance of wealth and dismayed by the realization that selling a candidate to the country was not the same as peddling breakfast cereal; and the vaunted influence of the press, rendered *hors de combat* by the personality of one man. Newspaper editors across the land were rudely jarred out of their smug belief they were powerful molders of public opinion.

The daily press had opposed Roosevelt throughout his first term, except for that brief and happy honeymoon period at the outset. And it opposed his reelection. That the press was anti-Roosevelt was more than mere allegation; it could be demonstrated statistically. Of the leading one hundred and fifty daily newspapers, those having a circulation of 50,000 or more, eighty endorsed Landon in 1936, fifty-five endorsed Roosevelt, and fifteen endorsed neither candidate. This meant Landon had a numerical margin of about 3 to 2, an edge of 53 per cent to 37 per cent with 10 per cent neutral. The margin was actually wider because most of those in the "neutral" category, papers like the Dallas *News*, the Houston *Post*, and the Jacksonville *Florida Times-Union*, supported Landon every way except by actual endorsement.[36]

There appeared to be a direct correlation between the size of the paper and its editorial line. The larger the paper the more likely it was to support Landon. Of the fifty dailies with a circulation of 135,000 or more, 75 per cent were pro-Landon, 20 per cent were for Roosevelt. The fifty dailies that might be considered medium-sized, those with a range of 80,000 to 135,000 went for Landon 52 per cent to 36 per cent. But the fifty smallest dailies, in the 50,000 to 80,000 range, divided their support 34 per cent for Landon and 54 per cent for Roosevelt. The eighty papers that endorsed Landon in 1936 represented 67 per cent of the circulation. Of the larger chains only the Stern papers and most of the Scripps-Howard papers supported Roosevelt.[37]

Despite this formidable array of powerful papers against Roosevelt, they bungled badly whatever opportunity they might have had to undo him, bungled it by waging war on the wrong battlefront, bungled it by trying to convince the reading public that Roosevelt was a Red.

The Chicago *Daily Tribune*, the voice of Colonel McCormick's animadversions, was not a typical example of a paper that fought the Roosevelt candidacy on the Communist issue; it was in a class alone, the worst of the bunch. In 1932 when he was first elected, the *Tribune* commented that Roosevelt was "not a strong man . . . but . . . was an honest and capable person."[38] And during the first hectic months the *Tribune* was remarkably restrained, giving Roosevelt the benefit of every doubt. Not until November, 1933, when Roosevelt extended diplomatic recognition to the Soviet Union, did the *Tribune* draw blood with its criticism. For the balance of his first term, criticism by the McCormick paper was more frequent and progressively bitter.

Following the Democratic National Convention in 1936 it appeared momentarily that perhaps a truce was in the making. COL. MC CORMICK ORDERS STRICT IMPARTIALITY DURING CAMPAIGN was the caption on a story in the July issue of *Editor and Publisher*. The story concerned a letter from McCormick to his managing editor, E. S. Beck. Posted for the entire *Tribune* staff to see, the letter urged "completely unbiased reports with an effort toward equal coverage. . . ." So far, so good. The letter went on to remind one and all that during his first term Roosevelt had "tried to control the Washington correspondents." In conclusion, McCormick warned, "there will be so much Roosevelt news created by his commissars that it will be necessary to see that Landon gets a fair share of the total. But the Roosevelt stories must be adequate and must be written without any animus against him."[39] What followed in the pages of the *Tribune* must have sent readers of *Editor and Publisher* and many *Tribune* staff

Reprinted with permission from the Chicago Tribune. *Cartoon by Carey Orr. Photograph courtesy of the Chicago Historical Society.*

members scurrying to dictionaries, convinced they were mistaken about the definition of "animus." The day after the story appeared the *Tribune* began a series of editorials under the heading, "Turn the Rascals Out."

On September 1, 1936, the *Tribune* launched a vicious two-month campaign against the Administration with a front-page editorial entitled "If We Want a Cheka." "Another senatorial investigation is underway under the congenial direction of Senator La Follette," it read. "Its ostensible purpose is to discover violations of civil rights in labor disputes . . ." That was the purpose of the La Follette investigation, an investigation into violations of the Wagner Act. The story of strike-breaking, union-busting and labor intrigue carried the La Follette Committee from coast to coast and continued, intermittently, until 1940. But to hear the *Tribune* tell it: "The real purpose ought to be obvious. . . . The senatorial investigation is campaign politics and fraud. . . . It is another New Deal importation of European methods employed by dictatorships. . . . If we want a Cheka we can have one by re-electing Franklin D. Roosevelt."[40]

Reprinted with permission from the Chicago Tribune. *Cartoon by Carey Orr. Photograph courtesy of the Chicago Historical Society.*

From September 1 until Election Day, the *Tribune* provided further evidence of its impartiality by featuring (with only the number changed) a daily page one box:

> Only 92 days remain to save your country. What are you doing to save it?

Tribune telephone operators cheerily answered the telephone with "Good afternoon, do you know there are only——days to save your country?"[41]

The theme of the *Tribune's* anti-New Deal crusade during the campaign —communism and dictatorship versus the American Way of Life—was by no means glowingly original. As early as April, 1933, Colonel McCormick, in a speech to the New York Bond Club, made the strong assertion that the government was "dominated by a communist element which is very close to establishing a stranglehold upon us. The grip is almost overpowering today."[42]

During Roosevelt's first term, the arch-enemy of the "American Way of Life," according to McCormick, had not been Earl Browder, head of the American Communist Party, but Rexford Tugwell. Tugwell had been pictured as a sinister Rasputin, carefully manipulating Roosevelt for the Russians, secretly receiving orders from Moscow, and ready, at the appropriate moment, to head up a Communist coup d'état. The meanest of all *Tribune* attacks on Tugwell was a front-page cartoon on September 12, 1936. Captioned "The Ugly Head is Beginning to Show Itself," the cartoon showed a cardboard cutout of Roosevelt, half-fallen, and supported by a New Dealer tagged "Tugwell Plotter No. 1." A leering, bearded Bolshevik loomed in the murky background and Tugwell was saying to him, "Shh-h-h, keep down until after the election." In the same issue the *Tribune* continued its series of articles purporting to prove a parallel between the views of Tugwell and Lenin.[43]

VIII

The New Republic described the campaign of 1936 as "one of the most slanderous campaigns in the entire history of American journalism." After reading the *Tribune* editorial for September 23 few would have been inclined to disagree. There appeared on the front page, under the title "In Fascist Berlin," the following:

> Protestants may not worship God as they see fit.
> Catholics are persecuted for daring to instruct their
>   children in their faith.
> Jews are outcasts without citizenship rights. . . .
> As long as the Constitution of the United States

> stands as the supreme law of the land . . .
> there can be no fascism in our country, no
> inequality on account of religion or race.
> Mr. Roosevelt thinks our Constitution is out of date.[44]

On October 14, 1936, the day following Roosevelt's campaign visit to Chicago, the *Tribune* printed a picture of a Chicago street littered with Roosevelt campaign buttons. The caption read: "Roosevelt buttons intended for coat lapels land on ground. A ragpicker helping himself to Roosevelt buttons on a street near the Loop yesterday. Apparently the buttons were tossed aside by pedestrians to whom they were handed by women members of Young Democrats of Cook County, who made wholesale distribution." The Chicago *Daily Times* moved quickly to prove the picture and story a fake. In a signed statement the ragpicker confessed he had been paid twenty-five cents to pose. The campaign buttons, allegedly "tossed aside by pedestrians," had been thrown on the street by the *Tribune* photographer who posed the picture. The *Tribune* ignored the charge, failing even to deny it.[45]

Two weeks later the *Tribune* printed a photograph of a dogtag embossed with a social security number. According to the story accompanying the picture the New Deal was planning to fasten dogtags around the necks of all American workers. The story brought immediate denials from the Social Security Board that there was any such plan. Characteristically, not a word of the denial appeared in the *Tribune*; in fact the *Tribune* reprinted the photograph on election day.[46]

During one entire week of the 1936 presidential campaign, Roosevelt's name appeared on the front page of the *Tribune* only once. In one issue his name was omitted altogether; and on another day he was mentioned only once, and this on page thirteen. But when an investigation exposed vice conditions in two Wisconsin cities, the *Tribune* ran the story with a choice headline: ROOSEVELT AREA IN WISCONSIN IS HOT-BED OF VICE.[47]

These attacks on Roosevelt were mild compared to perhaps the most slanderous news story of the campaign, a story charging that American Communists had been ordered by their Moscow puppetmasters to work for the reelection of Roosevelt. Though there is ample evidence that Communist preference for Roosevelt over Landon resulted, in large part, from Comintern instructions for a popular front, there is no reliable evidence that American Communists were specifically ordered to work for Landon's defeat or that the Soviet Union took an active part in the election.

Charges that Russia was interfering in the presidential campaign apparently began with a *Tribune* story on August 9, 1936. Under the headline MOSCOW ORDERS REDS IN U.S. TO BACK ROOSEVELT, the story revealed that Communist party leaders in Russia had instructed American Communists to work for the reelection of Roosevelt and for the defeat of Landon who represented "forces which oppose the development of class war and revolution in America." The story, sent from Riga, Latvia, was credited to the *Tribune's* northern European correspondent, Donald Day. On August 12, the Day story was repeated. "Why," the Tribune asked editorially, "do the communists desire the re-election of Mr. Roosevelt?"[48]

The charges, if true, represented a violation of a 1933 pledge by the Soviet Union, a pledge not to engage in any form of political agitation in the United States. The *Daily Times*, Chicago's only pro-Roosevelt daily newspaper, decided to investigate. In the original story, Day cited as his authority Number 13 of *Kommunisticheski Internatzional*, a Soviet journal published in Moscow. The *Times* investigation revealed that the article cited by Day did not urge the reelection of Roosevelt, did not order American Communists to work for Roosevelt's reelection, was not, in fact, even a statement of the Communist Party of the USSR as Day had implied. The article was simply a translation into Russian of a radio speech by Earl Browder in Chicago on May 29, 1936.[49]

On August 28, the front page of the *Daily Times* carried a challenge written by Richard Finnegan with a two-deck banner, PROVE TRIBUNE STORY—$5,000:

The Chicago *Tribune* has sounded and resounded an alarm that the Russian government is taking a hand in our American election.
If it's true, the *Tribune* has scored a notable scoop. If it's a false alarm, if the *Tribune* has had its leg pulled, that's equally notable, even in a campaign of false alarms.
The *Tribune's* story is that Moscow has ordered the Reds in the United States to back Roosevelt against Landon. It sounds fishy to us.
If the *Tribune*, or any other newspaper, can prove to the satisfaction of the American Society of Newspaper Editors and the American Newspaper Publishers Association that the *Tribune's* dispatch from Donald Day, datelined, "Riga, Latvia, Aug. 8," with its heading is true, the *Times* will donate $5,000 to the work of the Freedom of the Press Committee of the American Newspaper Publishers Association.[50]

The next edition of the *Tribune* ignored the challenge and continued to stress the Communist issue. A front-page story headed "Soviets Take an Active Hand in U.S. Election" was paired with a cartoon of Soviet Russia shouting, "Stop Landon," to American Communists.[51]

On September 2, the *Daily Times* repeated the offer of $5,000 for proof of the story, asserting that its investigation proved the Day dispatch was a hoax. The Republican National Committee, which by this time was distributing reprints of the Day story, was specifically invited to prove the *Times* was wrong. Needless to say, no one accepted the challenge. Many of the anti-New Deal newspapers, preoccupied with defeating Roosevelt, not only ignored the challenge, they picked up and repeated the Day story. Another colonel in the Chicago newspaper world, Colonel Frank Knox, published an editorial in his Chicago *Daily News* one week after the *Times'* $5,000 offer. "In plain English," the colonel editorialized, "the Communist International at Moscow has authorized American Communists to vote for Roosevelt, in order to play up to other American radical groups and to defeat Landon and Knox."[52]

The final footnote to the Day story was ten years off. In 1946, Day was arrested by United States military authorities in Germany and imprisoned for having broadcast for the Nazis during the war.[53]

IX

"Well, sir, you made a marvelous campaign," wrote William Randolph Hearst to Franklin Roosevelt on the eve of the 1932 election, "one that has stirred the mind and heart of the nation. I believe that you will be triumphantly elected, but in any case I shall retain an enduring admiration for yourself and your great work. . . ." Soon after, Hearst sent Edmund Coblentz, editor of the *New York American*, to Roosevelt with a personal pledge. Coblentz was instructed to tell the President-elect that "we are going to work with him and support him, and if he will let us know . . . what he wants newspaper help on, we will be glad to give it to him, when and in the way he wants."

In April, 1945, when Roosevelt died, Hearst wrote a moving tribute to the late President: "The work and name of Franklin Delano Roosevelt will live on, not only today or tomorrow but in all the annals of recorded time. . . . He loved his country above all else and labored in its service with utter disregard of his own well-being . . . of life itself."[54]

In the thirteen years between the two events, the birth of the New Deal and the death of Roosevelt, Hearst had few kind words for the New Deal, fewer yet for Roosevelt.

The Hearst-Roosevelt vendetta began in earnest in the spring of 1935. Early in April, Hearst wrote Coblentz: "I think we will have to settle down to a consistent policy of opposition to this Administration. . . . To accomplish anything we must speak frankly." By speaking frankly, Hearst meant referring to New Deal tax policies and efforts to redistribute the wealth as "plunder of the worthy well-to-do," as policies "pursued to the limit by Lenin." The New Deal was "a political socialistic system," "a system of dictatorial direction" elected "by false representations." A lot of talk passed between Hearst and Coblentz about how "to re-arouse the American spirit," about how "to re-assert the authority of the Constitution." "We have to do our best," Hearst urged upon Coblentz. And for about a month following, a series of strongly worded editorials appeared in the Hearst papers, all vigorously attacking the New Deal.[55]

In June, Hearst stepped up the attacks on the Administration. In a

June 19 memorandum sent to both Bainbridge Colby and Coblentz, Hearst called Roosevelt's proposed tax program "essentially Communism." It was not pure communism, said Hearst, but "a bastard product of Communism and demagogic democracy, a mongrel creation which might accurately be called demo-communism, evolved by a composite personality which might be labeled Stalin Delano Roosevelt." That blast marked the final break between Hearst and Roosevelt; from that date forward Hearst became the most prestigious spokesman of the Roosevelt haters, with the possible exception of Al Smith.[56]

The Hearst assault on the Administration begun in the spring of 1935 overreached itself in November when the Los Angeles *Examiner* of November 14 declared: "I do not know what catastrophe will be required to shock this nation into a realization of the enormous consequences which are being planned and ARE BEING EXECUTED by the Federal Administration and its little band of fanatical adventurers. . . . This band of revolutionary radicals propose to OVERTHROW THIS GOVERNMENT. AND THEY ARE DOING IT."[57]

During the campaign year, 1936, the total resources of the impressive and formidable Hearst publishing empire—thirteen magazines, eight radio stations, and twenty-eight newspapers with an estimated 28,000,000 readers—were turned upon Roosevelt and his "band of fanatical adventurers." Before the year was out Hearst would ponder a variety of ways to fight Roosevelt, ways which included the possibilities of a third party, a Constitutional Democratic Party, with someone like Al Smith as the candidate; a lawsuit against the Senate Committee investigating lobbying activities (the Black Committee) as an indirect means of embarrassing and harassing the Administration; and, of course, the "discovery" of Alf Landon.

But the election year was not many months old before the Hearst strategy for beating Roosevelt became clear to anyone who could read. Hearst was intent upon convincing the American people in print that Roosevelt was not just mistaken. Roosevelt was dangerous. Roosevelt was subversive. Roosevelt was a Communist dedicated to the overthrow of the United States government.

In January, in a letter to Coblentz, Hearst set the tone for the campaign year. It was ironic, he thought, that the "Socialist Democratic Party" should hold its national convention in Philadelphia and nominate ("in the city where American independence was declared") the man who "violated every American principle of liberty and individualism. . . .":

What a travesty of American ideals, what a burlesque of Jeffersonian Democracy, what a political farce, what a Christmas pantomine with administration clowns and pantaloons, all joking and laughing and playing Bolshevik pranks on the public. What a chance for Harlequin himself, attired in red and yellow patchwork of alien policies, to tell his bedtime stories.[58]

As the campaign waxed hotter, Hearst's attacks became increasingly extravagant. The same day the Donald Day story appeared in the Chicago *Tribune* Hearst ran a full-page editorial "to inform readers on the encroachments and conspiracies of Communist forces on your Government, property and liberty." Among the "encroachments and conspiracies" cited by Hearst was a FERA-financed college in Arkansas which was a hotbed of communism, where nudism, free love, and other indecencies were practiced on the campus.[59]

The Day story fitted the purposes of the Hearst anti-Roosevelt campaign too well to be ignored. It represented the happy combination of Roosevelt-baiting and Red-baiting copy he had been grinding out for months. Hearst could not resist. On September 19 a story appeared in the New York *American* stating that, while Earl Browder was the "titular nominee" of the Communist Party, "the real candidate—the un-official candidate of the comintern—is Franklin D. Roosevelt."[60]

Hearst was handicapped by treachery in the ranks of his own employees, many of whom liked Roosevelt and held views on the New Deal which were out of joint with the views of their employer. Every move of the Hearst press was reported to Democratic Party leaders well in advance.[61] Thus it was that two days before Hearst editors across the country were simultaneously to charge Roosevelt with Red support and repeat the Donald Day hoax, Stephen Early, secretary to the President, was able to counter the thrust with a statement to the press on behalf of the President:

My attention has been called to a planned attempt by a certain notorious newspaper owner to make it appear that the President passively accepts the support of alien organizations hostile to the American form of government.

The President does not want and does not welcome the vote or support of any individual or groups taking orders from alien sources.

The American people will not permit their attention to be diverted from the real issues to fake issues which no patriotic, honorable, decent citizen would purposely inject into American affairs.[62]

Being outflanked by the Administration did not deter Hearst. On September 21, as scheduled, the newspapers in his chain ran front-page stories outlining the "vicious plot" against the government under the headline MOSCOW BACKS ROOSEVELT. Subscribers could read the discredited Day story and "proof" that "through its Comintern in Moscow and its puppet organization in the United States, Soviet Russia is taking an aggressive part in the Presidential campaign—ON THE SIDE OF THE NEW DEAL."[63]

Unabashed, the Hearst newspapers not only printed the story but also criticized the President for having the effrontery to deny the charges. The Hearst Detroit *Times* ridiculed Roosevelt for "so unbecoming a performance as his White House statement of Saturday [the statement by Stephen

Early], with its nervous denial of charges not yet published." The *Times* summed up the story with "the FACT [of Moscow Communist support] is NOT DISPUTED."[64]

The day following the Roosevelt disclaimer, Hearst, traveling with his retinue in Europe, replied from Amsterdam. Although the President's statement had not named the "notorious newspaper owner," Hearst recognized his description and wired an angry reply to Coblentz. He was furious because Roosevelt had issued his statement "through a secretary" and "had not had the frankness to say to whom he refers. . . ." He resented, he said, being made a campaign issue by "his [Roosevelt's] conglomerate party of Socialists, Communists and renegade Democrats. . . ." "Wherefore," began one of the strangest denials of the decade, "let us state that I have not stated at any time whether the President willingly or unwillingly received the support of the Karl Marx socialists, the Frankfurter radicals, Communists and anarchists, the Tugwell Bolsheviks, and the Richberg revolutionists which constitute the bulk of his following." And in the next breath, "I have simply said . . . he has done his best to deserve the support of all such disturbing and destructive elements." He was compelled, he said, to print the truth because he was an "honorable and patriotic journalist" not "a shifty, prevaricating politician. . . ."[65]

Hearst's insistence that he had never stated whether the President "willingly or unwillingly" received support from radicals while true in fact was probably false in spirit. For example, on September 22, the day after Hearst's statement, the New York *American* had the following headlines on pages one and two: ROOSEVELT HAS BROWDER'S AID; REPRESENTATIVE REECE HITS AT ROOSEVELT'S RED FOLLOWING; DEFEAT ROOSEVELT REDS—MACNIDER; SOCIALIST-LABORITE SAYS COMMUNISTS BACK ROOSEVELT; and NEW DEAL STILL AIMS AT SOCIALIST STATE.[66] On October 8, the *American* printed a cartoon in which a hairy, apelike hand was writing "OK, Moscow" on a scroll bearing the hammer and sickle emblem. Below the cartoon was a poem of indifferent merit:

> A Red New Deal with a Soviet Seal
> Endorsed by a Moscow hand
> The strange result of an alien cult
> In a liberty-loving land.
>
> The truth is out, and there is no doubt
> Of the trend of the New Deal heads
> Their plans are made and their courses laid
> With the blessings of the Reds.
>
> All free men shrink as they pause to think
> Of the threatening Moscow tide
> But the evidence there stands red and bare
> And it cannot be denied.[67]

THE ENEMIES OF AMERICA WANT ROOSEVELT was the headline on an eight-column editorial in the *American* of October 31, in which it was asserted that "proof abounds that Socialists, Radicals and Communists are ENTIRELY SATISFIED with the Roosevelt administration and WANT IT CONTINUED."[68]

Shortly before the election Hearst bought full-page advertising space in leading newspapers across the country. Fairly typical of these last-minute campaign advertisements was the one appearing in the Buffalo *Evening News* on election eve, November 2. After the usual charges of extravagant spending and overpowering taxes, Hearst, predictably, repeated the old bugaboo "Mr. Roosevelt recognized Stalin. And later, Stalin recognized Roosevelt. The documents have been printed. Moscow has told all the Communists in America to vote for Roosevelt, the Friend of Russia, the camarade of Communism. Are you surprised at that?"[69]

X

Some newspapers, some very good newspapers, papers like the St. Louis *Post-Dispatch*, the Washington *Post*, the Kansas City *Star*, opposed Roosevelt on principle, fought him honorably, and stuck to the issues in the campaign. But the papers and the columnists who hated him most ignored issues, ignored principles. Theirs was a campaign of vilification, of personal abuse, of reckless charges of treachery and subversion. They agreed with Colonel McCormick's verdict that the New Deal was "a call to revolution." And they agreed with the cheerfully outrageous calumnies of Henry Mencken that Roosevelt was "a blood-brother of Lenin." "The smile of the sonofabitch in the White House and the smile of Holy Joe in Moscow," wrote Mencken, "have a great deal in common. You see that kind of smile on the faces of the barkers at Coney Island." "Your god-damn university, Harvard," Mencken told a friend during the campaign, "will have a lot to answer for to history for the Roosevelts." Theodore, said Mencken, had "the manners of a saloon bouncer and the soul of a stuck pig." But Franklin was "the synthesis of all the liars, scoundrels, and cheapskates of mankind." "If I were you," Mencken advised, "I'd hand back my diploma." And they believed, or at least they pretended to believe, that Roosevelt would be defeated in 1936, that Mencken was right: "From the solid gold offices of the Liberty League to the dismal cells of the Communist Party a roar of disapproval has been launched at the grinning Dr. Roosevelt until it swells to the proportions of a national raspberry. . . ."

But Roosevelt did not lose, and Hearst felt constrained to be magnanimous in defeat. Just one day after the election he advanced a generous offer: "If Mr. Roosevelt is a good President, if he is a democratic President, if he is an American President, the Hearst newspapers will support him again. . . ." Before Roosevelt really had the chance to ponder the surrender terms, his attempt to reform the Supreme Court restored him to his former status in the press as the destroyer of the American Way.[70]

Roosevelt critics had often applauded the Supreme Court as the guardian of all that was hallowed in the American system, and depended on it as a bulwark against dangerous tendencies in the New Deal. Roosevelt believed, however, that the roar of his 1936 landslide election had all but drowned out the cheers for the Supreme Court, that the time had come for a showdown, for a confrontation which would resolve the long impasse between the Executive and Judiciary. On February 5, 1937, at his regular semi-weekly press conference, Roosevelt abruptly announced his plan to reorganize the court system.[71]

Over his breakfast tray the next morning Roosevelt received the first inkling that he had misread the public mandate he had received three months earlier at the polls. Newspapers that morning were the first wave of what became a torrent of noisy national reaction and implacable public opposition to what the anti-New Deal press shrewdly called the Roosevelt "court-packing" plan.

It was not that court reforms were unnecessary. They were necessary. They were long overdue and knowledgeable people knew it. But buried in the President's proposed legislation was a plan to appoint an additional federal judge whenever a judge reached the age of seventy and refused to retire. The appointee was not to replace but to supplement the older judge, and the number of such appointees for the entire federal court system could not exceed fifty. The plan specified that in the case of the Supreme Court membership could not exceed fifteen. In 1937, six of the nine judges on the Supreme Court were beyond seventy. Under the plan Roosevelt would have been entitled to appoint six new justices at once. The considerable merits contained in other parts of the proposal were obscured by what seemed to many a brazen attempt to emasculate the Supreme Court.[72]

Warnings of dictatorship and prophesies of ruin filled editorial pages. The "tory" press, said Joseph Alsop wryly, "sounded like a swampful of banshees on a bad night." Middle-of-the-road newspapers, some of which, only a few months before, had called for the scalps of reactionary Supreme Court justices, now pictured them as paragons of virtue, demi-gods, far removed from the sweaty crowds, abstractly weighing legislation in the delicate scales of law. Even some liberal journals, behaving "like hens that had hatched out . . . a cockatrice," gave "excellent imitations of Mr. Gladstone hearing that one of his reformed harlots had hit the primrose path again." The idea implicit in the Roosevelt plan, the idea that the Court may change its interpretation of the Constitution in order to support legislation designed to meet national needs, was said to be as "false in

theory as it would be ruinous in practice." "No issue," said Walter Lippmann, "so great or so deep has been raised in America since secession."[73]

Anyone who could read knew Supreme Court justices were not the nine
vestal virgins. And there were many irreverent souls who strongly suspected
that the Constitution itself (like a young virgin) could come to full bloom
only by being violated. Despite considerable evidence that it was
judicial interpretation and not fundamental law that had shackled Roosevelt's attempts at national recovery and reform, the Supreme Court was
nonetheless regarded by the public as a sacred symbol of national unity
and stability, as a slender but impregnable barrier against personal government. This, they contended, is a government of laws, not of men.

The effusion of platitudes, had they been laid end to end, would have
reached from Times Square to Capitol Plaza. "The President wants to
control the Supreme Court," was the outraged cry of the New York
Herald Tribune and the rest of the anti-New Deal press. "It is," said
Albert Jay Nock, "simply a proposal to add a kept judiciary to a kept
Congress." The Dallas *Morning News* likened the President's plan to
"The Sad Fable of a Baseball Game That Ended Baseball." It was the last
crucial game of the season. The pitcher, the town idol, had broken all
records and seemed unbeatable. The umpire had called three balls again
when the pitcher turned to the bleachers and held up his hand for silence.
It was the eleventh such verdict in succession and he was tired of it.
" 'There is no sense in going on with this,' he cried. . . . 'We can't hope to
win until we get a new umpire.' 'You ain't puttin' 'em over the plate,'
yelled an opposition fan. 'I don't claim to be doing that,' said the pitcher.
'I only say that I can't win without strikes and this umpire calls it a ball
if it isn't over. He is living in the past and judging by rules that were
made a century ago. I demand a new umpire.' 'Why not change the rules
instead of the ump?' demanded the fan. 'There isn't time for that,' said
the pitcher. 'This is an emergency. . . .' " So a new umpire came in and
the game was won, but it killed baseball. David Lawrence, editor of *U.S.
News*, said the same thing in one line: "Traditionally the spirit of America
has been that if you do not like the rules of the game, change the rules—
but don't soak the umpire." Publisher Frank Gannett thought it little
wonder that all who understood the implications of the plan, a plan
which the Hartford *Courant* described as "destitute of moral sensibility,"
were "panic-stricken over the outlook for America."[74]

While much of the press opposed the plan conscientiously, arguing
against it solely on its merits, there were those papers which insisted on
injecting the threadbare alarms of dictatorship. One West Coast paper
described it as "a dark dawning," an "incredible omen" in which "not
a thing would stand between the ambitions of an unscrupulous man . . .
in becoming absolute dictator of this country." Publisher Paul Block, in an
advertisement in *The New York Times*, called the court bill "the most

un-American, undemocratic measure ever proposed to a Congress." In the Midwest the Cleveland *Plain Dealer* reprinted the old saw of its neighbor, the Chicago *Tribune*, "Down the road indicated by the President . . . lies dictatorship and the end of constitutional government." The *Tribune* explored another facet of the court plan, speculating irrelevantly upon the possibility that the next President might be a member of the Ku Klux Klan and the implications of this for religious and racial minorities.[75]

The court plan failed and Roosevelt was forced to accept a compromise. There were many explanations for the failure, all of which may be at least partly valid. One of the reasons was most certainly Roosevelt's disingenuous arguments for judicial reform which played into the hands of the opposition press, which seemed to lend credence to the suspicions of the press. "Because he is adroit and not forthright," William Allen White wrote, "he arouses suspicions, probably needless, about his ultimate intentions. . . ." Even so avid a Roosevelt supporter as the New York *World Telegram* resented his circuitous tactics, describing them as "Too clever, too damned clever."[76]

XI

The American people had spoken on Election Day, 1936, their voices echoing through a thousand editorial offices. "Do you realize what happened to you on election day?" asked the *Christian Century* in an open letter to publishers. "Do you know that thousands, perhaps millions, of ballots which American citizens thrust into boxes carried not only a vote for Mr. Roosevelt, but an equally discernible vote against you?" "The press," wrote Maury Maverick, ardent New Dealer and representative from Texas, "having reached the lowest level of degradation in national history, was thoroughly repudiated." To the anti-Roosevelt press, he announced triumphantly, "the people have one long razzberry."[77]

Soon after the election of 1936 *The New Republic* ran a survey of the daily newspapers in the fifteen largest cities across the country, those papers that inevitably came to mind whenever was mentioned "the power of the press." The survey did not support Roosevelt's own estimate in a *Liberty* magazine article that "about 85 per cent of the press of the nation supported the opposition." But it did confirm that better than two-thirds of the total circulation was openly hostile to Roosevelt. Yet in those cities the election results almost reversed the circulation ratio, 69 per cent of the votes going to Roosevelt, 31 per cent to Landon.[78]

The conclusion seems inescapable that the press was strongly anti-Roosevelt and that opposition did not change perceptibly during the next four years. There were perhaps a number of reasons for this, some more legitimate than others. Certainly one reason, a reason that may have been more serious than all the rest, was Roosevelt's attitude toward the press. Roosevelt lost support of a substantial part of the press early in the game when he indicated he believed newspapers were businesses not revered temples of sacred trust, lost it when he indicated he believed publishers deserved no more consideration than other persons engaged in money-making enterprises.

The noisy fight over the NRA code for the press symbolized the beginning of the estrangement, an estrangement not unlike the one that developed between Roosevelt and other businessmen. Newspaper ownership was, itself, big business. The problems of the businessman were also the problems of the publisher, who did not merely reflect but actually possessed the attitudes and prejudices of big business. Not only was newspaper ownership a matter of high finance, but owners and publishers were almost invariably involved in businesses other than publishing. Their economic interests, like those of their allies, their friends, their wealthy advertisers, were best served by protecting and defending the status quo. Roosevelt, with his dubious schemes for recovery, his talk of a planned economy, seemed a threat to the status quo and, therefore, to business, the publishing business included. Publishers felt they were in danger of being wounded by Roosevelt in the same tender, if not fatal, part of their anatomy so fiercely protected by the Liberty Leaguers and all the rest.

The story of press opposition to Roosevelt and the domestic New Deal was a study of American journalism at perhaps its lowest ethical ebb. "Newspapers," declared Mark Ethridge, general manager of the Louisville *Courier Journal*, "never so badly failed to give guidance and leadership . . . were never so unfaithful to their trust to present unbiased news, with editorials free from selfish interests."[79]

Because several of the large metropolitan newspapers deliberately slanted their editorials and distorted facts in their news columns, suspicions were cast on the ethical standards of all of American journalism and particularly on the anti-Roosevelt press. It was not true that the entire opposition press of the decade conducted itself unethically. There were newspapers that distorted little or no news, played up few or no scare headlines, did not resort to sensationalism, invective, or abuse. Such newspapers as the Detroit *News*, the Kansas City *Star*, the Emporia *Daily Gazette*, the Cincinnati *Enquirer*, and others took strong pro-Republican positions and vigorously opposed the Roosevelt Administration, but with factual, reasonable, logical arguments.

The right of a Hearst or a McCormick or a Mencken to utter the most blatant and arrogant nonsense in their editorial columns could not be challenged. They had a right to stomp through their columns snorting any brand of hell-fire and damnation they chose, for sophisticated readers were forewarned. If they entered those columns they were walking in paths of opinion. When opinions leaked through onto the news columns as they often did; when facts were distorted, colored, embroidered, suppressed; and when the whole sorry business was defended on grounds of freedom of the press, that was quite another matter.

In the 1930's it is unlikely the press could have altered much the course of events. Roosevelt and the New Deal were the great realities, the overriding issues of the decade. And they had a momentum; there was something irresistible and inevitable in the air that swept aside everything in sight. But even so, the enemies of Roosevelt could not be excused simply because hatred of him made all things seem plausible. This was singularly true of newspapers which, by their own ground rules, the freedom of the press, had a special responsibility to cherish truth and fair-play. In the 1930's, when journalistic ethics seemed lowest, it may have been more than coincidence that the power of the press to influence public opinion seemed weakest.

PART IV

What So Proudly
We Hailed...

"I F you believe what you hear around Washington," wrote Ernest K. Lindley in his Washington *Post* column for March 3, 1939, "President Roosevelt and his policies have lost the confidence of the country and the New Deal is all 'washed up.' The Republicans and conservative Democrats have built up such a bear market on Roosevelt that even some of the New Dealers are selling him short."

In the elections the previous fall many people thought they saw a mandate. In 1938 Republican manpower in the lower house of Congress was almost doubled. The Democratic majority dwindled from 227 to 87, and at least a hundred Democrats won reelection by embarrassingly slim margins. More important, Roosevelt did not have a working majority. The number of disenchanted Democrats, when joined with Republicans, formed an anti-New Deal majority sufficient, according to one knowledgeable observer, "to defeat, or vitally amend, important legislation, although it may have the aggressive, and even the belligerent support of the White House." The mandate seemed clear enough. Put on the brakes. Stop spending. Restore sanity. Dismantle. Retrench. One could even talk of a "return to normalcy" without apologizing for either content or diction.

In the first session of the Seventy-sixth Congress following the elections of 1938, the Administration was plainly in retreat. Appropriations for the relief programs (in which, according to Congressman Taylor, "political debauchery flourished like a green bay tree") were severely slashed. In May, 1939, amid much talk of "heading for a crash" and "spending the nation into bankruptcy," the Republican National Committee encouraged the commemoration ("One could scarcely say 'celebrating,'" remarked Karl Mundt of South Dakota) of something called National Debt Week when the debt for the first time topped $40,000,000,000. The President's tax program (which was likened to "some outsider taking six or seven chips out of every pot in a poker game") was overhauled. While complaining of Roosevelt's "gallery plays against business" and "a malicious small boy chasing the goose that lays our golden eggs around the national barnyard," the tax burden was lifted. The tax on undistributed profits, that is. But the most dangerous aspect of the revolt on Capitol Hill, according to Drew Pearson and Robert Allen's "Washington Merry-Go-Round" column of August 4, never made the headlines. It was the formation "by die-hard anti-New Deal Senate Democrats of a secret parliamentary organization of their own," an organization "with all the trappings," a floor leader, whips, and executive committee.

Roosevelt's trouble with Congress in 1939, its manhandling of his program with immunity, its very nearly contemptuous attitude toward the occupant of the White House, was not a phenomenon which occurred overnight. It was more like chickens coming home to roost. Seeds of congressional discontent were present from the beginning, from 1933 on.

As early as May, 1933, Arthur Krock wrote, "In 1934 there will be heard in the land Republican campaign assertions that the President has put Congress . . . on the shelf . . . that the constitutional duties imposed upon Congress were generally surrendered to the Executive." Most critics would not be so circumspect as Krock; they would say simply that Congress had become a rubber stamp.

What many did not understand was that, at the outset, Congress was like most of the country. It, too, was frightened, was willing to go along with Roosevelt, was willing to try almost anything that might cure the Depression. But there were also those in Congress who supported Roosevelt, not because they were paralyzed by fear, but because they agreed with him. For Congress and the President to see eye-to-eye did not make Congress subservient. But Congress was a proud body, delicately poised, quick to take offense, especially where its prerogatives, real or imaginary, were at stake. If enough people claimed Congress was a rubber stamp, claimed it often enough, appealed to congressional pride, aroused jealousies which always lurked just beneath the surface, Congress was capable of becoming sublimely obstinate.

Congress was not a "rubber stamp," not in 1933 and certainly not later. At the start, Roosevelt felt compelled to work largely through the regular machinery of party leadership, to work with men who were not always sympathetic toward the New Deal but who had wide influence, some sense of party loyalty and discipline, men who could make the cumbersome machinery of Congress turn. For men such as Robinson, Byrnes, Rainey, Bankhead, and others, cooperation was not subservience; it was a feel for the art of politics developed over years of practice. For men like La Follette and Norris and the others of that band who had tended the flame of Progressivism during the bad years, Roosevelt seemed an answer to a prayer. For them to cooperate with Roosevelt meant to participate in the fulfillment of a dream.

Sometimes Roosevelt got more cooperation than he wanted; on more than one occasion Congress took the bit in its teeth, outran the Administration, forced the issue. Some legislation, important legislation, like the federal deposit insurance plan, for example, started in Congress. There is little argument that Senator Hugo Black's thirty-hour work week proposal challenged the Administration to offer a countermeasure, the NRA. Occasionally, Congress went farther than Roosevelt was willing to go. This was the case with the veterans' bonus bill which he vetoed. (Congressional initiative would produce more than five hundred Executive vetoes by the end of Roosevelt's second term.)

The need for exercising Executive restraint on Congress became imperative after the elections of 1934. The Democrats increased their majorities in both houses. More important, a sizable number of the new men were an altogether different breed of Democrat, men who were fervently liberal and loyal to Roosevelt rather than to the party. For the time being

Roosevelt had both hands full trying to persuade, reassure, assuage old party wheelhorses whose hearts were not in the New Deal while trying to maintain some decorum among the Maury Maverick crowd and other clusters of radicals, most of whom were to the left of the President.

Serious deterioration of Executive-Legislative relationships began shortly after 1934. It was more than the deep pitfalls inherent in reconciling the conservative-versus-liberal impulse of the Congress. Roosevelt finally ran afoul of institutionalized serenity. A national calamity had forced Congress and the President to lay aside temporarily their traditional conflict, a form of internecine warfare carefully built into the system. When the crisis eased, Congress showed signs of wanting to get back to the old casual, pull-and-tug ways of doing things, back to the long-remembered placid pace of cloakroom and committee-room politics. Congress had its quota of men who had been there for years, who had seen Presidents come and go, who were in no way dependent on the Executive for their power or for their uncanny ability to be reelected term after term, men who had acquired squatters' rights in Congress when Roosevelt was only a handsome young law school graduate.

If Congress had any disposition to take things easy, the customs and practices (particularly the seniority system) made it comparatively simple. Powerful committee chairmen were likely to be men least obligated to the President, virtuosos of the parliamentary game who could cause the President no end of misery. When the Democratic Party held the majority, southerners were likely to dominate the committees and control the machinery. This was the situation which confronted Roosevelt in 1933. So long as he remained on reasonably good terms with the southern wing of the party, the New Deal had a chance. If these men should be alienated, made to feel betrayed, the New Deal might be in trouble.

Some southerners felt they had just cause for straying from the New Deal reservation. For one thing, the New Deal after 1934 was becoming increasingly radical, they thought. In this they were correct; in 1935, there began a perceptible shift leftward in New Deal policy. Men who were always too conservative to feel at ease in the New Deal were now genuinely alarmed. Southerners also resented the secondary role to which they were being relegated in the party, a decline in power and prestige symbolized by the abolition of the two-thirds rule in the convention of 1936.

The high tide of Roosevelt's influence in Congress came in 1935, the Second Hundred Days it would be called. To push through a program of social reform never before equalled, Roosevelt used every weapon he had—reason, charm, flattery, diplomacy, intrigue, patronage, undisguised threats. But the price of success came high and Roosevelt had little in reserve. His first term, despite appearances, was not a public relations triumph with Congress. He had used the Depression crisis until it was threadbare. And to get action he had dealt directly with the congressional leadership, largely ignored the rank-and-file (even the friendly ones), piling up enemies and political debts along the way. The landslide victory of 1936 was deceptive; it was a badly disorganized and divided Democratic Party that rolled over Landon.

1937 began with glowing promises and ended with humiliating excuses. Roosevelt himself provided the issue around which every congressman or senator who had a score to settle with the White House could rally without a second thought. The Supreme Court fight galvanized New Deal opposition; the enemy tasted blood and it had not cost a thing. The embarrassing circumstances surrounding the appointment of Hugo Black to the Supreme Court, and the sharp economic setbacks later in the year ("the Roosevelt Depression," the opposition merrily labeled it) kept Roosevelt in retreat.

The coalition of southern Democrats and northern Republicans which had scored heavily against Roosevelt in the court fight, became virtually a permanent arrangement in 1938. Blocked in Congress by members of his own party, many of whom owed their elections directly to his popularity, Roosevelt slowly came to a decision fraught with peril. The time had come for a showdown in his own party. "An election cannot give a country a firm sense of direction," he told the nation in June, 1938, "if it has two or more national parties which merely have different names but are as alike in their principles and aims as peas in the same pod." The "purge" was on with liberalism, New Deal style, the issue in Democratic primary elections across the land.

In this duel with Congress the "purge" failed; almost to a man his enemies won. While Democrats were staging their family row, the Republicans gained eighty more seats in the House and seven in the Senate. By 1939, coalition leaders in Congress were no longer content with stalemate, with merely blocking Roosevelt at every turn. Nor did they have to be. They could cut appropriations, and did. They could disrupt some federal programs and dismantle others, and they did that too. Where once they had whined about presidential control over the Legislative branch, about being a "rubber stamp," they were now in position to extend Legislative control over the Executive. And they tried.

Despite all this, a *Fortune* poll early in 1939 indicated that more than 60 per cent of the people approved, at least in a general way, of Roosevelt and his New Deal policies. "If the *Fortune* survey is even approximately correct," wrote Lindley as a final thought, "a great many Democrats in Congress have let themselves be stampeded into the anti-Roosevelt camp by trepidations based on incorrect readings of the public mind." Roosevelt's strength, as it had been from the beginning, was his love affair with the American people. So enduring was that bond of affection, wrote Lindley, that it should serve as "a warning to the members of Congress, and especially to the Democrats, that they should think twice—or three or four times—before they flout him." But they did that too.

CHAPTER VIII

Chaste Seduction or Lawful Robbery

The trouble is that . . . he may destroy the country and himself as well.
—David A. Reed

We are about to transform a democracy into a dictatorship.
—James M. Beck

This is just like mounting the guillotine on the infinitesimal gamble that the ax won't work.   *—Hugh Johnson*

M ARCH 4, 1933. The country had never seen anything like it. Wheels were already turning. Even while the new President watched the inaugural parade from a pavilion erected before the White House, at the other end of Pennsylvania Avenue the Senate was meeting in extraordinary session to confirm members of the new Cabinet. They were sworn in that night at an impromptu ceremony at the White House.

The next day, Sunday, Roosevelt issued the call for a special session of Congress to commence on Thursday, March 9. Early Monday morning he proclaimed a four-day bank holiday, an order which forbade foreign-exchange transactions and prohibited withdrawal of silver and gold for either domestic or foreign use. Even before the inauguration, Roosevelt people had been working on two emergency measures. One was to deal with the banking crisis, the other to fulfill a campaign promise to cut spending. When the special session convened, a session which would forever after be called the "Hundred Days," the Administration was ready.

And just in the nick of time. The final touches were applied to the Emergency Banking Act at an all-night White House conference. At dawn on Thursday it was finished. "Both bills are finished," Secretary of the Treasury William Woodin told reporters. "You know my name is Bill and I'm finished too."[1] When the bank bill was introduced at three o'clock that afternoon there had not been time to print it; a newspaper sufficed for the purpose. Less than six hours later the President signed it. Congressmen, who had not the slightest notion what they had voted into law, did know one thing: the New Deal was on its way.

The contagion of confidence, the desire for action animated the extra session; for more than three months Capitol Hill hummed with furious activity. By the time of adjournment on June 15 an exhausted Congress had passed legislation which all but overhauled the American system of government. In one day, May 12, the President signed into law the Federal Emergency Relief Act, the Emergency Farm Mortgage Act, and the Agricultural Adjustment Act. On June 16, the day following adjournment, the National Industrial Recovery Act, the Glass-Steagall Banking Act, the Farm Credit Act, and the Railroad Coordination Act became law.[2]

Never before in peacetime had a President so swayed the Legislature. Never before had Congress attacked national problems with such vigor and unanimity. Never before had the voice of opposition been so stilled. Congress all but stampeded in its eagerness to jump on the President's bandwagon, to put over the President's program.

It voted and, on occasion, shouted the New Deal into existence, sometimes without a roll call, sometimes without so much as a copy of the bill being voted on. Roosevelt sent fifteen major messages to Congress ("Count that day lost whose low descending sun views no new message from the President come," commented one congressional wag), and signed into law fifteen major bills. As he looked up from the last of the bills passed by the special session, Roosevelt remarked: "More history is being made today than in any one day of our national life." "During all time," amended Thomas Gore, Senator from Oklahoma. It was true. In one hundred days Congress had committed the government to a new philosophy.[3]

II

Even the Administration farm bill was speedily passed by the House. But in the Senate, where the agrarian tradition had remained strong since the days of William Jennings Bryan, the bill ran into real trouble. The farm bloc senators, the voluble Elmer Thomas of Oklahoma in the lead, were joined by the silver senators, led by insurgent Burton K. Wheeler of Montana, in demanding monetary inflation as their price for support of the farm bill.

"The nation," warned Wheeler, "must adopt bimetallism or face bolshevism." After a Wheeler amendment to remonetize silver at the old ratio of 16 to 1 had failed, Thomas presented an omnibus inflation amendment authorizing the President to remonetize silver, issue paperbacks, and alter the gold content of the dollar. Since the Wheeler amendment had received thirty-three votes (a similar amendment had received only seventeen votes three months earlier), it was obvious that inflationist sentiment was on the increase. Preferring the permissive features of the

Thomas amendment to compulsory silver legislation, Roosevelt handed Raymond Moley a copy of the Thomas amendment with instructions: "Have it thoroughly amended and then give them word to pass it."[4]

And they passed it. But not without the first serious congressional controversy of the Roosevelt honeymoon. To senatorial critics, piling inflation on top of the regimentation of the Administration farm bill was too much. This was, according to Senator Vandenberg of Michigan, "the most revolutionary proposal that has ever been presented in the history of the government." Carter Glass, ignoring his doctor's orders, appeared before the Senate and, with tears in his eyes, pleaded that Roosevelt not be given authority to reduce the gold content of the dollar. Calling the Thomas amendment "an unbridled expansion," Glass declared, "the rein is so loose that the steed will never stop until he goes over the precipice and kills his rider at the bottom thereof." "To me," he continued, "the suggestion that we may devalue the gold dollar fifty per cent means national repudiation. To me it means dishonor; in my conception of it, it is immoral."[5]

Representative Hamilton Fish, Jr., of New York called the Thomas amendment "The most amazing, daring, and dangerous piece of legislation ever offered to the American people." Senator Reed of Pennsylvania, calling on the country to reject "this insane plan," said it was like "a child playing with dynamite.' "He is trying to make prices go up. He may succeed. The trouble is that in doing so he may destroy the country and himself as well." When the country goes on an inflation "jamboree," he declared, "there is always a morning after."[6]

Reed was joined by three other Republican leaders—Senator Frederick Walcott of Connecticut, Representative Bertrand H. Snell of New York, and Representative Robert Luce of Massachusetts—in a public statement attacking the Thomas amendment. "The Administration inflation bill," they said, "violates the most elemental principles of sound monetary, credit, and financial policies. It is better designed to defeat than to promote business recovery." "It is inflation on a grand scale," the statement continued, and "it may well constitute the first step on the road to ruin."[7]

The Agricultural Adjustment Act was more than the "first step on the road to ruin," according to some congressional critics; it was the first step on the road to Moscow. "Is it true," asked Representative Knutson of Minnesota, "that the operation of this measure, in a large degree, would sovietize American agriculture, and that this whole plan is based upon the plan that is now in . . . operation over in Russia?" "Within two weeks," accused Minnesota's Representative Ray Chase, "we have placed in the hands of a dictator supreme control of the wealth of America. . . ." The Agricultural Adjustment Bill, declared Fred Britten of Illinois, "is more bolshevistic than any law or regulation existing in Soviet Russia."

"We are on our way to Moscow," warned Representative Joseph W. Martin of Massachusetts. "I cannot," cried Senator Simeon D. Fess of Ohio, "take this leap in sovietism."[8]

Not all the criticism came from the loyal opposition in Congress. Some of Roosevelt's advisers were also opposed to the inflationary features of the farm bill. Lewis Douglas, Roosevelt's Director of the Budget, when told of the decision to cut the gold content of the dollar, warned William Bullitt: "Bill, this means the end of western civilization."[9]

Western civilization survived—at least long enough to fulfill the dream of Senator George Norris of Nebraska, the establishment of the Tennessee Valley Authority with its multi-purpose dams to serve as flood-controlling reservoirs and its inexpensive hydro-electric power.

The TVA bill, introduced early in April, ran into stiff opposition in the House when Joe Martin charged it was "patterned closely after one of the soviet dreams . . . [and] will end as have most of the Russian industrial ventures—in failure. . . ." Other Republican members agreed TVA was another step on the road to Moscow. "Continue along these lines," warned Harry C. Ransley (Pennsylvania), "and you will have a socialistic government, destroying the initiative that has made this country great." According to Charles A. Eaton (New Jersey), TVA was "simply an attempt to graft onto our American system the Russian idea and make the government everything and the citizen nothing." "Not only does it scent of Communism," said Jesse H. Metcalf (Rhode Island), "but it is characterized by the cruel and destructive strokes always present when a government makes a violent change in its fundamental nature." "We are socializing this country today," charged Representative Robert F. Rich of Pennsylvania, "we are not only socializing it but we are Russianizing it." "The Tennessee Valley Authority," Rich prophesized, "will be one of the greatest boomerangs and one of the greatest monstrosities that has ever befallen the American people."[10]

Not only was the bill an attempt to Russianize America, but, on the more practical side, according to its Republican critics, it was economically unsound. "It is another deflationary measure," charged John Taber (New York), and will "create a situation that results in a further depression of the price of labor and commodities. . . ." "If you pass this bill," Harry Ransley warned, "you will put out of business many fertilizer plants, employing thousands. . . ." "This is no time," declared Carl E. Mapes (Michigan), "to start expenditures of this kind. . . . It is economically unsound. . . ." "The Muscle Shoals area," Allen L. Treadway (Massachusetts) reminded his colleagues, "is at present more than adequately served by existing private power companies." Besides, he continued (not meaning to be grimly humorous), the demand for power "has been steadily decreasing during the last few years." According to Edward W. Goss (Connecticut), the existing power capacity of the area was "more

than 33 per cent in excess of the market demand." "To those who advocate that our Government should engage in such an undertaking," declared Thomas Cochran (Pennsylvania), "I will say, by way of comparison,
banditry is an honorable profession." Dewey Short, Republican from
Missouri, told the House that "of all the crazy, cockeyed schemes hatched
from the diseased and disordered brains of the 'new dealers,' the T.V.A.
easily takes the prize. . . . This legislation . . . is false, fickle, flimsy, frivo-
lous, and fraudulent."[11]

Despite all opposition the TVA bill passed both houses by wide margins.
So did the Economy Act; at first, anyway. Roosevelt had been working
on plans to cut spending since before the inauguration. On March 10, in
his second message to the special session, he requested sweeping powers
to slice $400,000,000 from payments to veterans and another $100,000,000
from the pay of federal employees.

Convinced the proposed Economy Act reflected Wall Street demands
for wage slashing, demands of "big powerful banking racketeers," and that
it was cruel and unfair to veterans, "a slaughter of the disabled service
men of the United States," one congressman called it, the Democratic
caucus in the House refused to support the President. But that was only
big talk in the privacy of the caucus room. On the floor of the House
the attitude of the insurgents changed; those who protested so vigorously
in secret became docile in public. "I had as soon start a mutiny in the
face of a foreign foe," declared Representative John Brown of Kentucky,
"as start a mutiny today against the wishes of the President of the United
States." "When the *Congressional Record* lies on the desk of Mr. Roosevelt in the morning he will look over the roll call," warned Congressman
Clifton Woodrum of Virginia, "and from that he will know whether or
not the members of his own party were willing to go along with him in
his great fight to save the country."[12]

There were hisses and groans, and a few cat-calls, but the point struck
home. All but ninety Democrats heeded Woodrum's counsel, and the
House passed the economy bill after only two days of debate. The Senate,
where the long knives were, had no stomach for a fight either after
Roosevelt took to the radio for the first of his Fireside Chats.

Congressional revenge came later in the special session when, under authority of the Economy Act, the President pared an estimated $460,000,000
off the veterans' budget. This was the last straw to a Congress ripe
for revolt, revolt inspired by stacks of letters from disabled ex-soldiers
relating tragic stories of hardship resulting from the new regulations of
the Veterans Administration. As letters were received and read on the
floor of the Senate and House, pathetic letters, letters from yesterday's
heroes now lonely and forgotten, passion for economy in government
yielded to sympathy for destitute, maimed, bedridden ex-servicemen.

One thing they all objected to, to use Senator Huey Long's picturesque prose, was "authorizing some little two-by-four, two-bit, job-hunting politician" in the Veterans Administration to decide the compensation due ex-servicemen. Long, for the life of him, could not understand why the government "took four hundred millions from the soldiers and spent three hundred millions to plant saplings." "They went beyond all reason in their reductions," charged Senator Dill of Washington.[13]

In the Senate, compassion for the plight of veterans was expressed by adding an amendment to the appropriations bill restoring $170,000,000 from the Roosevelt reductions and placing a 25 per cent limit on cuts in compensation for service-disabled veterans. The House enthusiastically concurred. Although the President salvaged a compromise, refusal of Congress to accept his leadership in the matter represented the only serious congressional revolt of the special session.

Roosevelt had not heard the last of the veteran issue. It would arise to plague him again early in 1934. Prodded by ex-servicemen and federal employees, the second session of the Seventy-third Congress in April, 1934, demonstrated it could serve other masters than Roosevelt. It enacted a law which the President opposed and dramatically vetoed, a law that provided veterans an additional $83,000,000 annually and $100,-000,000 for federal jobholders. The House overrode the President's veto 310 to 72 and the Senate, 63 to 27. "That was the worst trimming any President has ever taken in any Congress," exulted Bert Snell, Republican leader in the House, with the exaggeration expected of opposition leaders.[14]

III

Although Congress emasculated one of Roosevelt's principal achievements, the Economy Act, and imperiled one of his original policies, the bringing of government expenditures—excluding those for emergency purposes—into balance with receipts, on other fronts real progress was being made against the economic crisis. Major steps had been taken in the fields of finance (Emergency Banking Act, March 9; abandonment of the gold standard, April 19), agriculture (Agricultural Adjustment Act, May 11; Emergency Farm Mortgage Act, May 12), conservation (Civilian Conservation Corps, March 31), power (Tennessee Valley Authority Act, May 27), and relief (Federal Emergency Relief Act, May 12). But industry, the touchstone of the American economy, was omitted from congressional consideration until virtually the end of the special session.

On June 12, after a long, uphill fight, the Senate finally passed the National Industrial Recovery Act by a vote of 49 to 39. The bill presented to Congress back in May was a double-barreled proposition. Title I was intended to promote industrial recovery by waiving the anti-trust laws and permitting cooperation in wages, hours, prices, markets, and the like through codes voluntarily adopted by the various industries on a nation-wide basis. Title II established a Public Works Administration, with an initial appropriation of $3,300,000,000.[15]

With little debate and few changes the House rushed the bill through in just over a week. In the Senate, however, the bill—particularly Section 7a, containing collective bargaining, maximum hours, and minimum wage provisions—encountered stiff opposition.

To most Republican congressmen the National Industrial Recovery Act was a dangerous and impractical regimentation which violated their concepts of government, of economics, and particularly of the role of government in the economy. As they had with the AAA and the TVA, so grim-faced congressmen pointed the accusing finger at this new effort to "sovietize America." "As the shadows of the evening are lengthening with us now, the shadows of a lasting night are falling upon the old constitutional edifice," warned Congressman James Beck, the brilliant constitutional lawyer, in funereal prose. "We are about to transform a democracy into a dictatorship." Beck, the most prestigious opponent of the bill in the House, protested against a measure that "barters away the constitutional functions of this House and the industrial liberties of the American people." "That is a contradiction in terms," he declared to those who argued that the NRA would create no more than a benign dictatorship. "You might as well talk of chaste seduction or lawful robbery or of peaceable murder. . . ."[16]

"We have made Mr. Roosevelt a dictator—a dictator," insisted Arthur R. Robinson, senator from Indiana. "The New Deal," accused Senator Henry Hatfield of West Virginia, "while it sings the praises of Jefferson and Jackson, is more in keeping with the preachings of Norman Thomas, Stalin, Mussolini, and Hitler. . . ." "Had Karl Marx risen from the grave to write the bill," he plunged on, "the triumph of his idea could not have been more complete." "The wonder is," said the senator who would soon join ranks with the Liberty League, "that Stalin . . . has not sooner cabled his congratulations to the White House, because this bill boldly flaunts the label, 'Made in Moscow.'" Later, not content with so simple and direct a criticism, Hatfield listed forty-two reasons for the Senate why he opposed this "ghastly folly of regimentation."[17]

On Bernard Baruch's recommendation, Roosevelt chose General Hugh Johnson to head the Recovery Administration and to get on with the business of negotiating NRA codes with major industries. Thick-necked, profane, pugnacious, with the gentleness of a master-sergeant and the tact of a bulldozer, Johnson greeted his appointment with a prophesy: "It will be red fire at first and dead cats afterward." The codes, Johnson hoped, would "eliminate eye-gouging and knee-groining and ear-chewing in business." He had no illusions, however. The chances, he remarked, were about "like mounting the guillotine on the infinitesimal gamble that the ax won't work."[18]

The ax worked; flying dead cats did fill the air; but it was the Administration's eyes that were gouged and groin that was kneed—from both sides of the congressional aisle. By November, 1933, criticism of the NRA was widespread. Critics suggested the initials stood for "No Recovery Allowed," "National Run Around," "National Racketeer's Association," and "National Ruin Act." Progressive Republicans like Gerald Nye and William Borah declared the NRA had become a breeder of monopoly. An old-school Democrat like Carter Glass deplored "the utterly dangerous effort . . . to transplant Hitlerism to every corner of this nation." Senator Patrick A. McCarran, Democrat from Nevada, warned the NRA was "an avalanche that sweeps away the structures fought for and reared by the great Jefferson. . . ." "The NRA," declared Senator Simeon Fess of Ohio, has "gone too far in the Russian direction."[19]

In March, 1934, no longer able to ignore mounting protests, Roosevelt appointed a temporary board with the legendary defense attorney, Clarence Darrow, as chairman to investigate the NRA. Hugh Johnson, in what he later called "a moment of total aberration," enthusiastically agreed.[20]

Darrow, now nearly seventy-seven years old, viewed this as his last case and gave it everything he had. For four months Darrow and his staff investigated everything in sight; held nearly sixty public hearings; considered some three thousand complaints; analyzed thirty-four codes; issued one report after another. The result was not, as Johnson had expected, a measured appraisal of the program but a scathing attack which branded the NRA an instrument of monopoly.[21]

The New York Times, reviewing the Darrow report, remarked, "Reversing the precedent of Balaam, Mr. Darrow, summoned to bless the Recovery Act, remained to curse it." General Johnson, nonplussed but at no loss for words, described the report as "superficial, intemperate, and inaccurate," and declared "this Board is not in good faith." "Bloody old Jeffries [sic] at the Assizes," he stormed, "never conducted any hearing equal to those for cavalier disposal of cases." NRA general counsel, Donald Richberg, had a more sophisticated criticism. The report, he wrote to Roosevelt, was compiled by "a noted Socialist who advocates complete Government control of business," and who was trying to please "philosophic anarchists who apparently opposed any Government control of anybody, including criminals."[22]

Congressional critics got good mileage from Darrow's embarrassment of the Administration. Republicans in Congress, men whose usual reaction to Darrow was that he deserved to be shot for his radicalism, now praised him for his wisdom and vision. His report at once became expert evidence justifying additional Republican assaults on the NRA. They were not long coming. Senator Nye, representing the left wing of his party, continued his attack on "the Blue Eagle . . . a bird of prey on the masses" in a series of speeches in the Senate. Right-wing Republican senators, men like Fess, Dickinson, and Hastings, chimed in with remarks about how the NRA was "impractical . . . bears out the general idea that monopoly is developed . . . it demonstrated the danger of abandoning the Federal Constitution." Senator Schall interjected a few lowbrow comments about "Brigadier 'Crack Up' Johnson," and about "fixing code prices for barbering, shoe shining, clothes pressing and cleaning. . . ." "The N.R.A. should be repealed," said Schall "and Clarence Darrow should be given a vote of confidence of the Senate."[23]

And so it went. Despite all Roosevelt's efforts to improve the NRA—he trimmed its powers, limited its jurisdiction, replaced Johnson with the more domesticated Donald Richberg—the whole industrial recovery apparatus was near administrative and political collapse by the time the Supreme Court delivered the *coup de grâce*.[24]

IV

Except for criticism by leaders in Congress, the Republican Party remained silent during the early days of the New Deal.

Republican House leader Bertrand Snell, commenting on the performance of congressional Republicans during the first hundred days, claimed the minority had resorted to no "captious criticisms," no "partisan obstructions," even when it "violently disagreed"; Republicans had registered their disagreements in a "dignified and parliamentary manner."[25]

Absence of strong opposition from Republicans until late 1933, was, according to Turner Catledge, the result of deliberate strategy. "These Republican leaders," he wrote in *The New York Times*, "make no secret of purposely sitting back and giving the administration a free rein in its efforts to dispel the depression. . . . Their philosophy is simple. . . . If the program works, it would be futile to resist it; if it does not work, it would be futile to resist us; there is plenty of time to tell."[26]

There was more to it than that. Besides this strategy of silence the party was torn by internal dissensions. For years the party had dominated national affairs. It had elected Presidents, controlled congresses, passed laws, taken credit for prosperity. Now that it was temporarily eclipsed it became a divided party, a frustrated factious minority. Except for list-less, almost melancholy opposition by congressional leaders, Republicans ventured no serious criticism of Democratic policies until autumn, 1933.[27]

In November the Republican National Committee issued a sharply worded pamphlet, *Let's Look at the Record*, blasting the Administration for failing to live up to Roosevelt's campaign promises of sound money and a balanced budget, for failing to make good its pledges on public works and agricultural relief. The next month, ignoring the Christmas spirit, the committee followed with another pamphlet, *Tories, Chiselers,*

Dead Cats, Witch Doctors, Bank Wreckers, Traitors, denouncing the Roosevelt recovery plan as dictatorial. This sudden burst of activity embarrassed congressional Republicans who thought the violent anti-New Deal tracts too extreme. Republicans in both houses hastily set up their own campaign committees, and the National Committee again subsided into inactivity.[28]

For the most part, criticism of the New Deal by conservative Republicans was negative and consisted chiefly of doctrinaire arguments, arguments that were legalistic, constitutional, and business-oriented, arguments that defined government in terms of what it could not and should not do regardless of urgent social needs.

As the congressional campaign of 1934 approached, the pat argument of Republicans was that the New Deal was contrary to traditional American values and principles. "Already liberty and the Bill of Rights have been ruthlessly destroyed," declared Mrs. Paul FitzSimmons, Republican committeewoman of Rhode Island. "The Constitution is a mere scrap of worthless paper. . . ."[29]

Chief among the destroyers of liberty and the Bill of Rights were the Brain Trusters. "If Wallace and Tugwell and Frankfurter and company are liberals," Henry P. Fletcher, Republican National Chairman, told his audience at a Lincoln Day dinner in Hagerstown, Maryland, "then Stalin and Hitler are liberals and Jefferson and Jackson were Tories." In June, 1934, the Indiana Republican state convention adopted a platform which opposed "unalterably and . . . unsparingly the sinister and hidden purpose of a so-called brain trust to change the fundamental law of the land by indirection and by implication."[30]

Republicans in Congress, fearful of making direct attacks on so popular a President, also found the Brain Trust (those "starry-eyed academicians" and "sinister Rasputins") a safe convenience. Brain Trusters were men "more interested in changing our form of government than . . . in recovery" (J. Will Taylor, Tennessee); men who were "at heart Socialists if not actually Socialists . . . [and] take all their principles and doctrines from Karl Marx just as the Communists do" (Hamilton Fish, New York); men like "Tugwell and Mordecai Ezekiel and . . . Frank and Frankfurter and all the other radicals who are leading us straight to Russian sovietism" (Thomas Jenkins, Ohio). Brain Trusters, men who "affiliate with the Civil Liberties Union," warned Jenkins, "want a dictator . . . their theories will Russianize America."[31]

The blanket indictment of the Brain Trusters was sufficiently broad to cover their sinister allies, the power-hungry bureaucrats. These were dangerous men, declared Henry Fletcher, at the eightieth birthday celebration of the Republican Party in Jackson, Michigan, to whom President Roosevelt entrusted "a vast maze of theorizing, meddling, directing, spending, lending and borrowing agencies, lettered on the Russian model."

In his Fourth of July radio address, Senator Borah blistered "that meddlesome, irritating, confusing, undermining, destructive thing called bureaucracy . . . which steals away man's rights in the name of public interest and taxes him to death in the name of recovery." Senator Arthur Robinson, campaigning for reelection in 1934, complained of the "arrogant dictatorship and ruthless destruction of our constitutional rights" by New Deal "bureaucratic busybodies" and their "mad schemes of collectivism and regimentation" in a "headlong rush of events carrying us on the road to Moscow."[32]

New Deal socialism, communism, and dictatorship were all some Republicans could find to talk about during the campaign of 1934. Without a salable program of their own, and not daring to attack Roosevelt directly, this was probably their only choice. So the country heard the charges over and over, charges lacking conviction, charges which people did not believe or did not give a damn about anyway, heard them until they were blue in the face. The New Deal, they said, was "a blind experiment" in which constitutional government was being "ravished and reduced to a travesty," in which state sovereignty and honest federalism was being "offered up to the Moloch of centralized government." Under the New Deal, they said, freedom for private business was "a thing of the past," individual liberty was "only a memory," replaced by a dictatorship which "must have made the noses of Herr Hitler, Stalin, Mussolini, and Mustapha Kemal of Turkey turn green with envy." The New Deal, they said, was based on a philosophy "not that of our fathers." It was an alien philosophy, "sired in Germany and damned [sic] in Russia," a freak species of "denatured communism imported directly from Russia and decked out with a few American trimmings." Senator Tom Connally of Texas, having listened wearily to one of Senator Dickinson's "strange and inimical to the American system" speeches, compared the Iowa senator and other anti-New Dealers like him to the swamp owl: "The more light you throw around him, the blinder he gets."[33]

The closest Republicans drew to a personal attack on the President came in late July when Henry Fletcher charged Roosevelt with using relief, drought aid, and crop reduction benefits as a "great campaign fund." He accused the Administration of deliberately delaying checks for crop reduction so they would reach farmers at the right psychological moment, just before the elections. "From now on in an increasing volume as the elections near," he added, "there will be a great outpouring of more government funds." Senator Fess of Ohio and a number of other senators claimed the New Deal was buying votes in their states with federal funds. Colonel Theodore Roosevelt, speaking at a Republican rally in October, stated, "The national administration is treating the billions placed at its disposal by Congress as a colossal campaign fund." "For the first time in fifty years," he added, "Washington lies in the shadow of Tammany Hall, and the methods of Boss Tweed, Croker and Murphy are being applied in our Federal government." "The lowest form of partisanship," charged Walter Edge, former governor of New Jersey, is "capitalizing misery, or permitting necessary relief to become a political racket."[34]

V

Whatever the causes, the Republicans lost in 1934, lost dismally. Chairman Fletcher, like every national chairman before him whose party had just absorbed a drubbing, tried to explain it away. Roosevelt's endorsement at the polls, he said bravely, "rests on a very narrow base." Republicans had done well, he insisted, better than could have been expected "in the teeth of the most cynical and shameless use of public money to influence votes." The leaders had tried hard enough. But the truth was that the Republicans lacked a positive program, lacked meaningful issues, lacked unity of purpose, and Fletcher knew it. Some Republicans had played it safe by remaining silent or by volunteering to support the New Deal "when it is right." Other Republicans, men like Charles McNary of Oregon, were known to be generally favorable toward the New Deal which created the anomaly of some candidates approving issues opposed by their party leaders. In any case, the Democrats won big in 1934; according to William Allen White, Roosevelt was "all but crowned by the people."[35]

The party in power traditionally lost seats in off-year elections. But instead of losing seats the Democrats gained thirteen in the House. In the Senate the victory was even more astounding. The Democrats won the greatest margin—better than a two-thirds majority—either party had ever held in the upper chamber. Arthur Krock assessed it as "the most overwhelming victory in the history of American politics."[36]

When Roosevelt addressed the country in January, 1935, it was with justifiable confidence, with "a strong hope . . . not empty optimism." "We can, if we will," he said, "make 1935 a genuine period of good feeling." Some of Roosevelt's advisers were even more enthusiastic. "Boys —this is the hour," Harry Hopkins exulted. "We've got to get everything we want—a works program, social security, wages and hours, everything— now or never."[37]

But Roosevelt was mistaken. So was Hopkins. So were a lot of others. The year 1935 was not going to be one of "good feeling." Congress, overwhelmingly pro-Administration on the surface, was going to be "far talkier and balkier" (as Raymond Moley put it) than anyone expected.[38]

By 1935 crucial programs of the early New Deal, programs like the NRA and the AAA, had lost momentum. The Blue Eagle, in the words of one congressman, had become "a Soviet vulture, perched on the smokeless factory chimneys of New England." The AAA was not faring much better. People were looking to the Administration and the new Congress for radical new approaches to recovery, for "super-New Dealing" according to one New England newspaper.[39]

The off-year elections had demonstrated more than Roosevelt's immense popularity; they had demonstrated as well the radical temper of the public. A number of new Democrats, elected on public-ownership and "production-for-use" platforms, stood well to the left of Roosevelt, and threatened to push the New Deal further than Roosevelt intended to go. Roosevelt had a tiger by the tail which prompted his remark to Raymond Moley that the only thing the New Deal had to fear now was its own excesses.[40]

As Roosevelt faced the first session of the Seventy-fourth Congress, political observers were predicting 1935 would be a year of reform surpassing even 1933 and the Hundred Days. But the State of the Union message did not indicate it. Roosevelt told Congress he would submit a new security program, new proposals for public works and work relief, and measures to extend the NRA and revise taxation "forms and methods." The New Deal, it appeared, was to be improved, clarified, consolidated, but not significantly broadened.[41]

The message seemed to fit the mood of Roosevelt's uncertainty. For the next few months he hesitated, procrastinated; for the first time he seemed unsure of himself. Buffeted from both left and right, Roosevelt attempted to steer a tentative middle course, moving first one direction then the other, reacting mechanically to specific problems and pressures. During the early months of 1935, months of "ordeal by indecision," the strong Roosevelt leadership was not evident; according to some, the Administration seemed to be drifting.

With conservatives insisting the New Deal had already gone too far too fast and radicals and progressives insisting it had done too little for too few too slowly, the recovery program was in danger of bogging down completely. Not only was Roosevelt assailed from all sides by external pressures, but there were internal troubles, troubles in the family. On one side was a group hot for recovery but cool toward reform, New Dealers who felt the most promising attack on depression could be made by restoring business confidence through discreet government-business cooperation. This group, including Donald Richberg, Raymond Moley, and Hugh Johnson, was joined by conservative Democrats in Congress. These were men who could nod in unison when, as early as the spring of 1934, Moley announced, "The New Deal is practically complete." On the other side stood Rexford Tugwell, Thomas Corcoran, Benjamin Cohen, and the congressional progressives who shared the belief that reform was at least as important as recovery, that reform should be instituted while public temper favored change. They agreed with Tugwell, agreed the New Deal was not only incomplete, it had hardly begun.[42]

Pressure for action came from all sides. Regardless of political persuasion all could agree, and did agree, that in the political year 1935 the New Deal had unfinished business. Millions were still unemployed; farmers were still drought-stricken; industrial workers were still restless and rebellious. The utopian schemes of Long and Townsend and the rabble-rousing of Father Coughlin were attracting millions of "true-believers." A new Congress, spoiling for a fight, had been elected in a campaign in which economy had hardly been mentioned. The business community, revived and breathing normally, was determined to stop any leftward movement of the New Deal.

The problems were there all right; but so were the self-anointed to make sure Roosevelt chose the right solutions. And in the super-charged atmosphere hung the threat that the Supreme Court might nullify important New Deal gains.

VI

Fear of the Supreme Court had nagged at New Dealers from the beginning. Four Court justices—Pierce Butler, James McReynolds, Willis Van Devanter, and George Sutherland—were arch-conservatives. Chief Justice Charles Evans Hughes and Owen Roberts seemed to be middle-of-the-roaders. The remaining three—Benjamin Cardozo, Harlan Fiske Stone, and Louis Brandeis—were usually on the side of liberalism. With the liberal trio, however, there were limits to their approval of reform measures that concentrated more power in the hands of the federal government. With the existing lineup the prospects were none too promising that certain New Deal measures would clear the judicial hurdles.

During the first two years no important piece of New Deal legislation came before the Supreme Court for judicial review. By 1935, test cases in the lower courts had worked their way up and several appeared on the Supreme Court calendar early in the year.

In January, the Court voted 8 to 1 against the government in a case challenging the "hot oil" provision of the National Industrial Recovery Act. From then until May, decisions in a number of other cases indicated the New Deal was in real trouble with the Court. In March, in a series of decisions, four in all, the Court sustained the Administration's repudiation of the gold clause in public and private contracts. But just barely; each time the vote was 5 to 4. The minority opinion, written by Justice McReynolds, was one of the bitterest on record; parts of the oral presentation were too bitter to be printed. At one point McReynolds lurched forward in his seat, face flushed, and proclaimed, "This is Nero at his worst. The constitution is gone!" Early in May the moderate Justice Roberts deserted his middle-of-the-road position, joined the four conservatives, and the Court (in another 5-to-4 vote) found the Railroad Pension Act unconstitutional.[43]

The most serious blow to the prestige of the New Deal came on May 27, 1935, "Black Monday," when the Supreme Court in a trio of unanimous decisions, struck down the Frazier-Lemke Farm Mortgage Act of 1934, ruled illegal the removal of William E. Humphrey from the Federal Trade Commission, and declared unconstitutional the general code-making procedure under the National Industrial Recovery Act.

It was the last of these decisions, *A.L.A. Schechter Corporation v. United States,* the celebrated "sick chicken" case, that was the most disconcerting to Roosevelt, but not because it effectively killed the NRA; Roosevelt had gotten about all the mileage he could from the NRA anyway. There were strong indications that Roosevelt was secretly glad the Court had spared him the embarrassment of scrapping the program. What was upsetting was the narrow construction the Court seemed to place on the commerce clause, a construction more restrictive than any decision in decades. It was this and the implications in it for other important parts of the New Deal that nettled the President, that led him into one of those infrequent but irretrievable faux pas. Roosevelt shot off his mouth. "We have been relegated," he petulantly informed his press conference, "to the horse-and-buggy definition of interstate commerce."[44]

VII

"Black Monday" was, so to speak, the last straw. For five disastrous months Roosevelt had succeeded in pleasing no one. The polls indicated his popularity was at its lowest since 1933; the Supreme Court had just laid low a major part of his program; the recovery program, after a fast start in 1933 and 1934, seemed to be slowing to a crawl. And while Roosevelt dawdled, indecisively, so did the Congress. By May the only major piece of legislation passed was the $5,000,000,000 relief act.

Early in the session Roosevelt's comfortable margins in Congress had begun to erode. The new Congress, to be sure, was composed of more radical members than its predecessor; but not everyone was committed to lavish spending. And there was a potent minority of conservatives, reduced in ranks but nonetheless formidable, determinably opposed to the reformist zeal manifested in the new Congress by left-leaning legislators.

In January when the House approved Roosevelt's request for nearly $5,000,000,000 for relief, Dewey Short, as usual, had plenty to say about "a supine, subservient, soporific, superfluous, supercilious, pusillanimous body of nitwits" handing over their powers and prerogatives on a silver platter "to a group of tax-eating, conceited . . . nincompoops out of Columbia University. . . ." Howard W. Smith, Democrat from Virginia, in more courtly language, deplored the "clear and complete abdication . . . and a delegation by the Congress to the President, or whomsoever he may select, of the legislative duties imposed on this body." John M. Robsion, Republican from Kentucky, agreed: "If this bill is passed . . . Congress ought to quit and go home." Giving Roosevelt a free hand with $5,000,-000,000, said Robsion, expansively, would mean giving him "more dictatorial power than Hitler in Germany or Mussolini in Italy."[45]

The bill for emergency relief funds was "must" legislation, and Roosevelt had asked for quick action. The Federal Emergency Relief Administration was so nearly broke, Harry Hopkins told Congress, that it could continue relief work for only two weeks more. The House acted accordingly. But the Senate took its own sweet time. The Emergency Relief Act did not pass until April, after two months of acrimonious debate.[46]

What happened in the Senate revealed wide cleavages in Democratic Party ranks. The Administration's majority, it developed, was largely a statistical myth. As Key Pittman of Nevada, chairman of the Senate Foreign Relations Committee, reported to Roosevelt, there was "no Democratic Party in the United States Senate." There were, Pittman reported, regular Republicans, Progressive Republicans, Democrats who sympathized more with the Progressive Republicans than with the Administration, and conservative Democrats who "conscientiously believe they are saving you by destroying you."[47]

There were Republicans and Democrats on both sides and in the middle. Republicans who opposed the relief bill were, of course, scathingly censorious. That was to be expected; and Republicans did not disappoint anyone. Senator Vandenberg said handing over so much money to Executive discretion was "a process of progressive surrender" of congressional prerogatives. Senator Hastings said, "I do not charge that this fund, or any part of it, will be deliberately and directly used for political purposes"; but Hastings could not imagine how that much money could be spent without Roosevelt's gaining "at least political advantage." And there was the customary humbug about "complete communism of the United States" and "destruction of all private industry." Senator Schall was almost happy to see the bill pass because it would hasten the collapse of the New Deal, and the sooner it collapsed the sooner it would be numbered "with jazz music, nudism, cholera epidemic, earthquake tremor, grasshopper plague, and passing fads, as one of those irrational experiences to which good countries are subject and . . . are glad to forget."[48]

Across the aisle, Democrats, particularly southern Democrats, bucked and pitched. If the relief bill was not a repudiation of the American Way of Life it was at least a threat to the Southern Way. Earlier experience with federal relief had already taught them to be wary; what they could not control they resented. They would rather do without than surrender their stranglehold on the blighted South. Theirs was a state of mind that led to warm applause when Senator Tydings of Maryland declared the bill was not a relief measure at all. "It is a pork barrel measure . . . an outrage on misery . . . an injustice on humanity."[49]

VIII

If the Emergency Relief Bill exposed wide cleavages in Congress, the bill to regulate public utility holding companies widened them further.

The Public Utilities Holding Company Bill (introduced in the House by Sam Rayburn of Texas and in the Senate by Burton K. Wheeler of Montana) was a tribute to the subtle influence of Supreme Court Justice Louis Brandeis who believed government should exorcise the curse of bigness in business and "come back to the little unit." The bill also meant a departure from the New Deal philosophy of 1933. Then the Administration would have attempted to tailor the holding company structure to fit a government-planned economy. In 1935 it wanted to change the structure to protect small business and individual enterprise and prevent manipulation of securities, to restructure holding companies into economically defensible units and eliminate speculation which had become possible through pyramiding of holding companies, sometimes to the seventh degree. Under the proposed legislation, holding companies would be reintegrated in such a way as to make sense both geographically and economically. The reintegration was to be voluntary for the most part; however, a clause in Title I, the "death sentence" clause, provided that if a holding company was unable, after January 1, 1940, to justify its existence on economic and geographic grounds the Securities Exchange Commission could force its dissolution.[50]

The bill was presented in February, 1935, without strong White House support. Though basically a conservative measure, the Wheeler-Rayburn proposal was bitterly opposed by conservatives who directed their main attack against the "death sentence" provision with such effectiveness that by mid-March it was obvious Administration support was necessary to bail it out of trouble. On March 12 the President sent a message to Congress urging its passage.

No longer, however, did the Roosevelt nod of approval mean automatic and immediate compliance; at least not for a bill described as the first step in an effort to nationalize all public utilities, an unwarranted attack on holding company investors, who, if you listened to the opposition, consisted primarily of widows and orphans. Was the bill, Senator Jesse Metcalf of Rhode Island, wanted to know, "a forerunner of complete domination of all our public and private utilities . . . ? Let us be fair with the widows and orphans who are dependent on these investments for the very necessities of life." Metcalf had reprinted in the *Congressional Record* excerpts from twenty-eight letters he had received from "widows and orphans."[51]

Senators, with greater vision than most people, did a lot of talking about the "ultimate end" and the "ultimate goal" of the bill. Their prophetic visitations told them that it would lead to "public control of all of the utilities in the United States," that it was "not a public utilities bill but a political power bill." Roosevelt's implacable foe, Senator Schall, reeled off his customary diatribe about "a bureaucratic dictatorship organized on Moscow and Tammany lines," and once more likened Roosevelt to Hitler, Mussolini and Stalin. In his strange logic, passage of the bill meant "to surrender the basic structure of this Republic. . . ."[52]

For every senator who thought the bill went too far there were others who thought it did not go nearly far enough. Huey Long for one. "It is not half strong enough," drawled the Louisiana senator. "This bill is not worth the paper on which it is written." But in the end he voted for it, he and a combination of Administration Democrats and Progressives. On June 11, after almost four months of debate, the "death sentence" passed the Senate—by only one vote—45 to 44. Following passage of its most controversial clause the entire bill passed the Senate, 56 to 32.[53]

At the other end of the Capitol, the bill remained deadlocked in the Commerce Committee until the third week in June. When it finally saw the light of day the "death sentence" had been seriously compromised, the House version transferring the burden of proof from the holding companies to the Securities Exchange Commission. The House, usually more susceptible than the Senate to White House blandishments, became almost rebellious on this occasion, a rebellion inspired by the public utilities lobby. "You talk about a labor lobby," fumed Roosevelt, "it is a child compared to this utility lobby. You talk about a Legion Lobby. Well, it is an infant in arms" compared to the utility lobby which the President branded "the most powerful, dangerous lobby . . . that has ever been created by any organization in this country."[54]

The Scripps-Howard press reported their count showed the ultilities lobby had 133 more representatives in Washington than there were members of Congress. Telegrams and letters, about 800,000 in all, flooded Congress during the last two weeks of June. Many of these were from concerned constituents. But a congressional investigation proved later that most of them were (as William Allen White said) "pure fake," sent and paid for by the utilities and their allies. It was at this stage of the game, while the House was hung up on the holding company bill, that the suggestion was made to the chairman of the board of Electric Bond and Share Company that a whisper campaign be started creating suspicion Roosevelt was insane.[55]

The pressure, fictitious or not, had its effect. Representative Jennings Randolph of West Virginia, apparently impressed by the "hundreds of thousands of letters . . . protesting against the enactment of this bill," said "these letters are the product of fear. They come . . . from lonely and despairing people who see their last dollar being taken away from them by Government fiat." Congressman Samuel Pettengill of Indiana, a conservative among conservatives, swallowed the utilities lobby arguments whole. To hear him and others tell it the entire course of American history was tied up in the bill. "No bill," he warned, "could be better calculated to impede recovery, deflate values, and freeze uncertainty. Business cannot go forward—men cannot go back to work with a death sentence over their head." "This proposed legislation," said George Darrow of Pennsylvania, "is the first step toward Government control and ownership of public utilities [and] will do more to retard recovery, and destroy public confidence, than any bill heretofore pending in Congress." "This bill," charged Congressman Charles Gifford of Massachusetts "was born in an obsession and reared upon the milk of destruction."[56]

For reasons not altogether clear, debate on the "death sentence" provision evoked more than the usual number of embarrassingly fatuous clichés, priceless gems of wisdom about how the Administration would unwittingly "burn down the barn to roast the pig," "kill the patient to cure the disease," "sink the ship to stop leaks," "kill the patient to cure appendicitis." John Hoeppel of California, who was perpetrator of the appendicitis analogy, thought he knew the reason: "Dr. Brain-trust is apparently a graduate of a different school of surgery."[57]

On July 1, the House voted down the "death sentence" 216 to 146 in what *The New York Times* called "the most decided legislative defeat dealt to President Roosevelt since he assumed office." The next day a watered-down public utilities holding company bill passed, 323 to 81. On August 1, with the bill in conference, the House again rejected the "death sentence," 255 to 210. House and Senate conferees finally decided on a compromise which retained a weakened version of the "death sentence," and on August 26 the President, somewhat unhappily, signed the bill into law.[58]

IX

Daniel Reed turned red above his high starched collar. "If this bill becomes law," cried the New York congressman, "the lash of the dictator will be felt." Senator A. Harry Moore of New Jersey opposed it for an entirely different reason. "It would take all of the romance out of life," he argued.[59]

Serious indeed was a legislative proposal that would lead to a dictatorship without romance. New Dealers could be forgiven much. But not this. What they were asking for was a distinct break with tradition, to be sure, and represented a new concept of social responsibility by the federal government. They wanted something that nearly every civilized country had had for years. Conservative countries. Countries with antiquated monarchies. Even imperial Germany. They wanted a national program of old-age and unemployment insurance. New Dealers were asking for passage of the Social Security Act of 1935.

Roosevelt asked the Congress to pass some kind of social security legislation as early as January, 1935. The same day, January 17, companion bills were introduced in the House by David Lewis of Maryland and Robert L. Doughton of North Carolina and in the Senate by New York's Senator Robert Wagner; the same day the battle began to save America from a romanceless dictatorship.

Conservatives attacked the social security proposal with unusual alacrity, pleading the cause of traditional American virtues, thrift, initiative, responsibility, self-help. "We might as well take a child from the nursery, give him a nurse, and protect him from every experience that life affords," was the way Senator Moore saw it. Delaware's Senator Hastings knew intuitively that "great grief is sure to grow out of . . . this new Act." It would not only destroy initiative and courage and defeat thrift, said Hastings; it would (for reasons not entirely clear) drive "worthy and courageous men from public life" and "end progress for a great country. . . ." Clare Hoffman, who had long since ceased to look for any merit in New Deal proposals, reduced it to even simpler terms. Social security was a scheme to take "from the thrifty, saving Peter to pay unfortunate Paul. . . ."[60]

According to Roosevelt's opponents the social security bill, like most New Deal measures, was at the very least a threat to recovery; for some of the uncompromising and unappeasable critics it was deliberately intended to retard recovery. In their unfriendly hands, social security was the "greatest single threat to recovery of all the administration's ill-advised policies" (Treadway, Massachusetts); a dangerous scheme that would "further and definitely increase unemployment" (Knutson, Minnesota); "wreck the nation as sure as the sun rises" (Rich, Pennsylvania); "threaten the integrity of our institutions" (Wadsworth, New York); "stop and clog recovery . . . prevent business recovery . . . enslave workers" (Taber, New York).[61]

Some of the more progressive-minded in Congress, objecting that the bill was too parsimonious, threw support behind other plans, notably those of Dr. Townsend and Congressman Ernest Lundeen of Minnesota.

John McGroarty, the poet laureate of California, sponsored the Townsend old-age revolving pension plan, an impossible scheme that would have provided pensions of $200 a month. Congress voted down the Townsend plan. And it discarded the even more radical proposal of Ernest Lundeen that would have provided unemployment benefits at prevailing wages, the program to be administered by a commission chosen from rank and file members of workers and farmers organizations.[62]

In the matter of social security Roosevelt had judged accurately the temper of the public. And the Congress, frightened by the growing support for people hawking a wide range of unworkable panaceas and sobered by the temporary flash of radicalism on the part of some of its own members, gave him what he wanted. In April, the House passed the bill overwhelmingly, 371 to 33; in June, the Senate concurred only a little less enthusiastically, and on August 15, the President signed it into law.[63] Social security had taken the play away from Townsend; but Congress and the country had not heard the last of the schemers with their quack cure-alls for the nation's ills. Other messiahs stood in the wings waiting for their moments of glory, waiting to build a new structure on the ashes of a burned-out New Deal.

CHAPTER IX

All Menu and No Meat

The New Deal is all menu and no meat. We have sung our song of a billion six-pence many times over, but there are no blackbirds in the New Deal pie.
—Harold Hoffman

We don't care one hurrah in Hades how they vote; the Literary Digest *is a fake, anyhow.* *—Jackson (Mississippi) Daily News*

We will therefore not support for reelection the candidate of the Philadelphia Convention. *—Resolution of National Jeffersonian Democrats*

PUBLIC enthusiasm for reform ran high in late 1934. But the first few months of 1935 were sorely disappointing to those who looked eagerly for new beginnings, who hoped and dreamed of radical departures from traditional economic and social institutions, who waited expectantly for the business of making over America to commence.

Discontent grew as recovery faltered. The New Deal was bewildering. Its promises outdistanced its achievements. It did not seem to be providing the kind of salvation many felt they had a right to expect. Moreover, millions of Americans—old people, migrant workers, sharecroppers, marginal farmers—were hardly touched by New Deal benefits. These were people who, for the most part, were even deprived of whatever consolation there was in Roosevelt's personal magnetism. They neither heard his reassuring voice on the radio nor saw his smile in newsreels.

Demagogues, quick to sense the discontent, offered simpler, more direct solutions. Their panaceas, presented dramatically amid the vulgar trappings of flag-waving and slogan-shouting, attracted millions. Or at least seemed to. Of the many who sought to capitalize on fear and sorrow one of the most successful was the flamboyant senator from Louisiana, Huey Pierce Long, Jr., with his "share-the-wealth" plan.

II

Long was an early and enthusiastic supporter of the President, fought for him in the Chicago convention against Al Smith, campaigned for him against Herbert Hoover.

228

In January, 1933, two months before the inauguration, Long called on the President-elect (to "talk turkey," he announced to the press). "I am going to ask him, 'Did you mean it or didn't you?'" he told reporters. "Goddam it, there ain't but one thing that I'm afraid of—and that's the people." As he left Roosevelt's suite he exulted, "We've got a great President. . . . He told me, 'Huey, you're going to do just as I tell you,' and that is just what I'm agoin' to do."[1] And that is just what he did—but not for long. "The Kingfish," as he loved to call himself ("Crawfish," his enemies insisted), for all his enthusiasm for Roosevelt, was no New Dealer at heart. Even abandonment of both a Senate inquiry into his campaign expenditures and a Treasury Department investigation of his income tax failed to land the Kingfish safely under the New Deal banner.[2]

Within a month after Roosevelt's inauguration, Long was in open rebellion against the New Deal. By June he was calling on the Senate to block Administration recovery plans and expressing a desire to "swap Roosevelt for Herbert Hoover." His break with Roosevelt was due at least in part to a real ideological disagreement ("We took four hundred millions from the soldiers and spent three hundred millions to plant saplings. . . . While millions have starved and gone naked . . . while babies have cried and died for milk . . . while people have begged for meat and bread, Mr. Roosevelt's administration has sailed merrily along, plowing under and destroying the things to eat and to wear.").[3]

For the most part, however, the breach was motivated by ambition and revenge. Tugwell, assigned the improbable task of keeping Huey happy, complained it was impossible; Long "wanted power, and he could get it only at Franklin's expense." Since Roosevelt occupied the only chair that would satisfy his ambition, Long directed his efforts toward unseating the President, made no secret of his plan to run for the presidency, maybe in 1936, surely by 1940.[4]

Of the two, ambition and revenge, revenge may have been the stronger motive. Neither Roosevelt nor congressional leaders showed any inclination to support Long's pleas for prorating the wealth. While letting the senator personally off the hook, the Administration pressed income tax inquiries involving some of Long's closest Louisiana supporters. To top off what Long considered unfair treatment at the hands of the Administration, James Farley (with Roosevelt's consent) shifted federal patronage in Louisiana to Long's political opponents. Long retaliated by becoming the most severe and intemperate senatorial critic of the New Deal.

Unlike other critics in the Senate, Long spoke to full galleries, his bitterness often concealed beneath a joke, a comic phrase, a droll story, or deliberate buffoonery. In Louisiana, the other ring of his political one-man circus, Long went so far as to propose that the remedy for his state was nothing less than secession from the Union.

In Washington, Long became increasingly bold and extravagant in his criticism. "We ain't goin' to get any place until we get rid of all those damn bureaucrats, hobocrats, autocrats and all those other 'crats. . . ." Long thought a good place to start was with Roosevelt himself, suggesting that Congress make a deal with Vincent Astor "to take the President out in the British waters to fish for a few weeks, but to keep him there for several more months and trust .to luck the country would find its way back to normalcy." From the Senate floor Long rattled off new titles for leading New Dealers more colorful than his clothes. On more than one occasion Long appeared dressed like a side-show barker—straw hat, silk poplin suit, mottled red and green tie, brown and white shoes, lavender shirt with a checked pattern—a "sartorial aurora borealis" *The New York Times* called him. Included in his glossary was: "Prince Franklin, Knight of the Nourmahal" (Franklin Roosevelt); "the Lord High Chamberlain," "the cinch-bug of Chicago" (Harold Ickes); "Expired and Lamented Royal Block," "Sitting Bull," "the new Oo-la-la of Oklahoma," "the erstwhile Prince of the Deranged Alphabet" (Hugh Johnson); "the Honorable Lord Destroyer," "the Ignoramus of Iowa" (Henry Wallace); "the Prime Minister," "the Nabob of New York" (James Farley). And all were high officials in "the Empire of St. Vitus," "the united order of crooks, thieves, and rabble rousers," the "blue buzzard government," a "brain-trust-bureaucratic-alphabetical conglomeration of everything except sense and justice." Frank-lin De-la-no Roo-se-velt, Long would say, half-humorously, half-satirically, placing unctuous emphasis on each syllable, "is a liar and a fake," a "no-good" who "hasn't a sincere bone in his body." They should, he once suggested, "hold the Democratic convention and the Communist convention together and save money."[5]

In January, 1934, Long launched his economic fantasy, the Share-Our-Wealth Society, on a nation-wide basis. In formalizing the program he hoped would eventually carry him into the White House, Long had a warning for chapter organizers: "Be prepared for the slurs and snickers of some high ups. . . . Be on your guard for some smart aleck tool of the interests to come in and ask questions. . . . To hell with the ridicule of the wise street-corner politician! . . . Who cares what consequences may come following the mandates of the Lord, of the Pilgrims, of Jefferson, Webster and Lincoln? He who falls in this fight falls in the radiance of the future."[6]

The plan brought immediate and enthusiastic response. Although the concept was hazy, the plan seemed less complex, less cumbersome than the New Deal. And far more direct. To many at the bottom of the economic pyramid it sounded the call to salvation. However impractical the plan may have been it made sense to hundreds of thousands. The poor, it seems, are seldom economic theorists. Within a year the society had more than 27,000 clubs, a mailing list of over 7,500,000 persons.[7]

The Long plan went right to the point: to correct economic inequity national wealth must be redistributed. Personal fortunes would be limited to $5,000,000; annual income to a maximum of $1,800,000 and a minimum of $2,000 to $2,500. The plan contained something for everyone: a $6,000 homestead grant for each family; for every veteran a bonus; free education at all levels for those who wanted it; pensions for the aged; radios, automobiles, inexpensive food for everyone. "Every neighbor a friend with every man a king" ran the chorus of Huey's anthem.[8]

Administration congressional leaders were more than cool toward Long's attempts to have his wealth distribution plan enacted into law. His first proposal received only fourteen votes in the Senate. At no time did it receive more than twenty votes.[9]

While the Kingfish's popularity grew rapidly across the country his influence in the Senate steadily receded. Single-handedly he filibustered for fifteen and a half hours against the National Recovery Act; his bill to set aside one billion dollars for college scholarships to needy students received only five votes; he failed to block appointment of Henry Morgenthau as Secretary of the Treasury; and the Senate refused, 62 to 20, to investigate his charges against James Farley. Senator Kenneth McKellar of Tennessee, summing up Long's flagging influence in the Senate, said; "I don't believe he could get the Lord's Prayer endorsed by this body."[10]

Long had little success at interesting Congress in his share-the-wealth scheme, but he was immensely successful (or so it appeared) at gaining the ear of a large segment of the American people. A dynamic, forceful speaker—vulgar, brutal, loud, flamboyant—Long could take the hide off when he wanted to. When Dr. Hiram W. Evans, Imperial Wizard of the Ku Klux Klan denounced him as "un-American," Long retaliated, "You tell the tooth-puller he's a lying sonofabitch. That ain't secondhand information and it ain't confidential." Such man-of-the-people talk endeared him to his followers. By 1935 he had become so popular—he claimed a membership of over 3,000,000 in his Share-Our-Wealth movement—New Deal advisers decided to conduct a secret poll of his strength. According to Jim Farley, the result of the poll, kept secret and shown only to a few people, was a real surprise. It indicated that, running on a third-party ticket, Long would probably poll between 3,000,000 and 4,000,000 votes for the presidency. A vote of that size, Farley warned, "could easily mean the difference between victory or defeat. . . ."[11]

Whatever threat the Share-Our-Wealth movement may have posed to Roosevelt and the New Deal, it ended in September, 1935, when Long was assassinated in the rotunda of the state capitol in Baton Rouge. Without him the movement lost its drive, its cohesiveness. Except for a few final gasps under the weaker leadership of Long's disciple, Gerald L. K. Smith, who appropriated the organization and moved its headquarters to Detroit, the movement died with the Louisiana senator.

III

By the end of May, 1935, mounting pressure from progressives, ominous threats by demagogues, and formidable opposition from business and other right-wing forces were pushing Roosevelt in a new direction. With the Supreme Court decisions on "Black Monday," five months of indecision and vacillation ended dramatically. Roosevelt, strangely becalmed, was moving again.

Since January the Seventy-fourth Congress had plodded a leisurely course and was—it thought—nearing its only apparent goal, adjournment. If the fault had been Roosevelt's lassitude he made up for it in June. At a White House meeting, congressional leaders—Speaker Joseph W. Byrns of Tennessee; House Rules chairman John J. O'Connor of New York; acting floor leader Edward T. Taylor of Colorado; and Ways and Means chairman Robert L. Doughton of North Carolina—were handed a list of "must" legislation by the aroused President. The Congress, he assured them, would act when the President told it what he wanted.

Roosevelt was again the President of two years past, taking the political bit in his teeth, laying down the political law, issuing orders, and doing it all with such obvious satisfaction and verve that the reporters at the White House could not miss it. "Everyone could see," *Time* reported, "that the winter of his discontent had ended." The "Second Hundred Days" was under way.[12]

The relief bill had already passed in April, but other Administration bills—the social security bill, the Wagner labor proposal, a banking bill, and the public utility holding company measure—had for months been gathering dust. These four bills were the core of Roosevelt's list of "must" legislation. To them he added a fifth, a wealth tax plan, a "soak the rich" scheme it was quickly labeled. When Congress did finally adjourn, Roosevelt had everything he wanted. But it had not been easy.

The first bill to profit from renewed presidential leadership was the Wagner-Connery Labor Dispute Bill, a proposal to establish a National Labor Relations Board and provide the right of workers to bargain collectively through representatives of their own choosing. Although the bill passed both houses by comfortable majorities and ran into less conservative opposition than expected, the same old clichés were dusted off and run by again. The bill is "manifestly unconstitutional," declared Congressman Frederick R. Lehlback of New Jersey, to which Howard W. Smith of Virginia, John Taber of New York, and Malcolm C. Tarver of Georgia nodded agreement. Not only was it unconstitutional, it was also "clear usurpation of Congressional power by the executive." Such a proposal, declared E. E. Cox of Georgia, "carries upon its face the most terrible threat . . . to our dual form of government that has thus far arisen."

With altogether confusing logic, critics of the bill insisted it was basically anti-labor. Senator Eaton explained this phenomenon by asserting that it "strikes a fatal blow at organized labor . . . for it plucks the labor union out of the plane of free, self-governing institutions . . . the labor union . . . becomes a mere cog in the vast political bureaucracy now being built up in Washington." According to Pennsylvania's congressman, Robert Rich, the Wagner-Connery bill would somehow inflict "new wrongs upon the workers," by denying them the "right of self-organization and association." It was, he charged, a "lopsided, arbitrary, and unjust provision approving coercion by one group and tolerating it when committed by another."[13]

With little delay but with plenty of opposition, Congress pushed through the rest of Roosevelt's "must" legislation. Easily the most spectacular and controversial piece was his unexpected proposal for tax revision. In a surprise message to Congress on June 19, Roosevelt asked Congress for an inheritance tax, a gift tax to prevent evasion of the inheritance tax, a corporation tax graduated according to the size of the corporation, and increased income taxes on "very great individual incomes," to achieve "a wider distribution of wealth" read the President's message, striking the keynote of his proposal. Vast personal incomes, the President declared, were attributable not only to individual ability or effort but also to "opportunities for advantage which the government itself contributes."[14]

Democrats in the House gave the message a standing ovation. But the Senate greeted the proposal with less enthusiasm, except for the cocky senator from Louisiana, who put on his usual sideshow. During the reading of the message, Long wandered around the Senate chamber—grimacing, grinning, pointing to his chest, and whispering *sotto voce* that Roosevelt was stealing his program. When the reading was concluded, Long addressed the chair: "I just want to say 'Amen,' " he announced, without cracking a smile.[15]

Critics of the New Deal really raised hell about his "soak-the-rich" proposal. Initial protests were directed at the speed with which Roosevelt apparently wanted action. Despite the summer heat in Washington, senators and representatives preferred a long-drawn-out session to precipitate action on such a politically dangerous measure. At the time of Roosevelt's proposal, a joint resolution to extend certain nuisance taxes (already adopted in the House) was pending in the Senate. Senators Joseph Robinson and Pat Harrison thought an effort should be made to attach the President's proposal to the resolution as amendments. There was an immediate whirlwind of protest from the House which complained that such a procedure would deprive it of its constitutional right to initiate all revenue legislation. Amid the uproar the President denied he had urged such action. The nuisance-tax resolution was approved without riders, and Administration leaders agreed to have the wealth tax proposal originate in the House.[16]

House opponents of the bill found their text in the Republican minority report of the Ways and Means Committee, which denounced it as a "face-saving" device. "If this bill serves no other purpose," the report stated, "it will at least demonstrate to the country that the extravagant and wasteful expenditures of the Democratic Administration cannot be met merely by 'soaking the rich.'" The Administration, the report added, would have to adopt a "sane spending program" before it had the right to increase the tax burden on either rich or poor.[17]

On the floor of the House, criticism was less temperate. Opponents of the bill, men like Isaac Bacharach of New Jersey, T. Alan Goldsborough of Maryland and others, denounced it as "partisan in origin, socialistic in purpose, unsound in principle, and detrimental in effect." Its purpose, they declared, was "not the distribution of wealth [but] the destruction of wealth." There was the usual immoderate talk about making everyone a dependent of Washington, of leading the country into socialism and bankruptcy. These were the inevitable consequences of legislation that was "uneconomic," that was "based on appeal to class hatred and prejudice," that would "kill all human incentive to work [and] wipe out the profit system." The tax proposal, said Goldsborough, with the worst indictment he could muster, was "un-American."[18]

Others saw it as a brazen attempt by Roosevelt to buy reelection in 1936. "This tax measure . . . is but another bid for votes," charged Clare Hoffman of Michigan, "a plain, shameless attempt to purchase votes at the next election." "It was never anything but a political gesture," agreed Tom Jenkins of Ohio. Although they protested the bill as a vote-buying device, they also were confident it would insure Administration defeat at the polls; it would, Hoffman said, "increase dissatisfaction . . . build up class hatred . . . destroy confidence."[19]

Ham Fish thought he saw a lot of Huey Long's Share-Our-Wealth notions in Roosevelt's proposal. And he may have been right. Not long before, Roosevelt had told Raymond Moley they would have to "steal Long's thunder." "The President caught Senator Huey Long and his Share-the-Wealth followers in bathing," Fish jibed, "and walked away with their clothes, leaving them naked and defenseless." Fish proposed the title of the bill be changed to read: "A bill to further destroy business confidence, undermine private industry, wreck the profit system, prolong the depression, impoverish the American people, and increase unemployment." The tax bill, "a gigantic hoax," according to Fish, intended to "deceive and bam-boozle the people" and to underwrite "the squandermania of the new deal," was "unadulterated socialism."[20]

August 5, after a little over a week of debate, the bill passed the House, 282 to 96, and was sent to the Senate where it passed, on August

15, by about the same 3 to 1 margin, 57 to 22, but not before a few dissident senators entered their disclaimers for the record. The tax bill, this "mid-summer madness," "conceived in political intrigue," was "a bid for the votes of those who have but little," a "mere appeal to mass prejudice," "mere sop to political strategy," "a snare and delusion to the average tax payer," "capricious and impetuous," "superficial."[21]

Whether the bill was any of these things, it was, all in all, an insignificant measure. It certainly was not a major means of raising revenue, since it would produce only $250,000,000 a year—barely enough to run the government for ten days in 1935. In its original form it would have pleased Justice Brandeis by emphasizing the distinction between big and small business. But the bill lost whatever social content it might have had when Congress sliced the corporation income levy to insignificance and removed the inheritance tax.

Although it failed to raise revenue or redistribute the wealth, it did have a significant result. It opened the floodgates of big business resentment toward Roosevelt. It provided Republicans with an additional issue with which to attack the Administration in the 1936 campaign. The President's message accompanying the proposal to Congress recognized taxation as a means of social control, even if the law in final form did not. And it helped set the tone of a new chapter in the history of the Roosevelt Administration, a Second New Deal where reform would take priority over recovery, and where security for the individual in a world not of his own making would be a first order of business for government.

At midnight on August 26, the first session of the Seventy-fourth Congress ended a session of "memorable achievement" boasted the Roosevelt supporters, a session of "ill-advised and extravagant legislation" lamented the opposition.

Either way, it had been a grueling session, and congressmen had good reason to be exhausted. In eight months they had plowed through 9,245 bills and resolutions in the House, 3,467 in the Senate; had acted on 15,000 appointments; had endured interminable hearings and investigations. Lobbying and the munitions industry had hogged the blackest headlines; but there had been others. They had enacted emergency relief appropriations, social security and holding company legislation, and a controversial tax bill; they had extended the scope of the RFC and HOLC, revamped the NRA, passed new legislation affecting labor relations, banking, and the coal industry; they had fought the President over the Patman bonus bill and lost, fought him on the "death sentence" clause of the holding company bill and lost again. They had increased the army by 40 per cent, authorized twenty-four new warships, and extended the borrowing power of the government by $11.5 billion.[22]

These major items interspersed with lesser matters meant the second major chapter in the New Deal was written; for all practical purposes the case for the New Deal was in. The remaining question was; what would the people think of it? For an answer both parties were already turning to the electorate.

IV

Following staggering losses in the 1934 elections Republicans attempted to reorganize to resume the offensive. One problem of serious proportions in 1935 was their perennial dispute: Should the Republican Party liberalize its position in response to changing public needs, or should it hold fast to its ancient conservative principles?

On the side of liberalizing the party were grouped such progressive reconstructionists and moderate Republicans as William E. Borah, Gerald Nye, Charles McNary, Gifford Pinchot, and William Allen White. "The trouble with our beloved party," said White, "is that it is shot through with plutocratic conquest. . . . It cannot live with fatty degeneration of the heart." Senator McNary agreed. "It should be plain," he said, "that a party cannot gain the attention of a people distraught by business and employment worries by extolling the nobility of our forefathers and the sanctity of the Constitution, and by spreading alarms over regimentation and bureaucracy." In March, 1935, William Allen White, reflecting on the dilemma of his party, could write: "If the Republican party has the courage to turn to the humanity of Lincoln and away from the property-minded leadership which has dominated it most of the time for twenty years, we can save America. But America cannot be saved by merely denouncing the faults of Roosevelt." What the party needed, he said, was "not a new platform, but a creed—a statement of old principles to fit the new issues of the new day."[23]

But the old-guard stalwarts—Henry P. Fletcher, the party national chairman; Herbert Hoover, its titular leader; Ogden L. Mills, its leading theoretician; and Charles Hilles, national committeeman from New York —believed the Grand Old Party could regain its strength only by remaining loyal to its ancient traditions. And their views prevailed. It soon became apparent the party would not be reformed and that "constitutional government" would be the primary issue in the coming campaign. "The Constitution is not so 'resilient' as Mr. Roosevelt imagines," Fletcher declared, "on the contrary, it is as rigid as every foundation should be." "[Mr. Fletcher] . . . is not in favor of moving forward," Senator Borah replied. "If he moves at all it is backward." "The Republican party," Charles Hilles wrote, "cannot stagger to the left." It would serve its "most useful purpose," he contended, by offering "absolute resistance to economic heresies." Borah answered, "No, . . . we are not going to stagger but we are going to the left as sure as I'm alive."[24]

But Borah was wrong. The party seemed impervious to change, due in no small part to the influence of a man like Herbert Hoover, who did not have to name Franklin Roosevelt when he told seven hundred Republicans at the Lincoln Day dinner of the National Republican Club that "whatever violates, infringes, or abrogates fundamental American liberty violates the life principle of America as a nation." Other speakers were not so reticent. President of the National Republican Club, Colonel Theodore Roosevelt, drew cheers when he asserted that the New Deal had "flouted the Constitution, emasculated Congress, assumed judicial powers, used the emergency legislation to break down important provisions of the Bill of Rights, and shaken the foundation of our liberty and democratic government." Following Roosevelt to the lectern, Glenn Frank, president of the University of Wisconsin, condemned "hastily improvised policies with which we have sought during the last two years to meet the emergency and make over the national future."[25]

But there was yet hope. "The Republican Party is alive!" At least Harold G. Hoffman, the young governor of New Jersey, thought so. "It is waiting," he beamed, "for new and aggressive and inspiring leadership to be touched into militant action." The Grand Old ("Young," suggested William Allen White) Party had already begun to put out feelers for a "new . . . aggressive . . . inspiring" presidential candidate for the 1936 election. It was a short list. Governor Alfred Landon of Kansas; Governor Harold Hoffman of New Jersey; Colonel Frank Knox, publisher of the Chicago *Daily News*, Senator L. J. Dickinson of Iowa; Senator Arthur Vandenberg of Michigan; Ogden L. Mills; even Congressman Hamilton Fish, Jr.; and, of course, the war horse himself, Herbert Hoover, were the best of a poor lot.

Little by little, it appeared Hoover was assuming the role of actual leader. In March, 1935, he had sent a message to the California Republican Assembly, asserting that the Republican Party had the greatest responsibility since the days of Abraham Lincoln, a responsibility "to raise the standard in defense of fundamental American principles." In April, Hoover left New York for a zigzag trip to his home in California (like a "modern Paul Revere," as someone called him) to arouse the natives against the New Deal. A similar trip in 1934 had excited little comment, but this one was different. Between the two trips Hoover had written a book and a series of scorching articles and had made numerous public statements attacking Roosevelt policies. He looked for all the world like a candidate.[26]

Strategy for the 1936 campaign, a strategy dominated by Hoover and the conservative bloc within the party, was to bear down with unearthly solemnity upon the New Deal threat to the Constitution. The theme, as Bert Snell phrased it, was that no Administration in the history of the country had been "so inconsiderate of the statutes [and] the Constitution. . . ." Efforts to avoid or to delay a showdown in the courts, said Snell, was conclusive proof the Administration "fears the worst for its legislation." In pursuing this headlong course, continued Snell, menacingly, "Mr. Roosevelt has come perilously close to what some people call impeachable grounds."[27]

Perhaps Roosevelt was inviting the Republican battle cry when, for example, he wrote Samuel B. Hill of the Ways and Means Committee on July 6, 1935, urging passage of the Guffey Coal bill: "I hope your Committee will not permit doubt as to its constitutionality, however reasonable, to block the suggested legislation."[28] But it seemed clear after "Black Monday" that any Rooseveltian threat to the Constitution, if it ever really existed, was past; if that immortal document were ever to take on mortality, it would be under dire circumstances that had little relation to the New Deal.

By the spring of 1935 the Republican pre-campaign offensive against the New Deal was beginning to pick up speed. In mid-June more than seven thousand Republicans from ten prairie states met at Springfield, Illinois for a grass roots conference. It promised to be a lively meeting from the beginning when Harrison E. Spangler, temporary chairman, gaveled the meeting to order and charged Roosevelt with "violating the confidence of the American people." A few days before, Hoover had conferred with Frank Lowden, powerful midwestern Republican and former governor of Illinois who had opposed Hoover for the presidential nomination at the 1928 Republican Convention. When a reporter asked what had been discussed, Hoover frankly admitted they had discussed "the Administration's proposals to change to a European form of government." Columnist Walter Lippmann, replying to the Hoover statement with more than a little editorial sarcasm, said it looked "wishful in light of the fact that there are no proposals to change to any other form of government. It does disclose Mr. Hoover's ambitions and his hopes. . . ." Although Roosevelt had made no such proposal, Republicans went on behaving as if he had. Frank Lowden, keynoting the Springfield conference, renewed the Republican challenge: "The saving of the Constitution from the menace of those who would destroy it is the supreme issue of the hour."[29]

The Springfield meeting, widely advertised as a "grass roots" convention, had little to do with "grass roots." Most of the eighteen points in a "Declaration of Grievances" adopted by the convention were grievances of big business against the New Deal: failure to reduce the cost of government; failure to keep government out of business; failure to maintain a sound currency; dangerous regulation of commercial banking; surrender of home markets to foreign competitors; destruction of free competition. Had Republicans meant business about a real grass roots program, they would have been more concerned with jobs, with relief, with human rights. As it was, the only "grass roots" evident, according to the Philadelphia *Record*, were "the grass roots—of Wall Street."[30]

Springfield was only one of many 1935 meetings at which Republicans sharpened their oratorical skills by grousing at the Administration. In May, at a meeting of nine hundred Republican county committee chairmen, Senator Steiwer of Oregon called the New Deal the "illegitimate child of State socialism." At a meeting of New England Young Republicans in New London, Connecticut, former senator Hiram Bingham accused Roosevelt of disapproving of the American Constitution, of wanting to change it "so as to give him the power possessed by the heads of the nations of Europe." Addressing the Union League Club in San Francisco in July, Harry W. Nice, governor of Maryland, branded the New Deal "totally insane," declaring that it was "little short of criminal," and was being run by "professional and political quacks." At a two-day meeting of some three hundred Republican women in New York in September, Senator Steiwer brought gasps even from Republicans with a comparison of the Roosevelt and Long administrations: "It is interesting to parallel the New Deal and the dictatorship in Louisiana. Both involve extraordinary concentration of power in the executive agencies; but as between them there is found in the rule of Huey Long a greater respect for constitutional authority. In subtle method and in furtive approach the New Deal excels. In candor, in consistent purpose and in fulfillment of promises it suffers by comparison." In October, at the Western States Republican Convention, Hoover hit hard at the New Deal's "dervish dance" of "riotous spending" and accused the Administration of "joy-riding to bankruptcy." In November, Hoover was back on the platform at the fiftieth anniversary celebration of the Ohio Society of New York at which he implied the New Deal was communism. "There are only four letters of the alphabet not now in use by the administration," he charged. "When we establish the Quick Loans Corporation for Xylophones, Yachts, and Zithers, the alphabet of our fathers will be exhausted." "But, of course," he added ominously, "the new Russian alphabet has thirty-four letters." In December, Governor Hoffman declared, "The New Deal is all menu and no meat. We have sung our song of a billion six-pence many times over, but there are no blackbirds in the New Deal pie." But there was no humor intended at a meeting of the New York State Chamber of Commerce when Senator Lester Dickinson charged the New Deal was run by a "secret junta" with "collectivist" designs on the United States.[31]

Nineteen thirty-five was not only a year of close communion for Republicans, it was also a year of encouragement. In mid-August Rhode Island produced a political sensation, the biggest since the Democratic landslide in 1934; and Republicans made the most of it. Returns from Rhode Island's First Congressional District, where a special election was held to fill a vacated seat, made Republicans—and not a few Democrats—

take a new look at Republican chances in 1936. A relentless foe of Roosevelt's policies, Republican Charles R. Risk, carried a traditionally Democratic district by 13,000 votes. "To call it an upset," said the Boston *Evening Transcript*, "is to use too mild a phrase. It is a change of popular sentiment of genuinely revolutionary proportions." Republicans were jubilant. "It is the beginning of the end for the New Deal," exulted Bertrand Snell; to Senator McNary the results strongly indicated "a Republican triumph in 1936."

The Rhode Island election was the first official test of New Deal popularity since November, 1934. If it meant anything, it meant, according to William Randolph Hearst's New York *American*, that "the America of George Washington, Thomas Jefferson, and Abraham Lincoln arose and delivered a smashing blow between the eyes of the proposed Socialistic America of Roosevelt, Wallace, Tugwell, and Frankfurter." Senator Hastings, chairman of the Republican Senate Campaign Committee, declared, "The vote in Rhode Island clearly proves that when the American people are convinced that traditional American principles and American liberty are in danger, they act promptly to destroy the persons responsible for such conditions."[32]

Maybe they were caught up in the enthusiasm of their own oratory, maybe they were prematurely encouraged by the Rhode Island victory, maybe they thought the "hate-Roosevelt" propaganda emanating from business sources and the extreme right was the voice of the people, or maybe they were beginning to believe rumors of third parties and anti-New Deal coalitions; whatever the reason, Republicans were convinced, by the end of 1935, the tide was running out for Roosevelt.

Pollsters and some prognosticators agreed. If the election were held in late 1935, Raymond Moley declared, Roosevelt would lose New York, Pennsylvania, Ohio, Indiana, Illinois, and all of New England. In December, *The Literary Digest* poll showed 57.69 per cent of the people opposed to policies of the New Deal; by January, 1936, revised statistics indicated 60 per cent of the people and 36 of the states were against Roosevelt. A week later, January 10, the anti-Roosevelt percentage had risen to 67.9.[33]

In the 1930's, *The Literary Digest* poll was a widely regarded opinion-gathering institution, its Delphic reputation buttressed by uncanny accuracy in previous political contests. But its prediction of a Republican victory in 1936 convinced few Democrats. "We don't care one hurrah in Hades how they vote; *The Literary Digest* is a fake, anyhow," stated an editorial in the Jackson, Mississippi, *Daily News*. "On the 4th of March, 1937, at the noon hour, on the front steps of the Capitol Building at Washington, Franklin D. Roosevelt will be inaugurated for his second term as President of the United States. That's as certain as sunrise tomorrow morning."[34] (The *Daily News* editor was wrong, of course. Neither Roosevelt nor anyone else would be inaugurated on March, 4, 1937. Ratification of the twentieth amendment had changed Inauguration Day to January 20.)

V

The second session of the Seventy-fourth Congress convened on January 3. Nine hours later, at nine o'clock in the evening, millions of radio listeners heard Speaker Bankhead's solemn words of introduction: "The President of the United States."

Only once before, in April, 1917, when Woodrow Wilson declared war against Germany, had a President addressed a joint session of Congress at night. Roosevelt was also declaring a state of war, not against a foreign enemy but against "powerful minorities" at home. "We have invited battle," he said; "we have earned the hatred of entrenched greed." He scorned those "who offer to lead us round the same old corner into the same old dreary street," those "who steal the livery of great national constitutional ideals to serve discredited special interests," those "who would 'gang up' against the people's liberties," and the "unscrupulous economic autocrats" who now wish to withdraw their "abdication" of 1933.[35]

Republicans and other Roosevelt critics greeted Roosevelt's State of the Union address with sneers. It was just a "political harangue," said Republican National Chairman Henry P. Fletcher. It was "good theater, good preaching, and, probably, good politics," stated Norman Thomas, "but it put forward no program at all." Harper Sibley, president of the United States Chamber of Commerce, thought the castigation of business "unfair and unreasonable." The *Christian Science Monitor* was not alone in criticizing Roosevelt for substituting national appeal for factual explanations, partisanship for statesmanship. "It is not necessary for government to knuckle under to malefactors of great wealth," the *Monitor* editorialized; "there may even be reason at the proper time to evoke popular support for curbs upon them." But Roosevelt needed reminding that capitalism could not be reformed "by calling capitalists names . . . by rousing resentment against individuals."[36]

Even before the speech was delivered, its timing was attacked in Congress. "The annual message," said Bert Snell, "has always been delivered at the convenience of the Congress in regular session. . . . Why this departure from the usual custom at this time? . . . Is there going to be anything in that message which will not stand the usual light of the midday sun?" With the gift of prophecy, Snell dismissed it as, "a cheap attempt on the part of the administration, under caption of an annual speech to Congress, to use the opportunity to make a purely political speech. . . ."

In retrospect, it was Hamilton Fish who about said it all for the Roosevelt critics. The Roosevelt innovation, he told the New York National Republican Club the next day, was "the high-water mark of all-time propaganda." The speech, he continued, was government by "propaganda and ballyhoo," a speech which served notice that "the New Dealers will continue this mad orgy of waste, extravagance, and squander-mania. . . ."[37]

With the State of the Union speech ritual out of the way, it was time to get down to business. But no one really expected much from Congress; it would, everyone agreed, be a political session from start to finish. The President had announced he would make as few recommendations for legislative action as possible. There was reason to believe it would be a short session, short so everyone could get on with the important business of the year, campaigning. Two years earlier the Administration could have controlled the situation; that time had passed. Though Democrats still held the same majorities in both houses they had held in 1935, White House control had slipped badly. Both houses resented having been called a "rubber stamp" Congress. True, they had been called that for almost three years, but it did not really start to hurt until the Supreme Court began declaring their handiwork unconstitutional. The vitality of the opposition had reached an all-time high in the last half of 1935. After three years the novelty of Roosevelt was wearing off; vociferous critics were crawling out of every wall.

All the predictions were right; the session was short, listless, and largely unproductive; Roosevelt pressed for little and got less. One item that had been around for a long time was the veterans' bonus. A week after Congress convened, the House approved the Vinson Bonus Bill. It was amended and passed by the Senate with what was almost unseemly haste. The House promptly accepted the amendments, and the bill was rushed to the White House. Although the President vetoed the bill, his veto message was perfunctory, and (probably with the election in mind) he indicated no disposition to fight. It took thirteen minutes for the House to override the veto by a vote of 324 to 61.[38]

As always, the plight of the farmer came in for its share of attention, only this time it was unintentional. On Monday, January 6, three days after the session convened, the Supreme Court passed judgment on the Agricultural Adjustment Act. U.S. vs. Butler did more than bring down the AAA; the tortured interpretation of the general welfare clause in the 6-to-3 decision endangered the entire New Deal program. Immediately following, the Department of Agriculture came up with a plan for soil conservation. The basic difference between the new program and the defunct AAA was that under the new arrangement farmers would receive benefit payments not for curtailing production but for replacing soil-depleting crops with soil-conserving crops.

Republican diehards repeated their usual shopworn diatribes. "Is the

New Deal trying to break the American farmer and make a slave of him through the use of 'a gentle rain of checks'?" asked Senator Metcalf. "Many of us are afraid that this rapidly growing bureaucracy will result in complete dictatorship and communism." "It is an attempt to enslave the farmer," said Congressman John Taber; "it is communistic." "[Farmers] ... are to be dominated and regimented for all time," charged Joe Martin. "No longer are they to be free men. . . . Give the farmer a chance to live happily but do not sell him into slavery." To the American Liberty League the new proposal was a "new AAA . . . risen from the ashes of the old, which offers even greater freedom of experiment than its predecessor to a group of theorists whose record has been one of tragic blunder."[39]

Compared to other criticisms these objections were only nominal; in March the Soil Conservation Act became law. Passage of the Bonus bill and abolition of processing taxes as a result of the AAA decision threw the budget out of line with estimates Roosevelt had presented to Congress. In a special message sent to Congress on March 3, Roosevelt asked for new taxes, declaring Congress would have to appropriate additional money to carry out provisions of the Soil Conservation Act and pay the veterans' bonus. As one method of raising the money, the President suggested a tax on undistributed income of corporations. Taxing undistributed corporation profits seemed an ideal tax plan for an election year, ideal because it struck at impersonal corporations and did not directly touch the pocketbook of the average voter.

The favorite arguments of those opposed to the tax plan were that it was unsound in principle, would undermine business stability, was another step toward regimentation of business; besides, it was unwise and useless to impose new taxes until the waste of public money was stopped. After much bickering about draining away rainy day reserves, about placing a penalty on prudence and a bounty on improvidence, about discouraging business rehabilitation and crucifying financially weak business enterprises, Congress adopted a weakened version of the corporate tax proposal.[40]

VI

On June 20, adjournment mercifully ended a dismal session of Congress enlivened only by a temporary recess for the Republican convention. For months the pre-convention campaign had been running full tilt; despite the debacle of 1934, Republicans began to recover hope as the 1936 campaign approached. They thought they discerned a weakening of the Roosevelt magic and a revival of conservative sentiment. The New Deal was not going well, or so it seemed to Republican optimists. Millions were still unemployed; business antagonism toward Roosevelt was never deeper; the national debt was still mounting; the budget was still out of balance;

Congress was restive; government spending had not produced prosperity; third parties, anti-New Deal coalitions, and radical splinter groups promised to drain off Democratic votes; and, of major importance, Republicans thought the public was beginning to see that constitutional government was endangered by Roosevelt and his Brain Trust.

To assist this growing tide of opposition Thomas G. Sabin, director of the Radio Division of the Republican National Committee, and Henry P. Fletcher, Republican national chairman, engaged veteran radio writer, Henry Fisk Carlton, to write a series of skits lampooning the New Deal. The first of the series, a half-hour program entitled "Liberty at the Cross-roads," had in its list of characters Jefferson, Samuel Adams, John Smith, Mary Jones, two farmers, a husband, a butcher, and the Voice of Doom. John and Mary decided not to marry because the nation was so overtaxed; a husband had to eat imported bacon because of the AAA policies of killing little pigs and because the processing tax made American bacon too expensive; and a rural storekeeper destroyed his business by adopting the New Deal method of spending its way out of debt.[41]

Both of the major radio networks, the National Broadcasting Company and the Columbia Broadcasting System, refused to accept the series. "These presentations," Lenox R. Lohr, NBC president, wrote to Fletcher, "would violate the policies upon which NBC has based its service to a listening public. . . . To accept such programs . . . would place the discussion of vital political and national issues upon a basis of dramatic license, rather than upon a basis of responsibly stated fact or opinion." William S. Paley, president of CBS, was more emphatic. "Appeals to the electorate should be intellectual and not based on emotion, passion, or prejudice. . . . We are convinced the dramatization would throw the radio campaign almost wholly over to the emotional side."

Republican reaction to the refusals was immediate. Fletcher, accusing both networks of unwarranted censorship, implied that the attitude of the networks was "affected by and perhaps involuntarily controlled by the political party in power." "We will go ahead anyway," declared Sabin. "We will take the issues of freedom of speech to the people." The first independent station to accept the program was WGN, the *Chicago Tribune* station, an affiliate of the Mutual Broadcasting System.[42]

Unable to get its voice heard on nation-wide radio, the Republican National Committee turned to the printing press, and early in 1936 issued a series of twenty-four pocket-sized booklets attacking the New Deal. The series began on a lofty, serious note with publications entitled *The National Debt, Influence of Merit, Women and the Coming Election* (this was subtitled: "Women oppose radicalism, inflation waste, excessive debt, spoils, dictatorship, war, and that's what Mr. Roosevelt offers"), *Why Blame Business,* and *The Cost of the New Deal.* Toward the end, however, the tone became less solemn and shifted to humor and derision with such titles as *Bark of the Mulberry Tree* (or, *How Kublai Khan Exchanged Paper Money for Treasure and What Happened*), *Some People Never Learn, And Nero Fiddles* ("It happened in Rome. It can happen here. Shall it?"), and the *New Deal Nursery*, a collection of verses modeled after Mother Goose:

> Little Boy Blue, come blow your horn
> There's a government agent counting your corn.
> Another one lecturing the old red sow
> On the number of pigs she can have and how.
>
> Pa's gone to town to find out what
> He can do next year with the old meadow lot.
> Ma's at the radio hearing them tell
> How under the New Deal there ain't no hell.
>
> Aunt Mame is in Washington dragging down pay
> From the PDA or the AAA.[43]

In February at traditional Lincoln Day ceremonies the New Deal caught it from Republican orators. Candidates for the Republican nomination invoked the hallowed name of the martyred President at Lincoln Day dinners all over the country. In Portland, Oregon, Herbert Hoover tapped a clenched fist on the lectern and indicted the New Deal for creating confusion and "a veritable fountain of fear." While Hoover was telling a nation-wide radio audience what he was against, Senator Vandenberg in New York was blasting the Roosevelt Administration in a speech carried by radio to three thousand other Lincoln Day dinners. Recalling he had supported Roosevelt in his original emergency program, Vandenberg insisted the New Deal had become "government by decree" that was retarding recovery.[44]

Vandenberg denied he was a candidate; his sights were on 1940. But other Republicans were not so reticent. Frank Knox had filed for the primary in Illinois before his Lincoln Day attack on the New Deal in Boston. Senator Borah extended his primary fight to California, declaring that if nominated he would insist on publisher Frank Gannett as his running mate.[45] Senator Dickinson, still hoping for the presidential nomination, joined the Lincoln Day barrage in Greensboro, North Carolina, declaring the New Deal was "socialism." With the shade of Lincoln so fervently enlisted for service against Communists and chiselers in government, it became increasingly difficult for Roosevelt critics to remember that Lincoln was also author of the phrase, "With malice toward none, with charity to all."

Alf Landon was clearly the leading candidate for the Republican nomination. As early as December, 1935, a Gallup poll had Landon out front, with Borah, Hoover, Knox, and Vandenberg following in that order. Landon, conservative in fiscal policy and states' rights, was called, somewhat unfairly, "the Kansas Coolidge." "I never like to be called 'the Kansas Coolidge,'" he wrote in 1939, ". . . my family were always insurgents." And they were. Landon was a veteran of the Bull Moose campaign. He had admired Wilson; had supported the League of Nations; had voted for Wheeler and La Follette in 1924. He was—or had been—sympathetic to not a few of the aims of the New Deal. He was, as the Cincinnati *Enquirer* put it, "not so much a 'Kansas Coolidge' as a 'Republican Roosevelt.'"[46]

By June, when Republicans gathered for their convention in Cleveland, Borah, Hoover, and Vandenberg were no longer serious contenders. Frank Knox, although his chances seemed somewhat less than slim, still considered his campaign very much alive—after all he had Hoover's personal assurance he would receive the ex-President's support if the contest narrowed to Landon and Knox. Landon's approach, one of aloof silence, Knox felt, was totally wrong. "If he is right," Knox stated, "I am entirely wrong because I feel the public psychology requires a slashing, frontal attack."[47]

VII

Keynote speaker Frederick Steiwer of Oregon led off the convention with an address that ranged far and wide, an uninspired assault against traditional New Deal foes like spending, unbalanced budgets, and inflation, and against some like the NRA and the AAA that no longer even existed. (*The New York Times* blandly pointed out that Steiwer had voted for the NRA and the AAA and had voted to pass, over a presidential veto, a bill killing most of the provisions of the Economy Act of 1933.)[48]

Steiwer failed to arouse the convention; and the platform, no better and no worse than most platforms, inspired no real enthusiasm. Though the substance of the platform was moderate, much of its rhetoric was couched in the usual synthetic gloom. "America is in peril," began the preamble. "The welfare of American men and women and the future of our youth are at stake. We dedicate ourselves to the preservation of . . . political liberty . . . individual opportunity . . . which today are being threatened by government itself." This solemn warning was followed by a detailed indictment of the New Deal (throughout the document the term "New Deal" was used instead of "Democratic"), and a plea for all Americans "to join in the defense of American institutions."[49]

During the first two days of the convention nothing the stage managers did seemed to strike fire. But on Wednesday, June 10, the convention came alive briefly, not with hope but with nostalgia, with a genuine outpouring of affection as Herbert Hoover made his way to the platform. Delegates to the convention differed somewhat from those of previous conventions. These were not Republican jobholders, for obvious reasons.

Many were small-town people, small businessmen, or lawyers and representatives of small business—men unaccustomed to but hungry for national power. The glue that held them together was a dislike and distrust of Roosevelt, and the former President was the personification of both.

Hoover, with a happy smile of vindication, waited for the demonstration to die down. Then, with knees visibly trembling and hands twitching in and out of his pockets, Hoover began a long and bitter recital of the New Deal's march toward fascism. As he invoked the "blessing of Almighty God" on this "holy crusade for liberty" a thunderstorm broke over Cleveland. It appeared almost as though Divine Providence were punctuating his words with claps of thunder.

"If there are any items in the march of European collectivism that the New Deal has not imitated it must have been an oversight," said Hoover in his halting style. If the New Deal were allowed to continue, he warned, America could expect "the succeeding stages of violence and outrage by which European despotisms have crushed all liberalism and all freedom." Hoover's reiteration of the evilness of the New Deal brought delegates to their feet, whipped them (according to *The New York Times* in the vocabulary reserved for national conventions) into "a wild and uncontrollable burst of frenzy."

After Hoover's long malediction the convention proceeded with its important charge—the naming of a Republican presidential nominee. From here it was all downhill. Landon was nominated on the first ballot after half a dozen favorite sons released their delegates. The only other opportunity for spontaneous fun came when Senator Vandenberg, in his seconding speech for Landon, shouted, "I belong to but one bloc and it has but one slogan—stop Roosevelt!"

Nomination of a vice-presidential candidate was perfunctory. Most of the hopefuls had either withdrawn or had been eliminated by Landon (*The New York Times* reported that Governor Styles Bridges of New Hampshire had been briefly considered until Roy Roberts, friend of Landon and editor of the Kansas City *Star*, pointed out what the opposition could do to a combination of Landon-Bridges). Colonel Frank Knox remained eager and willing. The country braced itself to "Get off the rocks with Landon and Knox."[50]

VIII

The convention, it turned out, was the high point of the Republican campaign. Landon's acceptance speech in Topeka set the pattern of his early campaign oratory, a quiet and earnest plea, something less than Hoover's call to arms in a "holy crusade." The speech disappointed most Landon partisans; the content was much too bland, the style of delivery was colorless. The inevitable comparisons with Roosevelt were already painful to many Republicans.

A few Republicans—and most Democrats—were pleased with Landon. Democrats were pleased because his speeches promised to be dull and not likely to inspire enthusiastic support among the noncommitted voters. Some Republicans were pleased because they believed the public would equate the monotonous performance of "Frugal Alf," the "cash and carry governor," with sincerity and sound common sense, a contrast to Roosevelt's transparent hypocrisy and slickness. "The public is getting tired of Roosevelt's personality," charged Mark Sullivan, representing the no-nonsense school, "of his evasiveness, his adroitness, his showmanship and especially of his everlasting smile." "If that is the best that Landon can do," countered Harold Ickes, "the Democratic campaign committee ought to spend all the money it can raise to send him out to make speeches." In July *The New York Times* described Landon's style, or lack of it. He used no gestures, spoke too fast, slurred his words, killed his applause by not pausing, looked at his script too long and too frequently, and, if that were not enough, said the *Times*, compounded it all with a disagreeable midwestern nasal monotone.[51]

The campaign technique of the vice-presidential candidate was more agreeable to the warhorses of the party. Frank Knox gave the voters what he thought they wanted, a "slashing, frontal attack." "We are not in a political campaign," he stormed, "we are in a crusade to save America" from "fanatics, theorists and impractical experimenters." At Denver, Knox described Roosevelt as "a man drunk with power." "Be on your guard," he warned. "Silently in the night they are creeping up, seeking to impose upon us, before we realize it, a new and alien kind of government."[52]

With Landon soft-pedaling criticism of Roosevelt, another high-ranking Republican joined Knox to take up the slack. John D. M. Hamilton, Landon's choice for Republican national chairman, charged up and down the land declaring New Dealers were attempting to supplant the Constitution. So different were the campaign styles of the two Republican candidates it was difficult to believe they were running under the same party banner or on the same platform. "The Republican gospel of salvation being preached by Alf Landon on one hand and that being preached by John Hamilton and Frank Knox on the other," according to *Time* magazine, "seemed about as dissonant and confusing to voters as competing Christianities of a Boston Unitarian and a hard-shell Southern Baptist would be to Hottentot bushmen."[53]

As the campaign entered the fall, Landon's moderation wore thin. Perhaps it was pressure from right-wing Republicans, perhaps it was the beginning of desperation, but for whatever cause Landon began to sound more and more like Hoover, Knox, and Hamilton. In Detroit he charged that Roosevelt had pointed the nation toward dictatorship. He pledged that if elected he would work for repeal of all laws giving the Executive "autocratic powers." In Los Angeles Landon warned of the menace to American liberties of increasing governmental power; criticism of the Supreme Court, control of business and agriculture, and abuse of the taxing power were undermining freedom. In Phoenix he declared that saving the American system of government was the fundamental issue of the campaign. The New Deal, he charged, in his most extreme statement of the campaign, "violates the basic ideals of the American system. . . . No nation can continue half regimented and half free. If we are to preserve our American form of government, this administration must be defeated."[54]

Although Landon never became as vituperative as Knox or Hamilton, his later speeches were hardly distinguishable from theirs. As the campaign entered its final stretch he yielded to strong pressures to join the hysterical cry that the New Deal was subversive. In the last month of the campaign Republicans were becoming desperate. It was apparent the campaign was not producing results. In their frustration they became progressively more violent. Republican orators began hitting hard at alleged radical support of the New Deal. The Pennsylvania State Republican Committee issued a statement that Roosevelt was supported by "Reds, Radicals, and Communists." The National Committee claimed that Earl Browder, the Communist Party candidate, had been ordered by Stalin to throw his support to Roosevelt."[55]

As such charges multiplied, some of Landon's friends became uneasy, disturbed that Landon had allowed "violent and ignorant prejudices" to enter his campaign. But apparently Landon had lost perspective in the heat of battle. Aboard Landon's campaign train in the late stages of the contest the conversation turned to talk that Roosevelt was a Communist. Raymond Clapper, the veteran syndicated columnist, is supposed to have turned to Landon: "That's terrible to spread that stuff. . . . It isn't true and you know it." Landon's reply allowed no rebuttal. "His policies are leading to dictatorship," he said emphatically. "When a President gets hold of the purse strings, you have dictatorship."[56]

IX

The Republican cause featured a sizable number of anti-New Deal Democrats. In August, forty-two dissident Democrats and confirmed Roosevelt-haters met in Detroit, men such as James A. Reed, former senator from Missouri; John Henry Kirby, Texas lumber magnate; recent converts to anti-New Dealism like Joseph B. Ely, former governor of Massachusetts; and habitual party-bolters like Bainbridge Colby and Henry Breckenridge, both New York lawyers.

The conference was called by Reed and Sterling E. Edmunds, St. Louis

attorney, to decide what action anti-New Deal Democrats should take in
the campaign. Two days of earnest talk led to a decision not to found a
new party. Time was too short for that. But southerners present were unwilling to endorse Landon because of the possible effect this would have on
local elections. They agreed only to urge other Democrats to vote for
Landon or stay away from the polls, a position which they reaffirmed in a
1,000-word resolution: "The Democrats of the nation see today a President calling himself Democratic . . . turning his back upon the party platform . . . replacing the doctrines of Democracy with the tenets and teach-
ings of a blended communism and socialism. . . . We will therefore not
support for reelection the candidates of the Philadelphia convention."
From their national headquarters in St. Louis the National Jeffersonian

Campaign Literature. *Reprinted with permission from the
Philadelphia* Inquirer. *Cartoon by Hutton.*

Democrats, as they now called themselves, boasted they could divert three million votes from Roosevelt.[57]

While the major parties played their game of political billingsgate and the Democrats grappled with schisms in their ranks, leaders of the new Union Party—Dr. Townsend, Father Coughlin, Gerald L. K. Smith, and William Lemke, the party standard bearer—unlimbered on both parties. The Union Party was a strange amalgam. Smith, having declared himself Huey Long's successor, found he was a leader without a movement when the Long machine politicians ignored him. After a short chase he caught

Tammany Practices
Under the New Deal

New Dealers boast that they have given more jobs to negroes in the last six months than any Republican administration ever did in a similar length of time. There are 431,257 negroes in Pennsylvania, and Pennsylvania has 36 electoral votes. Colored voters from Pennsylvania now living in the District of Columbia who will fill out the above blank are certain to get jobs with the New Deal—at least until after November 3rd. Read sections II, I and J and learn why.

Does Roosevelt want to help the colored people? Or does Roosevelt want the Help of the Colored Votes?

10

Reprinted with permission from The Trumpeter, *July 15, 1936, of the Republican National Committee.*

Townsend, announcing, "We here and now join hands in what shall result in a nationwide protest against this Communistic dictatorship in Washington." In June, 1936, Townsend and Smith were joined by Coughlin and his National Union for Social Justice. Proclaiming the formation of the Union Party, Coughlin bragged they would enter the campaign with more than twenty million votes committed against "the communistic philosophy of Frankfurter, Ickes, Hopkins, and Wallace."[58]

At Grand Rapids, Michigan, William Lemke (dubbed "Liberty Bill" by Coughlin, who undoubtedly knew the Liberty Bell was cracked) denounced the New Deal and its ties with "international bankers." Lemke optimistically estimated he would carry Michigan and Ohio, all of New England, most of the Middle West and Far West, Pennsylvania, and Illinois. With commendable modesty, he added, "Indiana will be nip and tuck." "I look upon Roosevelt," he said, with overtones of Dr. Wirt, "as the bewildered Kerensky of a provisional government. As for Landon he represents the dying shadow of a past civilization."[59]

"The dying shadow" was nonetheless displaying considerable liveliness. The Republican publicity division was particularly active, dispatching thousands of telegrams to newspaper and magazine editors telling them important material was on the way. It may or may not have been important, but it was voluminous. An estimated 361,000 press releases went out during the campaign. The Republican clip sheet, "Facts and Opinions," was sent to six thousand newspapers. By October, approximately 10,000 pieces of literature were being mailed each week from Republican national headquarters. The Republican Research Bureau in Chicago produced a volume of literature variously estimated at from 125 to 170 million pieces. The Industrial Division sent out approximately eight million pieces. Cards were mailed to employers destined, they hoped, for employee pay envelopes, cards with titles such as "Last Chance to Vote with the Spendthrifters," "Stop Waste and Misery," "Landon Will Change It," and "A Good Job . . . Instead of Charity."

Pamphlets were issued by the millions. No appeal, some quite unfair or distasteful, was overlooked. A pamphlet entitled *Death Flies the Airmail*, which recounted the misadventures of the air corps after James Farley had unwisely canceled airmail contracts with commercial air lines, pictured debris of a crashed air corps plane and blamed Roosevelt for the deaths of twelve Army pilots. A leaflet pictured a young, ill-clad Negro boy, fists clenched and jaws set with his foot on a newspaper with the headline LYNCH 2 MORE IN FLA. Under the picture was the caption "Who's a Democrat?" Even more repugnant was a leaflet issued by the Pennsylvania State Republican Committee picturing a Negro, the victim of a lynch mob, hanging from a tree, while a group of white people stood about looking at the gruesome sight. Under the picture was the title: "The More Abundant Life Under the New Deal!"[60]

Despite all Republican efforts it was apparent to nearly everyone that Landon would be decisively defeated. *The Literary Digest,* however, was not convinced. Just days before the election the *Literary Digest* poll, in its final prediction, indicated 57.4 per cent of the electorate would vote for Landon and 42.6 per cent for Roosevelt. Translated into figures that really mattered, this meant Landon would win hands down with thirty-two states and 370 electoral votes to Roosevelt's sixteen states and 161 electoral votes.[61]

Only two other major polls agreed Roosevelt would lose. A "grass roots" poll by about three-hundred country editors covering thirty-nine states and 919,441 votes gave Landon 60.5 per cent of the vote to 39.5 per cent for Roosevelt. The Republican-oriented *Farm Journal* conducted a poll of its own which gave Landon 57 per cent of the votes. The four big ones—the American Institute of Public Opinion, *Fortune,* Crossley, and the Baltimore *Sun*—predicted an easy Roosevelt victory. The *Fortune* poll was the most generous, conceding Roosevelt 74 per cent of the vote.[62]

X

The symbol of the Landon candidacy was the sunflower, the state flower of Kansas. Like the flower itself, Landon sunflower badges sprang up everywhere. In an off-the-record remark during one of his press conferences Roosevelt observed that the sunflower was yellow, its heart was black, and it was eaten only by parrots. To this description a newsman added that the flower died in November.[63] Death to the Landon sunflower came mercifully swiftly on November 3, 1936. The election went exactly as Jim Farley had predicted: Roosevelt 523 electoral votes, Landon 8. Only Maine and Vermont escaped the Roosevelt sweep. Roosevelt's 60.2 per cent of the popular vote, although a slightly lower percentage than Harding's 1920 vote, nevertheless gave him the largest plurality ever recorded—almost eleven million votes—a plurality which should have meant a new term of unprecedented harmony.

But it didn't.

CHAPTER X

Harmony, Hell!

Today even the Democrats themselves are split from top to bottom in every State into two warring camps—Roosevelt and anti-New Deal.
—Dudley A. White
(Republican, Ohio)

Looking at the Democratic Party in the most favorable light, no one can dispute that it is split wide open—not over fundamental economic problems of our time, but in a bitter factional fight.
—Philip F. La Follette
(Progressive, Wisc.)

Let me say in all candor to my fellow Senators, and to anyone else who happens to hear it, that this group is not going to run the Democratic Party. The day when it runs the Democratic Party, the Democratic Party will not be worth the respect of anybody. That group cannot run the party. They could not win an election. Let them drive out of the party the men who have served it all their lives, and see what happens to the party.
—Josiah Bailey
(Democrat, N.D.)

A party cannot exist half Roosevelt and half Democratic.
—J. S. Gray, Editor
Monroe (Michigan) Evening News

T HE two short years from November, 1936, to November, 1938, were lean years for Franklin Roosevelt and the New Deal. Roosevelt's unprecedented landslide in 1936 had swept the Democratic Party to the largest congressional majorities since Reconstruction days. The box score showed 333 Democrats to 102 Republicans in the House of Representatives. In the Senate, where there was standing-room only on the left side of the aisle and twelve freshmen had to swallow their pride and sit with the Republicans, there were seventy-five Democrats to twenty-one Republicans. Twenty-four months later, however, the political picture had changed significantly. In 1938, Republicans gained eighty-one seats in the House and eight in the Senate.

Looking back on the Roosevelt victory in 1936, it seemed impossible that his political fortunes could have ebbed so swiftly, so precipitously. But they had. Resistance to the New Deal had stiffened, had crystallized. The Republicans had taken heart and fought back. And members of

Roosevelt's own party, including some men who owed him their political lives had turned on him savagely, as if to disembowel a President bearing their own party label.

II

In late August, 1937, when Democratic Senator Theodore Green reported to the voters of Rhode Island on the accomplishments of the first session of the Seventy-fifth Congress, he began his radio speech with a pertinent question: "Why so lean a harvest from soil that promised such abundant fertility?" The meager results, he said, could not be attributed to the Republican opposition; during most of the session they had "sat silent." They knew from past experience that opposition from them was the best endorsement a New Deal measure could have. No, said the senator, the opposition came "mostly from those of the President's own party."[1]

Green was right; the first session of the 1937 Congress was a disaster for Roosevelt. "Rarely," stated *The New York Times* in its post-mortem, "has an Administration met so many failures." The casualty list included child labor legislation, the anti-lynching bill, a stronger food and drug bill, a ship safety bill, crop insurance and other farm legislation, and Administration proposals that would have made the Civilian Conservation Corps permanent, extended the TVA concept to other parts of the country, and transferred authority over air transportation to the Interstate Commerce Commission. But the most dramatic defeats were the wages and hours proposal, the plan for reorganization of the Executive department, and, of course, the Roosevelt court plan.[2]

That Roosevelt was so thoroughly manhandled may have been surprising, but that reaction had set in should have been expected. For one thing, it was assumed in every quarter that Roosevelt's victory in 1936 would be his last. Even in defeat Republicans could look with some optimism and relief to 1940 when they would not have to face a campaigner like Roosevelt. Some members of the Democratic Party entertained similar thoughts. It was customary for a President to experience a gradually diminishing influence during his second term as senators and congressmen began unhitching their wagons from a waning star. Ambitious men, men who aspired to the presidency themselves, had to begin beating retreat, seeking safe independence from their chief amid the shoving and elbowing of their colleagues for a place in the national spotlight. In the arena of politics, where calendars start in November and there are no prizes, only oblivion, for finishing second, loyalty is often a neglected virtue.

Jealousy and resentment, perhaps even honest fear, had something to do with the reaction to Roosevelt. Men whose own careers were built on the shifting sands of public opinion grew jealous of Roosevelt's incredible popularity, a public approval bordering on idolatry. It was resentment and fear which Herron C. Pearson of Tennessee was expressing when he called to the attention of the Congress that only eighteeen of the seventy-seven major bills passed during Roosevelt's first term had originated in Congress, "where all ought to have originated." The other fifty-nine, said Pearson, with venom in his tone, "had an illegitimate birth, conceived in sin and shapened in iniquity somewhere downtown, and were brought up here and the bastards laid on our doorstep with the command of the Executive that we acknowledge parentage."[3]

It was almost certain that Roosevelt would have trouble with the more conservative members of his party who were genuinely alarmed at the trend of the New Deal, the lavish spending, the mounting debt, the pro-liferating bureaucracy, and the casual disregard for traditional policies and time-honored constitutional procedures. Opposition of this type was certain to be strong, particularly in the southern wing. "You have my sincere sympathy," Representative Gifford of Massachusetts taunted; "I sympathize with you Democrats of the South who, in the victory of your party, have been forced to embrace the Democrats of the North."[4]

III

Roosevelt and the Democratic critics in the Congress began steering their collision course early in 1937. The issue at stake was defined in an article appearing in the *Saturday Evening Post*, written by Stanley High, a preacher-turned-writer, who had headed the Good Neighbor League during the recent campaign. It was High who had coined the term "eco-nomic royalists" which Roosevelt used with such devastating effectiveness against the Republicans. Annoyed by the President's apparent lack of gratitude, High broke with Roosevelt, to reappear in the Willkie camp four years later.

High's article "Whose Party Is It?" suggested that Roosevelt was little better than a traveling salesman who had run off with the farmer's wife. The long-suffering husband was pleading with her to come to her senses and return home. The article signaled the start of a two-year struggle to make the Democratic Party an honest woman, a struggle for Democratic Party control.

In the forefront of the effort to regain control of the party from the New Dealers was a powerful bloc of southerners, many of whom had suffered much at Roosevelt's hands, they thought; many of whom disa-greed with the philosophy of the New Deal and much of its specifics, sometimes violently. "I think there would be still greater differences," Gifford had needled, "if it 'were not for the plum tree. The tree is still shaken for your benefit."[5]

Gifford's jibes rankled because they were true. It was infuriating that, in a sense, they needed Roosevelt more than Roosevelt needed them. In a quite literal sense, the South had nominated Roosevelt in 1932. But the South certainly did not elect him. Had every southern state gone to Hoover, Roosevelt would still have won.

The elections of 1934 further reduced Roosevelt's dependency on the South. Of the 69 Democratic senators, the South had but 24; of the 322 Democratic representatives, the South had only 108. The classical Democratic coalition, it could be demonstrated, was yielding to one that was more northern than southern, more urban than rural; it was a new combination of forces which appealed to labor, to traditionally Republican Negroes, to the ethnic groups of the New Immigration, to women, and to intellectuals attracted by the imagination and pragmatism of the New Deal. It was a new political edifice of which the South was the frieze, not the cornerstone.

In 1936, a disastrous erosion of southern influence over the party took place at the Democratic National Convention in Philadelphia. The two-thirds rule had given enormous power to a section as single-minded as the South, the power of minority veto. The hasty, ill-conceived effort of the Roosevelt forces to eliminate the rule in 1932 had failed. But in 1936, Jim Farley's disciplined convention voted the century-old rule into oblivion with a minimum of fireworks; even southern opposition was perfunctory, listless, spiritless. With the two-thirds rule went the South's last important hold on the party; the face-lifting of the Old Democracy, it seemed, could proceed unimpeded.

That the South continued to support Roosevelt at the ballot box did not change the fact that he had on his hands a dissident group of old professionals at odds with the strange assortment of new leaders emerging within Democratic ranks, leaders with pigmented skin, thick accents, the smell of mine and factory about them, or the cultured pallor of the college classroom; new leaders with ideas as alien to southern traditionalists as if they were from another planet. "Democrats, Democrats," muttered Virginia's salty Senator Carter Glass of the New Dealers in 1935. "Why, Thomas Jefferson would not speak to these people."[6]

The senator's caustic remark went to the heart of the matter; it was more prophecy than pique. Roosevelt's new approach to the nation's malaise after 1935 stirred the hopes of classes of people untouched by the main current of politics since the golden days of Herbert Croly, Walter Lippmann, Robert La Follette, and the lesser gods of the Progressive pantheon. The South was singled out for special attention—the "economic problem No. 1 of the nation" Roosevelt once called it. This appraisal of the South was not remarkable. Anyone, assuming he was not half-witted, could see that it was true—or else the rest of the country was in a lot worse shape than anybody was letting on.

But one thing was remarkable. For years southerners had gathered at appointed times around the courthouse square to mop their brows and fan themselves in time to the pompous cadences of oratorical humbug. They had heard from their politicians more promises than a drunkard's wife. With the coming of the New Deal the promises took on meaning. The New Deal had meant action, action that reached down to the grass roots, action that astonished even the most langorous southern native. Suddenly politics became more than arm-waving speeches, hillbilly bands, and dinner on the grounds. In short, the New Deal began threatening the traditional political power structure of the South.

The threat took several forms. Relief, federally financed and administered, and public works involved patronage on an unprecedented scale, sufficient to make any good Democrat goose-pimply. But it was federal; and the Administration expected a certain amount of gratitude in exchange. Farley, the dispenser of patronage in those early years, wielded a heavy club; southerners like Huey Long and Eugene Talmadge, among others, had knots on their heads to prove it. Nor were the beneficiaries of federal largess likely to forget where to locate the windows of Heaven on the map. They were no longer in the offices of the county judge.

Many southerners reacted to this turn of affairs by explaining that the New Deal was undermining that southern tenet of the faith, states' rights. Roosevelt, said former governor Max Gardner of North Carolina, was "persistently attempting" to destroy local government and to substitute for it "all-powerful federal authority similar to the current dictatorships in several European countries." Albert Ritchie told the Ohio Bar Association in Toledo that unless New Deal measures were abandoned they would destroy the dual system of government and the integrity of the states. The transfer of power from the states to the federal government could end only in making the national government "master of our souls." "It is the complete reversal of the Jeffersonian theory of government," said the former Maryland governor. Those attending a United States Chamber of Commerce banquet in Washington applauded when Fitzgerald Hall, president of the Nashville, Chattanooga and St. Louis Railway, told them that it "was not Ulysses S. Grant who effected the near-destruction of 'States' Rights,' but rather the man who invented 'Federal Aid.'" Republican representative Will Taylor of Tennessee was more bitterly sarcastic: "What has become of the old Jeffersonian Democracy? Alas! It has gone the way of the dodo, the mastodon, and the ichthyosaurus. States' rights is now only a memory, and subsidy and centralized government are sweet morsels which our Democratic brethren roll on their tongues with increasing glee and gratification."[7]

However justified may have been these criticisms of the New Deal on ideological grounds, there were some southerners who feared it and attacked it for perhaps less defensible reasons. The New Deal was profoundly affecting the forgotten men of the South, particularly the Negro;

the New Deal, they said privately, was playing hob with white supremacy.

The change in the economic status of the Negro brought about by the New Deal was immediate. Direct relief and work relief generated considerable resentment among southern planters who complained that these programs made it almost impossible to get cheap Negro farm labor. "I wouldn't plow nobody's mule from sunrise to sunset for 50 cents per day when I could get $1.30 for pretending to work on a DITCH," was the way one farm worker explained it to Governor Talmadge in a letter which Talmadge forwarded to Roosevelt as proof that the New Deal was destroying the moral fiber of the people of Georgia.[8]

The effect of the New Deal on the Negro politically was more subtle. The success of Roosevelt in wooing him from his traditional allegiance to the Republican Party was obvious; in 1936, for the first time in history, a majority of Negro voters supported the Democratic candidate. This meant northern Negroes, obviously; southern Negroes did not vote in any significant number. But the phenomenon of 1936 was not lost on southerners, white or black. The handwriting was on the wall, and the *Grovey v. Townsend* decision of 1935 upholding the white primary could not erase it. The New Deal was hastening the day when the southern Negro would be a citizen in fact as well as in theory. Or perhaps it should be put the other way around. The New Deal was hastening the day when southern politicians could no longer count on using the Negro to frighten the masses.

IV

Thus for a number of reasons, Roosevelt and members of his own party in Congress were heading for a showdown, and the festive sounds of the 1936 victory had hardly died away when the trouble erupted.

It was the President who precipitated it. His first request of the new Congress was for judicial reform, legislation that seemed far removed from the need of "one-third of a nation" poorly fed, poorly housed and poorly clad, which he had talked about in his second Inaugural Speech. Roosevelt's court plan caught most people by surprise, including his own party leaders. Not until February 5, the day his message was sent to the Congress, did Roosevelt call a Cabinet meeting to explain the plan. Later in the day, when the President read details of his plan to White House correspondents, it was widely reported that he interrupted his reading on several occasions "to laugh uproariously," which left Republican Congressman Clarence Hancock of New York wondering whether the President's laughter was because of "the practical joke he intends to play on the Supreme Court—or on the American people."[9]

Recovering from their surprise, supporters rallied behind the President.

Congress was soon swamped by a flood of petitions favoring the plan; from the German Sick and Benevolent Society of Mansfield, Ohio, to the Mississippi State Bar; from the Bakery Salesmen (Local No. 335) of Kansas City, Missouri, and the United Mine Workers (Local No. 2098) at Antrim, Pennsylvania, to the German Assembly of Pennsylvania. As might have been expected, the country was soon assured that the President had support from another source. "Every Communist in America," generalized Congressman Usher Burdick of North Dakota, "is solidly behind the President's program to take over the Supreme Court."[10]

Opposition to the plan was equally instantaneous. Not from Communists and bakery salesmen, but from people like the Pennsylvania Society of Colonial Dames of America, the Sally Wister Chapter of the Daughters of the American Revolution, and the Society of Mayflower Descendants. The national commander of the American Legion, Harry Colmery of Topeka, Kansas, while conceding that he could not speak until after the next national convention, felt reasonably sure that the American Legion would not approve it.[11]

How accurately this kind of support and opposition pouring in on the Congress reflected public opinion was not easy to assess. At least one congressman, Maury Maverick of Texas, discounted it almost altogether. Maverick cited the case of the Sons of the American Revolution. The president-general of the organization, Messmore Kendall, had put the Sons on record as opposing the court plan and was sending out telegrams to the membership all over the country urging them to write their congressmen. "Nobody can throw a rock at me and say that I am subverting the Government," said the forceful south Texan, a vigorous supporter of the plan, "because I am a member of that organization. If we travel around the country, we will find various and sundry organizations operating this way. It is an old American custom."[12]

Roosevelt was in a position to take strong issue with the Supreme Court. It had already killed the AAA and had mercifully put the NRA to sleep. In the spring of 1936, it had strained a little to nullify the Coal Conservation Act. When, a month later, the Court invalidated a New York State minimum wage law by a 5-to-4 vote even conservatives were joyously amazed. Roosevelt was amazed, too. The Court had created an impossible situation in labor relations (a "no-man's land," Roosevelt called it) from which the Wagner Act would never get out alive. In such a constitutional climate, his plans for a wages and hours law were out of the question. Confronted by what seemed an intransigent Court set on dismantling four years of effort and of blocking future rebuilding, and buttressed, he believed, by overwhelming public approval, Roosevelt moved to break the stalemate.[13]

He could not have mismanaged it more had he let the opposition plot the strategy. In a way, the opposition did plot the strategy. His choice, to drive for legislative enactment rather than a constitutional amendment, was from the certain knowledge that only a little effort and a modest financial expenditure could bog down an amendment in a number of state legislatures, enough to smother it.

But it was Roosevelt's own fault that he made the issue one of crowded dockets and superannuated judges rather than the fate of his program in the hands of an unfriendly Court. If his purpose in pursuing an oblique approach was to divert the emphasis from court-packing to court reform, he misjudged badly. The less-than-candid tack seriously handicapped his friends while providing his enemies with an issue tantamount to finding the Holy Grail. Honesty, integrity, morality, and tradition all seemed to be on the side of the opposition.

Moral indignation was a safe and respectable banner under which any and all enemies of Roosevelt could rally. The hatred and resentment that his adversaries had pent up for years found a legitimate outlet; their visors were down and their swords drawn in a holy cause. What Roosevelt was asking, they said, was for dictatorial powers, powers "which no sane man a decade ago would have ever dreamed a President of the United States would ever covet, much less possess." "Upon what meat doth this our Caesar feed," asked Kansas Congressman Guyer, quoting the lean and hungry Cassius, "that he is grown so great?" The proposal, stormed Senator Glass of Virginia, was "destitute of moral sensibility and without parallel since the foundation of the Republic."[14]

The court proposal probably provoked more impassioned, intemperate language in the Congress than any issue since the Civil War. And most of it was coming from Democrats, Democrats (according to one story making the rounds of the cloak rooms) whose throats were permanently raw from swallowing policies which they did not approve and whose wrists were sore from pushing those same policies down the throats of their colleagues. Republicans, except for a very few like J. Parnell Thomas of New Jersey ("most insidious and diabolical political scheme ever concocted," "only a dictatorship or Fascist state will be left"), stayed out of the Democratic family fight. It was Democrats—men like Burton K. Wheeler, the Progressive warhorse, and Edward R. Burke of Nebraska, who had been elected to the Senate in 1934 as an ardent Roosevelt supporter after a bitter contest with Republican Robert Simmons on the merits of the New Deal; men like the tall Texan, Tom Connally and Joseph O'Mahoney of Wyoming (who referred to the Democratic opponents of the court plan as a "battalion of death to save the Constitution"); men like Harry Byrd, Millard Tydings, Carter Glass, Royal S. Copeland, and Pat McCarran. The fight against the President's plan was carried by these men, who for the most part, represented the Old Democracy, and they were joined by a few who, until now, had been reliable New Dealers.[15]

As the drama unfolded no one could touch Carter Glass for verbal artistry, the epithets flowing in a torrent from the corner of his mouth (a speech habit which had once caused him to be described as the only man in the history of the Senate who could whisper in his own ear). The court plan, he snarled, was "frightful," "shocking," "brutal," "infamous," "outrageous"; it was "sheer poppycock," "constitutional immorality," and those who proposed it and supported it were "political janizaries," "executive puppets," "amateur experimenters," "visionary incendiaries," "judicial sycophants," "judicial wet nurses." Glass swore he would never vote to allow Roosevelt to crowd the Court with "a lot of judicial marionettes to speak the ventriloquisms of the White House." It was estimated that more than 700,000 copies of one of his radio speeches delivered early in the debate were circulated by opponents of the plan.[16]

The President expected opposition from the more conservative wing of the party, but he was dismayed by opposition from otherwise loyal supporters. Early in March, at the Democratic Victory Dinner, he changed course. Putting the court fight on the issue that it should have been in the first place—the future of his New Deal program—Roosevelt argued that he was being prevented from carrying out his campaign promises because of the Court. Moreover, the judicial attitude, he charged, had encouraged a "widespread refusal to obey the law." "If we would keep the faith with those who have faith in us, if we would make democracy succeed, I say we must act NOW!" Five days later, in a Fireside Chat, a worried Roosevelt appealed directly to the people:

I want—as all Americans want—an independent judiciary as proposed by the framers of the Constitution. That means a Supreme Court that will enforce the Constitution as written—that will refuse to amend the Constitution by the arbitrary exercise of judicial power—amendment by judicial say-so.[17]

This tactical change was an old one, one that was always used sooner or later by those whose ox had been gored by the Court. It was weak and it was too late. The damage had been done. Time was on the side of the opposition. The longer the acrimonious debate was prolonged, the more certain was Roosevelt's defeat.

Enemies outside the halls of Congress joined in the battle. Father Coughlin, still embarrassed by the outcome of the election the year before, and hoping to use the court issue as the opportunity for a comeback, predicted that enactment would mean "the passing of a nation." Raymond Moley, once so close to Roosevelt, made their alienation of affections permanent by denouncing the plan. Others, such as James Rowland Angell, retiring president of Yale University, in his final baccalaureate address, reflected mournfully upon the impending "rape of the Constitution." John T. Flynn, moving steadily away from his faith of *New Republic* days, told a Camp Tamiment, Pennsylvania, audience that

the plan was "thoroughly dishonest and hopelessly inadequate." Not knowing when to quit, Flynn predicted there would be such a reaction to
Roosevelt that it would sweep a Republican into the White House in
1940. Governor Herbert Lehman broke his silence to denounce the plan
as "a greatly dangerous precedent" and to urge New York Senator Robert
Wagner to vote against it.[18]

In *The Assault on the Supreme Court*, one of the many pamphlets
distributed by newspaper publisher Frank Gannett's National Committee
to Uphold Constitutional Government, Douglas Wilson Johnson asserted:
"He wants power. . . . The President is at heart opposed to a constitutional
government. . . . He wants unlimited power to govern the people as he
deems best for the people's good." Walter Lippmann, solemnly declaring
that "no issue so great or so deep has been raised in America since
secession," described the court plan as "a bloodless coup d'etat." "If the
American people do not rise up and defeat this measure," Lippmann
pontificated, "then they have lost their instinct for liberty and their
understanding of constitutional government." Out in Kansas, Gerald Winrod was sending out 500,000 blanks with the heading "Hands Off the
Supreme Court!" for his faithful to mail to their representatives in
Washington. "The Crisis Hour is Here" was the slogan on the envelopes;
inside, Winrod warned (in capital letters, of course) that "THE END OF
CHRISTIAN AMERICANISM IS TODAY IN SIGHT!"[19]

While the debate was in progress, the New York Chamber of Commerce
announced that it was launching a nation-wide campaign to rally support
against the plan. In a letter from the organization's president to the
membership, Winthrop W. Aldrich asserted that the object of the court
plan was "to convert our government into an authoritarian one, run by
an Executive. . . ."[20]

The efforts of the Chamber of Commerce were probably unnecessary. It
seems reasonably certain that after the debate had gone on for some weeks
had a show of hands been taken among the general public the plan would
have been rejected. This was surely the case with a group of Yale
University undergraduates who, with appropriate pomp and ceremony,
organized a "Roosevelt for King" club which soon had chapters at Columbia, Princeton, and New York University before humorless college
administrators intervened. Their proposition was to abolish the Supreme
Court altogether and convert the Supreme Court building into a palace for
Franklin I.[21]

In mid-July the court fight was resolved, not by reasonable compromise
but by death. In his apartment across from the Capitol, the loyal Senator
Robinson, who had faithfully marshaled the President's forces from the
start, collapsed and died. Opponents of the bill admitted that until the
death of the Senate majority leader from Arkansas they were beaten.
With Robinson's death, however, those who were personally pledged to

him were free to vote their convictions. "They've got the votes," shrugged Senator Minton of Indiana. "It's up to them."[22]

Vice-President Garner, who despised the court plan and who had retreated to Uvalde, Texas, while the debate was in progress, negotiated the surrender. Senator Wheeler and his colleagues could write their own ticket on the court bill, Garner told Wheeler, provided they "save the President's face" and preserve some semblance of party unity behind Senator Alben Barkley, Robinson's successor.[23]

It was 2:55 P.M., Tuesday, July 22, when Senator Logan of Kentucky, co-author with Senators Robinson, Hatch, and Ashurst of the compromise bill, moved to recommit it with instructions to the judiciary committee to report a new bill with provisions for procedural reforms of the lower federal courts only. "The Supreme Court is out?" asked Senator Johnson of California, half-standing as if to protest. "The Supreme Court is out," replied Logan. "Glory be to God!" murmured Johnson, as he sank back into his chair.[24]

The motion to recommit carried, 70 to 20. The court fight was over.

V

The court fight was over, all right. And in the backwash all manner of explanations would be offered to explain what had happened.

One explanation that became increasingly popular with the passage of time was that the Supreme Court, by changing direction, had literally saved itself ("A switch in time saves nine" was the popular cliché), an explanation that seemed plausible, at least on the surface. On March 29, the court, with Justice Roberts joining with the liberals, upheld the Washington State Minimum Wage Act, a measure similar to the New York law which the Court had invalidated in the Morehead decision the year before. The same day, by unanimous vote the Court sustained the new Frazier-Lemke Farm Mortgage Act. Two weeks later, in a decision which even the most optimistic New Dealer would not have predicted, the Court put its stamp of approval on the National Labor Relations Act. In May, in the crucial test of the social security legislation, the Court once more nodded approvingly. Seventeen times during the Supreme Court session the Administration went to the whipping post and seventeen times it came back all smiles, destroying the notion that the Court was out to wreck the New Deal, or that there was any need to change the Court.[25]

Meanwhile, Justice Brandeis had quietly arranged a much-publicized exchange of correspondence between Senator Wheeler, the chief enemy of the court bill, and Chief Justice Hughes, in which Hughes declared convincingly that the Court did not have a crowded calendar or backlog of cases pending. In mid-May, the same day the Senate Judiciary Committee reported unfavorably (by a vote of 10 to 8) on the court plan, Justice Van Devanter, a stalwart conservative and implacable New Deal foe, resigned, creating the first vacancy on the Court since Roosevelt assumed office.

It could also be argued that Roosevelt's defeat, his losing control of the Congress for the first time, was due to his failure to take Democratic Party leaders into his confidence, his permitting Farley too free a hand in patronage matters as a way to force the senators in line. (Senator McCarran, for example, delivered a two-hour speech daring Farley to reduce his number of loaves and fishes in Nevada for opposing the court bill.) Roosevelt's absolute refusal to compromise in the early stages may have been decisive.[26]

All of these things probably had some part in Roosevelt's humiliation. But one thing was certain; it was inflicted by Democrats. In the last analysis, the reason may have been simpler than most observers realized. The American people had shown every disposition to follow Roosevelt through fire, flood, and pestilence. But when it came to defying the gods and tribal magic, of refusing to bow before the Ark of the Covenant, the people grew fearful, sullen, and refused to move. It was then that Roosevelt's enemies who had waited long for such an opportunity, joining with those whose motives were less vindictive, had inflicted a most damaging defeat. Those who were baffled to learn that some of the men who were opposing Roosevelt's court plan were among those who had supported a similar plan back in 1917 (a plan that had lost in the House by a narrow 200 to 192 vote) simply did not understand the real nature of the court fight. The civil war among Democrats was on for control of an unbeatable party machinery. As one Michigan editor had put it at the time, "We are witnessing in the Senate debate another turning point in the history of the country." "Out of this debate," he continued, "will emerge a New Deal Party and a Democratic Party . . . it seems practically certain that the Democratic Party, as it has existed almost from the beginning of the country, will be doomed." "A party," he wrote, by way of clarifying the issue, "cannot exist half Roosevelt and half Democratic."[27]

The first major engagement of the interregnum strife had gone to the opposition. But the failure of the court plan was not to be Roosevelt's only Supreme Court embarrassment in 1937.

In mid-August, when Roosevelt had an opportunity to make his first Supreme Court appointment since becoming President, his prestige received another staggering blow. In a surprise move he sent to the Senate the name of Alabama's Senator Hugo Black to fill the Van Devanter vacancy. Black, a liberal and friend of the New Deal, would certainly be confirmed by his colleagues; although some, particularly the southern conservatives, agreed privately with former President Hoover that Black's appointment would mean the Court was "one-ninth packed." Roosevelt, they fumed, was deliberately pouring salt on the wounds left by the court fight. There was enough grumbling over the Black appointment that the Senate refused to confirm him without first referring the matter to the Senate judiciary committee, the first time that the Senate had so embarrassed a sitting senator since the appointment of L. Q. C. Lamar of Mississippi in 1888.[28]

Black and his wife were in Europe when the story broke that he had once been a member of the Ku Klux Klan. His solemn confession later to a nation-wide radio audience that he had, in fact, been a member was not reassuring. Although the Senate accepted Black's explanation and confirmed his appointment, Roosevelt's critics had a field-day. Roosevelt was seeking the power to control the decisions of all federal courts, Hugh Johnson told the National Hardwood Association in a speech at Chicago, and particularly "of the Supreme Court by appointing to it a majority of puppets of his own choosing—hillbilly Ku Klux wool hats from the forks of the creek, like Senator Black." William Allen White, who had first looked kindly upon the Black appointment, was expressing the hurt and shock felt by many: "When Franklin Roosevelt is dead and buried and all his bones are rotted," wrote White, "the one thing for which he will be remembered is the fact that he played around with Black and appointed to the highest honorable office in American life a man who was a member of the Ku Klux Klan. . . ."[29]

VI

Roosevelt's court plan and his appointment of Black seemed, to his critics at least, to confirm what they had been saying about his determination to destroy the Constitution and the judiciary. Not only was Roosevelt trying to destroy the Constitution, they charged, but he was also trying to ruin the country by spending it into bankruptcy. Throughout the session attacks on the Administration and the President's program continued relentlessly. Criticism of New Deal extravagance was louder than ever before.

Congressman Charles A. Plumley of Vermont, who liked to preface his expansive generalizations with "If history teaches anything," was always good for a few words on New Deal spendthrifts, particularly the President himself. "He [Roosevelt] puts no premium on thrift or self-support," he said, in reply to the President's relief message, "nor does he draw a picture of hard work, self-sacrifice . . . [or] that man was put on earth to earn his own bread and not live on the bread of others. . . ." Clare Hoffman said he was getting "sick and tired" of voting against unnecessary appropriations, appropriations that Democrats used "to gain political credit, fix . . . political fences, and pose as friends of mankind in general. . . ." Dewey Short thought the House should know that Congress had appropriated only a little more than a billion and a half dollars to thirty Presidents in the first one hundred and forty-three years of the nation's history to spend as they saw fit. But since March 4, 1933, Congress had turned over $15,428,498,815 to one man to spend as he, "in his infinite, infallible, omnipotent, and impeccable wisdom," saw fit. That amount, said Short, represented more power "than any good man should want and certainly is more power than any bad man should possess." "We have got no government in Washington," Senator Glass told Senator Borah during the debate of the President's tax measure. "The last election was carried by people who were getting favors from the Government, people who were subsidized by the Government, people who were on relief rolls, and people who were sanctioning the invasion of private property. . . ."[30]

Roosevelt's request for $1,500,000,000 for work relief for the fiscal year 1938, was met with renewed claims of wasteful overhead, overlapping and duplication of efforts, and demands that relief efforts be restored to the states and local communities to free them of centralized bureaucracy and partisan politics. "Gentlemen," Congressman Ditter told his colleagues, "you can wrap up a skunk in a perfumed robe and it will still be a skunk, and you can wrap up a political relief racket in a robe of demagogic humanitarianism and it will still be a political relief racket."[31]

Work relief was not the only racket the New Deal was operating, according to some sources. The least efficient of the various types of relief and the type most difficult for Congress to reduce was the "high-salaried," "luxury relief" in the form of federal jobs for "a new army" of New Deal "faithful." When Roosevelt took office in 1933, the number of employees on the federal payroll was 563,000; four years later the number stood at 829,000, which was proof enough to anyone who could add and subtract that Roosevelt, during his first term, had bought 266,000 Democratic votes at the taxpayers' expense. Congressman Woodruff was still able to look on the bright side, however, pointing out that the way Roosevelt broke promises and the way his promises seemed always to work in reverse it was a good thing he had not pledged to cut government expenditures by 50 per cent (he had talked of 25 per cent during the 1932 campaign) otherwise the number of Democratic "faithful" on the payroll might be twice the number.[32]

Rex Tugwell and the Resettlement Administration came in for the usual share of hazing, Senator Bailey of North Carolina even suggesting that it would save the government money in the long run if they paid Tugwell a salary just to stay away from Washington. One of the funnier episodes in a session notably lacking of laughs was Congressman Guyer's dismay upon learning that the government was involved in the manufacture and sale of rum in the Virgin Islands, subsidizing the industry to the tune of about two and a half million dollars annually. It was bad enough, said Guyer, shaking his head, "all the vagaries and absurdities of the New Deal, its flirting with communism, its embrace of socialism, its adoption of collectivism. . . ." But for the government to be mixed up in the fermentation of cane squeezings revealed the New Deal's "utter lack of constructive genius."[33]

For the most part, Republicans had little to do during the session but let Democrats fight each other. But they enjoyed themselves immensely when it was learned that James Farley had been peddling copies of the 1936 Democratic campaign book—2,500 of them—autographed by the President, for $1,000 per copy. Such a display of righteousness and moral indignation as the Republicans put on had seldom been seen. The "campaign book scandal," as they called it, was a "nefarious scheme," "incredibly bold," "disgusting," "outrageous," "a cynical disregard of political morals and ethics," "contempt for law," "dangerous," "disregard for public opinion," "vicious," "demoralizing." "The camouflaged sale" was a "slick trick to evade the Corrupt Practices Act," a form of "political blackmail." It was bad enough, said Republicans, that for the first time in history a national committee had had "the effrontery to inveigle the President of the United States into such a piece of political chicanery"; for him then to plead that he had no idea what he had been signing was incredible indeed.

When the Rules Committee promptly refused to act on the demand (from the portly minority leader, Bertrand H. Snell) for an investigation of the campaign book affair, Republicans could only conclude ("inescapable conclusion" was a term frequently heard in the cloakroom and corridor) that there "was much to hide and Mr. Roosevelt knew it."[34]

VII

During the last week in June, 1937, the President met with three different groups of Democrats from the Congress on successive days at the Jefferson Island Club in Chesapeake Bay. Roosevelt was never in better form. But beneath the cordiality, the banter, and the horseplay were issues separating some Democratic congressmen from their chief of such serious nature that they were not to be resolved by a keg of beer, a few steamed crabs, and the Roosevelt smile.

The court fight was still in progress, that attempt "to circumvent the Constitution by judicial atrocity," J. Parnell Thomas called it, privately. And not a few agreed with Thomas that if Roosevelt won the country could expect a torrent of legislative proposals "more radical than anything we have yet seen." In one of the few speeches made by a Republican against the court bill, Congressman Roy Woodruff of Michigan had warned against supporting a plan that would allow six "wet-nurse" justices to approve a legislative program "now hidden carefully in the background," a program "so extra-constitutional, so revolutionary, as to be beyond anything the present liberal Court could possibly find constitutional." "It's the legislation that Roosevelt will shoot at us if he gets his court bill that worries me," Senator Burke confided to an ally. "That is the real danger of his plan. That is what I am against."[35]

It was not really relevant to speculate about Roosevelt's future legislative plans. Whether he won the court fight or not, the Supreme Court was not going to rule on the constitutionality of anything until a bill became a law and a test case made of it. Judging by the mood of the Congress in 1937, the Court was going to have considerable leisure since the President's legislative program for that session, one that was known, about which there was no speculation, would never reach the Court. It would never reach the Court because it would never reach the statute books first.

What the court battle did was provide moral justification for Roosevelt's enemies in both parties, particularly in his own, to oppose the entire New Deal reform program in 1937.

This appeared to be what happened in the case of the reorganization plan, a proposal for streamlining the Executive branch. The Reorganization Bill, which became the storm center of one of the fiercest parliamentary and propaganda battles of recent history, was eventually betrayed in the House at the crucial moment by the chairman of the Rules Committee, New York's John J. O'Connor, a Democrat, and brother of President Roosevelt's former law partner. Passage of the Crop Control Act, the new version of the AAA, with its permanent plan of soil conservation, crop insurance, national acreage allotments and subsidies, and ever-normal granary features, was delayed until 1938 because it "smacks too much of dictatorship" and "shows clearly the thinking, or lack of thinking, of one Franklin Delano Roosevelt." Although the farmers approved the program by overwhelmingly lopsided margins when referendums were held the next year, congressmen who pretended to speak for agriculture insisted that farmers would never stand for it, would never tolerate "license tags on every cow's tail."[36]

Southern Democrats charged the Wages and Hours Act as if Western civilization itself was at stake. When Senator Hugo Black introduced in May, 1937, a plan providing for a minimum wage and maximum hours, the debate centered on the southern demand for a "differential" which would justify paying southern workers less than was paid in other sections of the country. The desire to perpetuate a system of cheap labor had nothing to do with it everyone was told. It was because of "the splendid gifts of God to the South," South Carolina's "Cotton Ed" Smith told the Senate, meaning a congenial climate where the cost of living was much lower. It was because transportation costs were nearly double in the South what they were in other sections of the country. It was because the bill amounted to a tariff levied on southerners for the benefit of northern industrialists. It was because labor was hard enough to get, what with the competition of "Mr. Roosevelt's shovel-setting brigades," without having to meet the competition of "wage-controlled industries." It was because "this piece of legislative hybridism" hatched by "radical organized-labor leaders" and "sinister intellectuals with red leanings" would create "a huge bureaucratic Frankenstein" that would stifle worker and employer alike. The Brain Trusters, said Congressman Taylor of Tennessee, should be taught a lesson, that there is "a limit to their arrogance and ambition to foist their socialistic dreams and panaceas on Congress with impunity and carte blanche nonchalance."[37]

It was interesting that Taylor should have thought of the wages and hours legislation as socialism when Amos Pinchot, an ex-socialist crusader, was writing an open letter to the President prophesying that should the wages and hours bill pass it would "throw the country into fascism in a fortnight." And it did little good for someone like Maury Maverick to point out that were he to suggest that southern senators and congressmen accept voluntary wage cuts because of the southern climate they would think he had lost his mind.[38]

The Senate passed the bill, but southern Democrats like Howard Smith of Virginia, teaming with Republican opponents of the bill, successfully exiled it in the House Rules Committee until a successful discharge petition finally rescued it. Not until the spring of 1938, a year after it had been introduced, was the bill enacted into law, and only then in the form of an unsatisfactory compromise, the Fair Labor Standards Act. And not before the country had heard about how factories would close and industries would go bankrupt and unemployment would spread if this "bald piece of deceit . . . the real purpose of which was to put the effective control of both industry and labor into the hands of the Federal Government" became law. The wages and hours bill, said Congressman Fred Hartley of New Jersey, in disgust, "is based upon the New Deal obsession that there ought to be a law although no one gives a damn what kind of a law." Its title, he said, should be changed to "A bill to further harass industry and to extend the New Deal depression." Maury Maverick was more hopeful. If it did nothing else, he said, it might at least discourage chambers of commerce in southern towns and cities from advertising cheap labor and lack of union organization as advantages.[39]

VIII

Congressional opposition to Roosevelt's wages and hours legislation was not altogether sheer cussedness. It reflected in part genuine fear and distrust by some of the union movement and Roosevelt's apparent surrender to Big Labor.

There was something besides Christmas spirit in the air when workers struck the huge General Motors plant in Cleveland late in December, 1936. Two days later, when the workers at Fisher Body No. 1 in Flint, Michigan, occupied the plant instead of walking out, the "sit-down" strike was added to the vocabulary of labor. For six weeks jeering workers held the plant under near seige conditions, and every effort to dislodge them was met by a hail of nuts and bolts and scrap metal. On February 11, 1937, General Motors capitulated. By the end of the year every automobile manufacturer except Ford had made peace with the United Automobile Workers.

Less than a month after the General Motors strike, United States Steel negotiated a contract with its workers that sensibly spared them and the country the anguish of a bitter strike. There would still be strikes, and private property would be weighed against lives and bloodshed. But the inexorable weight of numbers and the badge of righteousness was on the side of labor; a social revolution was under way that, in a few short years, would unionize most of the industrial muscle of the country.

During those early months of 1937 Roosevelt remained silent. But his unwillingness to use force against the sit-downers seemed to place him on the side of lawlessness. Clare Hoffman, the arch-enemy (in the Congress) of Roosevelt's labor policies, interpreted White House silence to mean more than tacit consent to lawlessness. "A President of the United States, voluble on all other subjects and at all other times, remains silent," Hoffman told his House colleagues; "without a word of disapproval from Franklin D. Roosevelt," John L. Lewis and his "crew of wreckers" are going about the country "smashing the faces, breaking the limbs, and sending to the hospital honest laboring men, whose only sin is the desire to work." Lewis' dirty work, he said, was being supported by Senator La Follette's Civil Liberties Committee, a committee created to investigate violations of the Wagner Act, but which, according to Hoffman, was nothing more than an opportunity for La Follette to "vent his spleen against those who have provided jobs for the workers." This "illegitimate child of a Communist mother and a politically ambitious father" (Hoffman called the committee) was simply a way of forcing workers into the arms of the CIO, a way of forcing them to pay tribute to John L. Lewis.[40]

Roosevelt's calculated campaign "to beat industry to its knees," a campaign, Hoffman insisted, inspired by Secretary of Labor Perkins ("who was born only God knows where, but whose destination, if the predictions of many be true, is absolutely certain") was sure to hasten the spread of communism and dictatorship. Hoffman quoted Roosevelt as having told Governor Murphy of Michigan, "if communism breaks in America, it will be in the Detroit area where it will first manifest itself." What Hoffman wanted to know was how Roosevelt was so certain of this "unless John L. Lewis told him so." And knowing this, why did he remain silent, Hoffman asked, why did he grasp in friendship "those red, dripping, bloody hands" of John L. Lewis. why did Roosevelt refuse to lift a finger to halt what was happening?

Hoffman thought he knew. Roosevelt, he asserted, is "waiting for the situation to go on . . . waiting until the sentiment of the people is such that he knows there will be an uprising impossible to quell and then he will come forward . . . and with great ballyhoo, announce that he has been anointed to rescue us from our peril." "When the iron collar of the Red Communists has finally been fastened firmly on the neck" of the labor movement in the United States, Hoffman warned, "the real motives and purposes of the dictator will be disclosed." And dictatorship it would be. "That this administration intentionally or otherwise would establish a dictatorship," Hoffman raged, "is no longer open to argument."[41]

It *was* open to argument, of course. Summer came and went, labor disorders subsided, the Reds did not take over, and Roosevelt was not crowned emperor. If Hoffman interpreted the President's behavior as treasonous approval, he was mistaken. That Roosevelt approved of the unionization of industry was no secret; but that he approved of the tactics being used was quite another matter. His failure to support sit-down strikes (which he privately described as a "damned unpopular device") won him no friends on either side, particularly from labor.[42]

Certainly Lewis did not regard Roosevelt's policies as being overly friendly to labor. In the off-year elections, Lewis said ominously, labor would find out "who its friends are." Whoever its friends were, Lewis decided that Roosevelt was not one of them. In 1940, the bushy-browed labor leader, who had been denounced all over the place as a Communist, returned to the Republican camp and backed Wendell Willkie for the presidency.[43]

IX

Roosevelt's seemingly moderate stand on the labor strife in 1937 threatened the loss of significant labor support, at least for the time being. But it threatened the loss of perhaps even more important support in other quarters. In his first term Roosevelt had loyal allies among small businessmen, shopkeepers and proprietors, white-collar and professional people, those who, by some broad definition, would probably be called middle-class. If the pitch and yaw of the New Deal during that first term was reason for some uneasiness, they did not seem to waver. They stayed with Roosevelt, cheered him on, voted for him by the thousands in 1936, but not so much because they were convinced that the New Deal made sense. They were not ideological converts to some new brand of liberalism.

All they knew was that some way, some how, conditions were getting better.

But 1937 had been a disappointing year, and it was not yet over; faith in Roosevelt was to get another jolt before it was. For four years economic conditions had steadily improved. By the spring of 1937, the levels of production exceeded those happy days of 1929 before the crash. Then, in late summer, the economy plummeted earthward again, wiping out the gains of the previous two years. The usual statistics, business and industrial indexes, car-loadings, steel production, stock sales, inventories, exports, Dow-Jones averages, unemployment, and all the rest, were mute testimony that the Roosevelt Panic (as Representative Ham Fish first labeled it) was on.

Back in 1935, at Charleston, South Carolina, Roosevelt had exulted: "Yes, we are on our way back . . . because we planned it that way . . ."; a boast which was now coming back to haunt him as his enemies made discreet inquiry as to whether the New Dealers had also planned a new depression. "Bridget said she had a hard time watching her husband and the fire both," teased Congressman Charles Gifford of Massachusetts; "if she kept her eye on one, the other went out. And so prosperity and recovery have recently gone out."[44]

The reason for the sudden flight of prosperity, according to his critics, was not hard to find. If Roosevelt had not deliberately planned a depression he had at least invited it by his hostile policies toward business, policies that meant punitive "soak-the-rich" taxation, bureaucratic snooping, red tape and reprisals, government competition with business, unsound, experimental legislation, squandering of money, and unbalanced budgets. The greatest of all New Deal sins, for which depression was the punishment, said Congressman Ditter of Pennsylvania, was meddling: "We meddle into farms, into factories, and into finances. We meddle into production, into prices, and into pay rolls. Were the results not so disastrous, the efforts would be humorous." Ditter's cure for the depression was simple enough, "let the administration mind its business and let business mind a little more of its own business . . . a hand of helpfulness rather than one of hostility must be extended." "The gay joyride of the 'brain-trusters' and alien-minded uplifters is ending in a smash," said New Jersey's Congressman Charles A. Eaton, with unconcealed satisfaction; "the self-appointed saviours . . . are taking to the cyclone cellars . . . the pack of the political Santa Claus is nearly empty. Business, hamstrung and manacled by punitive New Deal legislation and class propaganda, is ceasing to function." Fish of New York suggested that the New Deal change its theme song from "Happy Days Are Here Again" to "The Merry-Go-Round Broke Down." The New Deal, he said was like a merry-go-round with its gaudy trimmings and painted horses which gave the people a good time while the music lasted, but it got nowhere. "The trouble," said Fish, "is that business, not only in Wall Street but on Main Street, is jittery and dizzy from being whirled around and around by the New Deal merry-go-round at Washington and getting nowhere."

Fish was not just being facetious. He launched into a list of "I accuse him [Roosevelt]" that made the indictment of George III read like a letter of commendation, finishing off with a parting shot, "If there is anything else the gentleman wants me to accuse the President of, I am willing to do that also." Fish's list of particulars agreed with Emanuel Celler's conclusion that the new depression was the result of Roosevelt's anti-business policies. "Business needs to be encouraged," said Celler, "and not harassed and browbeaten at every turn."[45]

Whatever may have been the causes of the sharp economic setback, there were growing suspicions that Roosevelt had lost his magic touch. "The old Roosevelt magic has lost its kick," Hugh Johnson rasped. "The diverse elements in the Falstaffian army can no longer be kept together and led by a melodious whinny and a winning smile." Congressmen, who had never understood Roosevelt's economic sleight-of-hand, were restive. All they knew, according to a humorous editorial in *The New Republic*, was that "in dry spells, Mr. Roosevelt would go into a tent, make unintelligible noises and presently there would be rain. Last September saw the start of the severest dry spell in nine years. Mr. Roosevelt made no move to go into his tent, or reach for the bag of magic feathers. The rank-and-file Congressman jumped to the conclusion that his power was no longer intact." The court-packing disaster, the frightening labor disorders, the dismaying turn of events in the Black appointment, and then depression had seemingly ended Roosevelt's hold over a Congress that was spoiling for a fight from the beginning. The President, Harold Ickes told his diary in late summer, "is punch drunk from the punishment that he has suffered recently." Roosevelt made one last try, calling the Congress back into special session in November. But the special session was no better than the regular one and adjourned just before Christmas without passing a single bill requested by the President.[46]

The irresistible leader of 1936 had become the repudiated leader of 1937.

X

Now it was 1938, a year of brutal intramural strife among Democrats and defections by La Follette-led liberals, a year of stalemated trench warfare against the New Deal, fought out agaist a backdrop of continuing depression (until a slow upturn set in in late summer) and impending elections.

Efforts to heal the rift between Roosevelt and the conservative bloc in the Democratic Party which, with its Republican allies, had becalmed the New Deal program, had failed. "The Party is divided hopelessly," Senator Bailey wrote Wyoming's Joseph O'Mahoney; "the points of view and the respective interests, the objectives, cannot be reconciled."[47]

Bailey's pessimistic note to O'Mahoney came late in August, 1937, less than two weeks after a notable attempt to restore party harmony. The occasion was a dinner in Washington attended by some sixty Democratic senators honoring the new majority leader, Alben Barkley. The dinner was less than a success despite the pretty speeches, the cordial message from the President, and the live pigeon which flew above the heads of the diners symbolizing the dove of peace. When the love feast was over and a newsman asked a prominent senator if harmony had prevailed, his reply was: "Harmony, hell!; and don't quote me." Republicans were delighted, remarking that it seemed particularly appropriate that the organist had begun the evening's entertainment by playing "The Last Round-up."[48]

When the President turned up empty-handed after the special session, it was the signal for the conservatives to move. In December they circulated privately their own recovery plan, a plan that was largely the bipartisan handiwork of Senator Bailey and Republican Senator Vandenberg of Michigan. In it were the customary admonitions about states' rights, balanced budgets, encouragement for business, cutting taxation, and the other Ten Commandments of conservatism. It was the kind of program that Democrats like Byrd of Virginia, Millard Tydings of Maryland, and the physician-turned-politician, Senator Royal S. Copeland of New York, could support whole-heartedly.

When the new session got under way in January, 1938, with the conservative coalition and the President eyeing each other like judo wrestlers, it was the farm bloc that moved first. The patchwork legislation hastily thrown together after the Court had ruled against the first AAA in 1936 was proving unworkable. The plan, to reduce production and cure the dust-bowl problem, had depended on voluntary cooperation by the farmers, a breed not noted for doing things voluntarily. Cotton, tobacco, and wheat surpluses continued to mount, and as they did prices correspondingly sagged. As the farmer, tightening the vise on his own finger, began to yell for help, his spokesmen started demanding legislation with built-in absurdities—unlimited production, higher subsidies, and overseas dumping of the even larger surpluses that were bound to result.

They did not get everything they wanted. By 1938, Secretary Wallace was beguiled with the "ever-normal granary" concept of storing surpluses during good years and distributing them like Joseph in Egypt during the lean years. Somewhere between the two points of view Congress passed a new AAA, a compromise that made soil conservation a permanent program, authorized a program of crop loans and crop insurance, and permitted the Secretary of Agriculture to assign acreage allotments and subsidies, subject to approval by referendum of the farmers involved.

Although the farmers approved the new plan by staggering margins when the time came, it was bitterly assailed by some members in the Congress. Senator Charles L. McNary of Oregon, apparently forgetting that he had sponsored some interesting farm legislation of his own during the 1920's, claimed the act would make Henry Wallace "the autocrat of the breakfast table." With the plan, Roosevelt was "sowing dragon's teeth," said Senator Bailey, because it was "a perfect model of fascism; and, of course, everyone knows it." Senator McAdoo predicted that the law was impossible of enforcement and would have to be repealed at the next session. Others thought that nothing should be done until President Roosevelt put a stop to the reciprocal trade agreements negotiated by Secretary Hull. They argued that the importation of foreign farm products permitted under the agreements more than offset the cutbacks achieved by taking land out of cultivation under the acreage allotments. Congressman Lord of New York called it an "agricultural merry-go-round." Congressman Wolcott of Michigan strongly opposed the new bill, and when it passed, lashed out at Roosevelt whom he described (using a quotation from Abraham Lincoln) as a "bewildered, confounded and miserably perplexed man," a breach of etiquette which brought from Congressman Rayburn a retort that not in his career under five Presidents had he heard "a member of this House carry partisanship to such a point of personal criticism."[49]

Republican Senator White described the farm bill as a "lollapaloosa." "The next thing we know," said the Ohioan, "the cows, the chickens, and all the farmers will have to be saluting Wallace every time they turn around." White was delighted to announce that a group of some seven hundred farmers from one county in his state were organizing to combat the plan, were going "to join hands with any and all non-partisan, non-sectarian, non-factional farm organizations in the United States to seek the repeal of the act," and were going to lead the way in organizing similar groups in other farm states. The fate of the venture could almost be predicted when it was learned they had first chosen the Corn Belt Liberty League as a name for the organization but changed it to Farm Independence League when they discovered that a Corn Belt Liberty League had already been chartered by Ilinois farmers.[50]

Meanwhile, the Roosevelt recession was entering its seventh month, with no signs of improvement. The only cheerful note, according to Massachusetts Congressman Joseph Martin, was that at least the grass was not growing in the streets "because now 11,000,000 idle wage-earners are wandering these streets in search of employment."[51]

And there was still no shortage of experts with easy explanations of what was causing the trouble. In May, Hugh Johnson told one thousand

bankers and their guests at the Waldorf-Astoria Hotel that the responsibility for the recession was "single and direct." It rested on the "semi-
Socialist, anti-business experimenters" with whom the President had surrounded himself. His formula for remedying the situation was for everyone who disagreed with the New Deal "to keep jumping up and down
and raising hell all the time." "If you don't," he warned, "the Washington experimenters soon won't have anything to experiment with." In
September, Colonel Theodore Roosevelt declared that the depression
resulted from the persecution of business through the schemes of "imported professors," "plug-ugly politicians," and "this swarm of office-hold-
ing parasites." Roosevelt's opponent in the 1936 election and his campaign
manager offered similar explanations, Landon maintaining that the President's "nagging attacks on business" were responsible, while John D. M.
Hamilton asserted that the Administration refused to "learn by its mistakes," or "recant its economic heresies."[52]

In Congress similar views were being expressed almost daily. "Mr.
Roosevelt," said Copeland of New York, "has never made any secret of
his antagonism to business." Others agreed with Copeland and with
Congressman Plumley of Vermont who asserted, "It is brutally and frankly
true that the policy of this Administraton . . . has served only to worry
business—big and little—to block initiative and stop the expansion of
industry." And Congressman Noah Mason of Illinois said he had consulted with Stuffy, the old gray squirrel who dominated the White House
lawn, about the depression. "Congressman," the squirrel had told him,
"something has happened. A decided change has come over the president
lately. He used to be buoyant, now he seems downcast. . . ." Stufly thought
he knew why; "if we stop to think at all, we must realize that we are
right back where we were in 1933." According to this remarkable rodent,
the cure for the country's ills was "Government cooperation with private
industry instead of Government competition . . . remove the shackles that
have handicapped industry . . . give both big business and small business
some hope for the future . . . the green light . . . to business . . . the red
light . . . to boondoggling and political squandering."[53]

The steady tune that the depression was the result of the Administration's anti-business policies seemed more than a reprise, the repetition
of an old refrain. It was in the nature of an answer to the charge that
business had artificially induced the depression by "ganging up" on the
Administration. The day after Christmas, 1937, Robert Jackson, head of
the Anti-Trust Division of the Justice Department, delivered a radio
speech in which he blamed monopolists for the depression. A few days
later, at the meeting of the American Political Science Association in
Philadelphia, Jackson accused business of waging a "strike of capital"
against the Administration. The day following Jackson's speech to the
political scientists, Secretary Ickes let loose a broadside against "big busi-

ness fascism" that was endangering the country. Ickes warned that the new depression had resulted from the resumption of "the old struggle between the power of money and the power of the democratic instinct" by a relative handful of economic titans ("America's Sixty Families," Ickes called them) who were determined to topple Roosevelt.[54]

If their charges sounded too far-fetched they could point accusingly and say "I told you so" at the Lincoln Day speech some weeks later at Knoxville, Tennessee, by Congressman Will Taylor. Taylor slashed wickedly at the Administration, characterizing it as "a political vampire" that was draining the life-blood of the nation. "The business people of the Nation," said Taylor, in an unguarded moment, "have already discovered that the New Deal is a fallacy, and regardless of politics, they are ready to enlist in a battle to overthrow it." They could also point to a sign of business bad faith of another kind. Municipal power projects were blocked in twenty-three states by injunctions that had retarded progress on the projects for three years while the litigation dragged through the courts. As another example, Attorney-General Homer Cummings reminded the country that to frustrate the effectiveness of the Public Utility Holding Company Act seven major suits were brought simultaneously in the District of Columbia and more than forty suits in twelve different judicial districts, when one test suit would have done just as well. "There seemed to be," said Cummings, wearily, "and I say it with regret, a deliberate purpose to engage the Government upon so many fronts that effective defense would be rendered difficult or impossible."[55]

Reaction to the Jackson-Ickes speeches in the Congress was instantaneous. Their "trial balloons," Congressman Arthur P. Lamneck of Ohio conjectured, were sent up "to determine the gullibility of the people." There were desperate attempts "to find a substitute tune for 'Happy Days Are Here Again.'" Lamneck predicted that the American people were not going to pay any attention to "these two foghorn-voiced advance guards of the red-herring brigade." Instead, they would demand that Congress "throw these cures and the foreign-minded specialists who prescribe them out of the window" and get back to "a diet of untrammeled American competition." The charges made by Jackson and Ickes were very serious, said New York Congressman Frank Crowther, and should not be passed off lightly. They were serious enough, in fact, that a concerted effort should be made to find out if they were true. "The burden of proof," said Crowther, "is upon the Administration."[56]

Jackson and Ickes had both acted apparently without any prior consent from the White House. They breathed easier when Roosevelt made no move to repudiate their actions; and those in the Administration with trust-busting in their blood were agreeably surprised and pleased when the President, in his State of the Union message, promised to send Congress a special monopoly message later. Late in April, 1938, Roosevelt asked Congress for an investigation into the matter of monopolies and concentrated economic power. Congress responded with the Temporary National Economic Committee, headed by Senator Joseph O'Mahoney of Wyoming, the most elaborate investigation of the national economy ever undertaken by the government. If, as Crowther had said, the burden of proof was on the Administration, the TNEC would attempt to provide that proof.

XI

In mid-April, with no natural recovery in sight, Roosevelt reluctantly primed the pump by seeking congressional approval of a new large-scale spending program. Congress approved the plan in June, staking Roosevelt to a $3.75 billion bankroll, nearly a billion for the reactivated PWA, almost a billion and a half for WPA, and smaller amounts for a host of lesser New Deal activities.

The omnibus spending bill climaxed "nine years of fiscal insanity" according to Senator Byrd of Virginia (which meant the spending aberration was not all Roosevelt's, apparently; it included two years of the Hoover Administration). Senator Davis of Pennsylvania told the Young Republicans in Harrisburg that it was "a wicked exchange of bread for votes," the kind of "political pandering of relief as was done in the days of imperial Rome." Fish of New York charged that the Administration was bankrupted of recovery ideas except "to pile debt upon debt, deficit upon deficit." What galled Fish was that the money had no strings attached. We turn the money over to Roosevelt, said Fish, "leaving Congress with no more legislative control over these funds than Gandhi has clothing." Short of Missouri drew laughs with his comments about using the money to set out saplings, harness moonbeams, and construct dog pounds and monkey houses. But he was deadly serious about his charges of "inefficient and uneconomical management," "unblushing fraud," "ignoble graft," "criminal corruption," "boondoggling projects," and "unattainable dreams of wild-eyed schemers." "Auctioneer" Farley was going to have a field day, Short warned; "This money is not for economic recovery," he shouted, amid wild applause from the Republican side of the aisle, "it is to be used for political rehabilitation."[57]

Senator Bailey of North Carolina injected a new argument. Why, he wanted to know, had western states, on a per capita basis, received more money from the New Deal than any of the other states? Displaying the easterner's usual ignorance about the needs of the West, he could only conclude that it was because they held the political balance of power and the charge that the New Deal had "spent and lent its relief and recovery billions in the way best calculated to keep itself in power is true."[58]

For all the grousing Congress did about the pump-priming bill, the most bitter attack came from Amos Pinchot. Pinchot dispatched to Roosevelt an open letter in which he charged that the spending bill was "clearly a scheme to restore White House power by buying support in the coming elections." Did the President realize, Pinchot asked, that if the jobless Americans were to march from dawn to dark in ordinary military formation it would take more than three months for them to pass a White House reviewing stand? Yet, Pinchot insisted, Roosevelt's only solution to this desperate situation was more spending, a "grandiose and costly excursion into socialism," "the longest step toward collectivism," a plan "to squander ourselves out of depression," which, at best, could provide work only for a fraction of the unemployed. If throwing money around

Bread Upon the Waters. *Copyright 1938, New York* Herald Tribune. *Reproduced with permission. Cartoon by Brown.*

was all that was going to be done, Pinchot suggested using a plan proposed by Tom Corcoran ("bill drafter extraordinary and adviser pleni-
potentiary—as well, I understand, as official guitar player—for that curious
mixture of error, energy, and ambition known as the Third New Deal").
Corcoran, according to Pinchot, had once approached him about a position on the Board of the Reconstruction Finance Corporation. During
the course of their interview Corcoran was supposed to have remarked
that to restore buying power and get money in the hands of the people
"the ideal thing would be for fleets of airplanes to fly over the country
discharging money as they went, so that anyone needing cash could pick
it up from the ground."[59]

Our Twenty-Five Billion Dollar Hunting Party

*Copyright 1938, New York Herald Tribune. Reproduced
with permission. Cartoon by Jay N. Darling.*

To the Congress the most annoying aspect of the new spending program
was the thought of turning Harry Hopkins loose with nearly a billion and
a half dollars for relief just before elections. The claim that the relief program was shot through with politics had been made many times before, it
was nothing new. Men like Congressmen Hoffman and Gifford and Short
had been saying it for years. Some Democrats, including men like Senator
Bailey and Senator Byrd and old Carter Glass, were strongly critical of
the relief program. And the young Rush Holt of West Virginia, at first
a vigorous New Dealer, was building a political career around criticism of
Hopkins and the WPA.

The issue was very simple. Roosevelt and Hopkins (as Bailey once
claimed) were guilty of "buying votes with borrowed money." They were
"playing politics with human misery"; they would use the funds "to
purchase the votes of the hungry . . . to provide new jobs for political
favorites . . ." (Hoffman, Michigan); they were playing the same game
as imperial Rome which was "one of the fundamental reasons for the
downfall of the Roman Empire" (Davis, Pennsylvania); they would
guarantee the election of friendly congressmen and senators by expending
money needlessly "to reindex the court files or . . . to drag the river to
see if there are any prehistoric rocks in it" (Holt, West Virginia). Holt
produced statistics showing that in election years the relief rolls expanded
at a rapid rate but contracted just as quickly in other years. If Hopkins
and Roosevelt were going to use voters on relief to fix elections why
not admit it openly and candidly, Holt wanted to know. "A highway
robber," he said, "is better than a pickpocket."[60]

Gifford did not think the gravest danger in the relief program was
its use for partisan politican ends. The worst aspect was the way it had
"spoiled" workers, taught them habits of "inefficiency," showed them
how to live "improvidently" and to "depend upon the supposedly inexhaustible resources of Government to care for them. . . ." He believed
relief should be direct, a dole, "the better method, as proven by the
experience of other nations," which meant, of course, it was cheaper than
work-relief. He chided Roosevelt for not accepting a recommendation
favoring direct relief offered by a group of businessmen who had recently
met with the President at Warm Springs, Georgia, a recommendation
which Roosevelt had dismissed because, said Congressman Jerry Voorhis
of California, the dole was "unsound economically, unfair, un-American,
and un-Christian." Congressman Aime Forand of Rhode Island indicated
that he and some others had received mail suggesting that not only
should relief be direct but also that those on relief for extended periods
be disenfranchised as a means of eliminating politics in relief. "Notwith-
standing that they are for the most part blameless for their situation,"
went one letter which Forand read to the House, "they certainly should
not be permitted to vote after, say, two years of feeding at the public
crib."[61]

If Roosevelt were going to be permitted to resume spending as a cure for the recession, there were those who insisted that he must also take another step toward recovery whether he liked it or not. There must be tax revision, specifically of the undistributed profits tax and capital gains tax. Republicans, particularly, argued that it was the Roosevelt tax policy (the "same old policy of excessive taxes, of destructive taxes, and of punitive taxes that has destroyed business confidence in this country, prolonged the depression, and retarded recovery," according to Congressman Fish), that had triggered the Roosevelt depression. Congressman Dudley A. White of Ohio, could show, by oversimplified logic, that the tax made it impossible for industry to expand and this in turn prevented the creation of new jobs, jobs that were "forfeited on the altar of Government short-sightedness," jobs that were "chained to the fence-post of Government-enforced inactivity by this brainless 'brain trust' brainstorm."[62]

The existing tax policy reminded Gifford of a little story about the teacher who asked Mary a question about grammar. If the sentence "My father had money" is in the past tense, what tense would one be using if he said "My father has money," asked the teacher. "Pretense," answered Mary. Congressman Crawford of Michigan drew guffaws with the story about the businessman, on the verge of bankruptcy because of the tax policy, who had staved off disaster a little longer by an unexpected turn of events. The wolf at the door had had pups in the kitchen, and he had sold them to stay in business.[63]

A few Democrats, including people like Bernard Baruch and the wealthy Bostonian, Joseph P. Kennedy, a sometime New Dealer, were likewise convinced that the profit tax had at least intensified the economic decline. Even a New Dealer like Marriner Eccles, the bold and imaginative banker from Utah and governor of the Federal Reserve Board, accepted this thesis. In such a confused atmosphere the conservative-Democrat-Republican coalition succeeded in pushing through a compromise measure reducing the capital gains tax and retaining the undistributed profits tax in shadowy form. Roosevelt, chastened by earlier defeats, and apparently unwilling to butt heads with both Congress and business over a tax measure that was obviously favorable to the rich and the big corporations, allowed the bill to become law without his signature.

Roosevelt would keep in mind that it was Democrats, southern Democrats mostly, like James Byrnes and Pat Harrison, who had turned the trick in betraying the Administration tax policy.

XII

Before the session of 1938 was over Congress had one final setback in store for Roosevelt.

If the defeat of the court plan had been Roosevelt's worst defeat in the

Senate, the emasculation of his Reorganization Bill would be his worst rebuke administered by the House. The plan to introduce greater efficiency into government by streamlining the Executive branch got side-tracked when it was first submitted in 1937. But 1938 was a different story. Reorganization was too pat an issue to pass up; to prove that Roosevelt had subversive designs on democratic institutions reorganization was as convenient as court-packing.

The debate had little or nothing to do with the merits of the plan. Regardless of motive—from a genuine fear of a Roosevelt tyranny to a fervent desire to humiliate the President—the bill would stand or fall on fictitious issues, on checks and balances, coordinate branches of government, and unchecked Executive power. In its most irrelevant form the issue became that of an incipient Roosevelt despotism, although for five years the country had been told that Roosevelt was already a despot.

Senator Vandenberg may have started it, condemning the proposals as an attempt to create a "civil service dictator," "a symbol" of the New Deal "march toward a totalitarian state." The bill passed the Senate by a narrow 49 to 42 vote, but not before Tydings of Maryland and Brown of Michigan and Borah and Wheeler and Burke all had their say on the "dictator" issue. Senator Hiram Johnson, old, benign, the fires of Progressivism burning low in his bosom, struggled to his feet with a poignant appeal to his Senate colleagues: "I have little time in this body to spend; I have little time to spend at all. . . ." The California senator could not bear the thought that his last official act might be that of conferring "arbitrary power upon the President of the United States, no matter who he is. . . ." For Senator Walsh, passage would mean "plunging a dagger into the very heart of democracy."[64]

Senator Matthew Neely of West Virginia interpreted the obstructionist behavior of his Senate colleagues as largely dangerous fraud. ". . . the oldest inhabitant can scarcely remember when the debate on the reorganization bill began," said Neely, sarcastically, near the end of the debate. ". . . voluble Senators . . . have compassed sea and land . . . have discussed practically everything in the animal, vegetable and mineral kingdoms . . . unfortunate Jews in Europe . . . German nazism . . . Italian fascism . . . American water-power projects . . . the sex life of the Alaskan salmon . . . the prosaic existence of an unoffending Tennessee jackass . . . nothing has escaped the bitter omnivorous senatorial discussion . . . no degree of forensic longitude that it has not reached . . . no parallel of political latitude that it has not touched . . . all the depths and shoals of truth and error, wisdom and folly, sense and nonsense, have been sounded." But even after all that talk, said Neely, the only way to demonstrate that the bill would make a dictator of Franklin Roosevelt was by "perverting the plain language of the bill" and by "attributing to the President motives that would dishonor Ananias or degrade Benedict

Arnold." Senate opposition to the reorganization plan, in Neely's opinion, was a combination of "political hatred, partisan jealousy, or groundless fear."[65]

By the time the bill reached the House, the campaign against it was reaching full swing, much of the public opposition, perhaps most of it, being inspired by publisher Frank Gannett's National Committee to Uphold Constitutional Government. In the two days before the Senate vote, members of the upper house were inundated by thousands of telegrams and letters protesting the bill, a performance that would be repeated when the House took up the bill and which netted, by conservative estimates, some two hundred thousand pieces of mail.[66]

The campaign bore some of the characteristics of the one staged when the Wheeler-Rayburn Public Utilities Holding Company Act was passed. The barrage of telegrams, said one editorialist, seemed "about as spontaneous as a world series baseball game." Many were signed only with first names, lacked addresses, and contained identical messages. Senators and congressmen reported that a number of their replies were being returned unclaimed. Congressman Bulwinkle of North Carolina had nearly half of his returned, stamped "No such address" and "No such person at this address." Some were being told by constituents that they had not sent telegrams nor had they authorized anyone to send telegrams for them. And there was the classic case of one congressman who received a telegram from his wife (whose name was apparently picked at random) although she was with him in Washington at the time.[67]

The messages contained in the letters and telegrams and the material circulated by the Gannett organization bore down hard on the "dictatorship" issue, in many instances trying to link communism and fascism in with it. One survey indicated that about 95 per cent of the newspapers of the country opposed the bill and joined in what Congressman Sabath of Illinois called the "game of destruction," the New York *World Telegram* using it as an excuse for comparing Roosevelt with Adolf Hitler. People were reminded of Dr. Glenn Frank's warning to a Republican Party rally in Topeka, Kansas, a few weeks before. Frank, former president of the University of Wisconsin and chairman of the National Republican program committee, had said that the Republican Party was the faithful expression of the American tradition rather than "the Fascist program of the New Deal which . . . threatens to Hitlerize what was once democratic self-government." In contrast was a widely circulated resolution adopted by the New York National Republican Club which asserted that for the first time in the history of the country assaults, "led by the President of the United States," had been made against the Constitution, and against the government. The country was witnessing "the doctrines of Karl Marx and of the Second and Third International put into effect by those from the President down, whose acts belie their words."[68]

The bill received rougher treatment in the House where there were angry words about the "cult of standardization" and "federal usurpation" which, according to one congressman from Maine would mean the end of America as "the people of our generation have known it." Congressman Wigglesworth of Massachusetts thought it pertinent to introduce an editorial by David Lawrence, listing eight evidences of Roosevelt's drive toward dictatorship. There were a lot of other things, wrote Lawrence, that Roosevelt had not yet achieved in his plan for totalitarian control, "but which he has had very much in mind. Ham Fish wanted to build into the bill a safeguard that would limit the President to two terms, a proposal that was promptly ruled out of order. Congressman Lamneck warned that this was no "innocent little plan for revising Government charts." "This scheme," he insisted, "is the culmination of the Administration's paramount dream . . . to enormously increase the cost of government, wreck the civil service system, and saddle upon the country a malodorous bureaucratic one-man control. . . ." Congressman Knutson's contribution was the information that Earl Browder, leader of the Communist Party, was in favor of passage of the bill. Pennsylvania Congressman Stack reported the only people in his district who favored the bill were the radicals of the CIO, which was, in his words, "nuff said." It was Stack who opposed the bill for reasons that were long on sentiment but short on historical accuracy. "What is the matter with our Government that it needs to be reorganized?" he asked. "We have gotten along fairly well with it since the days of Valley Forge, when Washington and his little army suffered untold tortures that he and the early fathers might hand us down the country that we have today."[69]

In April the House rejected the bill, 204 to 196, with 108 Democrats kicking over the traces to vote against it. "Jim," Roosevelt told Farley, "I'll tell you that I didn't expect the vote. I can't understand it. There wasn't a chance for anyone to become a dictator under that bill." In the postmortem there were many who agreed with him. Herbert Hoover, who was not one of Roosevelt's warmest admirers, had said, "I do not share the belief that it is equivalent or nearly equivalent to dictatorship." Considering the comparative unimportance of the issue, wrote Arthur Krock of *The New York Times,* if the opponents of the bill had kept "within bounds of truth and reason" the Congress and the country would have paid "only ordinary attention to the legislation."[70]

But they had not. "Propaganda and deliberate distortion of the truth" were used on a national scale to beat the bill, declared Speaker Bankhead. No bill in recent times had been "so flagrantly lied about," asserted Congressman Thomas Ford of California, a newspaper man of considerable experience with the Los Angeles *Times* before running for Congress. Earl Godwin, ex-president of the National Press Club, described the newspaper campaign against the reorganization bill as "incredible," and warned that "the continued publication of such deliberate untruths will someday end in disaster. . . ." Commentators like Arthur Krock and Walter Lippmann agreed that had the "sham issue of 'dictatorship'" not been raised the bill would have passed easily.[71]

But the opportunity to rebuke the President was too inviting. "The object of the opposition is not to prevent reorganization of the executive branch," wrote Lippmann, "but to put a spectacular and decisive check upon this President's authority."[72]

XIII

In his relations with Congress after 1936 there was little that Roosevelt could look back on with much satisfaction. The bipartisan coalition of conservative Democrats and Republicans had held firm through both sessions of the Congress, inflicting defeat upon defeat. In two years Roosevelt faced the dual frustration of an economic setback which he had not anticipated and for which he was unprepared (trapped by his own boast that "We planned it this way") and the defiance of members of his own party, some of whom owed their political lives to his popularity, who were taking delight in knifing him, who relished his discomfiture, and who were determined to wrest from him the initiative for party leadership. It was an intolerable situation, particularly galling because Roosevelt did not believe that his congressional opponents accurately represented the sentiments of the country. The people were still with him, he thought; the Congress was not.

In June, Roosevelt embarked upon a plan of direct action, a dangerous plan, one strewn with dark pitfalls and unseen perils. He would break the existing stalemate and assure New Deal control of the party machinery in 1940 by eliminating the conservative opposition. He would "purge" the party.

The struggle over the court-packing plan may have planted the purge idea. Roosevelt simmered for weeks after that rebuff. He was not likely to forget that Garner had stood in the Senate lobby with one hand holding his nose, the other turned thumb down on the court plan. Or that Hatton Sumners of Texas, chairman of the important Judiciary Committee, had told his House colleagues, "Boys, here's where I cash in my chips." Democrats who persisted in supporting the court bill, Sumners warned, would not have "hide enough left to bother about." As early as August, 1937, *The New York Times* speculated that Senator Guffey's speeches on the defeat of the court bill and the wages and hours bill in which he called his defecting colleagues "ingrates" were "the opening shot" in a plan to rid the party of anti-New Dealers.[73]

The impressive victory of Lister Hill, an enthusiastic New Dealer, over

Tom Heflin in the hotly contested Alabama Senate primary encouraged Roosevelt in the belief that the conservatives did not reflect the sentiment of the people, encouraged him enough to intervene in the Florida primary on behalf of Claude Pepper. Pepper won handily amid rumors that Roosevelt had put him over by pressuring citrus growers with the threat of withholding federal funds to combat the Mediterranean fruit-fly if the growers did not support Pepper. The Pepper and Hill victories seemed sufficient evidence to prove that a purge was possible if the President wished to undertake it.[74]

While Roosevelt wavered, the decision was made for him. If the court fight suggested the desirability of a party purge, the announcement by Governor Philip La Follette that he was launching a new party, the National Progressives of America, created the sense of urgency. La Follette's words were fighting words. In his stirring address to the Progressives in Madison, Wisconsin, late in April, La Follette did not blame Roosevelt. It was not his fault that the country desperately needed a new party. If the ills of the country could have been cured by brilliant leadership, said La Follette, the job would have been accomplished long ago by Roosevelt. The trouble, as the Wisconsin governor saw it, was "the dissension within the Democratic Party itself which has sabotaged, undermined, and hamstrung the administration." The party was "split wide open" in a "bitter factional fight."

But the La Follette words that stung the President, alarmed him, jarred him into action was the charge that "Progressive leaders within the Democratic Party are only an outer fringe that act as window-dressing. The real power within the Democratic Party is increasingly wielded by a group of politicians who see no more and who feel no more than the Old Guard of the Republican Party."[75]

Roosevelt genuinely felt that the La Follette move was a threat, that he might possibly lose those liberal and left-of-center groups on which he had relied after the election of 1934. He had to act and act fast to remove any doubt that the Democratic Party was a party of liberalism. In June, in one of his Fireside Chats, Roosevelt told the country: "As the head of the Democratic Party . . . charged with the responsibility of the definitely liberal declaration of principles set forth in the 1936 Democratic platform, I feel that I have every right to speak . . . where there may be a clear issue between candidates for a Democratic nomination involving these principles. . . ." He denounced the "Copperheads" in the party. The contest for control of the party would now be taken directly to the people; the "purge" was under way.[76]

"Happy" Chandler in Kentucky, "Cotton Ed" Smith in South Carolina, Maryland's Millard Tydings, and some smaller fry felt the scourge. Before a home-state audience, the number one target, Senator Walter George of Georgia, was told to his face by the President that "deep down in his heart" George was opposed to the "broad objectives of the party and of the Government as they are constituted today. . . ."[77]

Republicans immediately leaped to the defense of their beleaguered colleagues, unable to bear the thought of a Democratic President attacking Democratic legislators. The purge was an "audacious affront" according to the prim reaction of Pennsylvania Congressman Ditter. There was much shocked and disbelieving talk about "the Roosevelt vendetta" carried on by "his political satraps," and, of course, much head-shaking and finger-waving about such dictatorial behavior. Clare Hoffman, who always took the direct approach where Roosevelt was concerned, said the purge was characteristic of dictatorships. But, he warned, those "smiling New Dealers who think they are riding high should recall what happened to some of the big boys in Russia," implying that Roosevelt was a Stalin who would turn on a friend as quickly as he would on an enemy. "The purge," said Senator Vandenberg, ". . . has utterly sinister implications." Congressman Bacon of New York, complaining of "the Roosevelt heresy" that would require every member of Congress to "check both his conscience and his intelligence at the door," likened it to the "cult of the leader in Germany, in Italy, and in Russia." The "march through Georgia," Congressman Ditter had said, disclosed Roosevelt's "whole design for dictatorship."[78]

Late in August, at the Republican "cornfield conference" in Indiana, billed as the largest between-convention meeting in the history of the party, John D. M. Hamilton, New York Congressman James W. Wadsworth, and a dozen more discoursed at length on "the Russian technique," on "brazen tactics," on the ethics of Roosevelt's crusade "to browbeat and terrorize men in public life. . . ."[79]

Herbert Hoover, who understood the purge more clearly than most, recognized Roosevelt's underlying intent to reorient the Democratic Party and establish it firmly as the party of liberalism. In an address to the Missouri Republican clubs in September, Hoover went further, asserting that Roosevelt meant to form a new political party. The party, he said, would wear the garb of "false liberalism," liberalism that was "hoary with reaction," liberalism that was dangerous. If the purge was any sample of the new liberalism, Hoover continued, then "George III, Hitler, Stalin and Boss Tweed were all liberals."[80]

The press, particularly southern papers (since most of those on the purge list were southerners), were greatly incensed at the whole idea. They, too, leaned heavily on the idea that purging the party and dictatorship were one and the same. The usually generous Atlanta *Constitution* said the purge would turn the Senate into a gathering of "ninety-six Charlie McCarthys with himself [Roosevelt] as Edgar Bergen." The Nashville *Banner* editorialized about the "power-drunk Chief Executive," and the Macon (Georgia) *Telegraph* emphasized the "duplicity . . . sheer malice" of the purge. Virginia papers like the Norfolk *Dispatch*, the Charlotte *Observer*, and the Lynchburg *Advance* told their readers that the purge meant "personal ambition for unquestioned power . . . a New Napoleon . . . a national dictator." "What right has Mr. Roosevelt to dictate to the people . . . how they shall vote?" asked the New Orleans *States*. "If the citizens of Georgia do what President Roosevelt told us," wrote the Augusta *Chronicle*, "we must . . . reconcile ourselves to complete dictation. . . ." Even the prestigious *New York Times*, pondering what the Baltimore *Sun* called "an act of executive arrogance," remonstrated with mild sarcasm on "how great an intellectual servitude the President now requires from his followers." The Roosevelt critics were delighted with David Lawrence's four-line summary of the purge in his *U. S. News:* "Every now and then Hitler orders a purge in Germany. So does Mussolini in Italy. So does Stalin in Russia. Comes now the first Roosevelt purge."[81]

The objects of the purge responded to the threat on moral grounds; their tormentor was a tyrant, they the martyrs as innocent as Christians being fed to lions. They talked of dictatorship, states' rights, independence, and carpetbaggers, appealing to local pride and the ability of the people to make up their own minds. Senator George murmured simply that he accepted the President's challenge. The only easterner on the list, John J. O'Connor of New York, chairman of the powerful House Rules Committee (who thought the Reorganization Bill should be allowed to "slumber in some cob-webbed pigeonhole") campaigned on the purge issue ("an escalator to dictatorship," he called it) warning that if it were a success, it would lead to a communistic form of government in the United States. "Which shall it be," he would ask in his speeches, "democracy or monocracy?"[82]

The purge was a dismal failure; only O'Connor failed to survive it. Roosevelt had taken a drubbing, and he knew it. His efforts to shake the party out of its parochialism, to nationalize it, to make it more sensitive to what he regarded national needs had not only failed but at least for the time being had perhaps even intensified its localism and decentralization. His hope of defining the liberal posture of the Democratic Party somehow kept eluding him when it was applied to local situations. Moreover, his intrusion into the state elections had once more placed him unwittingly on the wrong side of the issue. In the court fight it was his enemies who called it "court-packing"; in the elections of 1938 it was his critics who called it a "purge," a term which conjured visions of concentration camps, castor oil, firing squads, and forced labor in Siberia. The notion of a party discipline and party responsibility had become as sinister as a Nuremburg rally.

The purge did more than fail. In the elections, the Republicans netted eighty-one seats in the House and eight in the Senate, which all but guaranteed that the conservative Democratic-Republican alliance in the new Congress would be stronger than ever. With the elections of 1938, the Republicans boldly emerged from the political storm cellar; the Grand Old Party was a national party once more. Despite the continuing numerical superiority of Democrats in Congress, Roosevelt appeared to be through, his New Deal neglected and abandoned. If the 1938 outcome proved anything, wrote the veteran newspaperman Raymond Clapper, it proved "clearly, I think, that President Roosevelt could not run for a third term even if he so desired."[83]

Clapper was wrong, of course. The drama unfolding in Europe, Hitler and all of that, would provide a new base for the Roosevelt leadership. He was not through; but his domestic reform program was. Except for some minor unfinished business it was time to audit the New Deal books.

PART V
All Said and Done

M E N respond in varied ways to the cruel test of adversity. Some, being stronger than others, more resilient, can absorb the shock, can rebound quickly. Some never recover. But in every case there will be a measure of self-justification, of rationalization. In the face of adversity men often retreat from reality, find novel ways to go on thinking the best about themselves; there is, perhaps, a little of the *Red Badge of Courage* in every breast.

Maybe in the 1930's, in those depression years, years of unprecedented disaster, the American people could be exonerated for the manner in which some of them rolled their eyes and fled the field of honor. The wonder is the heroic staying power of the many. But defectors made recovery all the harder; they could not have done more harm had they gone over to the enemy. Part of it was their inability (and sometimes their unwillingness) to understand what their government was trying to do. They were aware, some of them well aware, of their heritage. They knew the courage, the resolution with which the Founding Fathers launched something new under the sun; the joy, the romance, the back-breaking toil that tamed a wild land "before we were her people"; the irresistible optimism that marked every turning, in war, in business, in science, medicine, and all the rest; the broad tolerance, so often honored in the breach, that fashioned a nation from "the wretched refuse of your teeming shore." They knew all this. Yet they shrank from the challenge of the Depression.

Criticism of Roosevelt and the New Deal was, for some, self-justification, a rationalization of their predicament; criticism gave them wings for soaring flights from reality. Not all. Of course, not all. Some men confronted the Depression with level gaze and declared Roosevelt was wrong, dead wrong. But whichever way it was—honest difference of opinion, bankrupt escapism, or something in between—criticism made Roosevelt's job harder. It was infinitely harder to inspire the country with that judicious blend of idealism and disarming candor at which Roosevelt was so gifted. It was harder to strike a proper balance between the private property rights of the few and social justice for the many. It was harder to ameliorate the conscienceless indifference of economics with humanitarianism, to temper the brutality of the marketplace with kindness. It was harder to explain the difference between what could be and what ought to be, the difference between politics and technique. It was harder to restore hope.

The New Deal, with its emphasis on experimentation and imaginative change, was a direct challenge to those people with whom nothing was so painful as ideas and change. Criticism of Roosevelt and the New Deal meant resistance to change, a withering of the spirit of high adventure, an alteration of plans; it meant pursuing lesser goals with petty means.

This is not to say that Roosevelt failed to effect significant changes or that he did not add new ideas to the body of American political philosophy. He did. Making security of the individual by governmental action a part of democratic philosophy may have been his most meaningful contribution.

But the New Deal never did live up to its promise; it never really came to grips with the deeper problems afflicting the country. The critics would say that was a blessing and would claim the credit for having made it so. Roosevelt was to be little more than the boy with his finger in the democratic dike. He could deal with the superficial aspects of the Depression. He could spend money, feed people, make work, build post offices, treat symptoms. But the organic disorders that had put the country flat on its back were still without medication.

Massive opposition kept the New Deal from ever becoming much more than a spirited evasion of the overriding issues of the twentieth century. That same opposition eventually forced Roosevelt into the role of the Fabius Maximus of the Depression. The final verdict would seem to be that Roosevelt and the New Deal did no more than reprieve democracy in the United States. It would be up to other men to prove that it had been worth saving.

CHAPTER XI

A Second Honeymoon and After

The American has never yet had to face the trials of Job. . . . Hitherto America has been the land of universal good will, confidence in life, inexperience of poisons. Until yesterday, it believed itself immune from the hereditary plagues of mankind. It could not credit the danger of being suffocated or infected by any sinister principle. . . . —George Santayana

People will endure their tyrants for years, but they tear their deliverers to pieces if a millennium is not created immediately. —Woodrow Wilson

They are unanimous in their hate for me—and I welcome their hatred.
—Franklin D. Roosevelt

A COUPLE of days after his old friend Al Smith had bitterly attacked the New Deal, Roosevelt had asked an aide to dig up a vaguely remembered quotation from Lincoln:

I do the very best I know how—the very best I can; and I mean to keep on doing so until the end. If the end brings me out all right, what is said against me won't amount to anything. If the end brings me out wrong, 10,000 angels swearing I was right would make no difference.[1]

But there was little comfort in the quotation; the "very best he knew how" was not good enough, not nearly good enough for Roosevelt's critics. Even without criticism Roosevelt's problems and struggles were monumental; many of his efforts were frustrated; frustration made him irritable; and irritability made him react to the pinpricks of opponents.

Roosevelt was not "as a sheep before her shearers is dumb"; when his "very best" was not good enough, Roosevelt could parry with the best of them. He could and usually did ignore the irrational vilification of cranks and crackpots, the paranoid protests of native Fascists and others. But he was uncommonly sensitive to criticism from the press, from businessmen, from people of his own "class," from alleged friends, particularly members of his official family, and erstwhile New Dealers. He could be vindictive and petty—and often was. He could shred a man or an idea with ridicule and sarcasm, with stark and angry name-calling, with bitter and illogical criticism of his own. When moved by great resentment and exasperation, he could take direct action—as he did in the legislative "purge" of 1938.

The surprising thing is that Roosevelt reacted to attack so seldom. Never before had criticism of a President, his personality, his family, his administration, been so fully, so freely, and—too often—so viciously expressed. Roosevelt felt that the unremitting opposition to his best efforts were unfair, that much of the unreasoning hostility was a betrayal of democracy, that the whole democratic system was jeopardized by its apparent inability to develop a code of political etiquette, at least some concept of common decency and fairness.

II

Roosevelt maintained friendly, often affectionate, relations with the working press; but he could tongue-lash those who wrote uncomplimentary things about him. At press conferences he would occasionally tell them to put on dunce caps and stand in the corner or he would "award" them Iron Crosses.

His trust in reporters, however, was not reflected in his attitude toward what he referred to as "fat-cat" or "Tory" newspapers, toward publishers, or toward syndicated and byline editorial columnists. "As you know," Roosevelt once wrote Claude Bowers, Ambassador to Spain, "all the fat-cat newspapers—85 percent of the whole—have been utterly opposed to everything the Administration is seeking. . . ." Once, when his photograph appeared in a newspaper over a caption describing a beauty queen, Roosevelt clipped it out and sent it to Steve Early with the pencilled notation: "Accuracy of the American press." Of the editorial staff of *The New York Times*, he commented, "About fifteen years ago I attended one of the famous luncheons in the French mahogany-carved sanctum of *The New York Times*. In that rarefied atmosphere of self-anointed scholars, I had the feeling of an uneducated worm under the microscope."

Roosevelt attributed press hostility not to newspapermen, but to the prejudices of publishers. "It is not the man at the desk, in most cases," he said. "It is not the reporter. It goes back to the owner of the paper. . . . You know perfectly well that special bureau chiefs down here write what the owner of the newspaper tells them to write, and they leave out half the truth." As newspaper owners grew richer, he contended, they gradually lost their contact with average people and "soon the check book and the securities market supplant the old patriotism and the old desire to purvey straight news." In a letter to the St. Louis *Post-Dispatch*, Roosevelt wrote, "Newspapers cannot be edited in the interests of the general public from the counting room."[2]

Roosevelt often sang the praises of a free press, defended its right to be critical of governmental policies, even invited its criticism ("Feel free to criticize," he had once urged early in his first term). But press criticism, which he found far more palatable in theory than in practice, could sting him into intemperate, violent (though usually private) outbursts. Periodically he called attention to the sins of the press: it played fast and loose with its public trust; it told only part of the story; it distorted and exaggerated anything detrimental to the Administration and played down anything favorable; it manufactured anti-Roosevelt stories out of the whole cloth; it was controlled by men of predatory wealth.

Raymond Moley noted "a growing petulance about all criticism" in the President in 1935. "During those months, when I came into his bedroom," Moley reported in *After Seven Years*, "he would comment angrily about the papers he had read over his breakfast. This paper had said 'something untrue'; that paper was being 'consistently unfair' " and at a press conference in 1938, Roosevelt, flourishing some eight or ten different papers, declared: "There isn't one story or one headline in all of those newspapers that does not give, to put it politely, an erroneous impression—not one. . . . The American people are beginning to realize that the things they have read . . . have been pure bunk, b-u-n-k, bunk. . . ."

Often Roosevelt aimed his barbs at individual newspapers and publishers. On one occasion the President, according to a Scripps-Howard editorial, "got mad to the name-calling state—and talked rather tall and tactless about lies and boobs," and as usual directed his remarks to newspaper owners. An editorial in the New York *Herald Tribune* piqued Roosevelt into accusing the newspaper of lying and misrepresentation. When the *Herald Tribune* approved the Post Office's issuance of a baseball stamp, Roosevelt wrote Jim Farley: "Good for you! To draw a word of commendation from the *Herald Tribune* is like being allowed to sit on an iceberg for a whole day when you are in Hell." Of *Time* magazine Roosevelt declared, "Beginning with the first number . . . , I discovered that one secret of their financial success is a deliberate policy of either exaggeration or distortion. Pay no attention to them—I don't."

But perhaps because Hearst was a former friend, Roosevelt paid plenty of attention to his newspapers. Shortly after Hearst editors across the nation were instructed to charge Roosevelt with receiving support from Communists, Stephen Early issued a statement on behalf of the President charging that "a certain notorious newspaper owner" was attempting to raise "fake issues which no patriotic, honorable, decent citizen would purposely inject into American affairs." In August, 1935, word leaked to Roosevelt that Hearst had instructed his editors to refer to the Administration's tax program by the phrase "Soak the Successful" (Hearst's former phrase "Soak the Rich" had backfired) and to use the words "Raw Deal" instead of New Deal. Indignant, Roosevelt had a press release prepared— "The President believes that it is only fair to the American people to apprise them of certain information which has come to him. . . ." Cooler heads prevailed; the statement was not issued. "I sometimes think," said Roosevelt in retrospect, "Hearst has done more harm to the cause of Democracy and civilization in America than any three other contemporaries put together."[3]

After the 1936 elections the rift between Roosevelt and the press widened. In 1937, columnist Franklin K. Waltman wrote that virtually all presidential press conferences saw some sally at the expense of the press, that Roosevelt had written to editors complaining about individual Washington correspondents, that he had charged some writers of national reputation with only 40 per cent accuracy. "This man Kent [Frank R. Kent, syndicated columnist with the Baltimore *Sun*]," he charged, "not only has no regard for the truth, but uses the kind of poison pen and poison tongue which has alienated practically all of his friends." In a letter to Adolph Ochs, publisher of *The New York Times*, Roosevelt wrote, "This is not the first occasion on which Mr. Krock [Arthur Krock, editorial writer for the *Times*] has rendered a real disservice. . . . I am making this the first—literally the first—exception to my general rule of not writing to any Editor of any paper in regard to stories which their people send out of Washington."

Four years later Roosevelt's opinion of Krock had not changed. "Wasn't Krock terrible? However, I got passed [sic] the stage of writing him, correcting his articles about five years ago. It got to the point where I would have had to write him one a week!"

Henry Morgenthau would have been the first to agree. When *The New York Times* published a column by Krock stating that "influential people in business and finance" feared the radical trend in the Treasury, the irate Secretary told Krock: "I consider this one of the dirtiest pieces of writing . . . since I've been in Washington." Harold Ickes reserved the award for the worst newspaper to the Chicago *Tribune*, and, apparently, Roosevelt concurred. "He [Roosevelt] agreed with me," Ickes reported, "that it [the Chicago *Tribune*] was the rottenest newspaper in the whole United States."

In April, 1939, Ickes, on network radio, renewed his criticism of the press with a dissertation on "columnitis, that curious, endemic malady which, in these modern days, has infected one newspaper after the other." Finding prose inadequate to express fully his opinion of columnists, Ickes recited a ten-stanza verse that began:

> Wouldst know what's right and what is wrong?
> Why birdies sing at break of dawn?
> Ask the columnists.
> Does milk come from the Milky Way?
> Why do dogs bark and asses bray?
> Ask the columnists.

Through the medium of verse he taunted several of the individual columnists:

> Who run the earth and sun and moon?
> Just Thompson, Lawrence, Franklin, Broun,
> Just the columnists.
> When FDR you want to sock,
> Page Lippmann, Johnson, Kent, or Krock,
> Page a columnist.

His strongest denunciations were aimed at the "calumnists," who "waste good white space to spread injurious gossip and disseminate prevarications and even unpunished libels." The "calumnist's" stock in trade, he asserted, is "falsification and vilification." Walter Lippmann, for example, reminded Ickes of a biblical quotation. What better description could there be of Lippmann, he asked, than that contained in Revelations 3:15–16: "I know thy works, that thou are neither cold nor hot; I would that thou wert cold or hot. So then because thou are lukewarm and neither cold nor hot, I will spew thee out of my mouth." Frank Kent, Ickes charged, "delights in cruel jibes and acidulous comment that he will direct at a straw man if one of flesh and blood is wanting." " 'Croak' Carter [Boake Carter, radio commentator] with complete self-assurance could enter any intellectual goldfish swallowing contest," Ickes told his audience. He described Dorothy Thompson as the "Cassandra of the Columnists," "a sincere lady who is trying to cover too much ground . . . as a final authority on all social, economic, governmental, national and international questions."[4]

III

There were other occasions when Roosevelt needed the assistance of friends, occasions when he felt it impolitic to intervene directly. In early 1935, for example, with the New Deal slumbering and the whole recovery program apparently stalled on high center, Roosevelt seemed more of a sidelines observer than a dynamic leader.

There was plenty to observe. He watched closely the frenzied activities of the priest-politician-physician triumvirate of Coughlin, Long, and Townsend. "In normal times," Roosevelt wrote Henry Stimson, "the radio and other appeals by them would not be effective. However these are not normal times; people run after strange gods." But Roosevelt could watch with some detachment for he knew intuitively that at the crucial moment they would be unable to unite. "There is no question," he wrote Colonel House, "that it is all a dangerous situation but when it comes to a showdown these fellows cannot all lie in the same bed and will fight among themselves with almost absolute certainty."

Not only would they be unable to get together but their timing was wrong. It was far better, he wrote House, to have a "free side-show" in 1935 than in the following year during the main performance. "There is another thought," he confided to Ray Stannard Baker, Wilson's biographer, people "tire of seeing the same name day after day" and of hearing "the same voice night after night over the radio." If I had tried, he continued, to keep up the pace of 1933 and 1935, "the inevitable histrionics of the new actors, Long and Coughlin . . . would have turned the eyes of the audience away from the main drama itself." The time would come, he told Baker, to counterattack.

Meanwhile, Roosevelt maintained a public silence while instigating a flanking action behind the scenes. As early as 1932 Roosevelt recognized Long's mischief-making potential. He had told Rexford Tugwell that Long was one of the two most dangerous men in the United States (the other, he said, was General Douglas MacArthur). By January, 1933, he was suggesting to Tugwell that some effort should be made to tame Long. In February, 1935, he told a meeting of the National Emergency Council, "Don't put anybody in, and don't keep anybody that is working for Huey Long or his crowd. That is a hundred percent!" All Long supporters with federal, non-civil service appointments were fired, patronage in Louisiana was given to Long's enemies, and federal agents checked into the financial affairs of Long and his supporters. When Theodore Bilbo, the Mississippi politician given the job of keeping an eye on Long, reported that "that madman Huey Long" had been given his first treatment, Roosevelt replied, "I am watching your smoke." While Roosevelt maintained his public silence and quietly stepped up behind-the-scenes attempts to outmaneuver Long, others grew restive.

On March 4, 1935, Hugh Johnson, former National Recovery Administration chief, launched over nation-wide radio a headlong, hammer-and-tongs attack against New Deal critics. Johnson began by warmly recounting Roosevelt's accomplishments, but confessed that the New Deal was bogged down. "The push is gone. The drive is stopped," he declared. He blamed the slow-down on the "breakup of spontaneous popular cooperation," a breakup "engineered by the combination of . . . dangerous demagogy with the direct assault of the old social Neanderthalers." In Johnson's opinion there were two groups of "business and political guerrillas." There was the "Old Guard" who believe that "property and profits come first and that if you take care of them the humanities will take care of themselves." There was the "emotional fringe" moved by "emotions rather than beliefs"; they are "like a harp-of-the-winds upon which any breeze can play a tune." At the head of the "emotional fringe," he declared, were the "Pied Pipers," Long and Coughlin.

Using, according to the New York *World Telegram*, "every weapon in his bulging verbal armory from scimitar to meat-ax," Johnson hacked and slashed at his principal targets. "You can laugh at Father Coughlin—you can snort at Huey Long—but this country was never under a greater menace." He contended that an "open alliance" had been formed "between the great Louisiana demagogue and this political padre." Between this "couple of Catalines," he said, there was "the whole bag of crazy or crafty tricks possessed by any Mad Mullah or dancing dervish who incite a tribe or a people through illusion to its doom." He called Senator Long "a plausible Punchinello," "an able little devil" with "cast-iron cheek" and a "cane-brake drawl." Coughlin, he said, should "sever his revolutionary political activities from his priestly office."

The next day Long replied from the floor of the Senate in what Ernest K. Lindley, Washington correspondent of the New York *Herald Tribune*, called "a session such as the Senate has seldom seen in recent years." The Senate chamber sizzled "with insults, epithets and prophecies of disaster." Joseph T. Robinson, Democratic leader in the Senate, using what the Boston *Transcript* called "the only language the Kingfish understands," described Long's speech as "a demonstration of egotism, of arrogance, of ignorance." For months, he continued, Senator Long "has disgusted this Senate with repeated attacks upon men who are superior to him, with repeated efforts to discredit the President and humiliate him. And now it is about time that the manhood in the Senate assert itself."

At a press conference in early April, Harold Ickes leaped into the melee. If Long continued to use his "Longislature" to put federal spending in Louisiana under his control, Ickes told reporters, "The Emperor of Louisiana" is creating a situation down there where all allotments might have to be cancelled." "The trouble with Senator Long," said Ickes (a few days later), "is that he is suffering from halitosis of the intellect. That's presuming Emperor Long has an intellect."

There is no evidence Roosevelt approved in advance the attacks by either Johnson or Ickes; but he cheered them on from the sidelines. He told Ickes at a cabinet meeting that his comment about Long's intellect was the best thing that had yet been said about Long. Although he had "no objection" to what was being said about Long and Townsend, he told Jim Farley he regarded intemperate references to Father Coughlin as "very unwise." Roosevelt knew the power of the Catholic vote and feared a head-on collision with the "radio priest." He much preferred to work against Coughlin quietly through such prominent Catholics as Frank Murphy, ex-mayor of Detroit, and Joseph P. Kennedy, chairman of the Securities and Exchange Commission.

By May, Roosevelt was ready to take action. He told Bainbridge Colby, editor of Hearst's New York *American* and a New Deal critic of some reputation, that he was "fighting Communism, Huey Longism, Coughlinism, Townsendism." He referred, of course, to Long's plan for equalizing the distribution of wealth. "To combat this and other crackpot ideas,"

Roosevelt told Colby, "it may be necessary to throw to the wolves the forty-six men who are reported to have incomes in excess of one million dollars a year." Apparently Roosevelt meant the same thing when he later told Raymond Moley they would have to "steal Long's thunder."

At any rate, in response to the criticism and the popularity of Long and Townsend and to mounting pressure from progressives, Roosevelt proposed sweeping tax revisions that included inheritance and gift taxes, a graduated tax on corporate income, and higher personal income tax rates in the top brackets. These proposals signaled a major change, the beginning of a second New Deal—a New Deal of reform and an apparent swing to the left. With the change came bitter opposition. The ensuing public utilities holding company fight, the banking fight, and the tax fight intensified hostility from the business community.[5]

IV

By the beginning of the second New Deal, opposition from the business community was old hat to the President; his honeymoon with business had ended over a year before.

In August, 1934, when Jouett Shouse announced formation of the American Liberty League, "Big Business" criticism of the Administration began in earnest. Soon after Roosevelt had written a friend: "All the big guns have started shooting—Al Smith, John W. Davis, James W. Wadsworth, du Pont, Shouse, etc. Their organization has already been labeled the 'I CAN'T TAKE IT CLUB.'"

Though the Liberty League claimed nonpartisanship, no one doubted that it was founded for the purpose of harassing Roosevelt, embarrassing the New Deal, and trying to rid the country of both. At his first press conference after announcement of the League, the President resorted to mild ridicule, praising it, as one reporter wisecracked, "with faint damns." The League is fine, Roosevelt said, "as far as it goes." But it is like an organization established "to uphold two of the Ten Commandments," ignoring the Commandment that "Thou shalt love thy neighbor as thyself." They [the Liberty Leaguers] fail to mention anything, the President continued, about the responsibility of the government for "people who want to keep themselves from starvation, keep a roof over their heads, lead decent lives, have proper educational standards. . . ." The founders of the League, he said, failed to mention the protection of the individual against those who "seek to enrich or advance themselves at the expense of their fellow citizens."

Loyal New Dealers, following the lead of the President, also scoffed. The league of "right-thinking people," charged Harry Hopkins, was "so far to the Right" that no one would be able to find it. Harold Ickes, referring to the League's Lawyers' Committee, said sarcastically, "one thing about it, Mr. Shouse beats the Chief Justice of the Supreme Court in salary; but then, he is a greater constitutional authority." Shouse could probably, Ickes went on, "take on the work of the executive and legislative branches of government as well" if they would only double his salary. By the fall of 1934 Roosevelt's estrangement from the Liberty League seemed complete and irreparable; "Big Business," he told Ickes, was deliberately trying to sabotage the Administration.

Jim Farley saw in Liberty League obstructionism an excellent opportunity to make political capital for the Democratic Party and Roosevelt's coming campaign for a second term. The Liberty League, Farley wrote later, "seemed to be one of the most vulnerable ever to appear in politics and our campaign was developed on that theory." Thus, he continued, "the Democratic National Committee's first 'battle-order' was to ignore the Republican Party and to concentrate fire on the Liberty League."

The League's vulnerability was—to use labels pinned on it by Charles Michelson, Publicity Director of the Democratic National Committee, and his assistant, Edward Roddan—its "gold-coast complexion," its public image as a "millionaire's union." The strategy was simple (and, as it turned out, spectacularly successful): make the Liberty League synonymous with social and economic privilege, associate it closely with the Republican Party, then attack the Republicans by attacking the League. Once synonymity between the Liberty League and predatory wealth was established, the League could be attacked both directly by name and indirectly by blasting "economic royalists."

In late 1935 the word was out that Al Smith, as principal speaker at a Liberty League dinner to be held on January 25, 1936, would pull out all stops in attacking the New Deal. Roosevelt was prepared. On January 3, in his State of the Union message, he beat Smith to the punch. The President's message was a fighting speech, a slam-bang attack on "unscrupulous money changers," who offered to lead the United States "back round the same old corner into the same old dreary street." "Give them their way," he warned, and they will "steal the livery of great national constitutional ideals to serve discredited special interests . . . they will take the course of every autocracy of the past—power for themselves, enslavement for the public." The New Deal had, he contended, shifted the focus of government away from private interests to public concern, and in accomplishing this had "invited battle," had "earned the hatred of entrenched greed." This "resplendent economic autocracy," Roosevelt charged, had fought back by inciting fear, "a synthetic, manufactured, poisonous fear that is being spread subtly, expensively and cleverly by the same people who cried in those other days—'Save us, save us, else we perish.' "

A few days later at the annual Jackson Day dinner, Roosevelt cast himself in the role of a twentieth-century Andrew Jackson:

An overwhelming proportion of the material power of the Nation was arrayed against him. The great media for the dissemination of information and the molding of public opinion fought him. Haughty and sterile intellectualism opposed him. Musty reaction disapproved him. Hollow and outworn traditionalism shook a trembling finger at him. It seemed sometimes that all were against him—all but the people of the United States. . . . History so often repeats itself.[6]

V

Roosevelt's harsh words and Al Smith's Liberty League speech set the tone of the election year. It was to be a gloves-off, no-holds-barred campaign with the President winning by a knockout. One of his best punches was ridicule of his tormentors, and he used it with devastating impact. "There will be—there are," he warned, "many false issues." His critics, he charged, would drag out "red herrings—as they have always done—to divert attention from their own weaknesses." A frightened and malicious opponent, he continued, always resorts to dirty fighting. Other critics in other days had charged that George Washington planned to be king, that Thomas Jefferson "planned to set up a guillotine," that Andrew Jackson planned to surrender American democracy to the dictatorship of a frontier mob," that Abraham Lincoln fancied himself a "Roman Emperor," Theodore Roosevelt was a "Destroyer," Woodrow Wilson a "self-constituted Messiah." And now, the same kind of people, "desperate in mood, angry at failure, cunning in purpose," charged him with communism.

Such tactics reminded him of the story of a rich old gentleman who "fell off the end of a pier" in 1933. The old man, the story went, was "unable to swim," and a friend had to pull him out. The old man was "effusive in his thanks." But now, three years later, the rich man was "berating his friend because the silk hat was lost."

While Roosevelt attacked the American Liberty League indirectly by striking at "economic royalists," his friends concentrated their fire directly on the League itself. Two days before Smith's speech, for instance, Lewis Schwellenbach, senator from Washington, charged that Smith had been duped by "all the . . . leeches, rascals, crooks, and bloodsucking lawyers who control the American Liberty League." Pat Harrison, senator from Mississippi, labeled the league "the American 'Lobby' League," an organization of "griping and disgruntled politicians," "apostles of greed" masquerading as patriots.

One of the first of the New Deal fusiliers was Smith's vice-presidential running mate in 1928, Arkansas' Senator Joe Robinson. Roosevelt, accepting Michelson's position that a formal reply from the Administration "would be dignifying Smith unduly," chose Robinson to do the honors.

"The voice is Jacob's voice, but the hands are the hands of Esau," began Robinson's reply. The complaints that Smith had thrown at the Administration, Robinson charged, embodied the same principles of social justice that Smith himself, in the voice of Jacob, had called for in the past. But the campaign for the common man then, as now, Robinson continued, had been opposed by "stock-ticker patriots"; the voice of Jacob had been drowned out "by greed and privilege hiding behind a murky and malodorous smoke screen." Robinson expressed amazement that "the policies of the American Liberty League had become the platform of the Unhappy Warrior," that Smith, with the hands of Esau now firmly attached, was "enthroned in the camp of the enemy warring like one of the Janizaries of old against his own people, and against the men and women with whom he fought shoulder to shoulder in the past."

From Smith's speech the Republicans picked up many of their campaign slogans and charges—"government by bureaucracy," "class against class," "socialism," "communism" became familiar words in the Republican campaign lexicon. Farley was delighted. In the identification of the Republican Party with the Liberty League and the League with wealth and privilege, he found the "gaping hole in the battlelines of the opposition." "Our opponents," Farley predicted, "will make this the bitterest and certainly the dirtiest political struggle that any of us here can remember."

Farley was ready. The battlelines were drawn. The guns were loaded and aimed at the Republicans' weakest point, the Liberty League. "The Republican National Committee," he told a Democratic rally in St. Louis, "has a little cry baby brother called the American Liberty League. The brothers are always together. They pal around together, they think the same thoughts, they echo the same phrases, and they seek ·the same end. . . ." "The American Liberty League," he said at a banquet for the Kansas Democratic clubs, "ought to be called the American Cellophane League" because "first, it's a du Pont product and second, you can see right through it." Farley continued throughout the campaign to concentrate on the League. The American Liberty League, this ally of the Republican National Committee," this "center and soul of the predatory powers," he charged, "speaks as conclusively for the reactionaries and their party as does Mr. Hoover, the United States Chamber of Commerce and the National Manufacturers' Association."

Roosevelt had much help in his fight with right-wing opposition, but he was to get in the last telling blows. Campaigning in Chicago in mid-October 1936, Roosevelt attacked with withering sarcasm:

Some of these people forget how sick they were. But I know how sick they were. I have their fever charts. I know how the knees of all of our rugged individualists were trembling four years ago and how their hearts fluttered. They came to Washington in great numbers. Washington did not look like a dangerous bureaucracy to them then. Oh no! It looked like an emergency hospital. All of the distinguished patients wanted two things—a quick hypodermic to end the pain and a course of treatment to cure the disease. They wanted them in a hurry; we gave them both. And now most of the patients seem to be doing very nicely. Some of them are even well enough to throw their crutches at the doctor.

For his last speech of the campaign, Roosevelt switched from sarcasm to sharp anger. On October 31, 1936, only two days before he was returned to office by an overwhelming landslide, Roosevelt angrily denounced his critics in a speech at Madison Square Garden in New York. After listing some of the nation's ills and blaming them on reckless bankers, speculators, monopolists, and profiteers, he threw out a challenge:

Never before in all our history have these forces been so united against one candidate as they stand today. They are unanimous in their hate for me —and I welcome their hatred.

I should like to have it said of my first Administration that in it the forces of selfishness and lust for power met their match. I should like to have it said of my second Administration that in it these forces met their master.[7]

VI

Roosevelt could be cut to the quick by harsh words from the right, especially from businessmen, people he considered to be in his own class. "I wish you could have heard the dinner conversations in some of the best houses in Newport," he wrote to a friend. He often mentioned critical remarks his friends were reported to have made. In a letter to a former Harvard classmate he confessed, "because of what I felt to be a very old and real friendship these remarks hurt." But for the most part he could deal with such friends, in words sometimes stinging in ridicule, sometimes slashing in anger.

It was one thing to deal with malcontents off somewhere in New York or Boston or Chicago, with crackpots in Louisiana or Detroit, with columnists and publishers, but it was quite another matter when opposition developed at home. It was something else when his friends in the Senate or his advisers in the White House, when those who had fought the same battles, who had stood with him shoulder to shoulder, turned against him. Then his anger could rise to white heat.

Hugh Johnson, after leaving the Administration, joined the Roosevelt critics and turned into a fiery anti-New Deal columnist. Following the death of Joe Robinson rumors began to circulate around Washington that Roosevelt had planned to renege on his promise to appoint the senator to the Supreme Court. Roosevelt was furious, particularly when Johnson repeated in his column the charge of intended treachery. Roosevelt had the former National Recovery Administrator summoned to the White

House. With Johnson seated just across the desk from him Roosevelt went over the column, answering each point and occasionally throwing in sarcastic remarks. Harold Ickes later reported that the President came to him the next day and repeated the conversation:

Hugh, do you know what fine, loyal old Joe Robinson would have said to you if you had written that while he was alive?
No.
He would have said, Hugh, that you are a liar, a coward, and cad.

On November 11, 1935, George N. Peek, administrator of the Agricultural Adjustment Act and foreign trade adviser, addressed the War Industries Board Association in New York. In a speech entitled "America's Choice," he attacked the Administration's trade policies. Without specifically acknowledging authorship, Peek sent Roosevelt a memorandum covering the points made in the speech. In his reply Roosevelt wrote that he thought the memorandum "rather silly." "It sounds," he said, "like a Hearst newspaper." Roosevelt attacked each point—one was "advocated by no one of intelligence I know"; another was "impossible"; another was called "a trick, an unfair thing to say"; another was branded "a deliberate lie." The President concluded the letter vigorously: "In other words this kind of statement amounts to nothing more than the setting up deliberately of straw men, who do not exist in reality, and then making a great show of knocking them over with a firing of salutes and a fanfare of trumpets." Four days later Peek resigned.

Other advisers also broke with the Administration: O. M. W. Sprague, Treasury adviser; Lewis Douglas, budget director; Dean Acheson, Under Secretary of the Treasury; James P. Warburg, economic adviser. Roosevelt was particularly annoyed by the resignation of Sprague in 1933. Sprague had evidently attempted to organize meetings to protest against New Deal financial policies. Roosevelt wrote him a scorching letter, one that would take the hide off, telling him that had he not resigned he would have been dismissed and stating that Sprague's actions had closely approached disloyalty to the government. The letter, however, was never sent.

When Warburg resigned from the Administration because of differences over New Deal monetary policy, Roosevelt wrote him that he had read his book with interest. The President urged Warburg to buy a secondhand car, put on his oldest clothes, and tour the country. "When you have returned," Roosevelt advised, "rewrite The Money Muddle and I will guarantee that it will run into many more editions."[8]

VII

Roosevelt's reaction to critics occasionally took more direct and formal form than simple tongue-lashing. He could simmer and stew and strike out at "fat cat" publishers and business and financial moguls who "ganged up" on the Administration, who financed anti-New Deal organizations, who found legal loopholes to avoid taxes; he could verbally lash out at editors and columnists who wrote bogey tales to scare the people; at the "yes, but" fellows who agreed in general with the need for reform but disagreed with his way of doing it; at the demagogues who offered panaceas of quack medicine. By 1938 Roosevelt added another group to his list, obstructionists in his own party, men who had ridden to Washington on his coattails, who had campaigned as friends of the great vote-getter, but who, once safely seated in the houses of Congress, turned their back on the New Deal, on their campaign promises, and, in Roosevelt's opinion, on the people. Roosevelt could do little but talk about the former groups. But here, finally, were anti-New Dealers within reach of presidential retaliation.

After the defeat of his judicial reorganization plan in 1937, Roosevelt was forced back on the defensive with his Executive reorganization bill of 1938. He negotiated many compromises and bowed to the pressure to exempt many agencies. Even this was insufficient. The opponents whipped up a popular fear of presidential power. Many of the old charges of dictatorship and bureaucratic autocracy were dusted off and paraded before the public. Roosevelt moved quickly to calm popular fears. To a press conference called suddenly in Warm Springs, the President issued this statement:

A: I have no inclination to be a dictator.
B: I have none of the qualifications which would make me a successful dictator.
C: I have too much historical background and too much knowledge of existing dictatorships to make me desire any form of dictatorship for a democracy like the United States of America.

He denounced "a carefully manufactured partisan and political opposition" and "silly nightmares conjured up at the instigation either of those who would restore the government to those who owned it between 1921 and 1933, or to those who . . . seek deliberately to wreck the present administration."

Despite everything, the reorganization plan was gutted by Congress. All congressional action was slow in 1938; the New Deal congressional program bogged down. It was time, Roosevelt decided, for a party showdown, time to rid the Democratic Party of obstructionists, time to "purge" reactionary opposition. Only great resentment and exasperation could have moved Roosevelt to such action. Once he decided to act he moved on a grand scale. In Kentucky he campaigned against "Happy" Chandler, in Georgia against Walter George, in Maryland against Millard Tydings, in South Carolina against "Cotton Ed" Smith, and in New York against

John J. O'Connor. When it was all over he had lost. For the first time since 1932 he had turned to the people and the people had turned him down.[9]

VIII

It was not often that Roosevelt had appealed to the people to vindicate him before his enemies only to have the people turn away. He had done it before; direct appeal had always been one of his most effective weapons against criticism. In fact there were those who firmly believed Roosevelt relished criticism from some quarters, on occasion deliberately courted criticism to exploit the sympathies of the people. When Roosevelt told the crowds, with obvious satisfaction, "I welcome their hatred," he knew he was gaining friends for the enemies he had made. No President before or since had used the spoken word to rally popular support and muzzle opposition the way Roosevelt did. His speeches, while often lacking content, were unrivaled in eloquence. And as a psychological device the Fireside Chats were pure inspiration.

On other occasions Roosevelt had fought fire with fire. He could call names with the best of them; could wither with sarcasm; could humiliate with ridicule; could shock with petulant retort. And Roosevelt was an inveterate letter writer; sometimes it seemed he was determined, single-handedly, to set the record straight with his critics. More often, however, Roosevelt found it prudent to let others—Ickes, Farley, Hopkins, Jackson, Johnson, or some other sharp-tongued New Dealer—fight his verbal battles for him.

And Roosevelt had met his foes with more than words. A President has a tremendous reserve of power, sometimes subtle, sometimes naked, limited in variations only by the imagination of its wielder. Roosevelt knew how to wield power: leadership of the Democratic Party, presidential coattails, prestige of office, personal charm, patronage and federal largesse. At one time or another and in endless combinations pressure had been applied to the political heathens. If the "purge" of 1938, easily the boldest attempt by Roosevelt to exert political power, had proved anything it was that power need not be irresistible, certainly not when it it used so indiscriminately.

In the broader sense, the entire New Deal might be conceived as a response to criticism. Certainly the shortcomings of the first New Deal, shortcomings that were shouted from the housetops by a Greek chorus of the more conservative business community and its allies, the Chamber of Commerce, the National Association of Manufacturers, the Liberty League, as well as the extremists of both right and left, had forced Roosevelt's hand. Roosevelt had responded to criticism by altering New Deal policy. And if the emphasis of the second New Deal was on reform and security and the welfare of the "forgotten man" to curb the Townsends and Coughlins and to take "the wind out of Huey's sails," so was it a form of reprisal against the "economic royalists" and "fat cats," "The Enemy" as Corcoran called them on occasion. Running through the policies of unprecedented federal controls and regulation and "soak-the-rich" tax programs had been a streak of revenge, revenge to assuage the feeling of betrayal which Roosevelt nursed toward members of his own "class." The subtle change from a New Nationalism to a New Freedom orientation in the New Deal had not been entirely an intellectual exercise; there were insistent overtones of retaliation.

IX

Harold Ickes, who had known all the ups and downs in the battle for reform, could be forgiven his enthusiasm in the early days of the New Deal. "By God," he declared, "I never thought I'd live to see this. Why this is a second honeymoon." But the New Deal honeymoon of which Ickes exulted did not last, could not last. For many the romance faded, disenchantment set in, then estrangement, and, finally, total alienation.

Why, one wonders, had Roosevelt and the New Deal, grappling, as it were, with "the trials of Job," inspired such distrust, such massive opposition in some quarters, such savage criticism? An equally tantalizing question is why the torrent of criticism and abuse seemed to produce so little tangible results, so little action.

In the quest for answers the starting point would appear inevitable. It was the Depression: the shock, the despair, the disbelief that was a part of it. It was the Depression: the vulgar enormity, the sinister insidiousness of it. The American people reacted to the Depression and the nature of that reaction was clearly reflected in the nation's response to the New Deal. In the national calamity Roosevelt was either friend or foe; the New Deal left few people neutral.

Most of the Roosevelt critics fell into rather well-defined categories. This is not to say there were not some, perhaps many, who could not be easily catalogued, those who were critical of a particular program or policy, those who were unhappy because some special desire went unfulfilled, those who found unpalatable some personality in the Administration, even some of those, who, for whatever reason, disliked Roosevelt personally. But these were not the persistent denouncers and nay-sayers, nor were they the people who joined organizations, attended meetings, distributed literature, lent financial support, and in every other way possible sought to unhorse Roosevelt.

Among those who could be considered serious critics of the New Deal were three groups at one end of the political spectrum: the Communists, Socialists, and (for lack of a better name) the Radicals. It is true that after 1935, when the international party-line shifted to the Popular Front approach, American Communists were all sweetness and light, true-blue defenders of patriotic virtue. But this was only a matter of tactics. Roosevelt, they thought, was their best defense against home-grown fascism—for the time being. They supported Roosevelt. Some even voted for him in 1936 and 1940. But they despised him, and in the early years of the New Deal they attacked him openly and relentlessly. If the Communists despised Roosevelt, the Socialists and Radicals pitied him and were frustrated by him. To non-Communists on the political left Roosevelt was wasting precious time and opportunity, the time and opportunity to effect a substantial change in the political and economic system of the country.

At the other end of the political spectrum were the native Fascists, dreaming their dreams of an America, Nazi-style. And strung out at intervals along the spectrum were other groups of Roosevelt critics. They included a more than substantial part of the American business community, professions, the press, and the Republican Party, all rallying under the banner of what is traditionally described as political and economic conservatism. In the Congress this conservatism eventually assumed the form of a Republican-Southern Democratic coalition which, after 1937, fought Roosevelt to a standoff. Almost defying location was the wide variety of anti-Roosevelt lunatic fringe groups.

X

Criticism of Roosevelt by all of these opponents made sense, a great deal of sense, if one were willing to accept their premises. The Communists who, until the party-line switch, regarded Roosevelt a social Fascist and the New Deal a dictatorship designed to betray the working classes, to keep them enslaved (assuming they were enslaved), hated Roosevelt because they hated the system. Communists could hardly live with the thought that Roosevelt just might pull it off, just might save capitalism.

Socialists and non-Communist Radicals were frustrated by dreams of what the future could be. The golden opportunity, the opportunity to usher in a Socialist millennium or something approaching it, they lamented, was slipping through his fingers like sand. The dreadful consequence of this lost opportunity, they believed, would be some form of fascism in America. The right-wing extremists, the native Fascist crowd, opposed Roosevelt for a similar reason. They, too, were aiming for a new system. Despite their insistence that they sought only to save and preserve America from the heresies of the New Deal, their goal was revolution and Roosevelt stood astride their path. Motives of the fringe groups were more obscure; but they all shared the same desire to be rid of Franklin Roosevelt.

All these groups, extreme in their methods, revolutionary in their goals, seemed to make little headway against the New Deal. The explanation for this happy circumstance, while admittedly tentative at best, also explains much about the American tradition, a tradition which the Depression strained but could not break. Out of the American past had emerged a society perhaps unique among nations in its nearly uniform devotion to middle-class values, values which set the tone of American society, democratic politics, and capitalist economics. America did not share with most other countries a history of serious ideological conflicts which set one class against another. It had been characteristic of its national development that, despite the weaknesses and excesses of the capitalist economy, its endless bounty had spread to most groups before their grievances could become chronic, before they could become inflamed by ideology or revolution. In the American political tradition there was, historically, no political left or right on which to build, no important base from which to operate when the Depression thrust opportunity upon revolutionists of both extreme persuasions.

Another way of putting it is that in the United States ideologies get nowhere, not even during depressions. Third parties (and groups which seemed destined to become third parties), intense, idealistic, usually single-minded in their ideological commitments, have come and gone. They get nowhere because the rigid nature of the American electoral structure has made it impossible for a third party to succeed. They are incapable of combatting the sectional and parochial nature of American politics. Trying to operate only at the top with no strong local and sectional base and no way to accommodate local and sectional needs has always been a fatal flaw. Perhaps a corollary of this has been their inability to speak to the American people in democratic terms, terms the people can understand, that have a familiar ring to them, that sound right to the American ear. In any case, while ideologists have sometimes influenced the major parties they do not defeat them in elections.

It is true that Roosevelt was having a profound effect on party politics. The nature of his appeal and the uniqueness of the coalition he had put together by 1936 seemed to indicate that in the future politics in the United States would be more "national" with the emphasis on the attitudes and needs of large urban populations. The new role of labor, ethnic groups (particularly the Negro), and other groups that characterized urbanization and industrialization, also suggested that in the future American politics was likely to be less sectional and more class oriented.

But in the 1930's class politics had by no means crystallized. In other countries, notably those in Europe, where there was a long history of rigid class systems, class politics, and political parties based on class, ideological cleavages were a way of life. A political left, right, and center could operate with reasonable comfort, cheek by jowl. In the United

States, where there was really only a center, ideological extremes seemed alien, seemed (to use a uniquely American word) "un-American."

And they were. The Socialists and Radicals, working within the existing political framework, approached the problems of the Depression with intelligent seriousness and did not particularly frighten people. There was, in fact, a sort of embarrassed admiration for them and a protective, almost paternalistic attitude toward the country's resident Socialist, Norman Thomas. But the American people also recognized that their solution was an ideological one, a revolutionary one, that was not consistent with traditional democratic politics.

The other extremist groups were, from the outset, alienated groups for quite another reason. The Communists (despite their efforts to pass themselves off as a political party), the native Fascists, and the lunatic fringe had at least one thing in common. They had discarded the rules of democratic society. In their minds the social institutions and techniques for resolving problems by peaceful means, and the traditions from which those institutions and techniques evolved, were so corrupt, so evil, that they were not worth using, and certainly not worth saving. There was inherent in their ideologies a sense of alienation, of isolation, of being menaced by a society they did not understand. Every hand was against them, pluralistic politics in a democratic society was a great mystery—it was more than that, it was a conspiracy which it was their duty to unmask. Their fear of the ordinary, work-a-day world around them was pathological.

XI

Opposition to Roosevelt from the business community and its allies evolved from a significantly different rationale. The United States had come of age in the late nineteenth century when the basic assumption of laissez-faire economics held that man was essentially an economic creature, one whose behavior was largely a matter of self-interest. The public interest, ran the argument, was best served when individuals were free to pursue their own interests in a self-adjusting, self-regulating economy; by some mysterious chemistry the collective result was inevitably good. Thus "free enterprise" was the key to America's success and political interference could only imperil that success.

This proposition, without serious rivals, readily became assumption; it had long since been enshrined. It was a "self-evident" truth that that government governed best that governed least. Government, particularly national government, was dangerous and must be restrained, must be kept under constant surveillance. Or, to put it another way, economics was good, government was bad; problems arising in society could best be solved by individual action rather than political action.

Much of the opposition to Roosevelt could be explained in these terms, opposition from sincere men who had been conditioned to regard Roosevelt's use of governmental powers for problem-solving as dangerous. But this was not all of it. There was something else at stake. These people sensed an erosion of their power and prestige; Roosevelt was undermining their social position, was "a traitor to his class." The relentless urbanization of America, the pressures from below of ethnic and religious minorities, intensified by economic distress, were imperiling what one recent writer, E. Digby Baltzell, has described broadly as the Protestant Establishment.

In the 1930's an urban-ethnic revolution was in progress and Roosevelt was leading it, using it, building a new majority party with urban crowds, city machines, labor unions, Negroes, Catholics, Jews, immigrant groups, all seeking acceptance and respectability. And they were getting it. Eric Goldman, in *Rendezvous with Destiny*, has a well-heeled liberal saying: "For quite a while I have lived in a commuter community that is rabidly anti-Roosevelt and I am convinced that the heart of their hatred is not economic. The real source of the venom is that Rooseveltism challenged their feeling that they were superior people, occupying by right a privileged position in the world. I am convinced that a lot of them would even have backed many of his economic measures if they had been permitted to believe the laws represented the fulfillment of their responsibility as 'superior people!' " Goldman's anonymous "liberal" struck a nerve. With their political influence and social prestige ebbing away, they screamed bloody murder. It would be expecting too much for political and social power to pass (or appear to be passing) from one group to another without Hell to pay; other countries have had civil wars for less reason.

For a party which thought it had squatters' rights to the White House, Roosevelt was hard to take. Since 1860 there had been only two Democratic Presidents, Grover Cleveland and Woodrow Wilson. Slavery had caused the Republican Party. The abolition of slavery should have ended it. It did not, of course. For years the Republican Party marshalled majorities, won elections, controlled one or both houses of Congress, monopolized the White House, and did it as the party that had abolished slavery, crushed rebellion, saved the Union, dignified mankind. With such moral issues the party had found the political Holy Grail.

But in those postwar years it still lacked a *raison d'être* until the party discovered the Industrial Revolution. The Republican Party hitched its wagon to the rising star of business; it was an unbeatable team. Year after year, while business boomed with only temporary interruptions, the Republican Party dominated American politics. It was the party of business, eventually of "Big Business," and was proud of the alliance. Not until the Depression did the "Party of Business" become a sneer, a slander, a term of reproach. Reduced to the unaccustomed role of the loyal opposition, striving to recoup its lost position and prestige, the Republican Party could do little more than bide its time, seeking to reassert its moral superiority by claiming the New Deal was unnatural, immoral, dangerous, an attack upon tradition and "the American way." So complete was the humiliation of the Republican Party by Roosevelt that its traditional business allies exemplified by the Liberty League considered seriously the creation of a new party in the 1930's.

In some respects, opposition to Roosevelt from within his own party, especially from the southern wing of the party, was like that of Republican opposition. For a party that had spent so much time in the political wilderness purging itself of the taint of treason, atoning for its past sins, Roosevelt was a new Moses. But many southern Democrats were uncomfortable with a program that seemed to do violence to states' rights, to the traditional race arrangement, and the rigid power structure in the southern states. But this was not all of it, either. The Democratic Party emerging under the leadership of Roosevelt, with its urban-ethnic orientation, the exclusion of lean-year Democrats from the New Deal team, and the secondary political status of the South as a section (as symbolized by abolishing the two-thirds rule in Democratic conventions), was more than many southern Democrats could swallow. It was no accident that virtually all of those on Roosevelt's purge list in 1938 were southerners.

XII

Santayana was not exaggerating; except for the Civil War the United States had known little of the "trials of Job." The American, with his hand to the plow and one eye on the future, had never known defeat; his preoccupation with work, his mobility, his unbounded optimism, his almost fatalistic faith in progress, had always overcome every irritation, every frustration. A sense of the tragic was not part of his makeup. For the American, achievement had always meant individual effort, self-reliance, a minimal dependence on society or government. It followed, then, that in the prolonged economic disaster of the 1930's he was unwilling to accept the logical implication that he was a failure, that what had happened to him was his own fault; he desperately needed a scapegoat. At least he thought he did.

Roosevelt was almost ideal for such a purpose. No doubt much of the name-calling may be traced to the need for a scapegoat, a mindless sort of business which nonetheless served a purpose. Part of it probably stemmed from the "I-am-as-good-as-you-are" egalitarianism which is a part of the American style. Roosevelt, his name, his patrician heritage, his looks and mannerisms, his religion, his eastern background, his stand on Prohibition, his wife, his mother, family—there was no end to the list of things which might arouse and offend the self-righteous and self-conscious nobodies of the country.

Roosevelt's attitude toward Prohibition is an example of what was probably another dimension to the name-calling. In a country where Protestantism dominated, especially evangelical Protestantism of the Baptist and Methodist variety, the emphasis was on "saving" people. Theologically, this meant saving souls; in practice, it meant saving men. Theology consistently took a back pew to ethics; men were importuned to be moral, to behave themselves, to be "good." Even this had a uniquely restricted meaning, a meaning usually applied to certain sins of the flesh, to drinking, dancing, cardplaying, and cavorting with the girls. A large segment of Protestantism could thunder against the evils of nudist camps and liquor. But most of the time it could ignore the depredations of businessmen, the exploitation of neighbors and friends, the ghettoes and deteriorating race relations, the corruption in government at every level. When it became clear that Roosevelt intended to take men as he found them, that New Deal reform meant making men feel better, not making them behave better, he became the object of epithets usually reserved for brewers and brothel-keepers.

Much of the criticism of Roosevelt had been legitimate, in good taste, honestly motivated; it was the proper stuff of politics in a free society. The name-calling, the racism, the cultist approach with its absurd suspicions, its paranoid schemes, and the irresponsible ravings about subversion and treachery were something else entirely. And there really was not much that could be done about it. Such people who resorted to those tactics had (and continue to have) influence greater than they should have had, greater than their numbers deserved. It is at once the pride and the despair of America's democratic, pluralistic society that everybody, including the mean and unlovely, has the right to speak his piece. Such people could not be ignored. They were numerous enough to be part of the national picture, bizarre figures on the political landscape. The public had to listen. They listened because the press, the radio, the other organs of communication impelled them to listen. Lunatics made good copy, the cunning only a little less so. And it was morbid fun, a vicarious adventure, to discuss such things, things almost as exciting as a good murder or an extra-marital scandal. It was not so much that talk of Roosevelt's being a Jew, a "nigger-lover," a Fascist, the fall-guy in a Communist conspiracy, and all the rest, was irrelevant. It was that the whole ugly mess was a distraction, an unwelcome intrusion, a miasma that diffused urgent issues, blunted the attack on the main order of business. Theirs was a strange, private kind of politics just sick enough to give the whole body politic a low-grade infection. The country had to pay attention to extremists.

While it often appeared that the extremist critics of Roosevelt and the New Deal exercised more political leverage than they should have, more than their numbers justified, one thing is surprising. There was little violence. It was not that violence was unrelated to the American style. The country had survived slave rebellions, race riots, lynchings, labor disorders, the excesses of a frontier, vigilante-minded people moving West, gangster killings, and a lot more. The capacity of Americans for committing mayhem upon each other has always been enormous.

But violence directed against government has been isolated and infrequent. It is true that on more than one occasion a President has been assassinated and attempts have been made on the lives of others, including Roosevelt. With the possible exception of Lincoln's assassination these have not been the premeditated mischief of organized, politically motivated groups seeking redress of grievances or seizure of the government. Even the attempt on the life of President Truman by Puerto Rican nationalists would seem to be a special case that does not contradict the conclusion that presidential assassins are pathetic loners.

No, all of the talk about shooting Roosevelt and other open invitations to violence turned out to be just talk; there were, fortunately, few takers. The reason would appear to be related to the reasons why political extremists make no tangible headway in the United States in the first place. Americans may fight each other; but in the matter of their government, their political system, there had been amazing consistency. Unlike any other country, there has always been in the United States a unanimity, a consensus that has approached the absolute.

But there was a disturbing aspect to the whole matter of violent criticism in the 1930's. Acts of violence do not strike like a bolt of lightning. No, little by little, people become conditioned by violent language, reacting with diminishing moral indignation to outrageous and inflammatory verbal abuse. There was danger in that violent action, if it were to come, would undoubtedly follow violent talk. It may be that the deep reserves of unanimity and good will traditionally felt toward government combined with the positive attack by the New Deal on the worst of the Depression were sufficient to preclude violence, to keep words from being translated into action. But the lingering, uneasy suspicion remains that had the Depression dragged on, had the government not responded to it with alacrity, violence would have been the tragic alternative.

CHAPTER XII

...A Six-Month Answer?

We did not dare to breath a prayer,
Or to give our anguish scope;
Something was dead in each of us,
And what was dead was Hope.

—Oscar Wilde
The Ballad of Reading Gaol

I<small>N</small> the early years of the Depression a common experience united the nation. It was not the kind of unity which comes in the wake of some great calamity, some natural disaster which strikes suddenly and is over quickly. Nor was it the kind of unity which defeat by a foreign foe brings—the humiliation of surrender, the rape of national honor, silent tears.

This was a unity of erosion, an erosion of intangibles, of will, of pride, of self-respect, of confidence, the slow, insidious erosion of alert minds, skilled hands, trained muscles. It was an erosion measured in the melting away of life savings, in the foreclosing of mortgages, in searching for cheaper lodging, selling precious household belongings and family heirlooms, in borrowing and stretching credit to the breaking point, in pawning wedding rings and watches, in moving in with relatives, in peddling apples on downtown street corners, in "No Help Wanted" signs, in the shame, the unbearable shame, of honest men asking for relief. From it all emerged a unity of a people, uncommonly patient, numbly asking themselves if there was no end to it; if there was nowhere to turn for a people long stricken.

It was little wonder that no President ever came to the office with greater opportunities or amid so great an outpouring of popular support and trust as Franklin Roosevelt did. There were, of course, some who had misgivings. Walter Lippmann had spoken of Roosevelt as "an amiable man with . . . philanthropic impulses . . . without any important qualifications. . . ." Paul Blanshard, a practicing Socialist in those days, asserted that if Roosevelt were no better President than he was a governor the country "will be preyed upon as it was in the days of Harding." And there were others. But the gainsayers were ignored or quickly forgotten in the early, exciting, electrifying days of the New Deal, days filled with drama and at least the illusion of action, days of smiling reassurance and words of cheer. Of a sudden, it was great again to be alive.

The first year Roosevelt escaped significant criticism. Political enemies feared his enormous popularity. Businessmen, industrialists, the nation's shopkeepers, men who poured into Washington seeking favors that would keep their heads above water, feared his vast emergency powers, powers which could inflict pain as well as bestow pleasure. The public was smitten by the new President, by his wit and charm, his unflagging energy and enthusiasm, and by his obvious relish for the job. Here was a President whose personal triumph over physical adversity seemed to personify the American virtue of rallying, of never giving up no matter the odds, of scoring the winning touchdown in the last minute of the game. People seemed willing to overlook most of the mistakes, or to believe that they were the blunders of inept assistants not of Roosevelt personally. Most felt like the Mississippi Negro wandering along the streetcar tracks on Pennsylvania Avenue, waiting for the inaugural parade to begin. Finding two dimes, he hastily pocketed them, exclaiming, "Praise be Massa Roosevelt! De new deal has came!" After twelve days in office, Roosevelt had received in the flood of White House mail more than fourteen thousand telegrams praising his actions. Arthur Krock, reporting on those first hectic days, wrote, "There is danger in the pace, and we know we may not land precisely where we intend to. But we are getting somewhere. . . . Never was there such a change in the transfer of a government."

Overwhelming approval and a willingness to give Roosevelt a chance was enough to silence all but the most pessimistic, those who were committed to the working of natural economic laws to cure the ills of the country rather than to what seemed the drastic remedies of the New Deal. Even they were circumspect; like Herbert Hoover, surveying the scene from the thirty-third floor suite of his son in the Waldorf Astoria Towers, telling reporters there was just one thing to do. We must support the President, advised the sad, bone-weary hero of a happier day.

II

Roosevelt escaped censure at first for another reason. Conditions did improve. On the anniversary of his first year in office, *The New York Times*, with mock seriousness, noted only one major failure. Everything had improved under the New Deal except the weather; the winter of 1933–34 was the worst since 1888.

But from a reliable source came word that trouble was brewing. In

Brussels, the occult journal, *Demain*, revealed the President's horoscope. According to the astrologers, the future was not bright; there was peril ahead, unexpected complications "causing the President great difficulty and making him an object of criticism." These adversities, they explained, would come in late 1934 and early 1935, because of a conjunction of Venus and the sun, with a triple conjunction of Saturn, Jupiter, and Neptune. The whole universe was about to kick up a fuss over Roosevelt and the New Deal.

In April, 1935, in a radio address on the public works program, Roosevelt invited criticism. "Feel free to criticize," he had said. It was just as well; criticism had already begun in earnest during the fall and winter of 1934. Whether the planets had anything to do with it probably no one can say for sure this side of Glory. In August, 1934, the American Liberty League was formed, an articulate spokesman for the conservative business community which was beginning to recover its nerve. In the elections that fall, the Democrats made criticism an issue, an antidote to the Republican campaign in which candidates, fearing to challenge Roosevelt's popularity, tried to separate him from the New Deal. They liked Roosevelt, they said, liked his humanitarianism, his earnest concern for the underdog, his zealous attack against the Depression on all fronts. But they disliked specific parts of the New Deal. The Democrats based the campaign on the simple proposition that Roosevelt was the New Deal; the voter could not accept the one without the other.

The Democrats won handily in 1934, but reproach continued to mount. Although there were signs of recovery on every hand, the Depression was by no means over. The President hesitated, apparently undecided how best to use his phenomenal political success and personal popularity to get on with the job of recovery. In the winter of 1934 and the early months of 1935, he appeared to let the initiative slip away, the momentum dissipate; for a time the country seemed adrift once again.

In the spring of 1935, Roosevelt picked up the reins, moved off in a new direction, a direction from which retreat would be uncommonly difficult. In the months of inactivity, of near reverie, he was being pushed relentlessly toward a decision not altogether palatable to him. The decision was a philosophical one, a conscious choice to steer a leftward course, seizing the opportunity for reforms and for security that the depression crisis offered. With continual encouragement, recovery would almost take care of itself; but when it came, the propitious moment for crucial reforms and for built-in safeguards for the public against recurrent adversity would be past, gone with the twin by-products of prosperity—apathy and indifference.

Roosevelt's choice was reached amid a growing conservative mood on the one side, one that pressed the private view that recovery was being delayed by too much Administration radicalism, and an ever widening circle of opinion on the other held by those who had been hit hardest by depression and who had profited least by the New Deal recovery measures, who felt that Roosevelt had not gone far enough. Predictably, the choice begat the most extensive program of social and economic legislation ever undertaken in the history of the country. Roosevelt had not foreseen this turn of events. He was dismayed when his initial program, highly dramatic but largely conventional (the First New Deal, some would call it), did not bring the desired results. And he did not come easily to the role of the gay reformer. But this was to be his role until the rush of world events cast him in a new one, that of warrior.

"The United States, feeling much better, is behaving like all convalescents," wrote the widely respected Arthur Krock of *The New York Times* in the spring of 1935. "Its complaints are mounting." Krock was correct; by 1935, the Roosevelt honeymoon was long since over. Over, too, were the preliminary skirmishes and probing actions. Most people had made up their minds what the New Deal was, or, at least, what they thought the New Deal was. Opinions had crystallized. The verdict was in. What remained was the deadly serious business of acting out conviction.

III

If response to the New Deal was largely conditioned by what one thought the New Deal was, intelligent response was made more difficult because Roosevelt himself did not always seem clear about what the New Deal was and what it was trying to accomplish. Perhaps it was asking too much during days of national crises for him to think in purely abstract terms about the destiny of America, about its historic purpose. Yet amid efforts to effect recovery and reform it was inescapable that someone somewhere have in mind what sort of country was in the making. There had to be a dream; it was unthinkable that the New Deal be experiment, improvisation, expediency, and nothing more.

It was more than that, of course. The First New Deal, for all its trumpet flourishes, colored lights and carnival spirit, contained really few surprises; it was largely traditional methods. It was the speed, the *élan*, the sense of urgency, and Roosevelt's uncanny gift of dramatic timing that made it appear more daring than it was, perhaps even revolutionary. It was not so much what Roosevelt did as how he did it; it was Roosevelt's "imperial gesture" as one writer called it that made the commonplace seem important. Even the Second New Deal, which began in the spring of 1935, Roosevelt did not regard as being particularly radical. He sensed that the First New Deal had missed the mark, that something else was needed. But he was too close to his heritage, perhaps, too close to Groton, to his Latin grammars to ever be a convincing radical. Maybe he could not have spelled it had his life depended on it, but he still remembered *in medio tutissimus ibis,* and what it meant.

Roosevelt thought he was steering a slightly left-of-center course. In the preface to his book, *On Our Way*, published in 1934, he acknowledged that some people were calling the New Deal "fascism" while others branded it "communism." It was neither of these, he reasoned, because it was being executed "without a change in fundamental republican method." "We have kept the faith with, and in, our traditional political institutions," he wrote. Later in the year, he returned to the same theme. When people called the New Deal "fascism," "communism," "socialism," "regimentation," or whatever, they were making complex that which was really very simple. "I believe in practical explanations and in practical policies," he explained. "I believe that what we are doing today is a necessary fulfillment of what Americans have always been doing—a fulfillment of old and tested American ideals."

Roosevelt's soothing reassurances that his New Deals were nothing much out of the ordinary did not satisfy everybody. There was something in the air that made many uneasy; only a feeling perhaps, hard to pin down, not easy to put into words. It had something to do with Roosevelt himself, who seemed a little too good to be true. Such a man would bear watching.

It also had something to do with the people around him, in fact, with the whole new breed of people who enlisted in the New Deal cause. Years later, Harold Ickes recalled the widespread attitude of wonder and contempt toward New Dealers in general and the Brain Trusters particularly:

> You will recall that one of the funniest things that the Roosevelt administration ever did was to reach the insane conclusion that if there were brains available and for hire they could not be used to better advantage than in the service of their country. That elicited shrieks of derisive laughter. The country was not prepared for any such silly proposal. The first synonym of brains is "college professor," but who in the world would ever think of asking a college professor to formulate a sane opinion about the more serious affairs of government? It is notorious that college professors usually sit in their bathtubs with their hats on, or go to bed without taking off their shoes. Certainly, we shouldn't trust them to run the public's business.

They came from everywhere; young, for the most part, intensely enthusiastic, idealistic without being doctrinaire, long on ability but short on experience, and willing to work as if demon-possessed. Here were new people all over the place, interesting people who could appreciate good music, who had read books, were articulate, were full of ideas. They worked hard, played hard, drank hard, talked fast, and were willing to tackle anything. For the first time in anyone's memory the government was succeeding in attracting the brains and firing the imaginations of the college-bred class. They were a sharp contrast to the Washington stereotypes, the fluid-eyed and short-of-wind crowd that inhabited the halls of government; and they startled and frightened a lot of people, left others puzzled and bemused.

But it was more than the President himself, or a new cast of characters around him that was disturbing. The uneasiness also had something to do with New Deal technique. While most people admired, even applauded, Roosevelt's swift response to the crisis of depression, many resented and feared the tendency to perpetuate and to develop an entirely new method of conducting the business of government based on crisis. It was their sincere conviction that the President's practice of couching his program always, it seemed, in terms of emergency, of national peril, of grave danger, of critical urgency, or other scare phrases ("government by crisis" they called it) was altogether unhealthy and probably dangerous. In March, 1939, Congressman Bruce Barton pointed out that Roosevelt had used the terms "emergency," "crisis," "disaster," and "national peril" thirty-nine times in his speeches and state papers, which, commented Barton, meant some dreadful fate confronting the country every seven weeks for six years. "Any national administration is entitled to one or two emergencies in a term of six years," said Barton. "But an emergency every seven weeks means plain bad management."

Eventually (and this was particularly true after the election of 1936) to "government by crisis" was added "government by mandate." Because of the magnitude of Roosevelt's victories his friends found it easy to brush aside all objections, to justify almost anything on the grounds that the New Deal had a "mandate" from the voters.

The crisis and mandate concepts led to other techniques which members of the Congress particularly found offensive. They resented what came to be called "must" legislation, legislation written by the Corcorans and Cohens (or any of the swarm of Brain Trusters around the President who happened to be high on the pecking order at the time), legislation concocted somewhere along Pennsylvania Avenue or "the little Red House in Georgetown," or Hyde Park, or Warm Springs, or somewhere, anywhere, anywhere except on Capitol Hill. They resented being pressured, having their arms twisted by hot-eyed young presidential aides, seeing bills rammed through with little or no debate. This departure from the pull-and-tug, the give-and-take, the compromise and half-a-loaf legislative method that had always characterized congressional action, a departure that may have been justifiable, perhaps even been desirable in the early weeks of the national emergency, was continued for years.

IV

People could find much in the New Deal with which to disagree, honest people who were often not consciously aware that they even had a political philosophy. Their quarrel with the New Deal was on specifics, an honest difference of opinion on individual matters.

They were not so subtle, for example, as to understand how a party, once in power for a few years, can virtually pack the civil service with its own faithful so that a new administration finds its plans and policies quite at the mercy of the opposition. When the New Deal created new agencies and staffed them with Democratic political appointees so as to avoid entrusting the new programs to established governmental machinery —machinery populated by Republicans—it looked to many like a debauching of the civil service.

It was also easy to understand why people whose knowledge of economics might be no more than making change at the cigar counter were concerned about government deficits, deficits which mounted annually. The oversimplified argument concerning what happened to the man who consistently spent more than he earned made good sense to them, seemed entirely applicable to governments as well. It was an argument that gained plausibility with every example of New Deal waste and prodigality.

Any number of people were disturbed by an agricultural program that required slaughtering pigs, burning wheat, plowing under cotton, pouring kerosene on potatoes, letting fruit rot on the trees. They did not seem to resent a similar policy of scarcity involving business because fixing prices, dividing markets, adjusting wages, cutting production, reducing inventories, waiving anti-trust laws, did not look like quite the same thing. While people were starving in the midst of plenty, both here and abroad, it all seemed wrong; wrong, damn it, whether you were talking about "wrong" in terms of morality or simple error. New Dealers could talk about the policy of scarcity to raise prices and wages, about how the United States had reached some state of middle-age where the power to produce was outrunning the power to consume and the two had to be restored to some equilibrium, quickly, like jerking the adhesive tape from the patient, they could talk and explain until they were blue in the face, and it still did not make it seem right.

There were also those who took exception to Roosevelt's apparent lack of reverence for the Constitution. Some of them, probably most of them, had never read the Constitution, much less understood it; but they had a deep if vague affection for it, like the Bible, which they also had not read. When, for example, Roosevelt spoke peevishly of "horse and buggy" decisions, urged passage of the Guffey Act regardless of congressional doubts as to its constitutionality, and, with his court plan, undertook (in Hugh Johnson's picturesque words) "to reorient the whole constitutional universe as well," people balked.

It did little good to cite what other Presidents had said. Roosevelt never came close to Jefferson's retort on the occasion of the *Marbury* vs.

Madison decision: "The judiciary of the United States is the subtle corps of sappers and miners constantly working underground to undermine the foundations of our confederated fabric." No reaction by Roosevelt to a court decision had contained the bitterness and hostility with which Lincoln greeted the Dred Scott verdict: "If the policy of the Government upon vital questions affecting the whole people is to be irrevocably fixed by decisions of the Supreme Court . . . the people will have ceased to be their own rulers, having to that extent practically resigned their Government into the hands of that eminent tribunal." (Of course, it could be pointed out that Lincoln was not President at the time, either.) The President was modest in his criticism compared with the angry utterances of Theodore Roosevelt, who favored recall of judicial decisions. But all of that was long ago and since forgotten. To criticize the Supreme Court and to doubt the Constitution was "wrong"; it was a sin, like scorning Motherhood and nickel beer.

New Dealers were not without answers to specific criticisms. Nothing was ever done completely without rhyme or reason, although it may have seemed so at times. Government spending and the national debt was such a case. In 1936, in his remarks to the Chicago Union League Club, Harold Ickes parried a question about the debt and the national budget with a question of his own. In the 1920's we had always had balanced budgets and a declining national debt. Why, he asked, did the country have a depression at all if balanced budgets were the key to prosperity?

It was not all that simple, of course, and Ickes knew it. By 1939, the national debt, in round numbers, amounted to $40,000,000,000, of which $22,500,000,000, was left over from preceding administrations. At the same time, however, the banks were reporting assets and deposits totalling almost $32,000,000,000, an all-time high. Likewise, the total cash savings of the American people, as estimated by the O'Mahoney Committee (the Temporary National Economic Committee), was $69,000,000,000, also an all-time high. As Clarence Cannon, veteran member of the House Ways and Means Committee, pointed out in 1938, the per capita debt, local and national, was less than in 1929.

As for what the New Deal fight against the Depression had cost the country the TNEC also produced some surprising information. For the years 1931–38, inclusive, federal receipts totalled $50,700,000,000. Of this total, taxes produced $29,700,000,000; borrowing accounted for the remaining $21,000,000,000. During the same period, operational expenses (including national defense) totalled $29,600,000,000, almost the same amount collected in taxes. For day-to-day operation of the government income and expenses were about even.

The amount borrowed, $21,000,000,000, was almost equal to the amount expended for relief (6.6 billions), net plant (11.7 billions, including public works), and the estimated amortization on the net plant

(2.9 billions). If the amount for plant (for which the country would derive income or long-range social benefits) were subtracted, the real deficit for 1931–38 became approximately $9,000,000,000.

Admittedly, that was oversimplified bookkeeping. What it amounted to was this. Over the depression years, 1931–38, which included two years of the Hoover Administration, the government paid its running expenses with taxes, used over half its borrowings for useful public works and the rest for relief. New Dealers could ask, and with some justification, the relative merits of increasing the national debt by $21,000,000,000 for relief and public works over an eight-year period as compared to increasing the national debt by $24,000,000,000 to fight World War I.

These and other criticisms of a specific nature were serious enough that Louis Howe, shortly before his death in April, 1936, prepared a list of questions soliciting from friends of the Administration ideas on how best to answer the more troublesome ones, such as "Why does the Roosevelt Administration continue to leave the budget unbalanced while piling up deficits? . . . Won't the burden of new taxes, coupled with local and state levies, eventually send us downward into a new depression? . . . Why has the Administration persisted in ignoring the Civil Service? . . . Has the Administration really built up a vast patronage machine? . . . Why not go back to a straight dole instead of continuing the huge waste of boondoggling?" Such specific questions (eighteen in all appeared on the list) troubled the little Colonel, they troubled Roosevelt, and they were to continue to be troublesome throughout most of the New Deal years.

V

One source of bitter criticism was from within the ranks of his own party, criticism that had little to do with economic policy or other matters of state. It involved the Roosevelt concept of party leadership.

In his judicious selection of issues, in the style of his appeal to the whole spectrum of the American public, it was fairly evident that Roosevelt intended to avoid the traditional stereotypes and labels, including party labels. Despite his long association with the Democratic Party and with its leadership, Roosevelt was not a strong party man. In fact, Roosevelt had long before given up on parties as such; political initiative and responsibility, and the art of getting things done, had to center in the Executive not in party horse-trading. For this reason Roosevelt was intent upon being more than a Democratic President. He would be President of all the people if he could. Party labels (or anything, for that matter, which smacked of stereotype or ideology) were divisive; they did not fit Roosevelt's concept of leadership. It is perhaps true that the most original and distinctive characteristic of the New Deal was the almost adamant refusal to approach any problem in terms of identifiable ideology or label.

This approach to leadership, inherent in the Fireside Chats, the "mandate" idea, the Grand Ratification of 1936, implied a desire on Roosevelt's part to nationalize politics, rally the support of the masses, involve the whole people. This was the logic behind his reluctance to use the party name in his speeches; his nonpartisan acceptance speech of 1936; his infrequent reference to the party by name in the campaign of 1936. He sought, in a sense, to appear and remain "nonpolitical," to rise above traditional politics, to make the issue himself as he is quoted as saying; to make personal leadership the issue meant that he could not just win in 1936. He had "to win big"; had to make it "a crusade," not merely a plebiscite; the balloting must be akin to anointing Roosevelt.

When Roosevelt was charged with being a dictator it was only partly because of the enormous powers which he had assumed; it was also partly because of this approach to leadership. The breakdown of party lines, the diminishing dependence upon traditional party politics, the relative decline in the eminence of party leaders, the wheel-horses of the Old Democracy, all contributed to the idea that Roosevelt had dictatorial ambitions. "What will happen," one earnest writer asked, "if an 'accident' occurs and John Nance Garner becomes our President?" He meant that the traditional party machinery was in disrepair, there was no party discipline, no powerful Democratic inner circle, no hierarchy, no bishoprics that would perpetuate the New Deal gospel. "Let one man die," he wrote, "and the [New Deal] structure may well collapse overnight."

One practical consequence of his approach to leadership, a consequence that was hard to swallow for some and altogether indigestible for many others, was evident in the people whom Roosevelt gathered around him. They may have been disciples; they certainly were not apostles. They may have been loyal aides; they were not leaders in their own right. They were, as one longtime Democrat put it, in hurt and anguished tone, "a petty priesthood" who added nothing to the stature of Roosevelt, except, perhaps, by contrast.

They were not all Democrats, either. Albert Ritchie, Carter Glass, James Cox, John W. Davis, Alfred E. Smith were all excluded from the team. Few prominent Democrats were to be found in the service of the New Deal. When Al Smith looked at the New Deal leadership it did not resemble anything he could remember from his long years in the party. "Who is Ickes?" he fumed. "Who is Wallace? Who is Hopkins, and, in the name of all that is good and holy, who is Tugwell, and where did he blow from . . . ? Is La Guardia a Democrat? If he is, then I am a Chinaman with a haircut."

Roosevelt might be excused for not relying more heavily upon his own party on grounds that he wished to infuse new blood and fresh ideas into government, that he wanted to emphasize brains rather than political cunning. There were many who found the sudden elevation of the Brain Trusters refreshingly commendable, and the consequent discomfort and confusion of the Democratic Old Guard amusing. But many of the same people were dismayed by the patently political use of funds for partisan purposes, particularly the manipulation of relief funds for political advantage, by the heavy-handed use of patronage, and by the open alliance between the New Deal and discredited political bosses. Roosevelt seemed not at all embarrassed by Pendergast in Kansas City, or Dickmann-Hannegan in St. Louis, or Hague in Jersey City, Kelly-Nash in Chicago, the remodeled Long machine in Louisiana, and others, bosses and machines who could not have cared less about good government, men who shamed the idealism and humanitarianism impulses of the New Deal and marred the nobility of its aims.

VI

Sooner or later, informed criticism of Roosevelt, criticism of his New Deal, its personnel, its techniques, its specific programs, returned to the crucial matter of philosophy, to intent, to what the New Deal was and what it might become. The final verdict could not rest on whether people liked the man, Franklin Roosevelt. The New Deal could not stand or fall on the quality and caliber of men responsible for carrying it into execution, or judged solely on the basis of specific mistakes. It had to be weighed in larger scales, against a larger background. Decisions had to be reached regarding the whole New Deal, its aims and accomplishments, and the philosophy that motivated both. The crucial question remained: What was the New Deal?

Loud claims that it was "fascism" or "communism" or some other dangerous "ism" were tossed around indiscriminately during the 1930's. They represented a state of mind of many people, an unreasoning fear that any departure from the status quo, however tentative, was a giant stride toward some dreadful, consuming fate. Such charges could not be ignored. They were to be taken seriously, but not too literally. Obviously, the New Deal was not fascism. It certainly was not communism. But if it were none of these, what was it?

It was unfortunate, perhaps, but nonetheless true that the New Deal lacked a philosopher. There was enough written about the New Deal, to be sure, a pleonasm of words, a blizzard of literature, most of which was not worth writing and certainly not worth reading. It would be charitable to think that the New Dealers were not responsible for any part of the mass of barren prose; that they were too busy doing what had to be done to spend their time with petty explanations of what they were doing. It would be charitable to think so, but it would not be true.

New Dealers were among the most prolific writers of the decade. Like most of the others, what they wrote lacked the watermark of quality; it proclaimed much but conveyed very little of lasting significance. Rexford Tugwell might be an exception. And possibly Donald Richberg. Thurman Arnold, an able lawyer in the anti-trust division of the Department of Justice, may have been the most meaningful writer of the pack. But he appeared on the scene too late to be of much help. His *The Folklore of Capitalism* was not published until 1937. No, the charge still stands that the New Deal produced no philosopher, no Herbert Croly, no Walter Lippmann, no Walter Weyl, not even a Bruce Barton, who could explain what the New Deal was, explain it in language that made sense then and which would stand the test of time.

This meant that to discover what the New Deal was all about one was thrown on his own resources. The place to look was not in Administration propaganda, in campaign speeches, or Fireside Chats, or chummy press conferences with the President. The answer was not in New Deal elocution; it was in New Deal action.

The moment that the broad generalizations of politics and all the grand talk about the national interest ("the issues" as the politician is wont to call them) were reduced to legislation and the legislation subjected to the day-after-day strain of interpretation and administration, one could begin drawing comparisons and conclusions. No matter how opportunistic Roosevelt may have seemed, or how pragmatic or eclectic his programs may have been, inevitably they were going to look like something. How many alternatives were there, after all? So, to the observer, this program looked like progressivism, that policy looked like socialism, something else looked like fascism, the other thing seemed to be in the spirit of the New Nationalism, those over there looked pro-labor, or anti-business, or destructive of free enterprise, or contradictory to the laws of nature, and so on. For each one of these "looks like" comparisons Roosevelt won or lost support.

But watching the New Deal in action, like a spectator on the sidelines, was not an infallible test of what the New Deal was. The earnest seeker was likely to expect some sort of consistency. Consistent the New Deal was not. It was the lack of consistent direction that upset people like Amos Pinchot, who wrote to Felix Frankfurter in late summer of 1935, complaining that Roosevelt is "the Great Uncertainty. No one knows what he thinks or what he will do tomorrow." This was what Congressman Bolton of Ohio was concerned about when he pleaded fervently with his radio audience in 1935, "Let us have an end of government by experiment, government by trial and error, government by guess." In retrospect it might not be far from the truth to say that New Deal inconsistency was the stumbling block that kept tripping up the Republican

Party. With a will and a determination as grim as an adolescent piano recital the Republicans undertook to force Roosevelt to seek traditional goals by long-tried and time-honored principles of government at a time when the people wanted change and experimentation. The Republicans never learned that the public would not have settled for less.

Consequently, critics were amazed and frustrated when they pointed out inconsistencies, sometimes incredible contradictions in New Deal action, and nobody listened. It did not seem to matter, not matter at all, that TVA meant raising living standards by increasing productivity while NRA and AAA meant raising prices by decreasing productivity; that millions of dollars were spent taking millions of acres of productive land out of cultivation while other millions were spent on reclamation and irrigation projects that increased the number of productive acres; or that cotton acreage was restricted and cotton was imported; or that beef production was curtailed and beef was imported; or that the Economy Act was deflationary, but the pump-priming through borrowing was inflationary; or that work relief projects competed with private industry. The contradictions were legion; there was no shortage of examples.

Critics encountered the same kind of bland indifference when they cited, chapter and verse, important departures from tradition. During the first six weeks of the new Administration, Roosevelt cut spending by $1,000,000,000 with sweeping economies, after which balanced budgets apparently disappeared from the national scene as permanently as the spinning-wheel and the muzzle-loader. Pump-priming and deficit spending (with glib explanations of how "we owe it to ourselves") as a means to recovery through rising prices and business expansion became a permanent alternative to declining prices and liquidation of debts by write-off. A steadily mounting tax burden with its so-called "soak-the-rich" features became a way of life under the New Deal. Inflation of the dollar and other forms of currency tinkering, which involved defaulting on gold obligations brought cold shivers and stirred memories of Bryan and the Populists, a technique parried with the oft-repeated statement, "You can no more spend yourself rich than you can drink yourself sober." There was not a little grim satisfaction in being able to shock an audience in 1939 by pointing out that if one began counting dollars at the rate of one every second, eight hours each day, every day (including Sundays and holidays), it would take five thousand years just to count the national debt.

And, of course, there were the New Deal policies toward business. The mood of penitence and deathbed confessions among businessmen passed quickly. Where once they were disposed to fly to Roosevelt's bosom, by 1934 they went straight for his jugular. Talk turned to how the alien policies of the New Deal meant brow-beating industry, meant regimentation, interference, and strangling regulation by a bloated bureaucracy of spies and snoopers, meant no new jobs and idle capital because long-range planning was impossible. And the new militancy of labor, a manifestation of revived hopes under government encouragement, evoked talk of class dictatorship and the end of private property.

Businessmen took comfort in the hope that the end of New Deal business heresies were in sight. They could point to the Gallup Poll in 1939, in which a cross-section of voters were asked: "Do you think that, to create new jobs and reduce unemployment, it would be better to follow the ideas of big businessmen or the ideas of the Roosevelt Administration?" Fifty-five per cent favored following the lead of businessmen, including 36 per cent of the Democrats to whom the question was put.

Observing the New Deal in action could lead one to the conclusion that it was utterly chaotic, a hodgepodge, a political Hungarian goulash of experiments and contradictions and expedient leftovers. A patient, closer examination would show that it was some other, more desirable things as well. It was, for example (if nothing else), a stopgap. A favorite theme of New Deal critics was that recovery would have come about with or without the New Deal, that in the natural and immutable law of things there would have been a natural recovery, that President Hoover was right all along—prosperity was just around the corner.

That may be. In 1937, Senator Millard Tydings, who had his differences with Roosevelt and who was high on the 1938 "purge" list, looked back on those Depression years and conceded that Roosevelt had probably saved the country. Tydings, who was in basic agreement with the "natural recovery" philosophy, reasoned that something very much like the New Deal had been required at the time to ease the pain until recovery came. Criticism of the early New Deal measures reminded Tydings of the story about the drowning man. "A voice from the shore calls out to him, 'Don't be frightened. Be patient. In a few hours the tide will go down and you can wade ashore.'" Tydings' concept of the New Deal was that of a life-preserver, something to keep the victim afloat until the tide went out, until recovery came.

Critics could charge that the New Deal was pragmatic, eclectic, experimental, trial-and-error, and they would all be correct. As Hugh Johnson put it in 1937, Roosevelt would go down in history as "the man who started more creations than were ever begun since Genesis—and finished none." Johnson did not mean that, of course; but it was an interesting way of saying that Roosevelt was at least willing to undertake the new and untried, which usually implied that he did not know what he was doing, that he was frantically pushing buttons and pulling levers hoping that something might accidentally start the machinery.

But the experimental spirit of the New Deal did not mean that it had no sense of direction, no ultimate destination. After a year and four months in office, *The New Republic*, in an article entitled, "The Show Is Over," described the disillusionment and discouragement of Roosevelt's more radical supporters in the Administration, men who despaired of the New Deal, men who lamented over Roosevelt's failure to aim for complete nationalization at a dead run. The talk by Rexford Tugwell and others about rolling up their sleeves and making the country over was only talk. They would never get the chance. The evidence was mounting that Roosevelt was no Communist or Socialist, not even radical enough to suit the Radicals.

If Roosevelt's goals for the New Deal were not clearly socialistic neither were they designed to lead the country back to some imaginary golden age, an age of ancient virtues, political quietism, and McKinley-like piety. Few would admit that the system worked none too well even then for the great majority of the American people. Yet so many of the leaders of American business and industry and finance in the 1930's had begun their climb to wealth and power, and sometimes fame, in the late nineteenth century that Social Darwinism was bred in their bones. Their political vision was clouded by nostalgia for what they regarded as the good old days, the American way of life, the system that had made America great. This was the vantage point from which the American Liberty League and its allies viewed the New Deal. The New Deal was never cautious enough for them.

The goal of the New Deal was not socialism, neither was it geared to a return to nineteenth-century conservatism. Nor was it fascism. That the New Deal was assailed from both sides, from conservatives and radicals alike, is a fair indication that Roosevelt stood somewhere in the liberal center. To some this meant that the New Deal was an attempt to democratize industrial and finance capitalism, to see to it that its fruits were more fairly distributed, that its knavery was permanently curbed. It was, as Herbert Agar put it, a program to promote widespread prosperity without the "obscenities of Big Business."

Moderate as those objectives may have been, they nonetheless involved Roosevelt in one of the great issues of American political history. Broadly speaking, American Presidents have been of two types. The one conceived of a federal government with limited powers, viewed national government with suspicion, and considered the office of Chief Executive to be exclusively administrative. The other accepted an ever-expanding role for federal government, particularly for the Executive branch, as problems multiplied and as life in an industrialized society became increasingly complex.

The contrast was plainly evident in the case of Roosevelt and his predecessor, Hoover. To say, or even to imply, that Hoover did nothing to check the Depression is grossly unfair. But it is true that in his approach there was a strong tendency to let nature take its course, a tendency to distrust governmental power, and a reluctance to extend federal authority.

Such reticence was manifestly not the case with Franklin Roosevelt. On the contrary, Roosevelt regarded government, federal government, the great medicament, and the Chief Executive the confident physician applying its curative powers. In this sense the New Deal meant an acceleration of and the stretching of federal powers, a steady concentration of authority in Washington with equally steady decline of states' powers and individual rights, an expanding bureaucracy, an increasing emphasis on planning, and the inevitable charge that these things led the way to autocracy and dictatorship.

In the minds of many no objective, however commendable, justified the use of such means; in fact, the use of such means would inevitably defeat the objective. "In all bureaucracies," Herbert Hoover asserted, "there are three implacable spirits—self-perpetuation, expansion, and an incessant demand for more power." Wherever bureaucracy dominated, he said, the consequence was always the same, "this host of government agents spread out over the land, limiting men's honest activities, conferring largesse and benefits, directing, interfering, disseminating propaganda, spying on, threatening the people and prosecuting for a new host of crimes." Lawrence Sullivan, in his book, *The Dead Hand of Bureaucracy*, reduced these characteristics of the New Deal to a formula. The growth of power, the expanding bureaucracy, and the emphasis on planning were all the clues Sullivan needed to prove that the New Deal was headed for a managed economy, "a protective euphemism for totalitarian socialism." "Pervading all this tangled growth of bureaus, boards, commissions, authorities, administrations, councils, and committees," wrote Sullivan in 1940, "is the current deep instinct of government toward collectivism, managed economy and 'social planning'—the demand for the centralization of all power and authority in Washington." The cancerous, malignant growth of federal power without a clear concept of how the power was to be used or to what end had set the country upon the high road to dictatorship, said Senator Steiwer of Oregon, "and a bewildered Nation knows not which way to turn."

The image of the New Deal that began to emerge from more conservative critical sources was that of an alien, foreign-styled dictatorship. In his *American Ideals Versus the New Deal*, Herbert Hoover, without cracking a smile, could define the New Deal: ". . . it appears to be a coldblooded attempt by starry-eyed boys to infect the American people by a mixture of European ideas flavored with our native predilection to get something for nothing." Ogden Mills, with a similar lack of humor, talked about having to turn the clock back centuries "to the days of absolute autocrats to find so great a power over the lives of millions of men lodged in the hands of a single fallible being." The New Deal "maelstrom of centralized order-giving," wrote David Lawrence, ". . . more strongly resembles the dictatorship of the Fascistic and Communistic states of Europe than it does the American system." The New Deal, said Senator McNary on the Washington *Evening Star's* National Radio Forum, is "one foreign to democracy . . . beyond our Constitution . . . a radical and experimental program. Out of such a program may come communism or a dictatorship." A Republican congressman delivering an address on Lincoln's birthday in 1934, was quite certain that dictatorship was already upon the land:

I have seen constitutional government ravished and reduced to a travesty. I have seen hitherto boasted State sovereignty offered up on the Moloch of centralized power. I have seen the Congress of the United States absolutely abdicate its authority to the Executive. I have seen a dictatorship spring up which must have made the noses of Herr Hitler, Stalin, Mussolini, and Mustapha Kemal of Turkey turn green with envy. Independence in private business is a thing of the past, and individual liberty is only a memory.

VII

Roosevelt was not Il Duce; and the New Deal was not some foreign-style dictatorship. In his biography of Roosevelt, Emil Ludwig (who had had first-hand experience with dictators) aired his disgust with those who called the President a tyrant. "Only those can speak thus," wrote Ludwig, "who have never had the misfortune to breathe the air of an unfree country." What Ludwig and others were trying to say was that dictatorships in the modern world did not germinate inside democratic governments and mature by a steady accretion of powers. They sprang upon an unwary citizenry, from the outside, as receivers in bankruptcy for governments which had lost the confidence of their people. Modern dictators were loners, outsiders, men who scorned parliamentary procedures, men who had played no significant role in the governments which they seduced.

The last line of Congressman Taylor's statement, that "independence in private business is a thing of the past . . . ," reveals what the "dictator" charge really meant. Another way of saying it was that under the New Deal business was no longer free to do as it pleased, to write its own ticket. The New Deal implied regulation of business in ways previously unknown, to eliminate, as Agar had said, "the obscenities of Big Business." The anti-business bias which the New Deal was accused of having usually took the form of attacking privilege and the status of "economic royalists," of professing effusive concern for "the forgotten man" and his blood relatives, "the little people," of upgrading the laboring man, both economically and socially.

The anti-business policies of the New Deal, if that is what they were, were expensive. They cost money, lots of it. But they also seemed to imply a change in the course of the country's political development, a change that would alter both the status and the personal identity of the American people. Critics talked about the loss of liberty and of how the New Deal was reducing people to serfdom. But in their hearts they suspected (all but the left-wing radicals, that is) that the change was intended to exalt the people; that with the sometimes conspicuous pro-labor policies of the New Deal more was intended than merely good pay and good working conditions; that a dictatorship of the proletariat was in the making; although many people were convinced that never before had "the people" had as much to do with controlling and directing their own destinies through government. Whichever way it was, the people would cease to be American in the old, the traditional sense.

Opponents of the New Deal bore down hard on the cost of the New Deal. It was an obvious issue, something that lent itself to all kinds of broad generalizations, oversimplications, and tricky uses of statistics. But one might strongly suspect that opposition was not based solely on cost. The time was not far removed when the country would spend multiplied billions for war and for defense without batting an eye. Then there would be no talk of spending the country into bankruptcy. Spending for war was not a new and unknown experience for Americans. They had done it before. Moreover, they knew who would be the chief beneficiaries of the spending. Perhaps if business had been left alone to carry on as usual, without government interference and legislative mischief, there would have been less said about the cost of the New Deal. When business could not reap all the benefits of New Deal spending with a whoop and a holler and when expenditures seemed to be designed to create a new privileged class, there was strong opposition. To have to help pay for their own embarrassment and humiliation, their loss of status and prestige, their vaunted sense of superiority, was unbearable.

It was not so much specific acts of the New Deal or their cost that worried some people, it was the mood that created suspicion that the New Deal was drifting toward a break with tradition, if, in fact, that break had not already occurred. Whatever may have been the motivation for calling the New Deal a dictatorship, it was important that there be created the impression that it was "un-American," that it was some kind of break with the past, that it was not in the American tradition. The implication was that protest and reformism was an alien draught from the poisoned wells of Europe. Such ideas as the New Deal seemed to embrace could not possibly have been conceived anywhere within the geographical boundaries of the United States, including the three-mile limit. Such arguments were not chosen for their fairness or because they were logical or true. They were expected to be effective because of the universal ignorance of the public concerning protest and reform movements in American history. Critics were counting on the people never having heard of Greenbackers, or Single-Taxers, or Utopians of one species or another like Edward Bellamy, or even of Populists and Progressives.

With some critics the conviction that the New Deal was a break with tradition was sincere. Theirs was the concept of history as having run its course; the historical process was as finished and complete as the Great Pyramid. The American Revolution was the mighty groan of a people straining every muscle, every nerve, to shove the apex stone in place. And now it was finished, at last things were as they should be, a handsome thing to be admired and revered through the ages, its excesses and stupidities buried deep inside with the mummified Pharaoh.

Roosevelt and the New Dealers rejected the concept that America was a finished product. The New Deal was, if nothing else, committed to the fact of constant, steady change, the necessity for governmental action to accommodate to those changes, and the continuing need for explaining to the people, in simple, candid terms, what those changes were all about. There was, then, a strong element of relativity about the New Deal, the belief that democracy was a method, a process, that was ever in a state of becoming, not a fulfilled system of economics, or government, or society, reduced to commandments and preserved on stones, writ by the finger of God.

Roosevelt and the New Deal applied to the Constitution something of that same spirit of change, of relativity, of dynamism. It was not that Roosevelt was flagrantly unconcerned about the supreme law of the land, that he rejected constitutional methods, that he deliberately sought to flaunt it, circumvent it, and, when the moon was right, murder it. He recognized, however, that it was capable of many interpretations (at least it always had been in the past). And he did not intend to stand idly by if it meant letting people starve by strict constitutional methods. If honest men, who stood in awe of the inspired Word, could differ, sometimes vehemently, over its meaning, so other men equally honest could dispute the meanings of the Constitution, which, after all, was not Holy Writ. John Franklin Carter, the Unofficial Observer of the New Deal years, was fairly close to the New Deal position when, in his customary humorous forthrightness, he wrote: "The New Dealers have no designs against the Constitution, provided that it retains the elasticity of the original fabric. This elasticity has always been in evidence whenever a Philadelphia lawyer desired to drive a corporate caravan through it, but it has been remarkably rigid whenever the rights of the common men were up for consideration."

Just as the New Deal was committed to change, so was it committed to the proposition that governmental power was not automatically evil. Power and evil were not the same thing; power could be used for good as readily as for evil; power could only be judged in its specific applications. What the New Dealers were getting at was that there could never be in modern society a moratorium on the use of power. Power existed, it was; if it were not held in one place it would be held in another. There could not be a power vacuum. If government refused to exercise its powers, particularly in economic matters, there were those who would exercise it privately, as New Dealers believed had been the case for years. They believed, sincerely and conscientiously, that the default by government in its use of power had produced an economic situation grossly unfair, one in which the American people consistently got the short end of the stick.

Granted, that the New Deal meant changes and modifications in many areas of economics and social reform. Roosevelt broke more precedents than any President in history. He did more building, more tearing down, and more remodeling than any other President. Yet none, perhaps, believed more firmly in the essential soundness of the American system than Roosevelt. No one was more bitterly disappointed in him than the radicals on each end of the political spectrum. As Frank Kent of the Baltimore *Sun*, a bitter critic of the New Deal, was willing to concede, Franklin Roosevelt had done "more than any other President to preserve our institutions and stem the tide of both Socialism and Fascism in this country." At the other extreme of political persuasion, Roosevelt was welcomed at first as the executioner of capitalism. But the executioner's axe turned out to be a surgeon's scalpel. The patient returned to robust health.

Whatever effectiveness there was to these arguments that the New Deal was a tradition-shattering philosophy, the New Dealers themselves had to share much of the blame. They invited such an image of the New Deal, albeit for different reasons. The image they sought to create was one of boldness, daring, courage, imagination, a willingness to experiment, to try the untried, to launch out on uncharted seas. In this they probably went too far. And in singing the praises of Roosevelt they unwittingly created the image of a leader that was indeed too good to be true, of a leader such as had not been seen in the land since Isaiah.

VIII

Despite what often looked like a vendetta with business, industrial capitalism and the free enterprise system were never really in any danger from the New Deal. From the first, Roosevelt expected to save the system, to cure its malaise. But he did not intend to do so because private business was somehow sacred. His was a pragmatic choice, not a theological one; a choice that was based on experience, not a divine admonition that had been handed down from on high on a pillar of fire. A system of private business, if it were conducted properly, was the best system in America to serve the public interest. Roosevelt was convinced of that.

But business could no longer do as it pleased and call it free enterprise. The New Deal, he told the country, "will not restore that ancient order."

New Deal convictions toward business and the economic policies undertaken were based on a number of serious assumptions. Roosevelt, early in the game, discarded the proposition that the economy moved in mysterious cycles of boom and bust, governed by immutable laws that mere mortals could not comprehend. "No government," Hoover had declared categorically in 1936, "can legislate away the morning after any more than it can legislate away the effects of a tornado—not even the New Deal." The "morning after" was the inevitable hangover from a prosperity spree, as inevitable and irresistible as a tornado.

Roosevelt refused to accept the assumption—and the spirit of resignation to a blind destiny implied in it—that the economic system was some whimsical, capricious, unpredictable thing that could bring pleasure or pain as it wished, and that there was nothing anybody could do about it. The conflict here was between those who believed that operation of the economic system had to be automatic, that it was some kind of perpetual motion machine, and those who put their trust in legislation to regulate and to assist the functioning of the system.

This New Deal commitment led to the conclusion that by wise planning and precautions prosperity was a happy state that could be created and depression avoided. Planning, as in the case of the National Recovery Act and the Agricultural Adjustment Act, was one of the prime excuses for charges of dictatorship, of conflicting claims of fascism and socialism leveled at the New Deal. As an aside, it did little good to point out to critics that at the outset businessmen and farm leaders had favored such planning, that the NIRA and AAA were largely designed by businessmen and farmers to save themselves, not by New Dealers.

There was at least one other reason for the New Deal appearing to be anti-business. That was the assumption (a mistaken assumption, as everyone eventually realized) that the United States had reached its maximum economic growth; the mature economy principle, it was called. The ability of the country to produce had far outstripped the capacity of the country to consume. If prosperity were to be restored, production and consumption must be restored to some sort of equilibrium.

The alternatives were to stimulate consumption, reduce production, or some combination of both. The New Deal did both. But the emphasis was on limiting production. Some New Deal measures, such as plowing under cotton and slaughtering pigs, made little sense except in this context. But in any case, if the road to prosperity was through limited production and artificial scarcity, a large degree of government planning and government regulation was inevitable.

The attempt to restore economic balance and to reconcile individual freedom with twentieth-century industrialization invited, perhaps required, an emphasis on regulation and planning and on social welfare and security for the individual citizen. But none of this meant that business or capitalism or free enterprise had much of anything to fear from the New Deal. There might be substantial areas of disagreement regarding techniques, and there might be grounds for serious discussion of which political party and which group might best implement the techniques. But the Depression had hastened the day and had forced upon the country acceptance of the proposition that, like it or not, government was destined to play an ever-expanding role in the daily life, particularly the economic life, of the country. Only the politically ossified insisted it was not true.

The New Deal acted on this assumption. Roosevelt, despite charges of being a traitor to his class, undertook to apply it without disturbing the foundations of the existing system. The NRA fostered monopoly and combatted the dangerously deflationary effect of ruthless price-cutting. His crusades against parasitic holding companies, stock market riggers, dishonest bankers, and irresponsible employers were attempts to save the system from the vulgar avarice of its practitioners, to save it from perhaps even more extreme solutions. Mortgage relief, subsidy payments, minimum wages, ready credit, work relief, public works, and the like were designed to bolster the system as well as to provide security and a helping hand to the underdog.

One of the striking characteristics of the New Deal was its humanitarianism, its enthusiastic response to the needs of people, those people so well described by Gerald Johnson in *Incredible Tale* as "people who were not fighters at all, who didn't know how to fight—babies, and small children, charwomen and cooks and housewives in remote places and practitioners of the gentle arts, music, painting, sculpture, the dance. The government was always giving a break to people no one had ever thought of helping before, Negro singers, aspiring playwrights, blind people, all of the dispossessed and disinherited. . . ." And if to the list be added farmers, laborers, old people, and students, it would change nothing. To help them did not mean to ruin others in some devilish geometric progression.

The novelist James Boyd was speaking volumes about how successful the New Deal was in this enterprise in the lines he wrote in 1938, lines that summarized his feelings about Miami upon seeing it for the first time in five years. "Miami is pretty much the same," he observed. "Like the rest of the country, it is divided into the people Roosevelt ruined and the people he saved—those he ruined still living in Byzantine palaces in more than Oriental luxury, and those he saved still living in tar-paper shacks."

IX

For those who would be critics of Roosevelt and the New Deal there was something for everybody. Men found ample excuse (and sometimes just cause) for criticizing Roosevelt personally, for criticizing at least some of the people around him, for criticizing specific New Deal policies, techniques, attitudes. Any or all of these forms of criticism were to be expected; they happened to one degree or another in every administration.

The unpleasant fact, the deplorable fact, was that massive opposition mounted on so many fronts was the principal obstacle that prevented Roosevelt from achieving the ultimate goals of the New Deal. Roosevelt was never able to make clear to the American people where the New Deal was going, what it really meant to do; and men, unfortunately, were not able to fathom it merely by watching the New Deal in action. There was from first to last appalling misunderstanding about the philosophy of the New Deal.

It is true, of course, that most Americans understood and profited by some of the objectives of the New Deal. America was all the better for a social and ethnic revolution which for the first time revised upward the status of great groups of the "forgotten men" in American society, provided them with unprecedented opportunity for escaping a dull and humdrum existence, offered them fulfilment. America was a better place because Roosevelt succeeded in making security for the individual something more than an idle wish; it became an attainable dream, an acceptable part of American political philosophy. America was better off because the New Deal had championed the right of others besides businessmen to participate in decision-making, particularly those decisions affecting economic policy.

But most Americans, friends or foes of Roosevelt, missed the real point of the New Deal. Certainly the critics did. Roosevelt refused to accept the narrow economic determinism implied in both socialism (whether it be of the Marxist variety or whatever) and laissez faire with its mystical faith in immutable economic laws. Roosevelt rejected the economic fatalism of the arrogant rugged individualist and the doctrinaire collectivist. He was convinced there must be some other way, a middle way. A modified capitalism, a mixed economy was possible, he believed. And he caught hell from both sides for believing it. Once convinced that he was right, that there was a middle way, Roosevelt burned bridges all over the place. What began to emerge from the New Deal experiment was a society that had divorced itself from laissez faire but which refused to marry socialism. But this was as far as Roosevelt got. He was never able to apply the philosophy of the middle way to anything more than the symptoms of the Depression. The crucial problems of the twentieth century, the problems which had caused the disaster in the first place, were not confronted; they remained unsolved.

The most serious problem confronting the country, challenging the minds of statesman and theoretician alike, straining the fabric of the Constitution and the federal system to the breaking point, was how to reconcile traditional freedom for the individual (the freedom of an individual in an agrarian society which the country had inherited from the nineteenth century) with the challenge of industrialization, centralization, monopoly, the maldistribution of wealth, urbanization, of science and automation and technology, all of those things which threatened, which undermined the American dream, which challenged Herbert Croly's promise of American life. The individual versus the Industrial Revolution was the unseen fear, sensed but uncomprehended, felt but misunderstood by the Populists; it was uppermost in the minds of every smalltown Progressive businessman hunched over his accounts and ledgers; it was the nagging imperative which had commanded the attention of Theodore Roosevelt and Woodrow Wilson, had provided a cause for the Muckrakers, had produced the New Nationalism and the New Freedom. It was the one important reality which escaped Herbert Hoover, which was overlooked in the sentimentalities of Henry Ford and the vulgar, almost sacrilegious irrelevancies of Bruce Barton.

It was the prime domestic question of the twentieth century, and Roosevelt faced it in a time of economic disaster when the country was in no mood to listen to solutions that might right the country in some indefinite long-run. People wanted action, they wanted it quick, and they wanted results. There was no time for seeking a middle way by careful probing, by judicious weighing, by intelligent and selective trial-and-error. The critics did not believe there was a middle way. It was the crowning irony of New Deal criticism that the classical liberal and the Marxist could meet on common ground and solemnly agree that the middle way was impossible, suicidally impossible; for both, the middle way consigned America to a life of economic sin or worse. The pressure for quick results and the dead weight of all-or-nothing, either-or obstructionism meant the New Deal could never be much more than a grand postponement.

The night of Roosevelt's death, Samuel Grafton, the syndicated columnist of the New York *Post*, wrote an obituary. Grafton may have had deeper insight into the New Deal dilemma than any critic or apologist, then or later, when he wrote:

Leaf-raking was silly. You cannot tell me he did not know it was silly. He knew. But as against a concentration camp, it was noble. As against what happened in Spain, leaf-raking even had grandeur. I think he knew these things, and there was a knowledge of them in his smile when he was attacked and baited.

He had no answers that were good for a hundred years. But in a six-month crisis he always had a six-month answer. . . . Maybe he had a right to smile, and to think that a billion was not so much; maybe he knew what he had got for it, and that it was a bargain.

Under the circumstances, a six-month answer for a six-month crisis would have to do. Stall for time. Trade dollars for time. Time. Time for the country to collect its wits. Time for the people to pull themselves together, shake their fears, recover their sense of humor, take heart. Time so that America would not default to madmen and lunatics and their wicked dreams. Time so that honest men could find solid answers to pressing problems that the country had been ignoring and fending off for years. Time to vindicate Roosevelt's dream of the middle way. He had seen America through a great agony. Democracy had survived its severest test; it was to have a second chance. As Grafton said, the New Deal was a bargain; Roosevelt did have a right to smile.

NOTES

To avoid an unmanageable number of notes, we have followed the practice of collecting the references to a particular passage (usually a paragraph) in a single note.

Recurring references are made to the Valentine Collection, a large collection of Rooseveltiana assembled by the late John Valentine of Glendale, California, which probably includes more anti-Roosevelt material than any collection extant. The Valentine Collection is at The University of Texas Library, Austin, Texas.

The Franklin D. Roosevelt Papers are at the Roosevelt Library at Hyde Park, New York. References to them receive the following abbreviated citations throughout:

Roosevelt Papers	Franklin D. Roosevelt Papers
OF	Official File
PPF	President's Personal File

CHAPTER I: IF YOU WERE A GOOD HONEST MAN . . .

1. *The New York Times*, August 6, 1935.
2. *Time*, August 12, 1935 (XXVI), 11; *Congressional Record*, 74 Cong., 1 Sess. (1935), 14266.
3. *Ibid.*; *Time*, August 12, 1935 (XXVI), 11.
4. "Whispers," *Newsweek*, July 20, 1935 (VI), 5; Elliott V. Bell, "The Decline of the Money Barons," in Hanson W. Baldwin and Shepard Stone (eds.), *We Saw It Happen* (New York: Simon and Schuster, 1938), 137–138.
5. Washington *Daily News*, July 10, 1935; *Congressional Record*, 74 Cong., 1 Sess. (1935), 7600, 8754; "Whispers," *Newsweek*, July 20, 1935 (VI), 5.
6. "Whispers," *Newsweek*, July 20, 1935 (VI), 5; *The New York Times*, July 9, 1935; Roger Burlingame, *The Sixth Column* (New York: Lippincott, 1962), 55.
7. *Time*, July 22, 1935 (XXVI), 14; *The New York Times*, July 14, 1935.
8. *Ibid.*, July 9, July 26, 1934; "Whispers," *Newsweek*, July 20, 1935 (VI), 6.
9. *Ibid.*
10. Special Committee to Investigate Lobbying Activities, *Hearings*, 74 Cong., 1 Sess. (1935), 809–834.
11. Marquis W. Childs, "They Hate Roosevelt," *Harper's*, CLXXII (May, 1936), 638.
12. George F. Gundelfinger, "Wooden-Head Son of a Bitch" (n.d.), Valentine Collection; G. F. Gundelfinger, "Message to Democrats," *The New Fraternity* (June, 1937), PPF 200–A, Roosevelt Papers; Gundelfinger to Robinson, July 8, 1937, PPF 200–A, Roosevelt Papers.
13. "Number One Obsession," *The Nation*, CXLVII (April 30, 1938), 491; Esther Arthur, "Have You Heard About Roosevelt . . . ?" *Common Sense*, VII (August, 1938), 15; Marquis Childs, "They Still Hate Roosevelt," *The New Republic*, XCVI (September 14, 1938), 147.

14. Esther Arthur, "Have You Heard About Roosevelt . . . ?" *Common Sense*, VII (August, 1938), 15–16.
15. Quoted in *Congressional Record*, 75 Cong., 3 Sess. (1938), 2395.
16. Morris A. Bealle, *Fugitives From a Brain Gang* (Washington: Columbia Publishing Co., 1940), 160–161.
17. *The New York Times*, October 24, 1934.
18. Alfred E. Smith, "Common Sense in Convention and Campaigning," *Saturday Evening Post*, June 11, 1932, 7; "Whispers," *Newsweek*, July 20, 1935 (VI), 6.
19. *Ibid.*, 5.
20. OF (Talmadge), February 11, 1935, Roosevelt Papers; quoted in Reinhard Luthin, *American Demagogues, Twentieth Century* (Gloucester, Mass.: P. Smith, 1959), 193; Robert Hale, "But I. Too, Hate Roosevelt: A Reply to 'They Hate Roosevelt,'" *Harper's* CLXXIII (June, 1936), 272.
21. Paul Haber, *The House of Roosevelt* (Brooklyn: The Author's Publishing Co., 1936), revised edition, 66.
22. Gundelfinger, "Roosevelt 'Speedocity,'" *Interquadrangular* (1936), 629, Valentine Collection; Gundelfinger to Robinson, July 8, 1937, PPF 200–A, Roosevelt Papers; Ernest Fowler, "Lady Jane—Andy Gump—Mr. Roosevelt," *The Fox Valley Mirror* (1934), 167, PPF 200–A, Roosevelt Papers; Edwin Thomas Whiffen, *The New Squeal; Or, These Lunatic Years* (Paterson, N.J.: The Gayren Press, 1939), 20.
23. James E. Pollard. *The Presidents and the Press* (New York: The Macmillan Company, 1927), 790–791; Stephen T. Early, "Below the Belt," *Saturday Evening Post*, CCXI (June 10, 1939), 112–113; Dixon Wecter, *The Hero in America; A Chronicle of Hero Worship* (New York: C. Scribner's Sons, 1941), 459.
24. James J. Bolton to Roosevelt (n.d.), PPF 200–A, Roosevelt Papers; Gundelfinger, "Dictator's Diverse," *Interquadrangular* No. 16 (1936), 895–896, Valentine Collection.
25. Quoted in William Dudley Pelley, *Cripples' Money* (Asheville: Pelley Publishers, 1939), 6–7, 20–21.
26. Pelley, *Does Roosevelt Get Net Receipts From Birthday Paralysis Balls?* (n.d.), leaflet, PPF 1, Roosevelt Papers; leaflet (n.d.), PPF 1, Roosevelt Papers; Pelley, *Cripples' Money* 6–7; Early to O'Connor, April 24, 1939, OF 3206, Roosevelt Papers.
27. Jerome Davis, *Character Assassination* (New York: Philosophical Library, 1950), 28.
28. Gundelfinger, "Dictator's Diverse," *Interquadrangular*, No. 16 (1936), 845, Valentine Collection; Haber, *The House of Roosevelt*, 31, 104; David Milton Proctor, *Pay Day* (Kansas City: Brown Publishing Co., 1936), 110; Mark Granite (pseud.), *A Book of Granitegrams: Mark Granite Sizes Up Franklin Roosevelt* (Newtown, Pa., 1936), 7–9; W. Lloyd Clark, *From Belshazzar to Roosevelt* (Milan, Illinois: The Rail Splitter Press, 1935), 27; Robert Morris Pierce, *The Roosevelt Road to Ruin* (New York: Languages Publishing Co., 1934), 23, 27, 35, 45, 51–52.
29. Squire of Krum Elbow (pseud.), "Behind The Smile," editorial in the *Highland Post*, Ulster County, New York, January, 1935, Valentine Collection.
30. George Abell and Evelyn Gordon, *Let Them Eat Caviar* (New York: Dodge Publishing Co., 1936), 57; *The New York Times*, July 24, 1935.
31. George Wolfskill, *The Revolt of the Conservatives* (Boston: Houghton

Mifflin Co., 1962); Jerome Davis, *Character Assassination*; Samuel Karr, *The Roosevelt Haters* (unpublished doctoral dissertation, University of California at Los Angeles, 1956).

32. *Congressional Record*, 76 Cong., 1 Sess. (1939), 6378; 73 Cong., 1 Sess. (1933), 4539; 73 Cong., 2 Sess. (1934), 1294; *The New York Times*, November 10, 1938; *Congressional Record*, 75 Cong., 3 Sess. (1938), 9464, 2348, 202, 26, 642, 1729; 76 Cong., 1 Sess. (1939), 3576.

33. *Ibid.*, 75 Cong., 3 Sess. (1938), 1749, 1430.

34. *Ibid.*, 73 Cong., 2 Sess. (1934), 1780; 74 Cong., 1 Sess. (1935), 8574; 73 Cong., 2 Sess. (1934), 11648; 74 Cong., 1 Sess. (1935), 7824.

35. Quinn O'Brien to Roosevelt, May 13, 1935, PPF 1741, Roosevelt Papers; *Chicago Tribune*, May 14, 1935.

36. Malcolm W. Bingay, "Roosevelt, Landon: A Fascinating Study In Contrasts" (1936), PPF 200–A, Roosevelt Papers.

37. John J. Mangan, *Roosevelt and Bankruptcy* (Chicago: The Author, 1934), 16.

38. *Congressional Record*, 75 Cong., 1 Sess., (1937), 5738; 75 Cong., 3 Sess. (1938), 641.

39. *Ibid.*, 76 Cong., 1 Sess. (1939), 255; 74 Cong., 2 Sess. (1936), 7730.

40. *Ibid.*, 75 Cong., 3 Sess. (1938), 2701; 75 Cong., 1 Sess. (1937), 3980–3981; 75 Cong., 3 Sess. (1938), 101–102; *The New York Times*, March 3, 1938.

41. *Congressional Record*, 75 Cong., 1 Sess. (1937), 8857.

42. *The New York Times*, July 14, 1939.

43. Burl G. Cross to Roosevelt, July 2, 1936, PPF 200–A, Roosevelt Papers; *Congressional Record*, 75 Cong., 2 Sess. (1937), 1809; 75 Cong., 1 Sess. (1936), 2510; Stephen Early, "Chronology of Representative Fish's Attacks On The President" (1937), PPF 4744, Roosevelt Papers; Republican Service League, "Or Isn't There to Be One?" (1936), PPF 200–A, Roosevelt Papers; Marquis Childs, "They Still Hate Roosevelt," *The New Republic*, XCVI (September 14, 1938), 148; Stephen Early, "Below the Belt," *Saturday Evening Post*, CCXI (June 10, 1939), 112–113.

44. W. L. Thornton to Stephen Early, May 26, 1935, PPF 200–A, Roosevelt Papers.

45. *Congressional Record*, 74 Cong., 1 Sess. (1935), 7308–7309.

46. Republican Service League, *Or Isn't There to Be One?* (1936), PPF 200–A, Roosevelt Papers.

47. *Congressional Record*, 76 Cong., 1 Sess. (1939), 152, 2767, 8463–8464.

48. I. B. Leibson, *The Raw Deal; The Deal Mr. Roosevelt Forgot* (New York: Ideal Publishing Co., 1936), 42.

49. M. C. Wyman to Roosevelt, November 19, 1935, PPF 200–A, Roosevelt Papers.

50. Hal Walton, "The New Deal and Lindbergh Baby" (October, 1938), Valentine Collection; Early, "Below the Belt," *Saturday Evening Post*, CXI (June 10, 1939), 112.

51. Quoted in Gerald Johnson, *Incredible Tale* (New York: Harper, 1950), 188; Frank Sullivan, "The Cliché Expert as a Roosevelt Hater," in Milton Crane (ed.), *The Roosevelt Era* (New York: Boni and Gaer 1947), 239.

52. Franklin Martin, *Fun During Recession* (South Orange, N.J.: 1938), 12, 23, pamphlet, Valentine Collection; C. A. Paige to Roosevelt, undated letter, PPF 200–A, Roosevelt Papers; *The New York Times*, January 27, 1939.

53. *Congressional Record*, 75 Cong., 3 Sess. (1938), 1522.

54. *Ibid.*, 76 Cong., 1 Sess. (1939), 4274.
55. Martin, *Fun During Recession*, 5, 10, pamphlet, Valentine Collection.
56. *The Indispensable Man* (n.p., n.d.), unidentified leaflet, Valentine Collection.
57. Schlesinger, *The Coming of the New Deal*, 568; Unidentified business card, Valentine Collection; Business Card, New Jersey Color Card Company, November 11, 1939, PPF 200–A, Roosevelt Papers.
58. Ulysses Grant Vogan, *A Modern Hudibras; The New Deal in Rime* (Athens, Pennsylvania: Balch Publishing Co., 1939), 8–9.
59. Leaflet (1938), PPF 200–A, Roosevelt Papers; James Lucius Strang, *Priming the Pump* (April, 1938), PPF 200–A, Roosevelt Papers.
60. Martin, *Fun During Recession*, 23, pamphlet, Valentine Collection; Unidentified business card, Valentine Collection; Copies in PPF 200–A, Roosevelt Papers; *Congressional Record*, 74 Cong., 2 Sess. (1936), 2931.
61. *The New York Times*, July 28, 1935.
62. *Ibid.*, February 9, 1939.
63. Adelaide W. Neall, "Through the Looking Glass," *Saturday Evening Post*, December 16, 1933, 29; *Congressional Record*, 75 Cong., 2 Sess. (1937), 905.
64. *The New York Times*, December 9, 1934; Unidentified leaflet in Valentine Collection; Martin, *Fun During Recession*, 13, pamphlet, Valentine Collection.
65. "Traitors Three," anonymous poem, PPF 200–A, Roosevelt Papers; "Rejected," anonymous poem, Valentine Collection.
66. E. F. Spicer, *New Deal Parodies* (Spokane, Washington: Union Printing and Publishing Co., 1936), 3–4.
67. E. C. Riegel, *Franklinstein* (New York, n.d.), 13, Valentine Collection.
68. Tart Speer, *Dignity of the Old Deal* (Houston, Texas: Old Dill Publishing Co., 1938), 45.
69. *The New Deal Goes to the Privy*, (Elizabeth City, N.C., n.d.), unidentified leaflet, Valentine Collection: Martin, *Fun During Recession*, 30, pamphlet, Valentine Collection; slightly variant copies in PPF 200–A, Roosevelt Papers.
70. Edgar Kemler, *The Irreverent Mr. Mencken* (Boston: Little Brown and Co., 1950), 269.
71. *Congressional Record*, 75 Cong., 3 Sess. (1938), 553; Arthur, "Have You Heard About Roosevelt . . . ?" *Common Sense*, VII, No. 8 (August, 1938), 15–16; Childs, "They Still Hate Roosevelt," *The New Republic*, XCV (September 14, 1938), 147.
72. *Congressional Record*, 75 Cong., 3 Sess. (1938), 4030; True Economics of New York, "Petition to the Congress of the U.S.A." (May 7, 1935), PPF 200–A, Roosevelt Papers; *Congressional Record*, 75 Cong., 3 Sess. (1938), 1980; *The New York Times*, June 1, 1939.

CHAPTER II: WE DON'T LIKE HER, EITHER

1. Mary Hornaday, "Mrs. Roosevelt—A Campaign Issue," *Christian Science Monitor*, June 24, 1936.
2. Malcolm Bingay, "Good Morning" (1934), unidentified editorial, Valentine Collection; quoted in Abell and Gordon, *Let Them Eat Caviar*, 65–66; there are three versions of "The Lady Eleanor" in the Valentine Collection.

3. Clark, *From Belshazzar to Roosevelt*, 23, 60, Valentine Collection.

4. *Ibid.*, 23; Women's National Association for the Preservation of the White House, "Blunt Criticism" (1936), PPF 200–A, Roosevelt Papers.

5. *The New York Times*, April 24, 1934; *Congressional Record*, 75 Cong., 3 Sess. (1938), 2703; Abell and Gordon, *Let Them Eat Caviar*, 67; Ernest Fowler, "Lady Jane—Andy Gump—Mr. Roosevelt," *The Fox Valley Mirror* (1934), 167, PPF 200–A, Roosevelt Papers; R. H. Hibbert to Roosevelt, March 16, 1938, PPF 200–A, Roosevelt Papers; Malcolm Bingay, "Good Morning" (1934), unidentified editorial, Valentine Collection.

6. *Congressional Record*, 75 Cong., 3 Sess. (1938), 2457.

7. *The New York Times*, March 2, 1938.

8. Abell and Gordon, *Let Them Eat Caviar*, 67.

9. *The New York Times*, June 15, July 1, 1937.

10. Stephen Early, "Chronology of Representative Fish's Attacks on The President" (1937), PPF 4744, Roosevelt Papers; *The New York Times*, July 29, 1937.

11. Humphrey Shaw to Charles Michelson, October 22, 1936; *Some Reasons Why the Present Administration Can And Will Be Defeated*, anonymous pamphlet (n.d.), PPF 200–A, Roosevelt Papers.

12. Women's National Association for the Preservation of the White House, "Blunt Criticism" (1936), PPF 200–A, Roosevelt Papers.

13. Davis, *Character Assassination*, 53; Women's National Association . . . of the White House, "Blunt Criticism" (1936), PPF 200–A, Roosevelt Papers; "A Southern Democrat," *Racial Distinction Abolished* (n.d.), Valentine Collection.

14. *The New York Times*, January 19, 25, 30, 31, 1936; *Time*, XXVII, No. 7 (April 27, 1936), 10–11; "A Southern Democrat," *Racial Distinction Abolished* (n.d.), Valentine Collection.

15. Quoted in Abell and Gordon, *Let Them Eat Caviar*, 82–83.

16. Malcolm Bingay, "Good Morning" (1934), unidentified editorial, Valentine Collection; William M. Citron to Roosevelt, July 24, 1935, PPF 200–A, Roosevelt Papers; "Whispers," *Newsweek*, July 20, 1935 (VI), 6.

17. Quoted in Clark, *From Belshazzar to Roosevelt*, 130. "Dixie" to Roosevelt, October 8, 1934, PPF 200–A, Roosevelt Papers; Unidentified business card, Valentine Collection.

18. Quoted in Abell and Gordon, *Let Them Eat Caviar*, 74–75; Gundelfinger, "Speedocity," *Interquadrangular* (1936), Valentine Collection.

19. American Guild, Inc., *Franklin Delano Roosevelt* (New York, 1933), 2, PPF 1–A, Roosevelt Papers.

20. *Congressional Record*, 75 Cong., 3 Sess. (1938), 3558.

21. *Ibid.*, 75 Cong., 2 Sess. (1937), 199–200.

22. *Ibid.*, 75 Cong., 3 Sess. (1938), 2701, 1125; "Whispers," *Newsweek*, July 20, 1935 (VI), 6.

23. R. H. Hibbert to Roosevelt, March 16, 1938, PPF 200–A, Roosevelt Papers; *Congressional Record*, 76 Cong., 1 Sess. (1939), 1402, 3784; E. M. Biggers to Louis Howe, July 21, 1934, PPF 200–A, Roosevelt Papers.

24. Clark, *From Belshazzar to Roosevelt*, 27; *Congressional Record*, 76 Cong., 1 Sess. (1939), 3574; Ragsdale, *We American Voters . . .* , 23–24; *Congressional Record*, 75 Cong., 3 Sess. (1938), 1749; *The New York Times*, May 29, 1936; *Congressional Record*, 74 Cong., 2 Sess. (1936), 2211; 74 Cong., 1 Sess. (1935), 3488; Bealle, *Fugitive From A Brain Gang*, 150; *Congressional Record*, 76 Cong., 1 Sess. (1939), 2248; Fowler,

"Lady Jane—Andy Gump—Mr. Roosevelt," 166–167; Reeves, *Is All Well On The Potomac?*, 7; Herbert Hoover, *Morals In Government* (Address before Joint Republican Organizations, Kansas City, Missouri, September 28, 1938), 5, pamphlet, PPF 200–A, Roosevelt Papers; *Congressional Record*, 74 Cong., 2 Sess. (1936), 10033, 9820.

25. Haber, *The House of Roosevelt*, 105–107; *The New York Times*, January 14, 1936; *Congressional Record*, 76 Cong., 1 Sess. (1939), 3453; 74 Cong., 1 Sess. (1935), 6109–6110; Reeves, *Is All Well On the Potomac?*, 61, 64.

26. *Congressional Record*, 74 Cong., 1 Sess. (1935), 6109–6110; John Adams (pseud.), *The New Declaration and Why Pay Tribute to—Atic Dust* (San Francisco: Cooperative Bindery Co., 1936), 56; *Congressional Record*, 75 Cong., 3 Sess. (1938), 6661; *The New York Times*, February 16, March 20, 1935; *Congressional Record*, 74 Cong., 1 Sess. (1935), 7354, 7432.

27. *Ibid.*, 74 Cong., 2 Sess. (1936), 10094–10095; 10170; 75 Cong., 3 Sess. (1938), 1717.

28. *The New York Times*, February 26, 1933.

29. *The New York Times*, April 5, 1936; *Congressional Record*, 75 Cong., 1 Sess. (1937), 744; Ragsdale, *We American Voters . . .*, 20, 24; Bealle, *Fugitive From A Brain Gang*, 150; Helen R. Whitely, "Madame La Secretary Perkins," *The American Mercury* (December, 1937), 426.

30. *Congressional Record*, 76 Cong., 1 Sess. (1939), 702–703, 1209.

31. *The New York Times*, January 3, 1938; *Congressional Record*, 74 Cong., 1 Sess. (1935), 6109; 75 Cong., 3 Sess. (1938), 2401; *The New York Times*, April 28, 1935; *Congressional Record*, 75 Cong., 3 Sess. (1938), 8000; 76 Cong. 1 Sess. (1939), 1542–1543, 3201; 74 Cong., 1 Sess. (1935), 234; *The New York Times*, November 26, 1938; *Anonymous letter* (Re: Morgenthau) to Roosevelt (n.d.), PPF 200–A, Roosevelt Papers; *Congressional Record*, 75 Cong., 3 Sess. (1938), 1223.

32. Bartholomew Dornblazer, "PIP: The Raw Deal Jackass" (Galesburg, Illinois, n.d.), Valentine Collection.

33. *The New York Times*, June 29, 1933.

34. Ragsdale, *We American Voters . . .*, 22–23; *Congressional Record*, 73 Cong., 2 Sess. (1934), 5632; 76 Cong., 1 Sess. (1939), 3538–3589; 74 Cong., 1 Sess. (1935), 1987; Albert W. Atwood, "Government by Professors," *Saturday Evening Post*, October 14, 1933, 88; *Congressional Record*, 74 Cong., 1 Sess. (1935), 11509; 74 Cong., 2 Sess. (1936), 7467; *The New York Times*, August 30, 1933.

35. *Congressional Record*, 73 Cong., 2 Sess. (1934), 10620; 74 Cong., 1 Sess. (1935), 11209.

36. *Congressional Record*, 74 Cong., 1 Sess. (1935), 7295.

37. E. C. Riegel, *Brain Trussed* (New York, n.d.), 2, 6.

38. *The New York Times*, July 7, 1934.

39. Quoted in *Congressional Record*, 73 Cong., 1 Sess. (1933), 3311.

40. *Congressional Record*, 74 Cong., 1 Sess. (1935), 234, 1209; 75 Cong., 3 Sess. (1938), 8526; Reeves, *Is All Well On The Potomac?*, 87.

41. *Congressional Record*, 73 Cong., 1 Sess. (1933), 2715, 6122; *The New York Times*, July 7, 1934.

42. *The New York Times*, April 21, 1934.

43. *Congressional Record*, 74 Cong., 1 Sess. (1935), 2301.

44. *Ibid.*, 841.

45. *Ibid.*, 74 Cong., 2 Sess. (1936), 8870.

46. *Ibid.*, 75 Cong., 3 Sess. (1938), 6781.

47. *Ibid.*, 76 Cong., 1 Sess. (1939), 2481, 3453, 3822.
48. *Congressional Record*, 74 Cong., 1 Sess. (1935), 7046, 11509; 73 Cong., 1 Sess. (1933), 4596; 74 Cong., 2 Sess. (1936), 8866.
49. *Congressional Record*, 73 Cong., 2 Sess. (1934), 11452–11453, 11460, 9834–9835, 11160.
50. *The New York Times*, June 13, 1934.

CHAPTER III: "THE JEW DEAL . . ."

1. John L. Spivak, *Secret Armies* (New York: Modern Age Books, Inc., 1939), 91–92.
2. *Congressional Record*, 73 Cong., 2 Sess. (1934), 8042–8043.
3. Copy of McFadden speech reprinted and distributed by Crusading Mothers of Pennsylvania, Colwyn, Pennsylvania, in Valentine Collection.
4. Deatherage to Roosevelt, September 10, 1934, PPF 200–A, Roosevelt Papers.
5. Quoted in Robert Edward Edmondson, "Roosevelt's Jewish Ancestry" (October 20, 1936), 1, Valentine Collection.
6. *The New York Times*, March 14, 1935.
7. Quoted in Edmondson, "Roosevelt's Jewish Ancestry" (October 20, 1936), 3, Valentine Collection.
8. Roy Tozier, *America's Little Hitlers* (Girard, Kansas: Haldeman-Julius Publications, 1940), 49.
9. Edmondson, "Blame the Rosenvelts" (March 15, 1934), a one-page circular, Valentine Collection; *Ibid.*, "Moe Roosevelt Wins" (March 5, 1936), a one-page circular, Valentine Collection.
10. *Liberation*, VIII (October 7, 1937), 3; George Sokolsky, "America Drifts Toward Fascism," *The American Mercury*, XXXII (July, 1934), 263; Martin Dies, *The Trojan Horse in America* (New York: Dodd, Mead and Co., 1940), 325; Christian Nationalist Crusade, "Roosevelt Jewish Ancestry" (1936), Valentine Collection; Quoted in Edmondson, "Roosevelt's Jewish Ancestry" (October 20, 1936), 1, Valentine Collection.
11. Franklin Thompson, *America's Ju-Deal* (New York: Community Press, 1935), 31.
12. Quoted in John Spivak, *Plotting America's Pogroms* (New York: New Masses, 1934), 12; *Saturday Evening Post*, CCXI (May 27, 1939), 72.
13. *Congressional Record*, 74 Cong., 1 Sess. (1935), 10073.
14. Donald S. Strong, *Organized Anti-Semitism in America* (Washington, D.C.: American Council on Public Affairs, 1941), 125; *Time*, August 24, 1936 (XXVIII), 40.
15. *Industrial Control Report* (March 21, 1936), copy in OF 1200, Roosevelt Papers.
16. Quoted in Strong, *Organized Anti-Semitism* . . . , 125.
17. Silver Shirt handbill, March, 1934, copy in OF 3206, Roosevelt Papers.
18. Quoted in Strong, *Organized Anti-Semitism* . . . , 155–156.
19. Paul W. Ward, "Washington Weekly," *The Nation*, November 7, 1936, 541; William Dudley Pelley, "The Final Stroke," *Liberation*, October 28, 1936, 2.
20. Edmondson, *The Government of the U.S. is not a Democracy but a Republic*, Edmondson Economic Service (October 20, 1936), pamphlet in Valentine Collection; *Ibid.*, *Roosevelt's Supreme Council* (February 25, 1936), Valentine Collection.

21. The Squire of Krum Elbow (pseud.), *Toward Armageddon* (Charleston, South Carolina: Militant Christian Association, c. 1936).
22. *Ibid.*
23. Silver Shirts of America, form letter, November 22, 1933, OF 3206, Roosevelt Papers.
24. *Ibid;* Quoted in Strong, *Organized Anti-Semitism* . . . , 160.
25. Pelley, *The Key to Crisis* (Asheville: Pelley Publishers, 1939), 28; *Ibid.,* *Hidden Empire* (Asheville: Pelley Publishers, c. 1938) n.p.; *Ibid., There Is A Jewish Conspiracy* . . . (Asheville: Pelley Publishers, c. 1939), n.p.
26. Jacob Thorkelson, *Is This Nation Ruled by Invisible Government?* (Asheville: Pelley Publishers, c.1939), n.p.; Gerald L. K. Smith, *My Fight For The Right* (St. Louis: Christian Nationalist Crusaders, n.d.), 8.
27. Quoted in Strong, *Organized Anti-Semitism* . . . , 82; Nathaniel Weyl, *Treason: The Story of Disloyalty and Betrayal in American History* (Washington: Public Affairs Press, 1950), 327; E. N. Sanctuary, "The New Deal is Marxian Sabotage" (c. 1939), Valentine Collection.
28. Edmondson, "Franklinstein Debt Bondage" (July 15, 1935), Valentine Collection.
29. *Ibid.,* "American Vigilante" (1939), Valentine Collection.
30. Squire of Krum Elbow (pseud.), "Mercury for Roosevelt Malady" (1936), editorial clipping in Valentine Collection.
31. *Ibid.,* "Roosevelt Buys Lehman Support in Blood," editorial from *Highland Post,* Ulster County, New York, July 10, 1936, Valentine Collection; Strong, *Organized Anti-Semitism* . . . , 55; Squire of Krum Elbow (pseud.), "Mercury for Roosevelt Malady" (1936), editorial clipping in Valentine Collection.
32. Olov E. Tietzow, *Aryan Americanism* (Chicago: The Author, 1937), 5–7, 14.
33. *Time,* November 12, 1934 (XXIV), 32–35; *Ibid.,* November 14, 1938 (XXXII), 37; Lloyd W. Eshleman, "The Truth About the Protocols," *Living Age,* CCCXLVII (December, 1934), 290–299.
34. Strong, *Organized Anti-Semitism* . . . , 73–74.
35. *The New York Times,* July 30, 1938.
36. Squire of Krum Elbow (pseud.), *Toward Armageddon,* 13–14, 16, 19, 27.
37. *The New York Times,* September 6, December 4, 1933; Strong, *Organized Anti-Semitism* . . . , 58.
38. *The New York Times,* January 1, 1934; Coughlin to Marvin McIntyre, March 21, 1934, OF 306, Roosevelt Papers; Charles E. Coughlin (ed.), *Quadragesimo Anno* (Detroit: Radio League of the Shrine of the Little Flower, 1933). For a brief but idolatrous summary of Coughlin's political and economic views see, Ruth Mugglebee, *Father Coughlin of the Shrine of the Little Flower* (Garden City, N.Y.: Garden City Publishing Co., 1933).
39. Coughlin to McIntyre (telegram), August, 1934, OF 306, Roosevelt Papers.
40. Alfred McClung Lee and Elizabeth Lee (eds.). The Institute of Propaganda Analysis, *The Fine Art of Propaganda: A Study of Father Coughlin's Speeches* (New York: Harcourt, Brace, 1939), 9; Coughlin to Kenton County Relief Committee, Covington, Kentucky, form letter, September, 1934, OF 306, Roosevelt Papers.
41. Coughlin to Ruth Ewing, form letter, February, 1935, OF 306, Roosevelt Papers; Memorandum, Howe to McIntyre, February 12, 1935, OF 306, Roosevelt Papers.

42. Mugglebee, *Father Coughlin* . . . , 343, 346–347; *The New York Times*, March 4, 1935.
43. *The New York Times*, March 5, 1935; *Congressional Record*, 74 Cong., 1 Sess. (1935), 2943.
44. *The New York Times*, March 12, 1935; Mugglebee, *Father Coughlin* . . . , 349–350.
45. *Ibid.*, 354.
46. *The New York Times*, April 25, April 27, 1935.
47. *The New York Times*, May 23, 1935.
48. Elliott Roosevelt (ed.), *F.D.R.: His Personal Letters* (New York: Duell, Sloan and Pearce, 1947–1950), I, 451; Quoted in Walter Johnson, *1600 Pennsylvania Avenue* (Boston: Little, Brown, 1960), 85.
49. *The New York Times*, November 18, 1935; *Time*, November 25, 1935 (XXVI), 13.
50. M. H. McIntyre, memorandum for the files, January 29, 1936, OF 306, Roosevelt Papers.
51. *The New York Times*, February 17, 1936; *Congressional Record*, 74 Cong., 2 Sess. (1936), 2220; O'Connor to Coughlin (telegram), February 16, 1936, OF 306, Roosevelt Papers.
52. Wallace Stegner, "The Radio Priest and His Flock," in Isabel Leighton (ed.), *The Aspirin Age, 1919–1941* (New York: Simon and Schuster, 1949), 244.
53. *The New York Times*, July 17, July 24, 1936.
54. *The New York Times*, September 26, October 26, 1936; William C. Kernan, *The Ghost of Royal Oak* (New York: Free Speech Forum, 1940), 105–106; Stegner, "The Radio Priest . . . ," 247; "Father Coughlin Out of Bounds," September, 1936, unidentified newspaper editorial, Valentine Collection.
55. *The New York Times*, July 30, 1936.
56. *Ibid.*, August 13, 1936.
57. *Ibid.*, August 11, August 16, 1936.
58. Herbert Harris, "That Third Party," *Current History*, XXXV (October, 1936), 85.
59. *The New York Times*, August 16, 1936.
60. Stegner, "The Radio Priest . . . ," 247; Strong, *Organized Anti-Semitism* . . . , 59.
61. Stegner, "The Radio Priest . . . ," 247.
62. George W. Naumburg, Jr., *Fascist America: As Exemplified by Charles Coughlin, William Pelley, James True and Gerald Winrod*, unpublished Honors Thesis, Harvard University, March 18, 1940; *Social Justice*, July 31, 1939; *The New York Times*, July 24, 1939.
63. Strong, *Organized Anti-Semitism* . . . , 59.
64. *Franklin D. Roosevelt Collector*, VI, No. 1 (May, 1954), 18.
65. *Congressional Record*, 74 Cong., 2 Sess. (1936), 10842.
66. Arthur M. Schlesinger, *Age of Roosevelt: The Politics of Upheaval* (Boston: Houghton Mifflin Co., 1960), 432; *Congressional Record*, 74 Cong., 2 Sess. (1936), 4041–4042; 75 Cong., 3 Sess. (1938), 2135.
67. Schlesinger, *The Politics of Upheaval*, 432–433.
68. *Ibid.*; Henry L. Moon, *Balance of Power: The Negro Vote* (Garden City, N.Y.: Doubleday, 1948), 38; *Congressional Record*, 76 Cong., 1 Sess. (1939), 4042.
69. *Congressional Record*, 75 Cong., 3 Sess. (1938), 895–896.
70. *Congressional Record*, 74 Cong., 2 Sess. (1936), 10780; Republican Na-

tional Committee, "Negro Balance of Power Should Support Alf Landon and Frank Knox" (1936), 5–7, Valentine Collection.

71. Quoted in Republican National Committee, "Negro Balance of Power . . . . ," 15.

72. Moon, *Balance of Power: The Negro Vote*, 37; Philadelphia *Tribune*, The Time is Not Ripe," editorial, September 3, 1936, OF 93, Roosevelt Papers.

73. Rossyln (Virginia) *Chronicle*, January or February, 1936, an editorial reprint, PPF 200–A, Roosevelt Papers.

74. Hamilton Basso, "Our Gene," *The New Republic*, LXXXVI (February 19, 1936), 37.

75. Quoted in Ralph Roy, *Apostles of Discord* (Boston: Beacon Press, 1953), 68.

76. *Time*, April 27, 1936 (XXVII), 10–11.

77. Strong, *Organized Anti-Semitism* . . . , 165, 125–126; Squire of Krum Elbow (pseud.), "Roosevelt Buys Lehman Support in Blood," editorial from *Highland Post*, Ulster County, New York, July 10, 1936, Valentine Collection.

CHAPTER IV: . . . AND THE RED DEAL

1. *The New York Times*, September 9, 1934.

2. *Ibid.*, September 10, 1934; James True Associates, *Industrial Control Report* (May 26, 1934), copy in OF 1200, Roosevelt Papers.

3. Gerald B. Winrod, *Communism and the Roosevelt Brain Trust* (Wichita: Defender Publishers, Kansas, 1933), 7.

4. Elizabeth Dilling, *The Red Network: A "Who's Who" and Handbook of Radicalism for Patriots* (Chicago: The Author, 1934), 82.

5. *Ibid.*, 74, 79–80, 91.

6. Quoted in Weyl, *Treason: The Story of Disloyalty* . . . , 321.

7. Crusaders for Economic Liberty, form letter (1934), OF 950, Roosevelt Papers.

8. Christians to Crusader White Shirts, form letter (1934), OF 950, Roosevelt Papers.

9. Silver Shirts of America, form letter (December, 1934), OF 3206, Roosevelt Papers.

10. *Congressional Record*, 76 Cong., 1 Sess. (1939), 3631–3632.

11. *Congressional Record*, 73 Cong., 2 Sess. (1934), 11108.

12. *The New York Times*, September 7, 1934.

13. Special Committee on Un-American Activities. Investigation of Nazi Propaganda Activities, *Hearings*, 73 Cong., 2 Sess. (1934), 215–259.

14. *Congressional Record*, 76 Cong., 1 Sess. (1939), 1118; *The New York Times*, May 18, 1934.

15. *Ibid.*

16. Committee on Un-American Activities. Investigation of Un-American Propaganda Activities in the United States, *Extract from Hearings* 75 Cong., 3 Sess. (1938), 1–402.

17. House Committee on Interstate and Foreign Commerce. Stock Exchange Regulation, *Hearings*, 73 Cong., 2 Sess. (1934), 763–773.

18. *The New York Times*, April 11, 18, 1934.

19. William A. Wirt, no title, unpublished manuscript (March, 1934), copy in OF 965, Roosevelt Papers; William A. Wirt, *America Must Lose* (New York: Committee for the Nation, 1934), 3, 23.

20. Walter Winchell to James A. Farley, telegram, March 27, 1934, OF 965, Roosevelt Papers; *The New York Times*, March 29, April 6, 1934.
21. *The New York Times*, March 25, 1934.
22. *The New York Times*, April 3, 1934.
23. *Ibid.*
24. *The New York Times*, March 25, 1934.
25. Select Committee to Investigate Charges Made by Dr. William A. Wirt, *Hearings*, 73 Cong., 2 Sess. (1934).
26. "Calendar of Controversy," *Forum and Century*, XCI (June, 1934), 348.
27. *The New York Times*, April 11, 13, 1934.
28. "Winding Up the Wirt Case," *Literary Digest*, CXVII (April 28, 1934), 8; *Literary Digest*, CXVII (April 7, 1934), 10.
29. Schlesinger, *The Coming of the New Deal*, 460.
30. M. A. Crowley to Augustine Lonergan, February 2, 1935, OF 263, Roosevelt Papers; *Congressional Record*, 74 Cong., 1 Sess. (1935), 9822–9824.
31. *Ibid.*, 7939, 8753, 9539.
32. League for Constitutional Government, *International "New" Dealism* (1936), Valentine Collection; *Congressional Record*, 74 Cong., 1 Sess. (1935), 9277–9279; League for Constitutional Government, *The Genesis of the "New Deal" with Some Revelations* (1936), Valentine Collection.
33. Roosevelt to Homer Cummings, memorandum with pamphlet attached, August 7, 1935, PPF 1848, Roosevelt Papers; *Congressional Record*, 74 Cong., 1 Sess. (1935), 10332.
34. *The New York Times*, September 16, 1935.
35. *The New York Times*, December 12, 1935.
36. OF (Talmadge), April 18, 1935, Roosevelt Papers; *The New York Times*, IV, April 21, 1935.
37. *The New York Times*, April 23, 25, 26, May 18, October 10, 1935; OF (Talmadge), press interview, April 22, 1935, Roosevelt Papers.
38. *The New York Times*, September 1, November 6, December 1, IV, 1935.
39. Wolfskill, *The Revolt of the Conservatives*, 175–177; *The New York Times*, September 11, 1936.
40. Percy Crosby, *Defense of Administration Against the Charges of the Russian Ambassador* (1935), 8–14, pamphlet in Valentine Collection; Crosby, *Three Cheers for the Red, Red and Red* (McLean, Virginia: Freedom Press, 1936).
41. Crosby, *Essay on Roosevelt's Second Inaugural Address* (1937), 6–7, 32, 41, pamphlet in Valentine Collection.
42. Crosby, *Would Communism Work Out in America?* (McLean, Virginia: Freedom Press, 1938), 307. *Ibid.*, 12.
43. *The New York Times*, September 7, 1936.
44. McCoy, *Angry Voices*, 132–133, 149.
45. Gerald L. K. Smith, newspaper clipping, PPF 200–A, Roosevelt Papers; Herbert Harris, "That Third Party," *Current History*, XLV (October, 1936), 83; *The New York Times*, May 29, June 1, 1936; Gerald L. K. Smith, *Too Much and Too Many Roosevelts* (1950), 54, Valentine Collection.
46. *Ibid.*, *Too Much Roosevelt* (Detroit, 1940), 7, 21, Valentine Collection; Herbert Harris, "That Third Party," *Current History*, XLV (October, 1936), 85.
47. Quoted in Roy, *Apostles of Discord*, 69; Selden Rodman, "God's Angry Men," *Common Sense*, V (September, 1936), 11.

48. *The New York Times*, October 21, 1936; Herbert Harris, "That Third Party," *Current History*, XLV (October, 1936), 90.

49. Abraham Holtzman, *The Townsend Movement: A Study in Old Age Pressure Politics* (unpublished doctoral dissertation, Harvard University, 1952), 453.

50. Stanley High to Stephen Early, August 29, 1935, OF 1542, Roosevelt Papers.

51. Martin F. Smith to James A. Farley, October 21, 1935, OF 1542, Roosevelt Papers; Holtzman, *The Townsend Movement . . .* , 453, footnote 5.

52. Francis Townsend, *New Horizons* (Chicago: J. L. Stewart Publishing Co., 1943), 202.

53. Holtzman, *The Townsend Movement . . .* , 456; *The New York Times*, May 31, June 2, 23, 1936.

54. Holtzman, *The Townsend Movement . . .* , 464–465; *Congressional Record*, 75 Cong., 3 Sess. (1938), 4052; George W. Baker to Marvin McIntyre, October 8, 1936, OF 1542, Roosevelt Papers; *The New York Times*, October 12, 1936.

55. Luther Whiteman and S. L. Lewis, *Glory Roads* (New York: Crowell, 1936), 141; Harris, "That Third Party," *Current History*, XLV (October, 1936). 84.

56. Elizabeth Dilling, *The Roosevelt Red Record* (Chicago: The Author, 1936), 439.

57. Milton S. Mayer, "Mrs. Dilling: Lady of the Red Network," *American Mercury*, XLVII (July, 1939), 293, 295–297; *The New York Times*, June 10, 1936; George Seldes, *Witch Hunt: The Technique and Profits of Redbaiting* (New York, 1940), 157.

58. Quoted in Mayer, "Mrs. Dilling: . . . ," *American Mercury*, XLVII (July, 1939), 294.

59. Dilling, *The Roosevelt Red Record*, 5.

60. *Ibid.*, 3, 26–27, 350.

61. E. N. Sanctuary, *Is the New Deal Communistic?* (c. 1936), 3, Valentine Collection; Quoted in L. M. Birkhead, "Father Coughlin, Self-Condemned" (c. 1939), Valentine Collection.

62. E. N. Sanctuary, "Deceive! Confuse! Collapse! Dictate!" (1936), broadside in Valentine Collection.

63. *Ibid.*, *Revolution and The Real Fifth Column* (New York: n.p., 1940), Valentine Collection.

64. Quoted in Norman Thomas, *What's Behind the Christian Front?* (1939), pamphlet of the Socialist Party of New York, 15, Valentine Collection; Morris Schonbach, *Native Fascism During the 1930's and 1940's* (unpublished doctoral dissertation, University of California at Los Angeles, 1958), 192–193.

65. Pelley, "The President Is Not So Big That He Can't Be Impeached," *The New Liberation*, VII (August 21, 1937), 5; *Ibid.*, "Make John Garner U.S. President," *The New Liberation*, VII (August 21, 1937), 1, Valentine Collection.

66. *Ibid.*, *Indians Aren't Red! The Inside Story of the Administration's Attempt to Make Communists of the North Carolina Cherokees* (1938), pamphlet in the Valentine Collection.

67. *Congressional Record*, 76 Cong., 1 Sess. (1939), 1125–1126.

68. Harrison F. McConnell, *The President Knows* (1938), 2, 41, pamphlet in the Valentine Collection.

69. *Congressional Record*, 76 Cong., 1 Sess. (1939), 1125.

70. Martin Dies, *The Trojan Horse in America*; for a detailed analysis of the Dies investigation, see August Raymond Ogden, *The Dies Committee: A Study of the Special House Committee for the Investigation of Un-American Activities* (Washington: The Catholic University of America Press, 1945).

71. Christian American Patriots to Roosevelt, February 16, 1938, PPF 200-A, Roosevelt Papers; Martin Luther Thomas, *Shall Communism Take Over the U.S.A.?* (1939), 1, pamphlet in the Valentine Collection; William C. Kernan, *The Ghost of Royal Oak*, 59–60.

72. David Milton Proctor, *Riding High* (Kansas City, Missouri: Brown Publishing Company, 1939), 128.

73. House Committee on Un-American Activities. Investigation of Un-American Propaganda Activities . . . , *Hearings*, 76 Cong., 1 Sess. (1939), 3271–3284, 3343–3384.

74. *Ibid.*, 3455–3543.

75. *Ibid.*

76. *The New York Times*, June 1, 1939; House Committee on Un-American Activities. Investigation of Un-American Propaganda Activities . . . , *Hearings*, 76 Cong., 1 Sess. (1939), 3545–3703.

77. *Congressional Record*, 76 Cong., 1 Sess. (1939), 6606.

78. *Ibid.*

CHAPTER V: THE DEVOTED WALL STREET LACKEY

1. Eric F. Goldman, *Rendezvous with Destiny* (New York: Knopf, 1958), 352.

2. William Z. Foster, *The Words and Deeds of Franklin D. Roosevelt* (New York: National Election Campaign Committee, Communist Party, U.S.A., 1932).

3. Irving Howe and Lewis Coser, *The American Communist Party; A Critical History (1919–1957)* (Boston: Beacon Press, 1957), 180–86.

4. *Ibid.*, 189; Earl Browder, *What Is the New Deal?* (New York: Workers Library Publishers, 1933), 2; Benjamin Gitlow, *The Whole of Their Lives* (New York: Scribners, 1948), 255; Eugene Lyons, *The Red Decade; the Stalinist Penetration of America* (Indianapolis: Bobbs-Merrill, 1941), 301; Anna Rochester, *Your Dollar Under Roosevelt* (New York: Workers Library Publishers, 1933), 6; *Daily Worker*, Jan. 2, 1935.

5. Harold J. Laski, quoted in Schlesinger, *Politics of Upheaval*, 172.

6. Rochester, *Your Dollar* . . . , 6; Benjamin Stolberg and Warren Jay Vinton, *The Economic Consequences of the New Deal* (New York: Harcourt, Brace, 1935), 11, 85.

7. Israel Amter, *Industrial Slavery—Roosevelt's New Deal* (New York: Workers Library Publishers, 1933); Earl Browder, *Communism in the United States* (London: Martin Lawrence, Ltd., n.d.), 14; William O. Thompson and Mary Van Kleech, *The NRA from Within* [and] Earl Browder, *The Communist Position*. International Pamphlets, No. 41 (New York: International Publishers, 1934), 20.

8. Gil Green, *Youth Confronts the Blue Eagle* (New York: Young Worker, 1933), 3.

9. "Opposition Labor Conference Against Industrial Recovery Bill," brochure, August 1933, OF 263 (Communism), Roosevelt Papers.

10. *Ibid.*

11. Alex Bittleman, "The New Deal and the Old Deal," *The Communist*, XIII (January 1934), 86; Abe Bluestein, *Forgotten Men, What Now?* (Bronx, New York: Libertarian Publishers, n.d.), n.p.
12. Bittleman, "The New Deal . . . ," 86; Israel Amter, *Working Class: Unity or Fascism* (New York: Communist Party, U.S.A., New York District, 1935), 3.
13. Howe and Coser, *The American Communist . . .* , 190.
14. Earl Browder, *The People's Front* (New York: International Publishers, 1938), 12–13.
15. Howe and Coser, *The American Communist . . .* , 332.
16. Schlesinger, *Politics of Upheaval*, 180.
17. *Ibid.*, 177; Murray B. Seidler, *Norman Thomas, Respectable Rebel* (Syracuse, New York: Syracuse University Press, 1961), 76.
18. *Ibid.*, 107.
19. David A. Shannon, *The Socialist Party of America; A History* (New York: Macmillan, 1955), 213; Donald M. McCoy, *Angry Voices: Left-of-Center Politics in the New Deal Era* (Lawrence: University of Kansas Press, 1958), 4.
20. Schlesinger, *Politics of Upheaval*, 179; "The Failure of the Socialist Party" *Common Sense* (October, 1934), quoted by Schlesinger, *Politics of Upheaval*, 179.
21. Schlesinger, *Politics of Upheaval*, 180.
22. Norman Thomas, *Is the New Deal Socialist?* (New York: Socialist Party of America, 1936), 4; Norman Thomas, *After the New Deal, What?* (New York: Macmillan, 1936), 17.
23. *The New York Times*, July 5, 1934; February 26, 1936; July 11, 1936; Thomas, *Is the New Deal Socialist?*, 5.
24. Norman Thomas, *The Choice Before Us: Mankind at the Crossroads* (New York: Macmillan, 1934), 124; *The New York Times*, June 18, 1933; October 7, 1935.
25. Thomas, *The Choice Before Us . . .* , 164.
26. D. P. Berenberg, "Pie in the Sky," *American Socialist Quarterly*, March, 1935, quoted in Schlesinger, *Politics of Upheaval*, 179; Thomas, *The Choice Before Us . . .* , 164; Norman Thomas, *A Socialist Looks at the New Deal* (Chicago: The League for Industrial Democracy, 1933), 5.
27. *The New York Times*, June 12, June 18, 1933; N. Thomas to Rhoda E. McCulloch, January 25, 1934, quoted by Siedler, *Norman Thomas . . .* , 116–17.
28. *The New York Times*, June 18, 1933; June 3, 1934.
29. Shannon, *The Socialist Party . . .* , 229.
30. Norman Thomas, quoted in Schlesinger, *Politics of Upheaval*, 180; Norman Thomas, *Why Did NRA Go Wrong?* (New York: Socialist Party of America, 1934); *The New York Times*, June 18, 1933.
31. Thomas, *A Socialist Looks at the New Deal*, 14; Thomas, *The Choice Before Us*, quoted in *The New York Times*, March 27, 1934.
32. N. Thomas to H. Wallace, February 22, 1934, quoted in Shannon *The Socialist Party . . .* , 231; Siedler, *Norman Thomas . . .* , 2.
33. *The New York Times*, February 25, 1935; Shannon, *The Socialist Party . . .* , 232.
34. H. L. Mitchell, "Letter to the Editor," *The Nation*, CXLII (February 12, 1936), 184; H. L. Mitchell and J. R. Butler, "The Cropper Learns His Fate," *The Nation*, CXLI (September 18, 1935), 328–329; "National Affairs: Secession," *Time*, March 20, 1939 (XXXIII), 15.

35. *What Roosevelt Did for Us* (Chicago: Labor League for Thomas-Nelson, 1936).
36. Thomas, *The Choice Before Us,* 7.
37. McCoy, *Angry Voices* . . . , 4.
38. *Ibid.,* 37; Schlesinger, *Politics of Upheaval,* 144; "Social Control vs. the Constitution," *The New Republic,* LXIII (June 12, 1935), 118.
39. *Common Sense* (August, 1933), 27, quoted in McCoy, *Angry Voices* . . . , 37; Schlesinger, *Politics of Upheaval,* 145.
40. McCoy, *Angry Voices* . . . , 39.
41. "An Open Letter to President Roosevelt," *Common Sense,* II (March, 1933), 23.
42. Alfred M. Bingham and Selden Rodman (eds.), *Challenge to the New Deal* (New York: Falcon Press, 1934), 4; Alfred M. Bingham, *Insurgent America; Revolt of the Middle Class* (New York: Harpers, 1935), 184–85; "Franklin Delano Roosevelt," *Common Sense,* III (September, 1934), 4; "1936 Is the Time," *Common Sense,* V (April, 1936), 3; "How Shall I Vote?" *Common Sense,* V (October, 1936), 3.
43. Robert S. Allen, "Roosevelt: Talk Tough, Tread Softly," *Common Sense,* III (September, 1934), 9; "Franklin Delano Roosevelt," *Common Sense,* III (September, 1934), 4.
44. McCoy, *Angry Voices* . . . , 47, 52–53.
45. *Ibid.,* 54–55; Schlesinger, *Politics of Upheaval,* 99.
46. McCoy, *Angry Voices* . . . , 79–81.
47. Floyd Olson, "Why a New National Party?" *Common Sense,* V (January, 1936), 6.
48. "1936 Is the Time," *Common Sense,* V (April, 1936), 2; "How Shall I Vote?" *Common Sense,* V (October, 1936), 3; Schlesinger, *Politics of Upheaval,* 104.
49. Russel B. Nye, *Midwestern Progressive Politics* (East Lansing, Michigan: Michigan State University, 1959), 338–39.
50. *Common Sense,* VI (January, 1937), 24; *The New York Times,* October 15, 1936.
51. McCoy, *Angry Voices* . . . , 158–162, 181.
52. Eric Goldman, *Rendezvous* . . . , 345.
53. Schlesinger, *Politics of Upheaval,* 593.
54. Wayne S. Cole, *America First; The Battle Against Intervention, 1940–41* (Madison: University of Wisconsin, 1953), 215; William E. Leuchtenburg, *Franklin D. Roosevelt and the New Deal, 1932–1940* (New York: Harper, 1963), 189.
55. "Frankie and Johnny," *The New Republic,* CII (February 5, 1940), 181; Maxwell C. Raddock, *Portrait of an American Labor Leader: William L. Hutcheson* (New York: American Institute of Social Science, Inc., 1955), 212–213.
56. "The Nation: Hot to Cool to Cold," *Literary Digest,* CXXIV (July 24, 1937), 7; *The New York Times,* September 4, 1937.
57. "Congress Swan Song: Lewis Blast at Garner Spurs Revolt Against New Deal," *Newsweek,* August 7, 1939 (XIV), 16.
58. Eldorous L. Dayton, *Walter Reuther, The Autocrat of the Bargaining Table* (New York: Devin-Adair, 1958), 123.
59. "Labor's Lewis Condemns Roosevelt . . . ," *Life,* November 4, 1940 (IX), 32.
60. William H. Riker, *The C.I.O. in Politics, 1936–1946,* unpublished Ph.D. dissertation, (Boston: Harvard University, 1948), 179.

61. Max Lerner, "What Is Usable in Veblen?" *The New Republic*, LXXXIII (May 15, 1935), 10.
62. John Strachey, "To Explain—Or To Change," *New Masses*, XX (January 22, 1935), quoted in Schlesinger, *Politics of Upheaval*, 175.

CHAPTER VI: A TRAITOR TO HIS CLASS

1. "Mr. Roosevelt's Men," *Fortune*, IX (April, 1934), 91; Raskob to FDR, April 4, 1933, quoted in Schlesinger, *Coming of the New Deal*, 424; John T. Flynn, "Other People's Money," *The New Republic*, LXXXV (December 11, 1935), 129; *The New York Times*, May 3, 1933.
2. *Time*, September 24, 1934 (XXIV), 57.
3. Frederick Lewis Allen, *Since Yesterday* (New York: Harper, 1940), 162.
4. *The New York Times*, November 11, December 1, 31, 1934; March 14, 25, 1935.
5. *Time*, October 29, 1934 (LIV), 24.
6. Thomas L. Stokes, *Chip Off My Shoulder* (Princeton: Princeton University Press, 1940), 364–65.
7. Anonymous, *Surplus Prophets* (New York: Viking Press, 1936), 9, 47, 52, 63.
8. Joseph Stagg Lawrence, "Can the New Deal Succeed?", *Review of Reviews*, LXXXIX (March, 1934), 24.
9. Glenn Frank, *America's Hour of Decision* (New York: McGraw-Hill, 1934), 84; *The New York Times*, October 31, 1933.
10. Frank Kent, *Without Grease, Political Behavior, 1934-1936 and A Blueprint for America's Most Vital Presidential Election* (New York: Morrow, 1936), 36; Raoul Desvernine, *Democratic Despotism* (New York: Dodd, Mead, 1936), 1958;"Smilin' Through!", *Saturday Evening Post*, CCVII (September 22, 1934), 22; C. M. Chester, "Business—The Guinea Pig," *Vital Speeches of the Day*, I (June 17, 1935), 609.
11. *The New York Times*, May 26, 1939.
12. Merle Thorpe, "Speculating Upon Speculation," *Nation's Business*, XXII (May, 1934), 11; John E. Dowsing, *The New Deal—Shadow or Substance* (New York: The Author, 1938), 5.
13. *The New York Times*, February 13, 1934; Herbert Hoover, *The Challenge To Liberty* (New York: Scribners, 1934), 115.
14. James P. Warburg, *The Money Muddle* (New York: Doubleday, 1934); James P. Warburg, *Hell Bent For Election* (New York: Doubleday, 1935), 67; James P. Warburg, *Still Hell Bent* (New York: Doubleday, 1936).
15. Ralph W. Robey, *Roosevelt vs. Recovery* (New York: Harper, 1934).
16. Ogden L. Mills, *What of Tomorrow?* (New York: Macmillan, 1935); Ogden L. Mills, *Liberalism Fights On* (New York: Macmillan, 1936); Ogden L. Mills, *The Seventeen Million* (New York: Macmillan, 1937).
17. Mills, *Liberalism Fights On*, 67.
18. Howard E. Kershner, *The Menace of Roosevelt and His Policies* (New York: Greenberg, 1936); William MacDonald, *The Menace of Recovery; What the New Deal Means* (New York: Macmillan, 1934).
19. Ralph Thompson, "Books of the Times," *The New York Times*, June 27, 1936.
20. Isaac Lippincott, *Sold Out* (New York: Appleton-Century, 1936); Raoul Desvernine, *Democratic Despotism*.

21. Frank Knox, *We Planned It That Way* (New York: Longmans Green, 1938), vii, 14, 21.
22. Howard Wolf, *Greener Pastures* (Caldwell, Idaho: Caxton Printers, 1936).
23. Anonymous, *Frankie in Wonderland* (New York: E. P. Dutton, 1934).
24. Porter L. Ferguson and C. Harold Hopkins, *Rebirth of the Nation; or, What's to Become Of Us?* (Los Angeles: The Fred Henson Co., 1936).
25. Russell Moore, *Roosevelt Riddles* (Garden City: Doubleday, Doran, 1936).
26. John C. Bell, Jr., *What Do You Know About The New Deal?* (Wilmington, Delaware: The Star Publishing Company, 1934).
27. David Lawrence, *Stumbling into Socialism; and the Future of Our Political Parties* (New York: Appleton-Century, 1935).
28. Earl Reeves, ed., *The Truth About the New Deal* (New York: Longmans Green, 1936); Clayton Rand, *ABRACADABRA, or One Democrat to Another* (Newark: Press of the Kells, 1936); Fred R. Marvin, *Fools Gold* (New York: Madison and Marshall, Inc., 1936), 2–3; George Harrington, *Horse and Buggy Days Are Here Again* (Boston: Bruce Humphries, 1936), 5.
29. Frank Kent, *Without Grease . . .* , 36; Gertrude M. Coogan, *Money Creators: Who Creates Money? Who Should Create It?* (Chicago: Sound Money Press, 1935), 3; "Smilin' Through," *Saturday Evening Post,* CCVII (September 22, 1934), 22; Hugh S. Johnson, "Think Fast, Captain," *Saturday Evening Post,* CCVIII (October 26, 1935), 7, 85; *The New York Times* February 13, 1934.
30. *The New York Times,* April 11, September 18, 1934; October 4, 1935.
31. Harold Lord Varney, "Are the Capitalists Asleep?" *American Mercury,* XXXVII (March, 1936), 266; Edwin W. Kemmerer, "The Consequences of Inflation," *American Mercury,* XXXVIII (July, 1936), 265; A. B. Magil and Henry Stevens, *The Peril of Fascism: The Crisis of American Democracy* (New York: International Publishers, 1938), 97; *Time,* February 3, 1936 (XXVII), 14, Virgil Jordan, quoted in address by Robert L. Lund, President of NAM, clipping in PPF 8246, Roosevelt Papers; Hoover *The Challenge to Liberty,* 88; "Roosevelt Again Takes the Reins," *The Literary Digest,* CXVII (April 28, 1934), 6.
32. David Lawrence, *Stumbling into Socialism,* 5; *The New York Times* October 21, 1933; November 3, 1934.
33. J. Howard Rhodes, "Watch Your Step, Americans!" *National Republic,* XXIV (August, 1936), 32; *The New York Times,* May 25, 1934; April 26, 1935; Bainbridge Colby, address, November 2, 1936, PPF 876, Roosevelt Papers.
34. *The New York Times,* June 5, 1935; Merle Thorpe, "New Labels on Old Bottles," *Nation's Business,* XXIII (July, 1935), 53; Lewis Douglas quoted in Schlesinger, *Politics of Upheaval,* 515.
35. *Ware Wolf!* by an original member of the National Committee to Uphold Constitutional Government (n.p., n.d.), 33, Valentine Collection.
36. *The New York Times,* April 23, 1935.
37. Harry Woodring, quoted in Schlesinger, *Coming of the New Deal,* 339; John T. Flynn, "Other People's Money," *The New Republic,* LXXXVIII (October 28, 1936), 350.
38. Magil and Stevens, *Peril of Fascism . . .* , 97–98.
39. *The New York Times,* November 20, 1935.
40. Rinehart J. Swenson, "The Chamber of Commerce and the New Deal,"

Annals of the American Academy of Political and Social Sciences, CLXXIX (May, 1935), 136.

41. "Chamber of Commerce Weighs the New Deal," *Scholastic,* XXIV (May 19, 1934), 20; Swenson, "The Chamber of Commerce . . . ," 136.
42. "Chamber of Commerce: Organized Business and White House Draw Apart . . . ," *Newsweek,* May 11, 1935 (V), 5–6; *The New York Times,* May 3, 1935.
43. New York Chamber of Commerce, leaflet, March 3, 1934, PPF 200-A, Roosevelt Papers; *The New York Times,* September 26, November 26, 1935.
44. "Business and Finance," *Time,* May 11, 1936 (XXVII), 74.
45. *The New York Times,* May 25, 1934; "Manufacturers: Industry's Forces United," *Newsweek,* December 15, 1934 (IV), 38.
46. *The New York Times,* December 6, 15, 1935; Magil and Stevens, *Peril of Fascism . . . ,* 97–98.
47. "Business and Finance," *Time,* May 11, 1936 (XXVII), 73–74.
48. "Chamber of Commerce . . . ," *Newsweek,* May 11, 1936 (V), 6.
49. Wolfskill, *Revolt of the Conservatives . . . ,* 22.
50. *Ibid.,* 22, 25.
51. "Liberty League . . . ," *Newsweek,* September 1, 1934 (IV), 6.
52. George Smith May, *Ultra-Conservative Thought in the United States in the 1920's and 1930's,* unpublished Ph.D. dissertation (Ann Arbor: University of Michigan, 1954), 132.
53. "Liberty League . . . ," *Newsweek,* September 1, 1934 (IV), 5.
54. Wolfskill, *Revolt of the Conservatives . . . ,* 63, 65–66.
55. Schlesinger, *Politics of Upheaval,* 518; Wolfskill *Revolt of the Conservatives . . . ,* 137.
56. *Ibid.,* 62, 139.
57. Oswald Garrison Villard, "Al Smith—Latest Phase," *American Mercury,* XXXIV (February, 1935), 148.
58. Wolfskill, *Revolt of the Conservatives . . . ,* 15, 151–52.
59. *The New York Times,* March 22, 1936.
60. Schlesinger, *Politics of Upheaval,* 521; "Topics of the Day," *The Literary Digest,* CXXI (February 8, 1936), 5.
61. Wolfskill, *Revolt of the Conservatives . . . ,* 241; John Henry Kirby, quoted in May, "*Ultra-Conservative . . . ,*" 74.
62. "National Affairs," *Time,* February 10, 1936 (XXVII), 5.
63. "Topics of the Day," *The Literary Digest,* CXXI (February 8, 1936), 5.
64. Schlesinger, *Politics of Upheaval,* 642.
65. *The New York Times,* February 15, 1937.
66. *Ibid.,* February 27, 1938.
67. Statement of National Committee to Uphold Constitutional Government, March, 1938, OF (Gannett), Roosevelt Papers.
68. *Time,* June 15, 1936 (XXVII), 63–64.
69. "You Pay," broadside issued by the Independent Coalition of American Women (n.d.), Valentine Collection; *The New York Times,* June 19, September 11, 1938.
70. Paul W. Ward, "Washington Weekly," *The Nation,* CXLIII (November 7, 1936), 540.
71. Frederick A. Ogg, "Does America Need a Dictator?" *Current History,* XXXVI (September 1932), 641–648.
72. Wolfskill, *Revolt of the Conservatives . . . ,* 85–86.
73. Special House Committee on Un-American Activities, *Investigation of*

Nazi Propaganda Activities and Investigation of Certain Other Propaganda Activities: Final Report, February 15, 1935.

CHAPTER VII: ALL THE NEWS THAT'S FIT TO PRINT

1. Edgar Kemler, *The Irreverent Mr. Mencken*, 270; Henry L. Mencken, *Prejudices: Sixth Series* (New York: Knopf, 1927), 14, 15, 27.
2. Kemler, *The Irreverent Mr. Mencken*, 271–72.
3. H. L. Mencken to Louis Untermeyer, November 9, 1933, in *Letters of H. L. Mencken*, selected by Guy J. Forgue (New York: Knopf, 1961), 351; H. L. Mencken to Ezra Pound, November 26, 1932 in *Letters . . .*, 352.
4. Charles Angoff, *H. L. Mencken; A Portrait from Memory* (New York: Yoseloff, 1956), 132.
5. Kemler, *The Irreverent Mr. Mencken*, 269.
6. Angoff, *H. L. Mencken . . .*, 132; H. L. Mencken, *On Politics: A Carnival of Buncombe*, edited by Malcolm Moos (Baltimore: Johns Hopkins, 1956), 298, 312; *Current History*, August, 1934, quoted in *The New York Times*, July 22, 1934.
7. Leo C. Rosten, *The Washington Correspondents* (New York: Harcourt Brace, 1937), 281.
8. Stanley Walker, *City Editor* (New York: Frederich A. Stokes, 1934), 222.
9. S. W. Adams to FDR, July 17, 1933 in PPF-200-A, Roosevelt Papers.
10. "The Press and the Campaign," *The New Republic*, LXXXVII (July 22, 1936), 311; *The New York Times*, September 2, 1934; John K. Winkler, *William Randolph Hearst; A New Appraisal* (New York: Hastings House, 1955), 259–60.
11. George Seldes, *One Thousand Americans* (New York: Boni and Gaer, 1947), 44–45.
12. *U.S. Supreme Court Reports*, 81 Law Ed., 953–65 (301 U.S. 103–141).
13. Franklin D. Roosevelt, *The Public Papers and Addresses of Franklin D. Roosevelt*, compiled by Samuel I. Rosenman, 13 vols. (New York: Random House, 1938–50), III, 384–389.
14. George Michael, *Handout* (New York: Putnam's Sons, 1935), vii.
15. Samuel G. Blythe, "Ferment," *Saturday Evening Post*, CCVII (May 11, 1935), 5; Frank R. Kent, *Without Gloves* (New York: Morrow, 1934), 28; *The New York Times*, January 12, 1938; E. Pendleton Herring, "Official Publicity Under the New Deal," *The Annals of the American Academy of Political Science*, CLXXIX (May, 1935), 171–72; Albert W. Atwood, "The Great Propaganda Machine," *Saturday Evening Post*, CCVII (June 15, 1935), 23.
16. Bernarr Macfadden, "The Dole—A Great Calamity," *Liberty*, X (July 29, 1933), 4.
17. John Tebbel, *An American Dynasty; The Story of the McCormicks, Medills, and Pattersons* (Garden City: Doubleday, 1947), 238; Evelyn Harvey, "The Unbudgeted Cost of Relief," *Saturday Evening Post*, CCVII (February 16, 1935), 23; "The Sugar Bowl," *Saturday Evening Post*, CCVI (February 3, 1934), 22.
18. Schlesinger, *The Coming of the New Deal*, 277.
19. Donald S. Howard, *The WPA and Federal Relief Policy* (New York: Russell Sage Foundation, 1943), 154–55.
20. Tebbel, *American Dynasty . . .*, 151.

21. "This Way Recovery," *Saturday Evening Post*, CCVII (March 23, 1935), 26.

22. "Is Roosevelt Slipping," *The New Republic*, LXXXV (August 6, 1935), 22; "The Spirit of Prodigality," *Saturday Evening Post*, CCVIII (November 23, 1935), 22; *The New York Times*, April 2, 1939.

23. *The New York Times*, April 8, 1936.

24. H. L. Mencken, "Bringing Roosevelt Up To Date," *American Mercury*, XLVI (March, 1939), 260.

25. J. T. Flynn, "Other People's Money," *The New Republic*, LXXXI (January 9, 1935), 245.

26. Lawrence Dennis, "The Planless Roosevelt Revolution," *American Mercury*, XXXI (July, 1934), 1, 11; H. L. Mencken, "Notes on the New Deal," *Current History*, XL (August, 1934), 527.

27. *The New York Times*, May 10, 1934.

28. Stephen Early, "Below the Belt," *Saturday Evening Post*, CCXI (June 10, 1939), 7.

29. H. L. Mencken, "Three Years of Dr. Roosevelt," *American Mercury*, XXXVII (March, 1936), 257.

30. Angoff, *H. L. Mencken* . . . , 132–33; William Manchester, *Disturber of the Peace; The Life of H. L. Mencken*, with an introduction by Gerald W. Johnson (New York: Harper, 1951), 282–83.

31. *Ibid.*, 283, 335; H. L. Mencken, "Three Years of Dr. Roosevelt," *American Mercury*, XXXVII (March, 1936), 263–64.

32. Schlesinger, *Politics of Upheaval*, 526; *Toronto Globe and Empire*, 1938, clipping in PPF 210-A, Roosevelt Papers.

33. "The Great Illusion," *Saturday Evening Post*, CCVI (April 7, 1934), 24–25; Washington *Herald*, May 15, 1934, reprinted in *Congressional Record*, 73 Cong., 1 Sess. (1934), 9585.

34. New York *Evening Post*, August 1, 1934, clipping in PPF 200-A, Roosevelt Papers.

35. Manchester, *Disturber of the Peace* . . . , 270.

36. Betty Millard, "The Press Places Its Bets," *New Masses*, XXI (October 27, 1936), 14.

37. *Ibid.*

38. Quoted in Marshall Field, *Freedom Is More Than a Word* (Chicago: University of Chicago Press, 1945), 111–12.

39. Tebbel, *American Dynasty* . . . , 176–77.

40. Chicago *Daily Tribune*, September 1, 1936.

41. Chicago *Daily Tribune*, August 4, 1936; Tebbel, *American Dynasty* . . . , 225.

42. *The New York Times*, April 27, 1933.

43. Chicago *Daily Tribune*, September 12, 1936.

44. "The Press and The Public," *The New Republic*, XC (March 17, 1937), 182; Chicago *Daily Tribune*, September 23, 1936.

45. Tebbel, *American Dynasty* . . . , 177; George Seldes, *Lords of the Press* (New York: Julian Messner, Inc., 1938), 59–60.

46. Harold L. Ickes, *America's House of Lords; An Inquiry Into Freedom of the Press* (New York: Harcourt Brace, 1939), 66.

47. "The Press Loses the Election," *The New Republic*, LXXXIX (November 18, 1936), 63; Virginius Dabney, "The Press and the Election," *Public Opinion Quarterly*, IV (April 1937), 123.

48. Chicago *Daily Tribune*, August 9, 12, 1936.

49. W. Cameron Meyers, "The Chicago Newspaper Hoax in the '36 Election," *Journalism Quarterly*, XXVII, No. 33 (1960), 359.

50. Chicago *Daily Times*, August 28, 1936, quoted in Meyers, "The Chicago Newspaper Hoax . . . ," 359.

51. Chicago *Daily Tribune*, August 29, 1936.

52. Chicago *Daily Times*, September 2, 1936, cited in Meyers, "The Chicago Newspaper Hoax . . . ," 360; McCormick, quoted in George Seldes, *Lords of The Press* (New York: Blue Ribbon Books, 1941), 56.

53. *The New York Times*, December 24, 1946.

54. Winkler, *William Randolph Hearst* . . . , 252, 256–57.

55. William Randolph Hearst, *A Portrait in His Own Words*, edited by Edmund D. Coblentz (New York: Simon and Schuster, 1952), 169–172.

56. *Ibid.*, 179.

57. Los Angeles *Examiner*, November 14, 1935, quoted in Ernest S. Bates and Oliver Carlson, *Hearst: Lord of San Simeon* (New York: Viking Press, 1936), 269.

58. Hearst, *Portrait* . . . , 191.

59. Buffalo (New York) *Evening News*, November 2, 1936, clipping in Valentine Collection.

60. New York *American*, September 19, 1936, quoted in W. A. Swanson, *Citizen Hearst* (New York: Scribners, 1961), 478.

61. Ernest S. Bates and Olan Williams, *American Hurly-Burly* (New York: McBride, 1937), 233.

62. *The New York Times*, September 20, 1936.

63. Meyers, "The Chicago Newspaper Hoax . . . ," 361; "Topics of the Day: Hearst Barrage Enlivens Campaign," *Literary Digest*, CXXII (October 5, 1936), 5.

64. Detroit *Times*, September 23, 1936, clipping in OF-263, Roosevelt Papers.

65. Hearst, *Portrait* . . . , 309.

66. "Trying to Smear Roosevelt," *The New Republic*, LXXXVIII (September 30, 1936), 212.

67. New York *American*, October 8, 1936, quoted in "The Press and the Public," *The New Republic*, XC (March 17, 1937), 182.

68. New York *American*, October 31, 1936, quoted in "The Press and the Public," *The New Republic*, XC (March 17, 1937), 183.

69. Buffalo (New York) *Evening News*, November 2, 1936, clipping in Valentine Collection.

70. H. L. Mencken, "Three Years of Dr. Roosevelt," *American Mercury*, XXXVII (March, 1936), 257; Angoff, *H. L. Mencken* . . . , 132–33; *Congressional Record*, 76 Cong., 1 Sess. (1939), 1090.

71. James MacGregor Burns, *Roosevelt: The Lion and the Fox* (New York: Harcourt, Brace, 1956), 294.

72. *The New York Times*, February 6, 1937.

73. Joseph Alsop and Turner Catledge, *The 168 Days* (Garden City: Doubleday, 1938), 71–72; St. Louis *Star-Times*, February 19, 1937, quoted in Alpheus T. Mason, *The Supreme Court: Vehicle of Revealed Truth or Power Group* (Boston: Boston University Press, 1953), 45.

74. *Ibid.*; Albert Jay Nock, "The Autocrat vs. the Constitution," *American Mercury*, XLI (May, 1937), 1; Dallas *Morning News*, March 26, 1937; William R. Barnes and A. W. Littlefield, eds., *The Supreme Court and the Constitution* (New York: Barnes and Noble, 1937), 51; "Court and Press," *Current History*, XLVI (September, 1937), 20: Rochester *Democrat and Chronicle*, March 24, 1937, clipping in Valentine Collection.

75. *The Oregonian,* quoted in "Court and Press," *Current History,* XLVI (September, 1937), 23; *American Agriculturalist,* February 27, 1937, quoted in Mason, *Supreme Court . . . ,* 45; *The New York Times,* July 20, 1937; "Court and Press," *Current History,* XLVI (September, 1937), 23.

76. Emporia (Kansas) *Gazetteer,* February 6, 1937, quoted in Mason, *Supreme Court . . . ,* 45; New York *Herald Tribune,* February 9, 1937, quoted in Mason, *Supreme Court . . . ,* 45.

77. "To Newspaper Publishers of America," *Christian Century,* LIII (November 18, 1936), 5118, quoted in *New Republic,* XC (March 17, 1937), 178; Maury Maverick, "The Next Four Years in Congress," *The New Republic,* LXXXIX (November 25, 1936), 99.

78. *The New York Times,* March 13, 1938; "The Press and the Public," *The New Republic,* XC (March 17, 1937), 178.

79. Louisville *Courier-Journal,* editorial reprinted in *Congressional Record,* 76 Cong., 1 Sess. (1939), 1090.

CHAPTER VIII: CHASTE SEDUCTION OR LAWFUL ROBBERY

1. Leland D. Baldwin, *Recent American History* (New York: American Book Co., 1954), 221.
2. Schlesinger, *Coming of the New Deal,* 20–21.
3. *Congressional Record,* 73 Cong., 1 Sess. (1933), 738; Leuchtenburg, *Franklin D. Roosevelt . . . ,* 61.
4. Schlesinger, *Coming of the New Deal,* 249; Moley, *After Seven Years* (New York: Harper, 1939), 159.
5. Schlesinger, *Coming of the New Deal,* 44; "Topics of the Day," *The Literary Digest,* CXV (May 6, 1933), 4; *The New York Times,* April 28, 1933.
6. "Topics of the Day," *The Literary Digest,* CXV (May 6, 1933), 3; Schlesinger, *Coming of the New Deal,* 44.
7. "Topics of the Day," *The Literary Digest,* CXV (May 6, 1933), 3.
8. *Congressional Record,* 73 Cong., 1 Sess. (1933), 669, 676, 682, 693, 728.
9. Harold L. Ickes, *The Secret Diary of Harold Ickes: The First Thousand Days, 1933–1936* (New York: Simon and Schuster, 1943), 659.
10. *Congressional Record,* 73 Cong., 1 Sess. (1933), 2176–77, 2178, 2197, 1677; 74 Cong., 1 Sess. (1935), 10794.
11. U.S. Congress, House Committee on Military Affairs, *Hearings on T.V.A. Bill,* April 12, 1933, 48, quoted in Democratic National Committee, Research Division, *Scare Words: A Compilation of Republican Attacks on Progressive Legislation Since 1882* (Washington, D.C., The Committee, n.d.), 33; *Congressional Record,* 73 Cong., 1 Sess. (1933), 2176, 2181, 2253, 2285; 74 Cong., 1 Sess. (1935), 10869–10871.
12. Leuchtenburg, *Franklin D. Roosevelt . . . ,* 45; *Congressional Record;* 73 Con., 1 Sess. (1933), 206, 209, 211, 214.
13. Leuchtenburg, *Franklin D. Roosevelt . . . ,* 97; E. Pendleton Herring, *Presidential Leadership* (New York: Farrar and Rinehart, 1940), 66.
14. *Newsweek,* April 7, 1934 (III), 5.
15. Schlesinger, *Coming of the New Deal,* 101–102.
16. Morton Keller, *In Defense of Yesterday* (New York: Coward-McCann, 1958), 245; *The New York Times,* May 26, 1933; *Congressional Record,* 73 Cong., 1 Sess. (1933), 4196.

17. *Congressional Record*, 73 Cong., 1 Sess. (1933), 4593, 5554–5555; *The New York Times*, September 9, 1933.
18. Hugh S. Johnson, *The Blue Eagle, from Egg to Earth* (Garden City: Doubleday, Doran, 1935), 208, 280.
19. *Congressional Record*, 73 Cong., 2 Sess. (1934), 9246, 9248, 9650; Thomas D. Schall, radio address, August 23, 1934, in PPF 1741, Roosevelt Papers; Leuchtenburg, *Franklin D. Roosevelt . . .* , 67.
20. Johnson, *Blue Eagle*, 272.
21. Schlesinger, *Coming of the New Deal*, 133.
22. *The New York Times*, May 21, 1934; *Congressional Record*, 73 Cong., 2 Sess. (1934), 9246; Schlesinger, *Coming of the New Deal*, 134.
23. Schlesinger, *Coming of the New Deal*, 135; "Republican Big Guns Trained Against New Deal," *The Literary Digest*, CXVII (June 2, 1934), 5; *Congressional Record*, 73 Cong., 2 Sess. (1934), 9246.
24. Burns, *The Lion and the Fox*, 193.
25. Harry Wesley Morris, *The Republicans in a Minority Role*, unpublished Ph.D. dissertation (Iowa City: State University of Iowa, 1960), 46.
26. *The New York Times*, June 26, 1933.
27. Morris, "Republicans in a Minority Role," 16.
28. *The New York Times*, November 1, December 5, 1933; Schlesinger, *Coming of the New Deal*, 481.
29. *The New York Times*, May 22, 1934.
30. *The New York Times*, February 13, June 6, 1934.
31. *Congressional Record*, 73 Cong., 2 Sess. (1934), 5448, 5626, 5814.
32. *The New York Times*, July 6, 8; II, August 19, 1934.
33. *The New York Times*, March 6, April 4, 1934; *Congressional Record*, 73 Cong., 2 Sess. (1934), 9158, 12595.
34. *The New York Times*, July 28, August 7, October 14, 16, 1934.
35. *The New York Times*, October 7, November 11, 1934; Leuchtenburg, *Franklin D. Roosevelt . . .* , 117.
36. *Ibid.*, 116; Schlesinger, *Coming of the New Deal*, 507.
37. Moley, *After Seven Years*, 300; Leuchtenburg, *Franklin D. Roosevelt . . .* , 117; Sherwood, *Roosevelt and Hopkins* (New York, 1948), 65.
38. Moley, *After Seven Years*, 302.
39. *Congressional Record*, 74 Cong., 1 Sess. (1935), 3980.
40. Leuchtenburg, *Franklin D. Roosevelt . . .* , 117; Moley, *After Seven Years*, 300.
41. Burns, *The Lion and the Fox*, 277.
42. Schlesinger, *Politics of Upheaval*, 212.
43. Leuchtenburg, *Franklin D. Roosevelt . . .* , 143–144; Schlesinger, *Politics of Upheaval*, 6.
44. Burns, *The Lion and the Fox*, 223.
45. *Congressional Record*, 74 Cong., 1 Sess. (1935), 841; *The New York Times*, January 27, 1934; Garet Garrett, "Surrender of the Purse," *Saturday Evening Post*, CCVII (June 22, 1935), 7.
46. "News-Week's Front Page," *Newsweek*, March 2, 1934 (III), 6.
47. Schlesinger, *Politics of Upheaval*, 7.
48. Garet Garrett, "Surrender of the Purse," *Saturday Evening Post*, CCVIII (July 26, 1935), 72–73; *Congressional Record*, 74 Cong., 1 Sess. (1935), 3335, 3337.
49. *Congressional Record*, 74 Cong., 1 Sess. (1935), 4069.
50. Schlesinger, *Politics of Upheaval*, 220, 306–307.
51. *Congressional Record*, 74 Cong., 1 Sess. (1935), 751–752.

52. *Congressional Record,* 74 Cong., 1 Sess. (1935), 8752, 9040.
53. *Congressional Record,* 74 Cong., 1 Sess. (1935), 8935; Schlesinger, *Politics of Upheaval,* 313.
54. *Ibid.,* 314.
55. *Ibid.,* 314–315.
56. *Congressional Record,* 74 Cong., 1 Sess. (1935), 9795, 10376–10377, 10446, 19425.
57. *Congressional Record,* 74 Cong., 1 Sess. (1935), 10376, 19425.
58. Schlesinger, *Politics of Upheaval,* 316, 324–325.
59. Schlesinger, *Coming of the New Deal,* 311; Leuchtenburg, *Franklin D. Roosevelt . . . ,* 131.
60. *Ibid.;* Daniel O. Hastings, "If the Administration's Program for Old Age Pensions Sound Negative," *Congressional Digest,* XIV (March, 1935), 81, 83; *Congressional Record,* 74 Cong., 1 Sess. (1935), 5983.
61. *Congressional Record,* 74 Cong., 1 Sess. (1939), 5531, 5543, 5545, 5795, 6054, 6061.
62. Schlesinger, *Coming of the New Deal,* 255–256.
63. Leuchtenburg, *Franklin D. Roosevelt . . . ,* 131–132.

CHAPTER IX: ALL MENU AND NO MEAT

1. Leuchtenburg, *Franklin D. Roosevelt . . . ,* 96–97.
2. Tugwell, *The Democratic Roosevelt; A Biography of Franklin D. Roosevelt* (Chicago: University of Chicago Press, 1957), 349; Schlesinger, *Politics of Upheaval,* 55.
3. "The 'Crawfish' At It Again," New Orleans *Times-Picayune,* June 9, 1933, clipping in OF 1403, Roosevelt Papers; Leuchtenburg, *Franklin D. Roosevelt . . . ,* 97; *Congressional Record,* 74 Cong., 1 Sess. (1935), 3437.
4. Tugwell, *Democratic Roosevelt,* 350.
5. Schlesinger, *Politics of Upheaval,* 250; Huey Long, "Our Blundering Government and Its Spokesman," speech, National Broadcasting Co., Washington, D.C., Thursday, March 7, 1935; *Congressional Record,* 74 Cong., 1 Sess. (1935), 3436; *The New York Times,* November 7, 1934, April 23, 26, 1935; *Congressional Record,* 74 Cong., 1 Sess. (1935), 11517; Huey Long, radio address over WDSU, July 8, 1935, quoted in New Orleans *Times-Picayune,* July 9, 1935, clipping in OF 1403, Roosevelt Papers; *The New York Times,* July 9, 1935.
6. Schlesinger, *Politics of Upheaval,* 64.
7. Leuchtenburg, *Franklin D. Roosevelt . . . ,* 99.
8. Hodding Carter, "Huey Long: American Dictator," in Isabel Leighton (ed.), *The Aspirin Age, 1919–1941,* 353.
9. Thomas Martin, *Dynasty: The Longs of Louisiana* (New York: Putnam, 1960), 134.
10. *Ibid.,* 137–138.
11. *Ibid.,* Farley, *Behind the Ballots,* 249.
12. *Time,* June 24, 1935 (XXV), 9; *Time,* May 27, 1935 (XXV), 1.
13. *Congressional Record,* 74 Cong., 1 Sess. (1935), 9672, 9678, 9680, 9705, 9707, 9708.
14. "Topics of the Day," *The Literary Digest,* CXIX (June 29, 1935), 3.
15. *Ibid.,* 4.

16. "Topics of the Day," *The Literary Digest*, CXX (July 6, 1935), 3.
17. "Clamor Increases As Congress Debates Taxes," *The Literary Digest*, CXX (August 10, 1935), 5.
18. *Congressional Record*, 74 Cong., 1 Sess. (1935), 12448.
19. *Congressional Record*, 74 Cong., 1 Sess. (1935), 12314, 12322–12323.
20. Moley, *After Seven Years*, 305; *Congressional Record*, 74 Cong., 1 Sess. (1935), 12323.
21. *Congressional Record*, 74 Cong., 1 Sess. (1935), 10467, 13045, 13056.
22. N. T. N. Robinson, "Congress Finally Adjourns—Major Results of the Session," *The Congressional Digest*, XIV (August–September, 1935), 193; "Topics of the Day," *The Literary Digest*, CXX (August 31, 1935), 5.
23. Schlesinger, *Politics of Upheaval*, 524–525; *The New York Times*, March 28, 1935; "Topics of the Day: Political Camp Meetings . . . ," *The Literary Digest*, CXIX (April 27, 1935), 6.
24. Schlesinger, *Politics of Upheaval*, 525; *Time*, December 24, 1934 (XXIV), 10.
25. "Topics of the Day: Hoover Speaks in New York," *The Literary Digest*, CXIX (February 23, 1935), 5–6.
26. "Herbert Hoover's Call To Arms," *The Literary Digest*, CXIX (March 30, 1935), 8; "Topics of the Day," *The Literary Digest*, CXIX (April 22, 1935), 5–6.
27. "Topics of the Day: Partizanship Discounted," *The Literary Digest*, CXX (July 27, 1935), 5; *The New York Times*, July 21, 1935.
28. Schlesinger, *Politics of Upheaval*, 335–36.
29. "Current Opinion," *The Literary Digest*, CXIX (June 22, 1935), 1, 11; *The New York Times*, June 5, 1935; *Time*, June 17, 1935 (XXV), 15; "Current Opinion," *The Literary Digest*, CXIX (June 22, 1935), 1.
30. *Ibid.*
31. *The New York Times*, May 3, June 20, July 23, September 18, October 6, November 17, 22, December 15, 1935.
32. "Topics of the Day: Roosevelt's Rhode Island Reversal . . . ," *The Literary Digest*, CXX (August 17, 1935), 3; *The New York Times*, August 7, 1935.
33. *The New York Times*, November 17, December 20, 1935; January 3, 11, 1936.
34. "Digest Poll . . . ," *The Literary Digest*, CXXI (January 11, 1936), 9.
35. *Ibid.*, 1.
36. *Ibid.*, 1–2.
37. *Congressional Record*, 74 Cong., 2 Sess. (1936), 7, 82, 83.
38. N. T. N. Robinson, "Politics Dominates Opening of New Session," *Congressional Digest*, XV (February, 1936), 33.
39. *Congressional Record*, 74 Cong., 2 Sess. (1936), 2362, 2551, 4697; *The New York Times*, February 22, 1936.
40. "Should the Administration's New Tax Proposal Be Adopted?" *Congressional Digest*, XV (May, 1936), 151.
41. *The New York Times*, January 15, 1936.
42. *The Literary Digest*, CXXI (January 25, 1936), 35.
43. Henry O. Evjen, *The Republican Strategy in the Presidential Campaigns of 1936–1940*, unpublished Ph.D. dissertation (Cleveland: Western Reserve University, 1956), 18–19.
44. "New Deal Under Lincoln Day Barrage," *The Literary Digest*, CXXI (February 22, 1936), 6.
45. *The New York Times*, March 1, 1936.

46. Schlesinger, *Politics of Upheaval*, 532, 540; Cincinnati *Enquirer*, quoted in *The New York Times*, February 9, 1936.
47. Schlesinger, *Politics of Upheaval*, 541.
48. *The New York Times*, June 10, 1936.
49. Eugene H. Roseboom, *A History of Presidential Elections* (New York: Macmillan, 1957), 447.
50. *The New York Times*, June 11, 1936; Jonathan Mitchell, "The Republicans Hate Roosevelt," *The New Republic*, LXXXVII (June 24, 1936), 194–95; Edwin P. Hoyt, *Jumbos and Jackasses* (Garden City: Doubleday, 1960), 350; Schlesinger, *Politics of Upheaval*, 544–45; *The New York Times*, June 11, 1936.
51. *The New York Times*, July 24, 1936; Schlesinger, *Politics of Upheaval*, 602.
52. *The New York Times*, August 29, September 25, 1936.
53. *Time*, September 21, 1936 (XXVIII), 15.
54. *The New York Times*, October 14, 21, 1936; Evjen, "Republican Strategy . . . ," 193; Alfred Landon, quoted in Schlesinger, *Politics of Upheaval*, 623.
55. Evjen, "Republican Strategy . . . ," 194.
56. Olive Ewing Clapper, *Washington Tapestry* (New York: McGraw-Hill, 1946), 109–111.
57. *Newsweek*, August 15, 1936, 20.
58. Schlesinger, *Politics of Upheaval*, 553, 55:
59. *The Literary Digest*, CXXII (August 15, 1936), 5; Schlesinger, *Politics of Upheaval*, 560.
60. Evjen, "Republican Strategy . . . ," 117–144.
61. *The New York Times*, October 25, 1936; Schlesinger, *Politics of Upheaval*, 639.
62. *The New York Times*, October 25, 1936.
63. Schlesinger, *Politics of Upheaval*, 623.

CHAPTER X: HARMONY, HELL!

1. *Congressional Record*, 75 Cong., 1 Sess. (1937), 2381.
2. *The New York Times*, August 22, 1937.
3. *Congressional Record*, 75 Cong., 1 Sess. (1937), 3338.
4. *Congressional Record*, 75 Cong., 2 Sess. (1937), 1468.
5. *Ibid.*
6. Arthur Mullen, *Western Democrat* (New York: W. Funk, Inc., 1940), 316–318.
7. *The Redistribution of Power*, ALL Document No. 93 (January 24, 1936), 13, 18–19; Albert C. Ritchie, *The American Form of Government—Let Us Preserve It*, ALL Document No. 92 (January 18, 1936), 9; Fitzgerald Hall, *A Federal Union—National and State Responsibilities*, ALL Document No. 123 (April 20, 1936), 14; *Congressional Record*, 73 Cong., 2 Sess. (March 23, 1934), 5626.
8. Talmadge to Roosevelt, OF (Talmadge), February 11, 1935, Roosevelt Papers.
9. *Congressional Record*, 75 Cong., 1 Sess. (1937), 430.
10. *Ibid.*, 2532, 2735, 2187, 1517, 1519, 2977.
11. *Ibid.*, 1517, 2187, 3207, 4210.
12. *Ibid.*, 1377.

13. Samuel Rosenman (ed.), *The Public Papers and Addresses of Franklin D. Roosevelt* (13 vols., New York, 1938–50), V, 191–192.
14. *Congressional Record*, 75 Cong., 1 Sess. (1937), 285; Carter Glass, radio address, March 29, 1937; *Congressional Record*, 75 Cong., 1 Sess. (1937), 679.
15. *The New York Times*, May 2, July 11, 1937; *Congressional Record*, 75 Cong., 1 Sess. (1937), 1249.
16. *Congressional Record*, 75 Cong., 3 Sess. (1938), 37.
17. Quoted in Charles A. Madison, *Leaders and Liberals in 20th Century America* (New York: Frederic Ungar Publishing Company, 1961), 266.
18. *The New York Times*, March 8, June 21, June 28, July 20, 1937.
19. Douglas Wilson Johnson, *The Assault on the Supreme Court* (New York: National Committee to Uphold Constitutional Government, 1937), 60–61; Walter Lippmann, *The Supreme Court, Independent or Controlled?* (New York: Harper, 1937), 56; *Congressional Record*, 75 Cong., 1 Sess. (1937), 1658.
20. *The New York Times*, July 20, 1937.
21. See the comprehensive analysis of public opinion in Joseph Rice Saylor, *The Constitutional Crisis of 1937*, unpublished doctoral dissertation (Austin, Texas: The University of Texas, 1945), 329ff.; *The New York Times*, March 9, 1937.
22. *Ibid.*, July 22, 23, 1937.
23. *Ibid.*, July 22, 1937.
24. *Ibid.*, July 23, 1937.
25. *Ibid.*, May 20, 1937.
26. *Ibid.*, May 16, 1937.
27. *Congressional Record*, 75 Cong., 1 Sess. (1937), 6810, 1811.
28. Leuchtenburg, *Franklin D. Roosevelt . . .* , 238; *The New York Times*, August 13, 1937.
29. *Ibid.*, September 15, 17, 1937.
30. *Congressional Record*, 75 Cong., 1 Sess. (1937), 858, 4198, 4909, 6284.
31. *Ibid.*, 4891, 4915.
32. *Ibid.*, 4941
33. *Ibid.*, 757, 9047.
34. *Ibid.*, 2141–2142, 2162.
35. *Ibid.*, 1249, 3607; Drew Pearson and Robert S. Allen, *Nine Old Men at the Crossroads* (Garden City, New York: Doubleday, Doran, 1937), 34.
36. *Congressional Record*, 75 Cong., 1 Sess. (1937), 368–369.
37. *Ibid.*, 7882; 75 Cong., 2 Sess. (1937), 1466, 369, 1499, 1847.
38. *The New York Times*, July 26, 1937; *Congressional Record*, 75 Cong., 2 Sess. (1937), 1407.
39. *Congressional Record*, 75 Cong., 3 Sess. (1938), 7432, 9257, 7293.
40. *Congressional Record*, 75 Cong., 1 Sess. (1937), 5739, 5736, 2113.
41. *Ibid.*, 5736, 5737, 6160, 5177, 2223.
42. *The New York Times*, June 30, 1937; Thomas Greer, *What Roosevelt Thought* (East Lansing, Michigan: Michigan State University Press, 1958), 73.
43. *The New York Times*, September 4, 1937.
44. *The New York Times*, October 24, 1935; *Congressional Record*, 75 Cong., 2 Sess. (1937), 1868.
45. *Ibid.*, 2029, 142, 302, 1795.
46. Burns, *The Lion and the Fox*, 346; T. R. B., "Washington Notes," *New Republic*, XCIV (1938), 358–359; Ickes, *Diary*, II, 182.

47. Quoted in Leuchtenburg, *Franklin D. Roosevelt . . . ,* 252.
48. *Congressional Record,* 75 Cong., 1 Sess. (1937), 8715.
49. *Congressional Record,* 75 Cong., 3 Sess. (1938), 1870, 6225, 1352, 2039–2040; *The New York Times,* February 10, 1938.
50. *Congressional Record,* 75 Cong., 3 Sess. (1938), 1352, 2138.
51. *Ibid.,* 321.
52. *The New York Times,* May 6, September 5, July 7, April 18, 1938.
53. *Congressional Record,* 75 Cong., 3 Sess. (1938), 3637, 1229, 876–877.
54. *The New York Times,* December 27, 30, 31, 1937; Eugene Gerhart, *America's Advocate: Robert H. Jackson* (Indianapolis: Bobbs-Merrill Co., Inc., 1958), 125–127; Marquis Childs, "Jackson versus Richberg," *The Nation,* CXLVI (1938), 119–120; Ickes, *Diary,* II, 282–283.
55. *Congressional Record,* 75 Cong., 3 Sess. (1938), 664, 73.
56. *Ibid.,* 124, 9683.
57. *The New York Times,* December 11, August 21, 1938; *Congressional Record,* 75 Cong., 3 Sess. (1938), 9666, 6659, 6661.
58. *Ibid.,* 7705.
59. *Ibid.,* 7256–7258.
60. *America's Future,* I (November, 1938), 7; *Congressional Record,* 75 Cong., 3 Sess. (1938), 2399, 7538, 7548–7549, 7554.
61. *Ibid.,* 2041–2042, 72, 201, 2024.
62. *Ibid.,* 2929, 2946.
63. *Ibid.,* 2396, 2794.
64. *The New York Times,* March 5, March 29, 1938; *Congressional Record,* 75 Cong., 3 Sess. (1938), 4197.
65. *Ibid.*
66. *Ibid.,* 1547.
67. *Ibid.,* 1924–1925, 1731.
68. *Ibid.,* 1547, 1189, 1306; *The New York Times,* January 30, 1938; *Ibid.,* August 4, 1937.
69. *Congressional Record,* 75 Cong., 3 Sess. (1938), 9387, 1381, 1288, 5114–5115, 4492, 4867, 4782, 4598.
70. Farley, *Jim Farley's Story* (New York: Whittlesey House, 1948), 130; *Congressional Record,* 75 Cong., 3 Sess. (1938), 1338; *The New York Times,* April 9, 1938.
71. *Congressional Record,* 75 Cong., 3 Sess. (1938), 1547, 4893; *The New York Times,* April 9, 1938.
72. *Congressional Record,* 75 Cong., 3 Sess. (1938), 1440.
73. Burns, *The Lion and the Fox,* 294; *The New York Times,* July 14, August 24, 1937.
74. *Congressional Record,* 75 Cong., 3 Sess. (1938), 6704.
75. *Ibid.,* 2005.
76. *The New York Times,* June 25, 1938.
77. Burns, *The Lion and the Fox,* 363.
78. *The New York Times,* August 13, September 8, 1938; *Congressional Record,* 75 Cong., 3 Sess. (1938), 734, 440.
79. *The New York Times,* August 28, 1938.
80. *Ibid.,* September 29, 1938.
81. Quoted in Herbert Hoover, "Undermining Representative Government" (Reprint of address before the Joint Republican Organizations at Hartford, Connecticut, October 17, 1938), 11–12, Valentine Collection; quoted in *Congressional Record,* 75 Cong., 3 Sess. (1938), 2292.
82. *The New York Times,* March 29, August 19, 20, 22, September 10, 1938.

83. Raymond Clapper, "Return of the Two-Party System," *Current History*, XLIX (December, 1938), 14.

CHAPTER XI: A SECOND HONEYMOON AND AFTER

1. Burns, *The Lion and the Fox*, 246.
   1956), 246.
2. Jack Bell, *The Splendid Misery: A Study of the American Presidency and Power Politics at Close Range* (London, 1960), 44; Burns, *The Lion and the Fox*, 317; Schlesinger, *Coming of the New Deal*, 563–565; Pollard, *Presidents and the Press*, 811.
3. Raymond Moley, *After Seven Years* (New York, 1939); Samuel I. Rosenman (comp.), *The Public Papers and Addresses of Franklin D. Roosevelt* (New York, 1938–50), VIII, 111; *Columbus Citizen*, February 5, 1939, quoted in Pollard, *Presidents and the Press*, 813; Albert Samuel Karr, *The Roosevelt Haters* (unpublished doctoral dissertation, University of California at Los Angeles, 1956), 280–281; Schlesinger, *Coming of the New Deal*, 564, 565; *The New York Times*, September 20, 1936; Burns, *The Lion and the Fox*, 241.
4. Pollard, *Presidents and the Press*, 816; Schlesinger, *Coming of the New Deal*, 564, 566; John Morton Blum, *From the Morgenthau Diaries: Years of Crisis, 1938–39* (Boston, 1959), 319; *The New York Times*, April 12, 1939.
5. Schlesinger, *Politics of Upheaval*, 243, 249–250, 325–326; Burns, *The Lion and the Fox*, 214–215; Rexford G. Tugwell, *The Democratic Roosevelt: A Biography of Franklin D. Roosevelt* (Garden City, New York, 1957), 349, 320; " 'Demagogues': Johnson Lambasts Senator and Priest . . . . ," *Newsweek*, March 16, 1935 (V), 5–7; "Pied Pipers," *Vital Speech*, I (March 11, 1935), 354–360; "Topics of the Day: General Johnson fires flash against old guard and emotional fringe critics of the New Deal," *Literary Digest*, CXIX (March 16, 1935), 3–5.
6. Elliott Roosevelt, *F.D.R.: His Personal Letters, 1928–1945* (New York, 1950), I, 417; Wolfskill, *Revolt of the Conservatives*, 28–35 *passim*, 73, 151–152, 156, 210, 212; Burns, *The Lion and the Fox*, 206–208; *Time*, September 3, 1934 (XXIV), 19; Karr, "The Roosevelt Haters," 138; Farley, *Behind the Ballots*, 294; *Newsweek*, January 11, 1936 (II), 9; Rosenman (comp.), *Public Papers*, V, 8–18, 38–44.
7. Rosenman (comp.), *Public Papers*, V, 383–385; *Congressional Record*, 74 Cong., 2 Sess. (1936), 925–930; Wolfskill, *Revolt of the Conservatives*, 156, 210–212, 218–219; Joseph T. Robinson, "Jacob's Voice," *Vital Speeches*, II (February 10, 1936); *The New York Times*, January 3, 1936; Farley, *Behind the Ballots*, 294; Samuel I. Rosenman, *Working with Roosevelt* (New York, 1952), 109–112, 117–119, 130–135; Elliott Roosevelt (ed.), *F.D.R.*, I, 623–624; *The New York Times*, November 4, 1936; *Newsweek*, November 7, 1936 (VIII), 7.
8. Burns, *The Lion and the Fox*, 205–206, 316–317, 345–346; Letter, FDR to Peek, November 22, 1935, FSF George N. Peek, 1933–35.
9. Burns, *The Lion and the Fox*, 206, 345–346.

Index

Index